IN-CAR INSTRUCTION:
Methods and Content

WILLIAM G. ANDERSON
Teachers College, Columbia University

IN-CAR INSTRUCTION:
Methods and Content
A Manual for Teachers of Driver and Traffic Safety Education

Second Edition

ADDISON-WESLEY PUBLISHING COMPANY
Reading, Massachusetts · Menlo Park, California · London · Amsterdam
Don Mills, Ontario · Sydney

ISBN 0-201-00217-5
ABCDEFGHIJ-HA-7987

To Dorothy, Bill, and Agnes

PREFACE

Much has happened in the field of traffic safety education since the publication of the first edition of this book. Particularly noteworthy are the many studies, funded by the United States Department of Transportation, designed to evaluate and recommend improvements in driver education programs. Information emerging from these and other studies provided a rich resource for formulating the many changes contained in this edition.

Government-funded studies of the driving task and instructional objectives for driver education conducted by the HumRRO organization (see Bibliography) were especially useful in determining needed changes in the Unit Plan for In-Car Instruction (Part II of this book). In fact the objectives and content of the Plan were revised to incorporate, directly or indirectly, virtually all of the more critical instructional objectives contained in the HumRRO study. In addition, the follow-up study by HumRRO, which yielded specifications for a "Safe Performance Curriculum," was used as a basis for revising selected portions of the Unit Plan. Also, the Automotive Safety Foundation's "A Resource Curriculum in Driver and Traffic Safety Education" was used at an earlier stage to delineate interim changes in the Plan.

The original Unit Plan (first edition of this book) was based on a series of field tests conducted at Teachers College, Columbia University and in high-school driver education programs in the region. These field tests were continued and resulted in the subsequent publication of materials for student drivers: *Learning to Drive: Skills, Concepts, and Strategies,* and *Laboratory Manual for Learning to Drive* (Addison-Wesley Publishing Company). These student materials reshaped several features of the Unit Plan; the newer features are also a part of this second edition of the Unit Plan.

Back in the late 1960s this was one of the few, or perhaps even the first, texts to highlight the use of analyses of the driving task as a basis for curriculum development in driver education. Since then, task analysis has become quite fashionable in traffic safety education, and with good reason. Many excellent analyses have emerged, including but not limited to the HumRRO analysis. These newer analyses have been helpful in the reformulation of the task analysis on which the Unit Plan is based. Incidentally, it is gratifying to see that many of the concepts contained in the original Unit Plan (intended path, tracking, reduced risk, and so on) are now included both in current analyses of the task and in new curriculum materials.

In this edition more emphasis has been placed on the multiple-car method. Professor Richard Ellis of the State University of New York at Albany, using his extensive experience with the method, provided much of the information needed to design a new chapter on multiple-car instruction.

Some units have been added to the Plan to cover aspects of the driving task that were not specifically treated in the first edition, and on the basis of information from field professionals using the Plan, the order of the units has been changed somewhat to make the Plan easier to implement.

I am most grateful to the driver educators who field tested the Unit Plan in their schools; the prospective teachers and students who provided the invaluable feedback used to revise the Plan; and the colleagues who have carefully reviewed and suggested improvements in this manuscript.

January 1977   *W.G.A.*
New York City

CONTENTS

part I

THE SELECTION OF CONTENT AND METHODS FOR IN-CAR INSTRUCTION

INTRODUCTION

Driver educators face an enormous challenge. Within a relatively short period of time they must prepare novices to cope with an extremely complicated and inherently dangerous task—driving an automobile.

Not too long ago, the driving task was conceived of in rather simple terms. Good driving was thought to consist of the performance of certain basic manipulative skills of acceleration, shifting, steering, and so on; the execution of common maneuvers such as turning and parallel parking; and obedience to the law regarding such things as speed limits and signaling. Not surprisingly, this conception of driving resulted in instructional programs that concentrated almost exclusively on the teaching of basic skills and maneuvers and knowledge of traffic laws. In retrospect it is apparent that these earlier programs viewed driving primarily as a series of consistently and legally executed manipulative performances, and gave little attention to other features of the task. Of course, things are different now.

In recent years much attention has been given to careful analyses of the driving task (B 45–B 66)*. The intent of these analyses has been to identify the critical elements of the task. Perhaps the most crucial outcome of these studies has been the universal recognition of the *complexity* of driving. Today driving is viewed as a demanding task in which the driver continuously searches the environment, uses stored knowledge to interpret what is seen, predicts future events, surveys alternative actions and their consequences, makes decisions, and then executes those decisions by controlling the movement of the car. Furthermore, given the pervasive dangers inherent in the traffic setting (B 1–B 44), the task requirements for *safe driver performance* are remarkably exacting. To remain accident free over long periods of time, drivers must perceive, interpret, decide, and act in countless situations *without committing a serious error*.

Therefore, the dimensions of the challenge facing driver educators are more definitively prescribed than they once were. Driver education programs must be carefully planned to incorporate all critical components of the driving task. Learning experiences have to be scrupulously designed and implemented to enable students to achieve at least minimal levels of safe performance in each component. Considering the time constraints (normally only a semester of classroom and laboratory work is available), the sizable numbers of students

---

* The numbers in parentheses refer to the Selected Bibliography in the back of this book.

enrolled in most programs, and the substantial range in entry-level capabilities among students, there is no question that the job facing the teacher is formidable. Only a comprehensive program of well-integrated learning experiences is equal to this sort of challenge.

Most comprehensive driver education programs consist of several phases: classroom instruction, independent study, in-car instruction, and in some schools simulation instruction. The effectiveness of the total program depends heavily on the quality of each instructional phase as well as on the extent to which each phase is integrated with other phases. This text focuses on the planning and conduct of in-car instruction, perhaps the most critical phase of any driver education program. It is designed to enhance the quality of the in-car phase and, of equal importance, to facilitate the integration of in-car instruction with other program phases.

In-Car Instruction and the Total Program

To fully appreciate the scope and nature of in-car instruction, and thus of this text, we must view it in relation to all phases of a comprehensive driver education program. A brief description of those phases follows.

Classroom instruction consists of several normal high-school periods totaling at least thirty to forty-five hours. As in most other school classes, one teacher meets with about thirty students and devotes the time to lectures, discussions, small-group work, films and other audiovisual presentations, tests, and so on. Often these meetings take place in classrooms that are set aside specifically for driver education and thus contain traffic boards, special testing devices, models, and other equipment designed to enrich classroom learning activities. The content covered in the classroom phase encompasses a broad range of topics in traffic safety education. Some classroom sessions prepare students directly for upcoming practice driving experiences (for example, learning concepts related to making proper left turns); other sessions are devoted to studying topics related to the student's ultimate ability to function effectively as a driver (for example, the role of alcohol in traffic accidents).

Independent study includes all those learning activities that students carry out on their own. In most programs it consists primarily of reading and of written homework assignments and special projects. Independent study assignments are frequently designed to prepare students for classroom discussions or for in-car practice, or to encourage them to analyze their in-car performance by keeping careful, evaluative records of practice driving sessions.

Simulation instruction normally takes place in a laboratory equipped with several electronic simulator units designed to resemble the interior of a vehicle. Students sit at each unit and respond, as though they were driving, to films projected onto a wide-angle screen in the front of the laboratory. The instructor operates the projector and monitors a control panel that displays or prints out a record of each student's performance in terms of a limited set of parameters. A panel on each unit provides students with immediate feedback on selected performance errors that are detected. Teachers often provide supplementary instruction during simulator periods by interrupting films to emphasize critical elements or discuss student performance. Simulator programs cover various aspects of the driving task from basic skills and maneuvers to expressway driving and emergency maneuvers. However, because the car on the film does not respond to the control actions of the drivers, many authorities believe that the utility of simulators is limited to training in certain perceptual and procedural elements of the task, and that they are not useful for developing control skills (B 146). Training time on simulators might vary from six hours to twelve hours depending on how this phase is integrated with other program phases.

Single-car instruction takes place in a dual-control driver education vehicle. The teacher occupies the right front seat and instructs the student driver, who occupies the driver's seat. Normally, two or three student observers occupy the rear seat and alternately become the student driver. In most programs, students receive at least six hours of practice driving instruction (that is, actual time spent as the student driver) and spend many additional hours observing other students drive. When single-car instruction is the only form of in-car instruction, it is divided between off-street and on-street instruction. Usually the student's first few driving sessions are devoted to practice of basic skills in an off-street area. Then, once the student achieves a certain level of proficiency, the practice sessions are moved to the on-street setting.

Multiple-car instruction takes place on a multiple-car driving range. Several driver education cars are in operation simultaneously; each one is driven by a student driver who normally is accompanied by one other student. The teacher is positioned outside the vehicle at a vantage point that permits a clear view of all the vehicles and communicates with students via an FM transmitter that uses the car radio as a receiver. The time allocated to multiple-car instruction varies depending on how it is integrated with other laboratory phases of the program. In most programs with ranges, students spend from four to six hours at practice driving on the range. In some programs practice on the range precedes and is prerequisite to on-street practice; in others, range practice is alternated with on-street practice. The content of multiple-car instruction varies with the design of the facility. Limited facilities provide practice in basic control skills and maneuvers; more elaborate facilities provide for greater amounts of "traffic mix" and a wider array of environmental conditions that permit practice in the more advanced elements of driver performance.

All too often these phases of instruction are treated as separate entities within a program: the phases are planned separately, different teachers are assigned to each phase, the content of one phase does not mesh with the content of another, and students arbitrarily alternate their time among phases without regard for the logical sequencing of learning activities. Indeed, in such instances driver education is actually a conglomerate offering of several discrete programs, instead of a single program consisting of integrated and mutually dependent phases. Such practices are often the result of administrative policies that place excessive priority on increasing student-teacher ratios and efficiently scheduling as many students as possible into the program. As a consequence, many multiphased programs fall short of their ultimate potential.

To be effective, driver education programs must integrate instructional phases. Above all this means that each phase should be used to accomplish those objectives that it is best suited to accomplishing. Basic concepts and information that can most efficiently and effectively be dealt with in the classroom should be covered in the classroom. Perceptual and procedural skills that can be best be taught on simulators should be taught on simulators. Basic skills that are amenable to acquisition in a range setting should be allocated to the multiple-car phase of a program. More advanced elements of driver performance that require on-street settings should be practiced on-street. In addition, programs should be sequentially arranged to optimize the transfer of the skills and concepts learned from one phase to the next. For example, students might study the risk factors associated with making turns at intersections as part of their homework, then discuss and clarify these concepts during a classroom session, apply the concepts to performance of turning maneuvers during range practice, extend the application to practice in several on-street settings, and finally review their in-car performance during a subsequent classroom session.

Fig. 1.1 Instructional pattern for each unit of in-car instruction

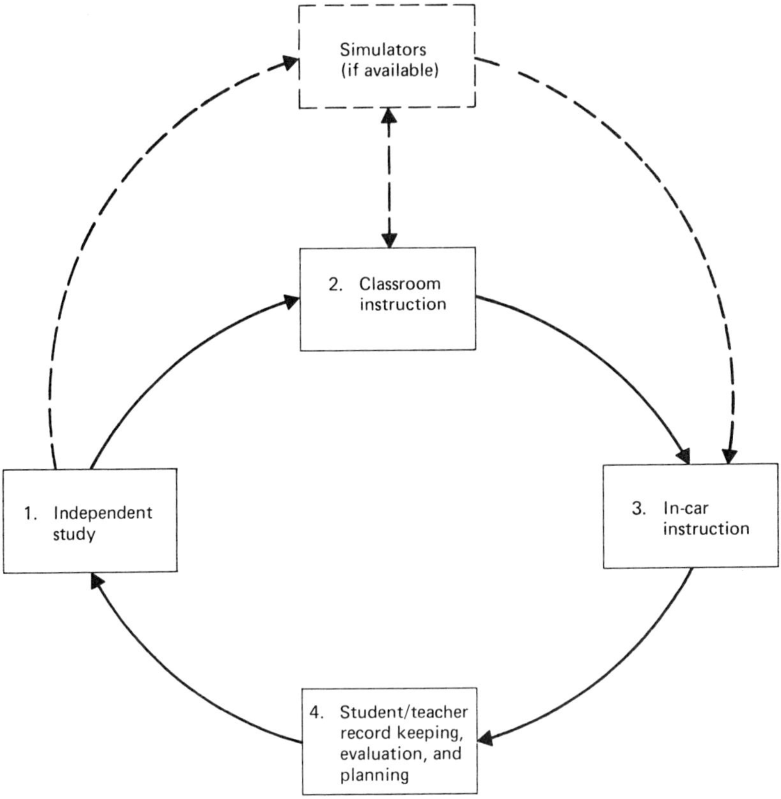

The Unit Plan

The Unit Plan for In-Car Instruction (Part II of this book) contains a series of fifteen units that serve as guides for in-car instruction. Each unit defines objectives in terms of student knowledge and performance; describes the skills, concepts, techniques, and other elements of performance to be learned; discusses common student errors and suggests corrective measures; and provides an instructional plan for selecting methods, organizing content, and guiding student practice.

While the Unit Plan is primarily concerned with the methods and content of the in-car phases of driver education (single-car off-street, single-car on-street, and multiple-car instruction), it also provides for the integration of in-car instruction with other instructional phases. For each unit of in-car instruction, appropriate independent study assignments are suggested, preparatory classroom sessions are outlined, related simulator lessons are identified,* and

---

* It should be noted here that this text does not deal specifically with simulator content or methods and that no attempt is made to prescribe the ways in which discrete elements of simulation content should be integrated with elements of in-car content. Thus teachers who use this text to guide in-car programs and offer simulation instruction as well will have to bear the major responsibility for integrating the simulation program with other program phases. (See further discussion in the section entitled "Using the Unit Plan.")

procedures for record keeping and evaluation are recommended. In fact, a basic instructional pattern or cycle is suggested for sequentially integrating the various phases in the coverage of each unit of in-car content (see Fig. 1.1). Hopefully, this approach will guide the development of an in-car program that fits well within the content of a total driver education program.

The Unit Plan was developed over a period of several years. An attempt was made to utilize the best available sources of information (see Chapters 3 and 4) in making decisions about the content and methods to be included. In addition, the plan was subjected to several field tests at various stages of its development. It was used by beginning and experienced teachers to guide their instruction of student drivers.* These teachers systematically evaluated each unit—in some cases student drivers took part in the evaluation. Substantial revisions were made in the plan on the basis of these evaluations. In a subsequent stage of development, written materials for students were developed and field tested. These include a student text, entitled *Learning to Drive: Skills, Concepts, and Strategies,* and a laboratory manual containing practice guides, practice record forms, evaluation forms, and other materials.

Of necessity the plan is flexible—it allows teachers considerable latitude in conducting their in-car programs. Teachers are encouraged to use the plan selectively according to the requirements of their own teaching situations and personal competencies as teachers.

Although the plan is designed to promote safe driver performance, no claims can be made with respect to its effectiveness. One thing is clear as a result of field-test evaluations: the effectiveness of the plan is significantly influenced by the capabilities of the teachers who use it. It will not compensate for poor teaching, and good teachers will use enough of their own imagination in implementing the plan to ensure its effectiveness.

---

* Beginning teachers enrolled in the basic teacher preparation course at Teachers College, Columbia University, used various forms of the plan as guides to their in-car student-teaching experience. Other experienced teachers in the New York City area used the plan in public and private high schools.

2

THE SELECTION
AND ORGANIZATION OF CONTENT

SELECTION OF CONTENT

Among the most important decisions made by driver education teachers are those that determine the content of the program. The limited amount of time available for instruction necessitates the careful selection of learning experiences that are likely to be most valuable for students, and the judicious rejection of less valuable experiences. In addition, once decisions are made to include certain elements of content, further decisions are required to determine the relative importance of these elements and to allocate instructional time accordingly. As a result of these decisions, particular skills, concepts, maneuvers, strategies, attitudes, and so forth are chosen that students are expected to learn and that together comprise the content of the program. The quality of the student graduates is likely to depend very heavily on the content to which they are exposed.

The selection of content for a driver education program should depend on the prior establishment of broad objectives for the total driver education course. Once the course objectives are determined, the teacher is in a position to select and devise learning experiences on the basis of their probable contribution to the accomplishment of the objectives. For example, the decision to include the learning of a particular maneuver (perhaps parallel parking) as part of the student's in-car experience, and the further decision as to how much time should be devoted to it, should depend on a prior evaluation of the maneuver in relation to course objectives. In the absence of a clear statement and understanding of course objectives, there is no rational basis for including or excluding the maneuver, or for deciding on the proportion of time it should consume.

The failure to carefully establish course objectives and to use these objectives as a guide to content selection can lead to several undesirable consequences. One possibility is that tradition will dominate the selection process—instead of actively engaging in the selection of content, teachers may accept what has been done in the past as the inflexible model for what must be done in the future. Another potential consequence is that objectives that have not been carefully scrutinized may guide content selection. For example, passing the state driver's license examination may assume a disproportionate degree of significance. Teachers may select experiences exclusively because they will help students pass the test, and in so doing fail to prepare students for the great variety of other driving experiences they will encounter.

The central objective of a driver education course should be to develop the student's capacity for safe driver performance. The classroom phase of instruction, together with independent study, should provide for the acquisition of knowledge, understanding, and attitudes that best contribute to this central objective. In the same way, in-car instruction should provide learning experiences that most effectively develop the student's capacity for safe performance. Driving skills, maneuvers, and techniques should be selected (or rejected) on the basis of their potential influence on safe performance.

But what are the constituents of safe driving? What knowledge and abilities should students acquire to enable them to become safe drivers? One way to approach this question is to start with a careful analysis of the driving task.

The Driving Task and Content Selection

The subject matter of driver education is the *driving task*. Fundamentally, the driving task is all of the things a driver has to know and be able to do to move the vehicle from one place to another, safely and efficiently. A comprehensive driver education program should provide instruction in all of the important components of the driving task, and should place special emphasis on those components that contribute significantly to accident avoidance (safe performance). Obviously, then, a clear conception of the driving task is one of the first prerequisites to determining content for a driver education program.

Many analyses of the driving task have been developed (B 45–B 66). Most of these analyses use relevant sources of information as a basis for identifying the crucial components of the task. Normally, the key sources of information include studies of accident causation, accident statistics, normative studies of driver performance, existing traffic laws and regulations, and authoritative opinion. In effect, then, a good analysis is a careful synthesis of what is known about drivers and driving. Although the consequent task analyses differ from one another in some respects, the more recent and comprehensive analyses have much in common. They all emphasize the accident preventive features of driver performance by viewing as the most important aspects of driving those driver actions that are crucial to accident avoidance. Thus, for example, most analyses regard the driver's perception and interpretation of potentially hazardous situations as being central to the task.

It would be marvelous to be able to report that our sources of information are impeccable, that research and careful study have yielded information that specifies precisely which components of the task are crucial and exactly how all drivers should perform each of those components. Unfortunately, this is not the case. There are many features of the driving task that as yet are not well understood. We do not have all the answers. Furthermore, given the inherent complexity of the traffic setting and, particularly, the complicated nature of the human operators (drivers), it might be quite some time before we do have most of the answers. Nevertheless, a good deal more is known today about the driving task than was known a few years ago. Competent analyses of the task reflect this new knowledge and provide a sound basis for determining content for driver education programs.

Development of the concept

The Unit Plan for In-Car Instruction (Part II) is based on a careful analysis and conceptualization of the driving task. Several key sources of information were used as a basis for developing the analysis. First, previous analyses of the task (B 45–B 66) were carefully examined. Common elements in these analyses, applicable to driver education, were isolated and used as the basic framework for the conception of the task. Malfetti's description of the task (B 58)* was particularly useful in the early development of the concept. The HumRRO study of the driving task (B 59) and the Automotive Safety Foundation's analysis (B 127) were used later on to expand the basic concept. Second, supporting evidence from a variety of sources was used to validate and refine the analysis. Studies of accident causation and accident statistics (B 1– B 44) were used to (1) isolate driver actions that contributed to accidents and therefore should be the focus for preventive training, and (2) identify common circumstances surrounding accidents that pointed to the kinds of situations drivers should be trained to deal with. Studies of driver performance (B 67–B 118) that record elements of the task as they are being performed (for example, eye fixations, steering and braking responses, and so on) were used to develop more specific descriptions of task components. Third, since driving is in large part a social phenomenon governed by specific rules and regulations, traffic laws (B 139) provided an important basis for conceptualizing the task. In addition, professional literature dealing with how people should drive (selected entries within B 119–B 147) was useful in identifying those features of the task that professional consensus indicated were most crucial to safe driving. Finally, extensive field explorations that tested the emerging concept by applying it to instructional settings provided information that was used to make the concept more suitable for beginning drivers.

The concept: an overview

A detailed presentation of the conception of the driving task, upon which the Unit Plan is based, is contained in the plan itself, particularly in those sections that describe the skills, techniques, strategies, and concepts to be learned. What follows here is a brief description of some of the essential features of the concept.

The overall concept of the task is divided into two major parts, readiness tasks and in-car tasks (see Fig. 2.1). The *readiness tasks* identify those things drivers should know about and/or be able to do in preparing themselves and their vehicles for driving. For the most part, knowledge related to readiness tasks is dealt with during the classroom or independent study phases of driver education. As they are not part of the Unit Plan, these readiness tasks are not a major focus of this text and thus need no further explanation at this point.

In-car tasks identify those features of the overall driving task that commonly occur during active driving performance. At the heart of the in-car tasks are the *fundamental elements of performance* that recur almost continuously during driving (see Fig. 2.1). The driver knows the vehicle's *intended path* (that is, where the vehicle is going). With this path in mind, the driver *scans* the environment in the vicinity of the path in search of *obstacles and potential obstacles* that might necessitate a change of path or adjustment in speed. What is seen is *evaluated* by the virtually simultaneous process of *identifying* critical elements in the vicinity, *predicting* the actions or movements of those elements (particularly the potential obstacles that might enter the intended path), *considering the alternative* actions available, and *deciding* to choose the alternative that *reduces the risk* of an accident. Then the decision is *executed* by controlling the *speed, direction, and position of the vehicle,* and when appropriate by *communicating intentions.†*

---

* This author was a major contributor to the development of this task description.
† This delineation of fundamental elements of performance is similar to the currently popular concept of IPDE (Identify, Predict, Decide, Execute) used in many other texts and programs. I have chosen to use the "fundamental elements" as depicted above because they emphasize the importance of "knowing the intended path" and "scanning techniques," which necessarily precede "identification." Also, I've included "identify," "predict," and "decide" under one larger operation, "evaluation," because these cognitive and judgmental operations so often occur simultaneously and in mixed sequence.

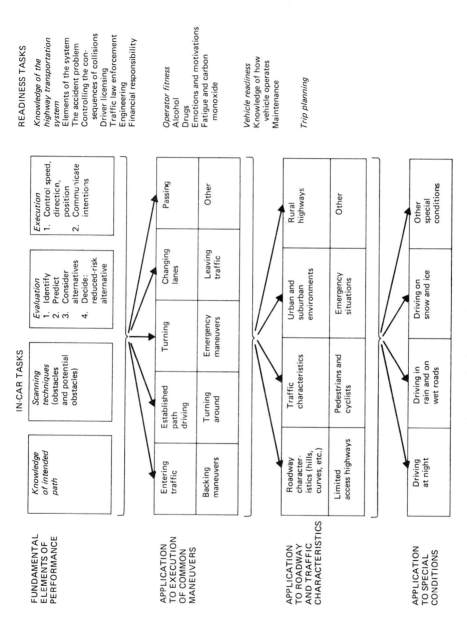

Fig. 2.1 The driving task: an overview

These fundamental elements of performance are applied in different ways during the *execution of common driving maneuvers.* For example, the scanning techniques and speed control patterns used in changing lanes differ from those used in making right turns. Yet within each type of maneuver there is considerable similarity in the ways the fundamental performance elements are applied. For example, the scanning techniques used in preparation for a lane change are similar from one lane change to the next. However, within each maneuver there are also differences in the application of the fundamental elements depending on the particular driving situation encountered. For example, a left turn in the face of oncoming traffic is executed differently than one executed when the roadway is clear.

Fundamental performance elements and the maneuvers they comprise must be applied in different ways to conform to the demands of various *roadway and traffic characteristics* such as hills, curves, heavy traffic, pedestrians, and so forth. For example, scanning techniques, evaluation procedures, and speed control used during established-path driving on a clear, straight, level road have to be adjusted when approaching a sharp curve in the road or when a pedestrian threatens to enter the car's path. Furthermore, adjustments in performance must be made to conform to *special conditions* (night, rain, snow, ice, and so on) that might exist on a particular roadway at a particular time of day. For example, entering traffic from one's own driveway might be performed in a certain way at noontime on a clear day, but would have to be performed in a different way at midnight when the driveway is covered with ice.

The effective performance of all of these in-car tasks depends on the driver's ability to execute certain *basic psychomotor skills* (braking, accelerating, tracking, and so forth) in an efficient and consistent manner. In addition, drivers must have a store of *related concepts and information* that enable them to (1) know where to look, (2) interpret what they see, and (3) make the right decisions in relation to the great variety of roadway, traffic, and special conditions they encounter.

Derivation of Specific Objectives

Once the subject matter for a curriculum has been clearly established (in this case the critical components of the driving task), the next stage in curriculum development normally entails the identification of objectives for students; that is, the specification of the things that students are expected to know and be able to do as a consequence of instruction. In most instances, specific objectives can be derived directly from the analysis of the driving task by identifying those aspects of the task that should be covered in the program and translating them into specific objectives.

Modern educational theory suggests that these objectives should be as specific as possible—preferably stated in precise behavioral terms—and should include a criterion level of acceptable (or passing) performance. Thus, for example, an objective dealing with knowledge of right-of-way rules might read: "Given a ten-item multiple-choice test on five basic right-of-way rules, the student will achieve a score of at least 90 percent." By specifying objectives in this way, the teacher gives precise direction to the program of instruction and clearly establishes the standards to be used in evaluating students. Furthermore, in a subject like driver education where the performance of psychomotor tasks is a central concern, specification of objectives helps clarify the distinction between cognitive, affective, and psychomotor objectives, and in so doing encourages teachers to be thorough in their specification not only of what the students should be able to *do*, but also of what they should *know*. A recent study sponsored by the Department of Transportation (B 138) resulted in an extensive specification of hundreds of instructional objectives, derived from an analysis of the driving task, to be used as guides in developing driver education programs. They make an excellent resource for teachers interested in clarifying and spelling out objectives.

While the specification of behavioral objectives has many advantages, it also has some inherent limitations. Specific objectives are only as good as the knowledge base from which they are derived. Although we know a good deal about the driving task and the *general* constituents of good driving, we do not know enough about the task to set very specific criterion levels that are indicative of acceptable driving performance. For example, although we know that accurate tracking (keeping the car on the intended path) is an important component of good driving, precisely how accurate a student should be in tracking in order to qualify as "acceptable" in this performance component has yet to be determined. Anyone who tries to write a specific behavioral objective that indicates precisely how accurately a student must stay on an intended path before his or her tracking performance is judged "acceptable" will have to do so in the absence of any clear supporting evidence.

The Unit Plan enumerates objectives for students in connection with each unit and each major segment of a unit. The objectives are written at a moderate level of specificity. That is, they are intended to be specific enough to give direction to each instructional segment and to the evaluation of student progress, and yet general enough to allow the teacher some flexibility in using them. Also, the objectives are written in such a way as to distinguish between cognitive and psychomotor objectives. In using the Unit Plan, teachers may wish to define the objectives further by deriving subobjectives that reflect the specific instructional elements included in their own programs or the specific criterion levels they use in evaluating student proficiency.

Limiting Factors in Content Selection

In the process of selecting content for a driver education program, teachers encounter several factors that limit the choices available to them. Although some of these factors are more evident in certain teaching situations than in others, they affect all programs to some extent. It would seem advisable for teachers to be acutely aware of these limitations so that their instructional plans provide for the best possible program within existing limitations. Since this text deals primarily with in-car instruction, only those factors that directly limit the in-car phase of instruction are discussed below.

Time   All driver education teachers are limited in the amount of in-car practice time they can provide for each student (see Chapter 3). This time limitation is important. In many cases it means that the teacher will be forced to omit elements of content for which there is no time, even though these elements are judged to be potentially valuable components of an in-car program. Of course, the teacher's responsibility in this regard is to make certain that those elements of content that are included deserve the priority they receive.

Available roadways and traffic conditions   Much of what persons learn about driving depends on the roadways on which they practice. Learning to drive on urban streets, expressways, rural roads, or on hills and curves is best achieved by practicing on these facilities. The same can be said for traffic conditions. Learning to drive in heavy traffic requires exposure to this condition.

The teacher's selection of content is limited by the roadways and conditions available within a reasonable distance of the school. Considering the fact that most in-car periods last approximately forty to fifty minutes, and that the time from and to school must be allowed for, the teacher usually cannot afford to venture to relatively distant areas. This means that some elements of content may have to be omitted in cases where the school is not located at a point accessible to various road and traffic conditions. The inventive teacher will find ways of reducing the influence of this limitation by, for example, scheduling back-to-back driving periods that permit more distant travel.

Available environmental conditions   Closely related to the previous limitation is the fact that teachers must provide instruction under the temperature and weather conditions that happen to prevail in their locale at times when practice is scheduled. A teacher in Florida is not likely to be able to conduct practice in driving on snow and ice. Furthermore, teachers in more northerly regions are not likely to have just the right type of snow conditions available at just the right time in the semester (when the student is ready to practice under these conditions). Even when conditions and time are right, they are not likely to stay that way long enough to permit most of the students to have the opportunity for adequate practice.

Uncontrollable traffic elements   Although teachers are in a position to exercise control over where the students drive, the maneuvers they perform, and how long they drive, the teachers are not able to control the movement of other vehicles, pedestrians, and objects in the vicinity of the driver education car. This has an important effect on which elements of driver performance can be taught systematically. For example, teachers might wish to provide instruction in defensive responses to the unexpected movements of other vehicles. To accomplish this, they might wish to expose all students to a series of common situations in which other drivers make these unexpected movements. Unfortunately, however, teachers cannot control the movements of other drivers. Instead, they must accept what happens and to this extent must allow chance to govern the situations that confront students. As a consequence, some students will be exposed to one type of unexpected vehicular movement, other students will be exposed to other types; some students will be exposed to several such unexpected movements, and others will be exposed to none.

As another example, teachers might wish to provide systematic instruction in passing another vehicle that is moving in the same direction. To do so, however, requires a lead vehicle, traveling at a certain speed on a certain portion of a roadway, at a time when there is a sufficient gap in traffic coming from the opposite direction. These variable elements are not under the control of driver education teachers, and hence instruction and practice in passing must await the opportune moment—a moment that may arise for some students and not for others.*

Exposure to unreasonable risk   Most important decisions in education are made on the basis of which alternative will provide the best possible learning experience for students. However, one principle that overrides educational desirability is the necessity to protect the student against unreasonable risk of injury or harm. This is a particularly important principle in determining content for in-car instruction. The in-car setting is inherently dangerous to begin with. The teacher's primary responsibility is to ensure that at no time is the level of risk unreasonably high. As a consequence teachers may be forced to reject elements of content that involve excessive risk—even though these elements otherwise represent valuable learning experiences. For example, providing practice in skid control, running off the roadway, and collision avoidance responses is educationally sound—especially when safe driving is the

---

* There are instances when a second driver education vehicle (and teacher) might be used as the "other" vehicle and thereby permit more control of the situation, but these instances are relatively rare and require extensive coordination between teachers.

major objective. Furthermore, with respect to these elements of performance, more realistic practice conditions are likely to result in more effective and transferable learning. However, teachers are limited in the amount of realistic practice they can provide in controlling skids, and so forth, because there is a point beyond which such practice incurs unreasonable risk.

Capabilities of beginners   The capabilities of beginning drivers to perform skills and to cope with traffic and road conditions develop gradually. The students' rates of development determine their readiness to perform the more complex skills and to be exposed to more difficult road conditions. One of the teacher's principal functions is to control the introduction of new content to suit the individual student's developing capabilities. It is inadvisable to encourage students to perform difficult on-street maneuvers before they have gained reasonable control of the accelerator and brake pedals. Nor is it wise to allow students to drive at high speeds before they are able to guide the vehicle accurately at lower speeds.

Teachers who follow these rules soon discover that during a driver education course the content to which a student is exposed is limited significantly by the student's own rate of progress. In particular, slower students are less likely to be exposed to the advanced elements of content and, indeed, the majority of students who progress at an average rate may have limited exposure to advanced elements. Although there are several procedures a teacher might use to reduce the influence of this limitation, it is likely to remain a problem as long as the course consists of approximately six in-car hours and students have a normal range of capabilities.

ORGANIZATION OF CONTENT

Sequential order of content

Existing analyses of the driving task have effectively pointed to the many components of driving that need to be mastered, eventually, by all competent drivers. But where does one begin, and how does one progress from the learning of one component to the next? Clearly, what is needed here is an analysis of the *task of learning to drive*. Ideally, such an analysis would be based on empirical evidence and would specify not only what should be learned, but the optimal order in which it should be learned. Components would be arranged in sequence to provide for maximum transfer from one learning experience to the next and thus optimally facilitate the student's eventual acquisition of all required competencies.

Unfortunately, however, while researchers and theorists have devoted much attention to analyzing the driver's task as it confronts the experienced driver, little attention has been directed toward determining the learner's task. Perhaps at some future point studies will emerge that demonstrate the superiority of certain sequential arrangements of learning experiences. To date there are no such studies. In their absence we have to rely on professional experience and intuition, logic, and some general principles of learning theory as the bases for our decisions about how to order and arrange subject matter in driver education. The professional literature (B 119–B 147) contains many examples of how the content of the overall program might be organized; teachers should examine these resources carefully before making final decisions about how to organize learning experiences.

Since this text is concerned primarily with the in-car phase of instruction, some general guides for sequencing the content of this phase are listed below. They in part represent the consensus found in the professional literature, and in part stem from our own experiences in field testing the Unit Plan.

1. *Cover the logical prerequisites to moving the vehicle first.*   There are certain elements of performance and knowledge that should logically precede any attempts to move the vehicle. These elements include knowing the location of controls and how to operate them, adjusting mirrors, adopting a suitable driver's position, and so on. Failure to cover such items at an early point in the in-car program frequently leads to problems later on. For example, drivers who adopt an unsuitable driving position may have difficulty in seeing or in reaching controls, and drivers who are unfamiliar with the location and operation of control devices may have problems performing maneuvers that require the use of these controls.

2. *Cover basic (component) skills prior to the more complex skills that are dependent on several components.*   Some driving skills are basic in the sense that they are components of many other more complex elements of driving. For example, achieving the ability to control the speed of the car might be considered a basic skill since speed control is involved in most types of driving performance. It is usually advisable to provide for the acquisition of such basic skills at an early stage of in-car instruction so that students will be equipped to undertake the subsequent learning of more advanced maneuvers. For example, the performance of on-street turning maneuvers is complex. It requires effective application of scanning techniques, evaluation procedures, signaling, steering techniques, speed control skills, and so forth. It is most helpful if students acquire some mastery of these component skills prior to attempting on-street turns. Otherwise they are faced with having to learn all the components at once, which may result in the commission of a variety of interrelated errors and may eventually lead to confusion and frustration. Indeed, as Gagne (B 128) suggests, all in-car content should be arranged so that "the learning of higher-level skills is substantially facilitated by the previous learning of lower-level skills."

3. *Cover related concepts and information prior to in-car performance.*   The effective performance of many driving skills, maneuvers, and techniques depends on a knowledge of related information or concepts. The plan for in-car instruction should take this fact into consideration. Provision should be made for students to acquire essential related information and concepts before attempting to perform the particular skill or maneuver in the car. For example, the safe performance of a lane change requires a prior understanding of the potential dangers involved in the maneuver and the appropriate scanning and assessment techniques designed to overcome these dangers. It is most helpful if the student driver comes to the in-car lesson equipped with such knowledge before attempting a lane change. Prior independent study and classroom work are convenient ways of providing for the acquisition of these related concepts and information in advance.

4. *Arrange content in order of its level of difficulty.*   Some skills, techniques, and maneuvers are more difficult to master than others. It is generally advisable to arrange the sequence of content so that students are exposed to the easier tasks first. This procedure should help ensure student progress during the early stages of instruction and at the same time should enable students to improve basic skills to the point where they are better able to cope with the more difficult skills. Introducing exceptionally difficult tasks at an early stage in the learning process can lead to repeated failure on the part of the student and to a consequent sense of frustration. For example, most students (and experienced drivers) find it more difficult to guide the vehicle on backward paths than on forward paths. Therefore it is usually advisable to permit the acquisition of a reasonable degree of skill in forward driving before requiring the student to master intricate backing maneuvers.

5. *Arrange content with regard to the level of risk involved.* Some elements of driving performance and some driving situations are more dangerous than others. Practicing at low speeds in a vacant off-street area is inherently less dangerous than practicing at high speeds on busily traveled streets. In addition, the amount of risk involved in practicing a particular skill at a particular location is increased or decreased by the beginning driver's capability for coping with the skill and the location. As a general rule, therefore, it is advisable to organize content so that students first learn less dangerous skills and perform in less dangerous situations. Then, as their capabilities develop, gradually expose them to more dangerous skills and situations.

Assignment of content to instructional phases

Once the objectives and content for a driver education program are mapped out and sequenced, there remains the task of assigning that content to appropriate instructional phases (that is, classroom, independent study, simulators, in-car). The real question facing the teacher is, How should the students' learning experiences be arranged within and across program phases to best facilitate the accomplishment of program objectives? Several general rules might be followed in making these decisions.

1. *Each instructional phase should be used to accomplish those objectives that it can most effectively accomplish.* For example, independent study and classroom discussion sessions are probably most appropriate for facilitating a thorough understanding of the problem of alcohol and accidents. Acquisition of the psychomotor skills involved in controlling the speed and direction of the car, on the other hand, must occur in the car, while practice in the perception of dangerous emergency situations may be feasible only in simulators.

2. *When two or more instructional phases can accomplish the same objective with approximately equal effectiveness, choose the one that is most efficient.* For example, it would be more efficient for the teacher to give instruction in "preparing to drive" to twelve students at once (in a simulation laboratory or on a multiple-car range) than it would be to provide the instruction for each student separately during single-car instruction.

3. *Avoid conflicts in content.* In any multiphased program there is the potential problem of introducing instructional information in one phase that conflicts with information in another phase. For example, "procedures for making a right turn" may be treated one way in the textbook, somewhat differently by the teacher in class or in the car, and still differently by the simulator program. The teacher's responsibility is to resolve these conflicts beforehand by carefully selecting, eliminating, and revising elements of content to the point where there is consistency across phases.

4. *Optimize positive transfer from one phase to another and minimize negative transfer.* For example, a classroom discussion of "scanning procedures at intersections" might include specific variations in scanning procedures that should be used at particular intersections along the practice driving route. On the other hand, do not allow students to develop stereotypical scanning habits that are suitable for a multiple-car range or simulator laboratory but not transferable to on-street driving. For example, the student may develop a routine scanning procedure for the one major intersection on a driving range and attempt to use the same routine in a variety of on-street settings where it is not appropriate. Or, when using simulators, students might get used to orienting their search procedures directly ahead (where the film is projected) and subsequently neglect to turn their heads to scan at on-street intersections.

The Unit Plan contains a general prescription for assigning content to various instructional phases, and attempts to present a reasonable plan for effectively and efficiently integrating program phases. Obviously, however, teachers will have to adapt this plan to suit the unique conditions at their own schools. Ultimately the decision to incorporate different phases and the assignment of content to those phases will depend on a number of factors uniquely related to the particular school, such as the available facilities (off-street area, range, simulators), the number of driver education teachers, the number of students to be trained, scheduling procedures of the school, and so on. An optimal program in one school may not be optimal or even feasible for another school.

THE SELECTION AND ORGANIZATION OF CONTENT FOR THE UNIT PLAN

The Process

The Unit Plan for In-Car Instruction is the product of a careful process of content selection and organization. All of the factors discussed in the previous parts of this chapter were taken into consideration during its development. Figure 2.2 illustrates the major steps involved in the process.

The major objective that guided the entire process was "to provide the basic preparation for driving that will enable each student to drive as safely as he or she possibly can." An early decision was made to limit the scope of the Unit Plan to in-car instruction, and as a consequence the analyses of the in-car tasks (Fig. 2.1) were used as the basis for selecting and sequencing content and for deriving specific objectives. Thus the Unit Plan is conceived of as a part of a total driver education program that would also provide for the learning of readiness tasks (Fig. 2.1) in other parts of the program.

Relevant and valid sources of information had a substantial influence on content selection and organization. Wherever possible, decisions were based on the implications of existing research findings, although, as mentioned earlier, the applicability of research findings to the teaching of driving is limited and indirect. In addition, existing professional literature and analyses of the driving task had a particularly significant influence on content selection. Some of the more important sources of information used in developing the Unit Plan are included in the References and Notations at the back of the book.

In order to ensure the practicality of the Unit Plan, limiting factors were taken into consideration. Elements of content and organization were rejected in cases where they were judged to be unrealistic in terms of existing iimitations in the majority of driver education programs.

In addition, the Unit Plan was subjected to a series of field tests. These tests were designed to evaluate each unit in terms of its effect on student performance and its usability by teachers. Several major revisions in content and organization were made on the basis of field-test findings.

The Product

Figure 2.3 presents a schematic overview of the essential features of the Unit Plan. The top horizontal line of boxes indicates the sequential ordering of concepts and elements of performance to be learned. These concepts and elements are cumulatively ordered so that

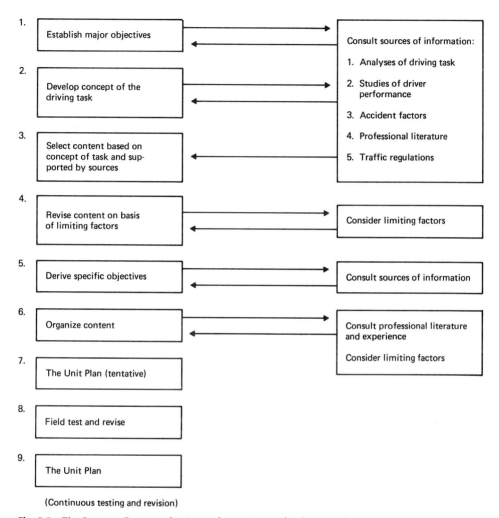

Fig. 2.2 *The Process:* Content selection and organization for the Unit Plan

subordinate skills and concepts precede higher-level skills and concepts of which they are a part. Thus, for example, the "elements of reduced-risk performance" incorporate and are dependent on prior mastery of all of the preceding concepts and elements of performance.

The lower rows of boxes indicate the specific units in the plan. The arrows from upper to lower rows identify the concepts and elements of performance covered in each unit. Notice particularly that the key reduced-risk elements of performance (scanning, communicating, evaluating, and control skills) are applied continuously throughout the later units (Units 6–15). What this means is that these key elements of performance are emphasized in all of the units dealing with maneuvers and strategies for environments and conditions. So, for example, learning to perform turns involves learning appropriate scanning techniques, communication

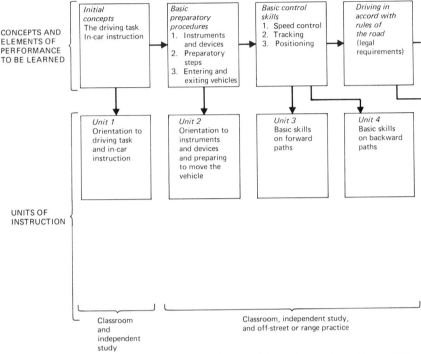

Fig. 2.3 Schematic overview of the Unit Plan

of intentions, evaluation procedures, and control skills; the same is true for learning to drive on curves. Of course, however, these key elements are differentially applied to each maneuver and strategy. For example, the scanning techniques for lane changes are different from those for backing maneuvers, which in turn are different from the scanning techniques used on limited access highways. Thus there is a continuity and yet a progressive differentiation in the learning of these key elements of performance.

Also notice the relationship between units dealing with basic maneuvers (Units 6, 7, 9, and 10) and units dealing with driving strategies for various environments and conditions (Units 8, 12, 13, and 14). The units on maneuvers are subordinate to subsequent units. The basic assumption here is that the student first learns to perform these maneuvers under a relatively restricted set of conditions and then learns to perform them in a variety of ways to suit various roadway, traffic, and environmental conditions.

The units are also arranged to provide for gradually increasing the level of difficulty of the tasks performed and the risk of exposure to accident. Initial units are designed for off-street and range practice. Later units, particularly those dealing with road and traffic characteristics, rely primarily on on-street practice.

Since effective in-car practice depends on the students' prior mastery of concepts and information directly related to in-car performance, the plan includes descriptions of those

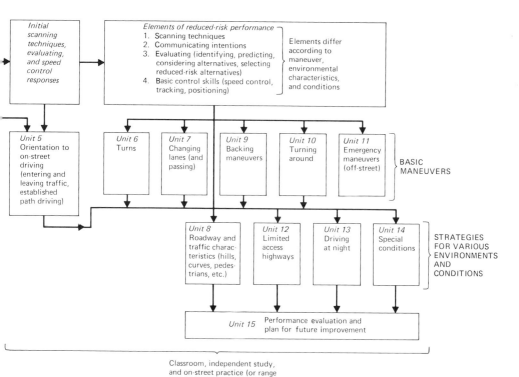

concepts and outlines classroom sessions and independent study assignments that focus on them.

Do not be deceived, however, by the way in which everything seems to fit neatly into boxes. This is done to help clarify the conceptual model that undergirds the plan, and to indicate the features of the driving task that are emphasized at each stage of instruction. In reality, there is a good deal of overlap in terms of the concepts and performance elements actually dealt with during instructional periods.

3

SINGLE-CAR METHODS

Any consideration of in-car teaching methods must begin with the understanding that a moving vehicle is a unique educational setting. Although it has some elements in common with the normal educational setting (the classroom), there is much that distinguishes the two. During in-car instruction the "classroom" moves; its movement is controlled to a large extent by the student; the outside environment is continuously changing; events in the environment cannot be controlled or, in many cases, predicted by the teacher; both teacher and student are faced with the ever-present danger of an accident; the teacher's job is to protect as well as to teach; and the subject matter itself is unique. Consider the following incidents that occurred during in-car instruction in high-school driver education programs.* They illustrate a few of the distinguishing features of this setting.

A high-school teacher in California reported:

We were in the latter stages of instruction and so were driving on a two lane highway, and a transcontinental truck was coming toward us from the opposite direction. We were going at 55 mph and the truck was going at least as fast. As we approached the vehicle I said, "We are a bit too close to the center line, better swing over." The girl's hands gripped the wheel a bit tighter and turned—*to the left.* I do not take the wheel as a general rule, but I grabbed the wheel with my right hand, swerving the car back to the right, and hit the dual control brake with my right foot. Just then the trucker gunned his motor and swung out too. It was a close call.

A high-school teacher in Wisconsin reported:

A girl student had three hours of good driving experience before we attempted the parallel parking problem. This was during my fourth consecutive hour of behind-the-wheel

---

* These illustrative incidents, and most others appearing in this chapter, were reported by high-school teachers and students. They describe actual events that took place during in-car instruction in high-school driver education programs. These reports were collected in connection with a study by Anderson and Malfetti (B 126). For the most part the incidents appear exactly as they were reported by teachers and students. In some cases, minor editorial changes have been made to provide a more readable incident. (All quotations from the files of the Safety Research and Education Project, Teachers College, Columbia University. Quoted by permission.)

instruction and followed a rather hectic morning of poor driver-students. I found my student, for some unknown reason, very ineffective. She made error after error, and was not getting any closer to parking the car. My patience was thin, and my instruction was a combination of caustic comments and forceful remarks to the point of indicating complete loss of confidence in her ability. The student became quite unnerved and began to cry. The addition of three smirking student observers in the back seat was no help and the lesson had to be discontinued.

A high-school teacher in Indiana reported:

We were passing a car and trailer traveling in the same direction. The student was instructed to pass when she felt all was safe. This she did, but failed to take into account a curve in the distance. As we pulled out to pass—progressing nicely—two cars appeared around the bend. The situation alarmed her, but she was well advanced in the procedure and if the oncoming cars would cooperate we could make it. I calmly encouraged her to speed up, remain calm, give signal to driver being passed and to pull back gently and steadily. The precarious mission was accomplished.

The discussion of teaching methods that follows focuses on the unusual demands of the in-car setting and the more important aspects of teacher performance in that setting. Much of the information upon which the discussion is based stems from a study of teacher performance in the car.* In addition, the author's experience in training teachers has provided relevant and useful information.†

BASIC CONSIDERATIONS

The process of making decisions about teaching methods should take into consideration some of the fundamental characteristics of the in-car setting discussed below. An awareness and understanding of these characteristics should enable the teacher to make a more appropriate selection and application of methods.

The Efficient Use of Available Time

No doubt the most formidable enemy facing the driver education teacher is time. The problem is especially critical for in-car instruction. The average teacher might expect to have available six hours of behind-the-wheel practice driving time per student.‡ Recognizing the complexities of the driving task, the problems of slow learners, the variety of driving experiences to which the student must be exposed, and the problems of retention from week to week, this is an extremely limited amount of time in which to train drivers effectively. (Motor vehicle departments recommend at least twenty hours of practice driving prior to applying for a road test.)

---

* This study (B 126) collected reports from thousands of teachers and students of driver education describing critical incidents that took place during in-car instruction.
† Records resulting from several years of in-car supervision of beginning teachers provided useful data. These records include accounts of the teaching methods used, the characteristic actions of teachers, and the performance of students.
‡ In 1974, 87 percent of all eligible students in the United States were enrolled in courses that provided at least six hours of behind-the-wheel practice per student (B 141).

Furthermore, unlike most other courses offered in the high-school curriculum, driver education is not offered repeatedly at several grade levels. Students cannot make up for time limitations by enrolling in a subsequent driver education course. Normally, they have one opportunity (a single course) to benefit from the expert guidance of a trained driver education teacher.

Obviously the most direct approach to this problem is to schedule as much in-car time as possible for each course. Beginning teachers should recognize this problem in advance and attempt to plan their courses accordingly. Experienced teachers are, no doubt, already familiar with the problem and have made attempts to extend the time devoted to in-car instruction. In addition to extending the total amount of in-car time, the teacher might further reduce the problem by adopting methods that efficiently use the time available.

Since learning to drive depends so heavily on the amount of actual practice of the skills and techniques involved, an efficient plan for the use of in-car time should devote as much of that time as possible to student practice. There are countless ways in which teachers can ensure maximal amounts of student practice. They can organize the total driver education course so that all material that can be covered in the classroom is covered there and does not use valuable in-car time. They can organize practice driving sessions so that time is not wasted getting to the car, changing seat positions, getting to the driving area, and so on. They can carefully select the driving route that offers the best opportunity for uninterrupted practice of the skills being taught. Most important, they can adapt their entire pattern of teaching to the demands of the limited time at their disposal—sometimes this may mean avoiding the use of an effective but time-consuming technique. For example, a student may experience difficulty in backing and steering; that is, she may turn the wheel in the wrong direction. One way to deal with this problem is for the teacher, through a series of questions, to encourage the student to analyze the effect of her steering actions on the front wheels and its consequent effect on the movement of the rear end of the car. This encouragement of student analysis through questioning is ordinarily a valuable teaching technique. However, it can be extremely time consuming, especially if the student is not quick to grasp the basic concept. It is entirely possible that a simple verbal cue from the teacher would have helped the student correct her performance and that a subsequent classroom discussion might be used to enhance the student's understanding of the principles involved.

Individual instances of wasted time may appear to be a relatively trivial matter to the inexperienced teacher. But when all separate instances are added together, the total waste is appreciable. In fact, a teacher who consistently makes efficient use of the available time might be able to devote 20–30 percent more in-car time to practice driving. The following guides emerge from a consideration of the limited amount of time for in-car instruction.

Guide 1   *Organize and conduct in-car instruction to provide maximal time for student practice of safe driving skills and techniques.*

Guide 2   *All material that can be dealt with effectively in the classroom, as independent study, or during observation time in the car should be covered in these phases of the course and should not be allowed to consume valuable in-car practice driving time.*

Teaching in an Inherently Dangerous Environment

Perhaps the most distinctive feature of in-car instruction is the influence of the inherently dangerous environment in which it takes place. The "classroom on wheels" moves— sometimes at relatively high speeds. Other vehicles and pedestrians within the teaching environment are also mobile. Not only is there the danger of a student error resulting in a collision, but there is the added threat created by the mistakes of other drivers and pedestrians. Obviously, the degree of danger varies with the capabilities of the student driver and with changes in roadway and traffic conditions. Nevertheless, danger is always present to some degree and makes for an unusual educational setting.

This element of danger must be considered in the planning and conduct of the entire in-car program. For example, the decision to allow a student to progress from the performance of a simple maneuver on an empty street to the performance of a more complex maneuver in heavy traffic must be based not only on the educational soundness of the plan but on the potential risk involved. While it might be educationally valid to provide a challenging learning experience for the student driver, the teacher cannot do so when it poses an unreasonable threat to the safety of the people in the car.

Students are affected by this ever-present danger. A reasonably large segment of student drivers feel nervous, tense, or frightened when they get behind the wheel, and this emotional stress frequently acts as a formidable barrier to learning. Furthermore, some teachers appear to be completely unaware of the student's emotional distress and behave in a way that aggravates the student's condition. There is no easy remedy for this problem. The inherent danger in the driving environment cannot be eliminated, nor can teachers do much to alter the basic emotional makeup of the student. They can, however, avoid aggravating the situation, and may even help to reduce the anxiety and fear. The first requirement for the teacher is to be alert to the problem and to recognize that in any group of students there will be some who approach the driving task with considerable apprehension. The teacher's job is to identify these individuals—sometimes this can be done by simply asking them how they feel; in other cases careful attention to the student's posture and movements may be revealing. Once the identification is made, the teacher might deal with the problem by adopting an especially calm and soft tone in making comments and corrections, or by explaining to the student that he (the teacher) has the dual-control brake available to prevent accidents, or by being careful not to permit the student to get into difficult traffic situations. Notwithstanding all these precautions, the teacher must be ready to accept the fact that some students simply will not calm down—until, perhaps, they have had extensive experience behind the wheel.

The effect of the ever-present danger also appears to produce unusual emotional strain on teachers. Instructing beginning drivers for five periods a day, five days a week in a dangerous environment can be an exceedingly trying experience. Many high-school teachers report instances in which they "lost their patience" or "blew up at the student," and they point out that these incidents proved to be severely detrimental to student progress. Once again there is no easy solution to the problem, but the least teachers can do is to be alert to it and to the disastrous consequences that may result if they lose their temper. In fact, teachers who find that they frequently lose their temper with students should give serious consideration to the possibility that they are not emotionally suited to the task of giving in-car instruction.

The following incidents reflect some of the problems that arise in connection with teaching in a dangerous environment.

A high-school teacher in Georgia reported:

We were driving along *on the city streets* three weeks after we began the behind-the-wheel phase of the program. There were four of us in the driver training automobile, three students and myself. When at an intersection after having stopped, a bus zoomed by in front of us completely terrorizing the driver, I realized that this had upset her greatly, because of the reaction on her face; before I could react she had pressed the accelerator pedal to the floor, she had a death grip on the steering wheel and we were soaring across the intersection. Luck was with us for no cars crossed our path. Very calmly I said to her in the midst of the panicking students in the rear of the car, "Ease your foot off the accelerator and let me have the steering wheel." I believe to this day that it was the calmness in my actions, excited to death as I was, that prevented a bad reaction on the student's part. She responded to my instructions perfectly. I gained control of the car, pulled over to the curb, allowed her to compose herself, and let her continue to drive the rest of her time.

A high-school student in Texas reported:

One time I was driving along a dirt road and came to a hill which was very steep and a railroad track was on top of the hill. I drove up the hill in high gear and when I got on top of the railroad track, the car stopped. Finally, when I managed to drive the car off, the teacher started shouting at me never to stop on a railroad track and that he wanted to live longer whether I did or not. He never did tell me what I should have done—that I should have shifted into second before going up the hill. I had to ask someone afterward what I should have done.

A high-school student in Pennsylvania reported:

Our object of the day was to learn how to correctly turn corners. It was our first time in the car (as far as handling it ourselves) and we were truly afraid. The girl who drives with me took her turn first. Everything came pretty easy to her. Then it was my turn. I started the car all right, but I couldn't see how I could be expected to turn a corner properly. As you may have expected I went way into the middle of the street. A car was coming and it was up to me to get out of the way. I got panicky. My instructor calmed me, gave me the right direction for making turns, and I passed that crisis still in one piece. I've been grateful ever since.

A high-school student from Florida reported:

It was our first try at turning corners. Our instructor turned several to show us the proper way to do it. I tried second; I am nervous when I try something new. I tried and tried, finally the instructor told me to stop the car. I did so at once. He started talking to me at first, then yelling until I was almost in tears. He said, "Try it again!" I did, but now my heart was not in it. I was hurt and overcautious. Whenever I am driving (without my teacher or with), I am afraid to turn corners, and I usually do a bad job. I don't know if it is right to blame it all on the teacher, but I am still trying to turn corners correctly and failing. This tends to make driving a task rather than a pleasure.

The following guides relate to the problem of teaching in an inherently dangerous environment.

Guide 3   *In making all decisions relative to the planning and conduct of in-car instruction, take into account the inherent danger in the teaching environment. Never expose students to an unreasonable risk of harm.*

Guide 4   *Be alert to the emotional strain that can affect any teacher and to the potentially disastrous consequences of such strain.*

Guide 5   *Be alert to the possibility that many driver education students approach the driving task with considerable fear and anxiety. Make an effort to identify these students and to treat them accordingly.*

Individualizing Instruction

Unlike the normal classroom situation where the teacher must contend with twenty-five or thirty students at once, the in-car setting provides an opportunity for individualized instruction. Only two, three, or four students are likely to be in the car during an instructional period. Furthermore, the teacher's principal responsibility is to guide the performance of the one student who is behind the wheel. This is the kind of ideal teacher-pupil ratio that most other teachers crave, but rarely experience. This one-to-one relationship between teacher and student driver should enable the teacher to tailor instruction to the individual needs, capacities, and characteristics of the student. To take advantage of this unique opportunity, however, the teacher must recognize the differences among students and develop alternative approaches suited to these differences.

While experienced teachers are likely to have become sensitive to individual differences among students, beginning teachers may not be able to anticipate the great variety of types of students they are likely to encounter. Some students approach the driving task with extreme apprehension, while others are blatantly overconfident. Some students lack motor coordination and struggle to gain control over the vehicle, while others seem to acquire accurate control skills almost immediately. Some students seem to be unable to maintain their attention on the driving task; others are so attentive to their driving that they fail to listen to the teacher. In response to the teacher's criticism, some students will argue, others will cry. Figure 3.1 indicates *some* characteristics of a selected group of 527 student drivers, as reported by high-school teachers and students in the study cited earlier (B 126).

Once the teacher acknowledges the substantial differences among students and the unique potential for individual instruction provided by the in-car setting, the next step is to make appropriate decisions about how to adapt the methods and procedures.

Since the variety of student types is so substantial, it would be impractical to attempt in this text to outline methods for dealing with each type. Instead, the guides listed below relate to general teaching procedures that should help to ensure the individualization of instruction.

Characteristics of Student Drivers	Number of Students	Percentage
1. Unfavorable temperament for driving or learning to drive; nervous, frightened, excited, emotionally upset, etc.	231	43.8
2. Unfavorable attitude for driving or learning to drive; reckless, overconfident, no confidence, over-cautious, know-it-all, reluctant to learn, etc.	99	18.9
3. Not competent for driving or learning to drive; uncoordinated, slow learner, poor vision, etc.	56	10.6
4. Inattentive	32	6.1
5. Inexperienced driver under present conditions	67	12.7
6. Experienced or competent driver	42	8.0
Total	527	100.0

Fig. 3.1   Characteristics of Student Drivers*

* These characteristics apply to 527 of the 2,122 students involved in the study. They should not be regarded as representative of the total driver education student population (B 126).

(The reader should notice that almost every section of this chapter discusses the aspects of teaching methodology in relation to individual differences among students.)

Guide 6   *Keep records of the driving performance of each student during each in-car period.*

The record should indicate the content practiced, an evaluation of the student's performance, and suggestions for what to cover in the subsequent practice period. A driving record of this sort can be condensed into a page or two and might be in checklist form to expedite the recording process. An accurate record of the student's past performance encourages the teacher to design each in-car practice with due regard for what has gone before. (In addition to or in place of the teacher's records, students might be encouraged to keep records of their own in-car performance—see the discussion in the section of this chapter entitled "Encouraging Student Self-Analysis.")

Guide 7   *Use periodic individual student-teacher conferences to discuss the student's performance and to plan for improvement.*

The individual student-teacher conference provides an opportunity for both student and teacher to discuss problems that they might otherwise not discuss during an in-car session (in the presence of other students). In particular, the conference should enable the teacher to discover how the student feels about the driving task in general. Conferences might be held before and after school, or the teacher might set aside one school period per week for the exclusive purpose of holding individual conferences.

Guide 8   *Use independent study assignments.*

Many problems that arise during in-car instruction can be dealt with partly by having students carry out independent study projects related to their performance problems. The projects might involve the study of written materials (perhaps a careful review of relevant traffic laws), a written assignment (possibly a paper dealing with the risks involved in performing a certain maneuver), or reviewing a film (perhaps an 8-mm film dealing with driving at intersections). In all cases the projects should be designed to help reduce the particular problem facing the student.

Methods in Relation to Content

In the same way that individual differences among students demand variations in methodology, differences in content require appropriately selected methods. In-car instruction encompasses a substantial variety of skills, techniques, procedures, judgments, and so forth. Some of these are relatively simple acts (turning the ignition key), while others are exceedingly complex (guiding the car backward into a parking space). Some elements of performance are overt (hand-over-hand steering), while others are covert (recognizing potential hazards). Some are connected with relatively stable elements in the environment (maintaining a centered position in a marked traffic lane), while others are concerned with continuously changing elements (responding to other vehicles and pedestrians). Some actions require a relatively high degree of motor skill (accurate guidance on a turning path), while others involve little or no motor performance (judging when it is safe to change lanes). These variations in the nature of the content call for the use of methods that best fit the type of skill, maneuver, or technique being taught.

One of the most common errors made by beginning teachers is the tendency to approach all skills and maneuvers using almost identical teaching methods. For example, I have observed many teachers who approach parallel parking in much the same way that they approach less complex maneuvers; that is, they demonstrate and thoroughly explain the elements of performance involved just prior to allowing the student to practice. The unfortunate result is that the "thorough" explanation and demonstration of this complex maneuver turns out to be so lengthy and so involved that by the time the student takes the wheel she is totally confused and hardly knows where to begin. This confusion might have been avoided had the teacher been more sensitive to the complexity of the maneuver and the consequent need to simplify the demonstrations and explanations.

The many variations in methodology that might be adopted to suit different content are too numerous to discuss here. The Unit Plan attempts to coordinate methods with content. It contains several variations in method designed to meet the unique characteristics of the skill, technique, or procedure being taught. (See the section in each unit titled "Instructional Plan.")

Guide 9   *Select methods that are best suited to the elements of content being taught.*

Determining the Amount and Distribution of Practice

When practice conditions are favorable, the more opportunities students have to practice specific skills or techniques, the more likely they are to master them. Unfortunately, however, driver education teachers are not in a position to provide unlimited practice time for each student on each element of content. As a consequence, one of their most crucial responsibilities is to effectively allocate available practice time.

A major variable affecting a teacher's decisions about practice time is the substantial difference in learning capacity among students. Some students are able to master a particular technique after two or three practice trials, while others require an entire semester to achieve the same degree of proficiency. For example, it is not uncommon for some students to become adept at smooth braking during their initial five minutes behind the wheel, while others struggle to acquire control over the brake for five or six lessons. Teachers should be attuned to these differences among students and should be ready to adjust the amount of practice time spent on each skill to suit individual capacities. One of the most naive assumptions made by beginning driver education teachers is that all the students in a driving group will learn a particular skill on a given day and then will move on to learn a subsequent skill or technique on the following day.

Apart from the need for individual variations in practice time, the question still remains, How much practice of a given skill is necessary before moving on to the next skill? Obviously, there can be no definitive and final answer to such a question because of the countless variables involved. However, it is usually advisable to develop some general procedures for determining appropriate amounts of practice. One such procedure might be to continue practice of a skill or technique until the student can perform it, without serious error, on several successive attempts. Once the student receives instruction and guidance in the performance of a skill and appears to have mastered it, have her perform the skill four, five, or more times without any comment or aid; if her performance contains no serious errors she may move on to the next skill. This amounts to giving the student brief but concentrated driving tests on each element of performance as a prerequisite to moving to new material. Inexperienced teachers often make the mistake of assuming that a student has learned a skill because she performs one or two correct repetitions—only to discover later that the correct performance was due to chance.

Even five or ten successive correct repetitions, however, are no guarantee that the student will be able to perform the same skill effectively at a later time. It is not unusual for a student to perform a maneuver well on Monday only to have considerable difficulty with the same maneuver on Wednesday. A logical procedure to follow in dealing with this problem is to have the student perform previously learned skills at the beginning of each driving lesson. This can serve as a test of how well the student has retained the skills, while at the same time it provides her with a valuable review.

Another useful rule to follow in determining amounts of practice time is to have the student continue to practice fundamental skills to the point where they will facilitate (and not interfere with) the learning of more advanced skills. In the process of learning to drive there is a hierarchy of skills; that is, the successful performance of advanced and complex skills partly depends on the prior mastery of more fundamental skills. When students are permitted to move on to more advanced skills before acquiring proficiency in the fundamentals, they frequently meet with considerable difficulty. They are attempting to coordinate four or five basic skills (such as braking, steering, acceleration, and position judgment) in the performance of a single maneuver (such as turning), when they have not yet acquired reasonable proficiency in the basic skills. Teachers who find themselves in this predicament of having allowed a student to progress too quickly are faced with two alternatives: either start all over by working on fundamentals, or allow the student to continue her futile attempts to perform the complex maneuver. Both alternatives can be detrimental to the student's progress. The entire problem can be avoided by providing adequate amounts of initial practice in fundamental skills.

While there is a danger in advancing too quickly from the practice of one skill to another, insisting that the student continue to practice the same skill for unreasonably long periods of time may also be detrimental. Driver education students are anxious to progress, and they judge their progress in terms of their ability to perform increasingly complex maneuvers and techniques. They are easily discouraged by having to perform the same maneuver over and over again. In fact, it is not uncommon for a student's performance of a simple skill to deteriorate when she is forced to practice it continuously—not because her ability decreases but because she loses motivation. While students should not be allowed to advance too quickly, neither should they be forced to practice simple skills for unreasonable periods of time. The teacher's task is to discover optimal amounts of practice time for each student on each skill that avoid both of these deleterious extremes.

Other important decisions must be made with respect to the distribution of practice time for a given skill. Most driving skills appear to lend themselves to initial massed practice followed by subsequent distributed practice. *Massed practice* refers to a concentrated practice session during which the student performs several continuous practice trials. *Distributed practice* refers to shorter practice periods with time intervals separating the periods. In the driver education setting the typical pattern of massed and distributed practice might resemble the following: On Monday the student is introduced to a new skill and allowed to practice it for a concentrated period of time (perhaps ten or twenty practice trials). On Wednesday and Friday and periodically thereafter the student reviews the skill by completing one or two practice trials before proceeding to learn other skills.

Although the practice pattern (first massed, then distributed practice) may not be suitable in all cases, it has advantages for the learning of many elements of driver performance— particularly the more complex ones.* Turning, parking, and other complex maneuvers are

---

* The issue of massed versus distributed practice in the learning of motor skills has a long history. Despite a substantial accumulation of data, however, most researchers are forced to conclude that the choice of massed or distributed practice is very much dependent on the type of skill involved and the capacities of the learner. The position stated above, which favors massed practice followed by distributed practice for learning most driving skills and techniques, is based on the author's experience in training beginning drivers.

composed of several elements of performance including speed-control skills, tracking ability, scanning techniques, and so forth. Ordinarily students require several practice trials to coordinate and integrate all the component elements of performance. The initial massed practice session provides an opportunity for this integration to take place and helps ensure the student's initial progress. Furthermore, the student's interest is sustained during the continuous trials because the skill is new and challenging. The subsequent distributed practice aids retention and also provides a convenient opportunity to concentrate on improving the performance of those components that have yet to be mastered.

The following guides relate to determining the amount and distribution of practice.

Guide 10   *Be prepared to adjust the amount of practice time spent on each skill to suit the individual learning capacities of each student.*

Guide 11   *Provide the student with sufficient practice on a given skill to enable her to perform it correctly on several successive trials.*

Guide 12   *Periodically check to see that skills that were learned earlier have been retained and when necessary provide additional practice.*

Guide 13   *Have the student practice fundamental skills until they are learned well enough to permit efficient progress in the learning of more advanced skills.*

Guide 14   *Avoid continuous and repetitive practice of the same skill to the point where the student loses motivation.*

Guide 15   *In planning for the practice of most driving skills, provide for initial massed practice followed by subsequent distributed practice.*

ASPECTS OF TEACHER PERFORMANCE

The following topics deal with the overt actions of teachers. Each topic covers a type of teacher action found to occur frequently during in-car instruction (B 126).

Control of the Automobile

Ordinarily most in-car instruction time is spent with the student in the driver's seat and with the instructor in the right front seat. Although the student is in the normal position for controlling the automobile, the teacher also is in a position of control. He has the dual-control brake available and is within easy reach of the steering wheel. During the average driver education course the teacher frequently has occasion to seize control of the automobile from the student. The way in which he takes control, the conditions under which he takes control, and the frequency with which he takes control have an important bearing on his effectiveness as a teacher.

The teacher's paramount obligation while in the car is to provide for the safety of its occupants and other persons in the driving environment. He must be ready to assume control at all times when danger is imminent. Allowing the student to commit a serious error that results in an accident may turn out to be a very valuable lesson for the student, but the teacher is hardly in a position to provide such potentially expensive and injurious lessons.

To facilitate the assumption of control when it becomes necessary, the teacher should maintain a ready position. This position entails having the right foot on the floor close to the brake and keeping the left arm in a position close to the steering wheel—either on the back of the seat or extended at his left side. In addition, the proper assumption of control depends on the adequacy of the teacher's scanning procedures. He continuously scans for hazards just as he would if he were driving himself. This includes scanning in front, to the rear, and right and left blind spots at appropriate moments. In this regard, extra rearview and side mirrors for the teacher are invaluable pieces of equipment (Fig. 3.2). The techniques involved in scanning and controlling the vehicle from the right front seat are unique—beginning teachers would be wise to devote considerable time to practicing them before they attempt to guide the on-street performance of beginning drivers.

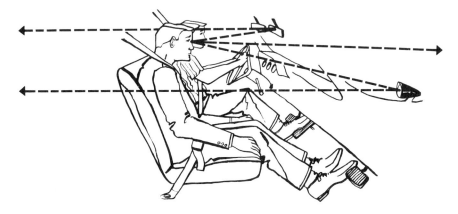

Fig. 3.2

While the prevention of an accident should be uppermost in the mind of the teacher, overcontrol by the teacher can seriously hinder the progress of instruction. Often teachers assume control when there is no imminent danger and no apparent educational benefit to be gained. Such behavior frequently leads to undesirable student responses. One outcome is that the student develops an aggressive attitude toward the teacher, and the driving lesson becomes a battleground for control of the vehicle. This creates an intolerable learning climate. Another common consequence of a teacher's overcontrol is the overdependent student—she learns to depend on the teacher to take the necessary precautions for safe driving. Once the student graduates from the course and starts to drive on her own, the consequences of such dependency could easily prove disastrous. In-car instruction should be a continual process of weaning the student away from her dependence on the teacher so that by the end of the course the student is an independently safe driver.

There are several ways to avoid the consequences of overcontrol. The teacher can avoid taking control in anticipation of student errors until he has given the student adequate opportunity to take the appropriate action himself. Or the teacher might alert the student to the impending danger by using a simple verbal cue instead of the dual brake. This allows the student to select the appropriate response and perhaps to learn by doing so. In addition, the teacher can avoid a good deal of confusion and antagonism by making certain that the student knows when the dual brake is being used, and when necessary, by explaining to the student the reasons for taking control. Teachers may take control for subtle reasons that are not obvious to the students; a favorable learning climate can be preserved by a simple identification of these reasons.

The following incidents illustrate some of the important aspects of teacher performance in connection with assuming control of the vehicle.

A high-school teacher in California reported:

We were practicing left- and right-hand turns. A young lady was driving and was told to make a right turn at the next corner. She was well in the right-hand lane and giving a right turn flashing light signal. She glanced in the rearview mirror but did not glance in the side mirror. Then, of all things, she started to turn *left*. A car was on our left ready to pass. When I saw what the student's intention was, I took hold of the wheel and kept her going straight down the road. This was a near miss, as the car on our left cleared us by only a few inches.

A high-school student in New York reported:

My teacher keeps telling me that I brake too fast. Well, I feel that I have to beat him to the brake because many times he has braked the car suddenly while I was driving, not giving me a chance to get to the brake and, almost all the time, it was not a situation which warranted a panic stop. Besides stopping the car suddenly himself, he blamed me. This makes me nervous because every time I brake a car I expect him to have done it first and I expect to feel the brake down already. I think this has ruined my judgment.

A high-school teacher in Illinois reported:

Our driver education car was approaching a corner to make a left turn. The student driver put on the turn signal but did not check the mirrors. A woman was following us in a station wagon, there were two youngsters in the front seat. When we were about to make the turn, I saw the car behind us pulling out to pass us. I looked at the young driver, waiting for him to check the mirrors, but he did not. She [station wagon] was at our side . . . the student driver began to make the turn . . . I stepped on the brake and stopped the car. [The teacher then explained the importance of checking the mirrors before turning.]

The following guides relate to effective control of the automobile.

Guide 16   *Assume control of the vehicle whenever an accident is imminent and there is reason to believe that the student is unaware of, or unable to cope with, the danger.*

Guide 17   *Continuously be in a "ready position" that facilitates the assumption of control through application of the dual-control brake and by grasping the steering wheel.*

Guide 18   *Equip the driver education car with a right side-view mirror and a second rearview mirror for the teacher.*

Guide 19   *Avoid overcontrolling the driver education car by assuming control in non-dangerous situations, assuming physical control when a verbal cue would suffice, and unreasonably anticipating student errors.*

Guide 20   *When the dual-control brake is used, make sure the student knows it is being used and, when necessary, explain the reason for its use.*

Providing Directions

Another unusual feature of in-car instruction is that while giving instruction the teacher must also think about the route that the car takes and the selection of appropriate times and places for the performance of different maneuvers. To carry out this function, teachers give directions; that is, they tell the student where to drive, which maneuver or skill to perform, and when to perform it (for example, "Pull into the curb and stop behind the green car ahead"). Although the actual giving of directions has little to do with the teaching process, it can have an indirect effect on the efficiency of instruction. Several reports indicate that teachers giving vague or poorly timed directions confuse the student and waste considerable time (see examples below). When one appreciates the demands placed on the beginning driver to concentrate on her own correct performance and at the same time be responsive to the teacher's directions, the need for precision in direction giving is apparent.

No doubt the best way to avoid the problems involved in directing student driving is for teachers to plan ahead. They should know the driving route and the sequence of maneuvers to be performed before the lesson begins and, when feasible, should convey these to the student at the outset of the lesson (for example, "We are going to drive down Main Street to the corner of Spruce Street, make a series of three right turns, then a left turn back onto Main Street, and come back here to school"). Of course, in those instances where the sequence of directions would be too complex for the student to retain, the directions will have to be divided into smaller segments.

Frequently the teacher finds it necessary to give directions on the spot, as the student drives from one situation to the next. In these circumstances the directions have to be clear, concise, and well timed. It is usually advisable for teachers to develop a "direction-giving technique" so that they have an effective repertoire of commands at their disposal. The contrast between the clear, concise direction and its less efficient counterpart usually resembles the following: "At the next corner, turn right," versus "I think you had better turn . . . up ahead . . . at the corner . . . I mean the next corner. . . ." Vague and drawn-out direction giving has several obvious disadvantages. Also, as a general rule, it is wise to indicate where a maneuver is to take place before designating the maneuver itself; this reduces the possibility of an instantaneous and premature execution of the maneuver. The timing of directions is equally important. For the most part, directions need to be given well in advance. For example, if the student is going to be asked to make a right turn, she should be warned at least a block in advance so that she has time to signal, get into the proper lane, scan the intersection, and evaluate conditions.

Since under normal conditions experienced drivers direct their own driving, teachers should plan to gradually relinquish the responsibility for direction giving to the student driver. This suggests that at appropriate times during the course, the student should be allowed to select her own driving route and be allowed to follow it without any directions from the teacher.

The following incidents illustrate some of the problems that can arise when inadequate directions are given.

A high-school teacher in California reported:

When approaching an intersection I told the student to "turn left here." The student did exactly as I said. He turned before reaching the corner and was approaching the inner lane on the opposite side of a double center line (the divider is about eight feet) before I stopped him.

A high-school teacher in Texas reported:

I have learned to use the word "right" sparingly. For example, once I told a student to "Go two blocks and make a left turn." Seconds later the student asked, "Did you say turn left?" I replied, "Right." After giving a signal to turn left, at the last moment the student thought I meant to *turn* right and did so. I have since used the word "correct" when I mean correct.

The following guides relate to providing adequate directions.

Guide 21   *Whenever possible, plan the driving route in advance and communicate this plan to the student before the lesson begins.*

Guide 22   *Develop and practice a "direction-giving technique" that includes a repertoire of clear and concise directions.*

Guide 23   *Give directions well in advance to permit the student to get mentally and physically ready to perform.*

Guide 24   *At appropriate times provide students with the opportunity to direct their own driving.*

Demonstrating

Ordinarily, the first step in teaching complex motor skills is to provide a model of correct performance that students can use to guide their performance. In driver education this model is frequently a teacher's in-car demonstration of the skill or maneuver. It is important for teachers to recognize, however, that demonstrations can have only a limited effect on the student's eventual acquisition of the motor skills involved. Learning the skills and techniques of driving depends primarily on the student's practice of those skills. Prolonged and repeated demonstrations can detract from valuable practice time. Furthermore, the student is usually anxious to get behind the wheel and try it herself and is, therefore, not receptive to prolonged demonstrations. In addition, many of the more elementary skills and maneuvers do not require any in-car demonstration because they can be taught as efficiently by simply telling the student what to do. Finally, in many instances, it may be possible to have an advanced student in the group demonstrate the skill or technique for others—this contributes to efficiency by allowing for student practice (by the demonstrator) at the same time the demonstration is taking place.

When a teacher demonstration is clearly called for it should be expertly performed so that the student has an appropriate model to follow. This does not imply, however, that the demonstration should be done at the speed at which an expert might normally perform the skill. A beginner's initial performances of a maneuver or skill are usually done at a much slower pace than the characteristic pace of the experienced driver. The demonstration, therefore, should be slowed down to meet the needs of the student. Teachers who demonstrate at normal speeds often find that the students attempt to emulate that speed and as a consequence make many mistakes. In addition, the effective demonstration usually is accompanied by appropriate comments that point to the critical features of the performance. This concurrent commentary is as important as the physical performance itself. It directs the students' attention to the important actions and thus keeps them from being distracted by trivial details. Also, it focuses attention on some of the subtle elements of performance that the students would not otherwise recognize. The demonstration and commentary should break down the performance into its simplest and most critical components and should not attempt to point out all the variables involved—especially in the case of complex skills.

Guide 25   *Demonstrate only when necessary—use student demonstrators whenever appropriate.*

Guide 26   *Demonstrations should be models of expert performance, carried out at slow speeds appropriate for student drivers, and accompanied by appropriate comments that point to the critical elements of performance.*

Guide 27   *Demonstrations of complex maneuvers and techniques should be simplified and should emphasize only the most critical aspects of performance.*

Using Verbal Cues

One of the more effective ways to encourage the acquisition of skills and knowledge is to structure the learning situation so that students respond correctly and then are reinforced for their correct responses. Although learning through one's mistakes (by trial and error) certainly has a place in education, recent evidence suggests that as a general rule the reinforcement of correct responses is more efficient—especially during the initial stages of learning.

The driver education teacher's careful use of verbal cues is a particularly effective method for encouraging correct student driving responses. Verbal cues are statements by the teacher that tell students how to perform the maneuver while they are performing it. For example, the teacher can ensure relatively correct performance of a lane-change maneuver by using a sequence of cues like "signal . . . check mirror . . . check blind spot . . . gradually steer left," and by timing the cues to coincide with the moments at which the actions are called for.

Effective verbal cues have much in common with effective directions; they must be clear, concise, accurate, and well timed. The amount and frequency of verbal cues given by the teacher appears to be critically important. Some teachers fail to take advantage of this teaching device. They simply provide an initial demonstration or description of the skill or maneuver and then permit the student to struggle the rest of the way on her own. This often results in a lengthy trial and error period that, at best, is grossly inefficient. At the other extreme is the teacher who continuously and indiscriminately provides a barrage of verbal cues. In such cases the teacher retains full control over the car by dictating every action that the student must take. This not only places limitations on the learning that can occur, but it also encourages the same kind of undesirable student reactions (hostility and overdependence) as overuse of the dual-control brake.

It would seem advisable *to provide cues only when they are necessary to help the student perform correctly a skill or maneuver that she would otherwise perform incorrectly.* There are several situations in which verbal cues can be quite helpful. During a student's initial attempts to perform complex maneuvers in traffic (such as left or right turns) there are so many things for her to remember at once that an appropriate sequence of verbal cues can be of assistance. When a student persists in repeating a specific error (for example, delayed recovery of the steering wheel in a turn), a simple cue may help to eliminate the error. When a student is confronted by a difficult traffic situation (such as the car stalling in the middle of a busy intersection), a series of specific cues that amount to "talking the student through" the maneuver can guide the student out of difficulty without placing her in the embarrassing position of having to relinquish the driver's seat to the teacher.

As the student becomes more proficient at driving, the need for verbal cues diminishes. If the teacher finds himself giving as many verbal cues at the end of the driver education course as he did at the beginning, it generally means one of two things; either the teacher fails to recognize that such cues are no longer appropriate, or for some reason the students have not progressed appreciably during the course.

The following are some examples of the appropriate and inappropriate use of verbal cues.

A high-school teacher in Virginia reported:

While driving with a student-driver who had driven for five days, we came upon some road repairmen and trucks. These obstacles were taking up the right side of the road. The road was torn up in spots and very rough. I told the student quickly and quietly to stop and wait until the man directing traffic waved us on, then to proceed slowly and cautiously. She, at first, was scared and nervous at the sight of a new driving challenge, but as I began "talking her through" the situation she became too involved in following instructions to be nervous. I feel that by my guidance and through her application of learned skills in a new situation, her confidence received a needed boost.

A high-school student in Michigan reported:

Whenever I'm driving and am about to do something (turning a corner, coming to a stop street) he tells me what to do. It's all right if he would tell me the first three or four times but after that I wish he would let me think for myself a little bit.

Guide 28   *Provide verbal cues only when they are necessary to help the student perform correctly a skill, maneuver, or technique that she would otherwise perform incorrectly.*

Guide 29   *Be ready to use verbal cues during the student's initial performance of a complex skill, when a student tends to repeat a specific error, in difficult traffic situations, and in other comparable circumstances.*

Guide 30   *Recognize that the need for verbal cues diminishes as the student's driving proficiency increases.*

Guiding Improvement through Analysis and Correction

Learning to drive is not unlike learning other complex motor skills. It involves gradual modifications in performance through practice. In effective learning situations these gradual modifications represent relatively consistent improvements in performance. The driver education teacher's task is to guide student practice in a way that encourages continuous and efficient improvement from one practice trial to the next. These gradual improvements depend on several important factors: students must be aware of the correct elements in their performance so that they can retain them in subsequent trials; conversely, they must be aware of their errors in order to eliminate them in future trials; they must know what kinds of changes in performance are most likely to produce improvements; and they should have the opportunity to apply the changes in subsequent practice trials. In effect, this suggests that the teacher should see to it that the students know what they are doing right, know what they are doing wrong, know how to correct their errors, and have an opportunity to correct them. As elementary as this process may seem, some beginning as well as advanced teachers make more mistakes in this phase of teaching than in any other.

When the teacher effectively guides improvement, the critical components of the process are easily recognized. The best way to illustrate these components is through an example of effective guidance. Suppose the teacher is intent on improving the student's performance of a right turn. As the student performs, the teacher carefully observes the critical elements of the performance. Suppose that he detects three errors in performance: (1) speed too fast, (2) wide turn, and (3) late recovery. He then analyzes and evaluates these three errors and decides that the error in speed has precipitated the other two errors. Before the student attempts the next turn the teacher tells her, "You approached the turn too fast; this time decelerate to a slower speed." The teacher has the student perform several right turns and may provide a timely verbal cue, "slow," at the appropriate moment. When the student achieves the proper speed the teacher says "correct" or "good speed" to reinforce the student's correct response.

The above example illustrates how the process *should* work. At various stages of this process, however, many things can and do go wrong. Because the total process is relatively complex, it is discussed further under three subheadings: "observation and analysis," "providing feedback and indicating corrective actions," and "subsequent practice."

Observation and analysis   Accurate observation of the key elements of student performance depends on the teacher's readiness to make such observations. In most cases the teacher can base his observations on the movements of the car (for example, he can detect a wide turn simply by observing the path of the car). Frequently, however, critical elements of performance are not immediately reflected in the car's movement (for example, checking mirrors, scanning techniques, foot position, and so on). In the latter cases, the teacher needs to look directly at the student driver to evaluate performance. Inexperienced teachers often neglect this need for direct observation and as a consequence are totally unaware of many critical driver errors.

Once the teacher has observed performance, he must be able to analyze it. Effective analysis depends on the teacher's thorough knowledge of the elements of good and bad driving performance. In addition to this knowledge, however, analysis involves identification of the causes of variations in performance. This is no easy task. It is one thing to recognize that the student failed to get the car into the parking space, but it is entirely another matter to determine the reasons why she failed. The example given earlier of the student performing a right turn in which the fundamental error was improper speed is a case in point. In similar circumstances, teachers frequently fail to notice the speed problem and attempt to correct the student's performance by dealing with steering control. This amounts to treating the symptoms instead of the cause—since it is the speed that causes the other errors. This problem of identifying the central causes is especially evident in dealing with beginning drivers who often make a series of mistakes in the performance of a complex maneuver.

The author observed:

A student was having considerable difficulty in parallel parking the car. The right tire of the car kept hitting the curb. At first the teacher thought it might be due primarily to the student's failure to recover the steering wheel quickly enough (i.e., turn it quickly to the left at the appropriate moment in the maneuver). But then he realized that the road surface was crowned and as the car was starting in toward the curb it was gaining momentum because it was traveling slightly downhill. In addition, the student did not have sufficiently fine control over the brake pedal to keep the car moving at a slow enough pace. This resulted in the student not having enough time to turn the steering wheel to the left and park successfully. Therefore, the teacher had the student practice the maneuver concentrating on controlling the car's speed with a slight pressure on the brake pedal. Once the student gained adequate control in using the brake, he was able to successfully complete the maneuver.

The author observed:

The student was attempting to parallel park in a space behind a red convertible. The teacher directed his attention to the movement of the driver education car in relation to the red convertible and in relation to the curb. That is, the teacher was constantly looking out the right side window and neglected to observe the actions of the student driver. The student failed to park the car successfully—the right rear tire hit the curb. The teacher proceeded to explain to the student what had gone wrong. His analysis was completely erroneous because he had failed to observe three critical errors made by the student driver. First, the student driver was looking forward during the entire maneuver. Second, she had turned the steering wheel one and one-half revolutions to the right before starting to back the car. Third, she lost control of the steering wheel midway through the maneuver. All of these factors had gone unnoticed by the teacher, however, because he never looked at the student.

Providing feedback and indicating corrective actions   In order to improve their performance, students must have information (feedback) about the correctness of their actions. In many cases the student receives direct feedback from the vehicle's movement or from other elements in the driving environment that indicate the appropriateness of her actions. For example, if the student applies the brake in such a way that the car and its occupants lurch to a stop or if the rear wheel jumps the curb during a turn, the student knows immediately that something is wrong. In such cases the teacher need only supplement this existing feedback by telling the student *why* things went wrong. In many instances, however, students are totally unaware of their mistakes. For example, errors such as failure to check the blind spot or failure to signal go unnoticed by the student. In such cases it is the teacher's responsibility to make the student aware of the error and, if necessary, explain the reason for its occurrence.

As a general rule the feedback provided by the teacher should be precise and immediate. Considerable evidence indicates that the immediacy and precision of the feedback are important to skill learning. Much of the feedback can be provided at the time of or immediately after the student action by a simple one or two word phrase. For example, in the previously mentioned case involving the right turn, the teacher might have said "too fast" and "too wide" as the student was making the error. This is generally a more effective procedure than to have the student continue to perform other skills and then have to say, "Remember a while back when you turned, you were going too fast and the turn was too wide." During the intervening time between the commission of the error and the teacher's comment the student is likely to have encountered other situations that make it difficult for her to recall what happened during the turn. Of course, there are occasions when the feedback must be delayed to permit the student to concentrate on other elements of performance or to provide more time for a detailed consideration of the student's actions.

Although the teacher should observe and be aware of all errors in student performance, this does not imply that he should immediately tell the student about *all* of the errors that are made. On the contrary, the teacher should limit the amount of feedback he provides in terms of the student's capabilities for absorbing and using information. When the beginning student makes three or four errors at once, it is usually a mistake for the teacher to identify all the errors immediately and have the student attempt to correct them all at once. Usually, the more advisable procedure is to identify the one or possibly two most crucial errors, concentrate on these, and then attend to the less significant errors.

An additional consideration is the teacher's responsibility for suggesting corrective actions. In some situations the mere identification of the error will suffice. For example, telling the student "You forgot to signal" is sufficient feedback because the corrective action is implied and obvious. In many other situations, however, the corrective action needed is not immediately apparent and therefore needs to be specified. For example, merely telling the student that the turn was too wide may not be adequate because the alternative corrective actions are several: slower speed, earlier initial steering, or quicker steering. In such circumstances the teacher needs to follow up the identification of the error with a clear indication of the appropriate corrective action.

The following incidents illustrate the consequences of inadequate or inappropriate feedback.

A high-school teacher in Michigan reported:

I observed this incident which involved another teacher. The girl who was driving at the time the incident occurred was very unsure of herself. She had been told many times at home by her brother and father that she would never make a good driver. She had been progressing nicely when the instructor in the front seat began criticizing her on almost her every move. She touched the brakes too much and too hard, starting was too rapid and jerky, she was not giving her full concentration to driving, were just a few of the faults he was finding. When her turn was over (ten minutes), she gladly gave up the job of driving. Her whole outlook on the situation had changed dramatically in just those few minutes. In this case too much was said at the wrong time. It has taken the girl almost a year to even regain enough confidence to desire to try again to drive.

The author observed:

The student was attempting to perform a backing maneuver. The objective was first to back the car in a straight line and then to gradually steer the car into a position parallel to and close to the curb. The student started the maneuver, noticed the car was drifting to the left, tried to correct for the drift, but turned the steering wheel in the wrong direction (that is, to the left instead of the right) and increased the severity of the error. The car ended up perpendicular to the curb instead of parallel to it. The teacher made no comment as the student was making the error, but after the student was hopelessly stuck the teacher said, "Okay, let's try it again, but this time watch your oversteering." The student tried to perform the manuever twice more, each time he made the same kind of error, and each time the teacher made the same irrelevant comment. Finally, the teacher suggested that the student try a different maneuver. After the lesson the student revealed that he knew he had been making an error but did not understand how to correct it and further, that the teacher's comments were not meaningful to him.

Subsequent practice   When the student commits a serious error and the teacher identifies it and indicates the appropriate corrective actions, it is generally advisable to provide an immediate opportunity to perform the skill or technique again. The performance may consist of one or several practice trials during which the student's principal intent is to correct the error. The actual length and number of additional practice trials should depend on the seriousness of the error and the student's progress in correcting it. The objective of this additional practice should be to provide the student with a reasonable opportunity to perform the skill or technique correctly, and then to reinforce this correct performance. The reinforcement might be in the form of a simple comment by the teacher, such as "good turn" or "good speed control," or it may come from the student's own perception of the correctness of her performance. Considerable evidence supports the value of such reinforcement in the acquisition and retention of skills and concepts.

At this point it seems appropriate to mention the importance of an occasional encouraging word from the teacher. The reports of high-school students clearly indicate that they attach considerable significance to the teacher's commendation of their performance. This seems to be especially true for slower students. An occasional comment indicating that the student "is progressing nicely" or "performed that maneuver well" can have a profound effect on the students' confidence as well as their entire outlook toward driver education. On the other hand, the teacher who concentrates exclusively on pointing out student errors and never seems to notice progress can easily discourage students and destroy their confidence.

Guide 31   *Be in a position to observe all the important elements of student performance, including those elements that are not reflected in the movement of the vehicle.*

Guide 32   *Thoroughly analyze all elements of the student's performance to determine the underlying cause of improper performance.*

Guide 33   *When the student is not aware of her error, clearly identify it for her.*

Guide 34   *As a general rule, verbal feedback should be immediate and precise.*

Guide 35   *Limit the amount of feedback in terms of the student's capabilities for utilizing it.*

Guide 36   *Whenever necessary, as a part of the feedback process, indicate the appropriate corrective action.*

Guide 37   *Provide the student with an immediate opportunity to correct errors by performing the skill again.*

Guide 38   *Whenever appropriate, verbally reinforce corrected performance.*

The Amount of Verbal Instruction

For the average driver education student, the task of learning to drive is a relatively demanding experience. When she is behind the wheel she confronts new and complex tasks that require her full attention. In addition to concentrating on her own performance and on the various elements in the driving environment, the student must attend to the teacher's verbal instruction. These three elements—her own performance, events in the environment, and the teacher's instruction—compete for the student's attention.

Some teachers, especially inexperienced ones, are not aware of this competition for the student's attention, and in their eagerness to be good teachers they simply *talk too much.* The usual result is that the student has difficulty attending to her driving and eventually becomes irritated by what she considers continual harassment. The solution is relatively simple. The teacher needs to be aware of this competition for the student's attention and periodically to ask himself, "Am I talking too much?" In fact it may be advisable for the teacher to seek confirmation of his suspicions by asking the same question of his students. When the answer is "yes," the alternative should be clear.

A high-school student in Michigan reported:

Once while driving on a main highway which had very heavy traffic, my instructor was talking very fast on what to do next, and so on, and I was trying to concentrate on what he was saying and also on the other traffic. Suddenly another car pulled in ahead of us and I hit the brake. He bawled me out and said I should have been paying more attention. Ever since I have been extremely nervous driving.

A high-school teacher in Connecticut reported:

There is a narrow street and as we drive along it I keep telling the students "watch the parked cars," "don't come too close," "watch out for the oncoming cars," etc. A couple of students recently told me that it made them nervous when I talked to them so much. Could they be right?

Guide 39   *Do not talk too much.*

Encouraging Student Self-Analysis

Eventually students will graduate from driver education and will have to take full responsibility for their own driving. At that point it is important for them not only to be competent drivers, but to be capable of continued guidance of their own improvement. One of the teacher's key tasks, therefore, is to develop the students' talents for self-analysis and self-evaluation. Students who can identify their own errors, diagnose the causes, and plan for improvements on their own are in a position to continuously improve their performance without direct assistance from a teacher.

During in-car practice, teachers can help students develop their ability for self-analysis by periodically asking the kinds of questions that encourage student drivers to review their own performance, identify their errors, and suggest improvements. In addition, an excellent technique for facilitating the students' careful examination of their performance is to have them maintain their own practice records. Figure 3.3 contains a sample practice record form that can be filled out by students after each practice lesson, or perhaps once a week.

Guide 40   *Periodically ask questions that encourage students to examine, diagnose, and plan improvements in their own driving.*

Guide 41   *Have students keep their own practice records.*

Special Methods for Special Problems

Occasionally special problems arise during in-car instruction that seem to resist solution via normal instructional methods. That is, the use of demonstration, verbal cues, and analysis and correction of student performance result in little or no improvement. The special problem may be the consequence of one or any combination of factors—usually related to deficiencies in the capabilities of students. The student may be excessively anxious to the point where she is unable to pay attention to the teacher; she may lack the coordination necessary to master a particular skill; or she may be unable to comprehend the teacher's description and explanation of a concept related to performance. Irrespective of the nature of the problem the results are the same: repeated use of normal instructional methods produces no progress.

Two distinct patterns of teacher behavior seem to emerge in response to such problems; one pattern is characteristic of effective teacher performance, the other is characteristic of ineffective performance. The principal distinction between the two is that the effective teacher tends to be flexible and to employ special methods designed to cope with the special problem, while the ineffective teacher remains inflexible and stays with a single approach despite its continued failure. For example, a typical problem involves the student who is apparently unable to master a relatively simple skill, such as gradual braking. Despite the student's continued difficulty, the ineffective teacher persists in his use of the same instructional method; that is, he demonstrates, describes, uses cues, and verbally identifies errors. Eventually he tends to become impatient and either reprimands the student or abandons his efforts altogether. The effective teacher, on the other hand, utilizes normal instructional methods up

PRACTICE RECORD

1. NAME _____ DATE _____ PRACTICE LESSON NO. ____

2. Indicate the skills practiced during the lesson by placing a check mark (√) next to those performed correctly, or an ex (X) next to those on which you made at least one serious error. Circle (√)(X) those skills which you were practicing for the first time during the lesson.

BASIC SKILLS		BASIC ON-STREET SKILLS		REDUCED-RISK MANEUVERS		DRIVING STRATEGIES		OTHER SKILLS	
Preparatory steps		Entering traffic		Changing lanes		Roadway and traffic characteristics		Emergency responses	
Basic skills in moving forward		Establishing path driving		Right turns		Limited access highways		Other skills (list):	
Basic skills in moving backward		Basic scanning techniques		Left turns		Driving at night			
Parking vehicle		Evaluating and responding to obstacles		Backing maneuvers		Driving under special conditions			
				Turning around					
				Passing					

3. Identify errors in your performance. (Be specific.)

_____

_____

_____

_____

4. What will you do to correct them next time? (Be specific.)

_____

_____

_____

_____

5. Identify the most important things you learned during the lesson (i.e., things you should remember in the future).

_____

_____

_____

_____

6. Other comments (improvements, road and traffic characteristics, performance of others, etc.).

_____

_____

_____

_____

Fig. 3.3 Source: *Laboratory Manual for Learning to Drive,* by W. G. Anderson, Addison-Wesley, 1971.

to the point where he recognizes that the student is not going to respond to them. At this point, he employs alternative approaches. In the case of the student's inability to master gradual braking, he might utilize a special simulated practice braking drill, vary the speed of the vehicle during the practice trials, or have the student practice on a downgrade, controlling the vehicle's speed using only the brake pedal. In addition to providing potentially more effective approaches to the solution of problems, such special methods are usually cause for renewed hope and interest on the part of both student and teacher—thus avoiding the frustration and impatience that so often accompany repeated failure.

The variety of special methods that might be devised to meet special problems is limited only by the ingenuity and imagination of the teacher. The effective teacher has a repertoire of such methods at his disposal for dealing with a considerable range of problems. In view of the substantial number and variety of special methods that might be employed, no attempt has been made here to itemize or even to categorize them. Instead a few of the techniques used successfully by high-school teachers are listed below; other special techniques are suggested in various parts of the Unit Plan.

1. Special drills are devised to help the slow student master various skills and techniques. These drills normally provide for concentrated practice of that aspect of performance that is most difficult for the student.

2. In cases where students have difficulty following directions, some teachers have them repeat the directions and/or point in the direction of an intended turn.

3. Charts and diagrams are used to clarify explanations.

4. Students who have difficulty judging the vehicle's position are encouraged to view it from a different perspective; that is, from outside the car.

5. Special competitions are established that assess demerits (or actual fines) for driving violations.

6. Individual conferences and individual driving lessons are devoted to the solution of a student's problems.

7. Checklists are used to help students retain information related to performance.

8. Various devices and markings are added to the interior of the car to enable the student to follow directions better, avoid looking at controls, assume the proper seating position, and so forth.

Guide 42   *Develop a repertoire of special methods designed to cope with special problems.*

EVALUATING STUDENT PERFORMANCE

The process of evaluating student performance is closely associated with the total teaching process. In effect, all of the judgments about student performance made during an in-car program are part of the evaluative process. This is evaluation in its broadest sense. The word *evaluation*, however, is more often used in education to refer to more formal types of assessment procedures such as testing and systematic rating.

A road test is the most common type of formal evaluation used to assess a student's driving performance. It normally consists of having the student drive over a prescribed route while the teacher uses a rating form to record and make judgments about the student's performance. Assuming that the test is well designed and administered, it should make an important contribution to the effectiveness of in-car instruction. In particular, it provides the teacher with a relatively objective method for determining the degree to which the student has achieved the objectives of the course.* The careful attention required to develop a good test, however, should not be underestimated. Poor or inappropriately used road tests are not uncommon in driver education, and they can be a significant detriment to an otherwise effective program. Some of the most important features of good road tests are discussed below.

Curricular validity   A valid test in any course should measure student progress in relation to the objectives and content of that course. The road test, therefore, should closely reflect the objectives and content of the in-car program. Items in the test should correspond to the elements of content covered during instruction and the items should be weighted† to reflect the relative importance of the content. A test developed in this way has "curricular validity"; that is, it is a true reflection of the student's performance in the course.

The need for curricular validity places limitations on the common practice of using standardized road tests in driver education programs. Such tests are valid only to the extent that they reflect the content of the course. When items on standardized tests relate to elements of performance not covered in the course, or when important aspects of the course are not part of the standard test, such tests are not appropriate for use as a final measure of student progress. A case in point is the rather common practice of using a facsimile of the state motor vehicle department road test as a "final test" in the in-car program. This would seem to be a rather unfortunate practice. A state road test is developed for the purpose of detecting those drivers who fail to meet minimum standards of performance for licensing. It may not have relevance for much of what transpired during the in-car program.

All of this implies that the driver education teacher must assume responsibility for developing a road test that has curricular validity for his course. He may use a few or several items from standardized road tests depending on the extent to which they correspond with the content of his course. Unit 15 of the Unit Plan contains a "driver rating form" developed for use in connection with the Unit Plan. The items on this road test closely reflect the content of the Unit Plan. However, this form is useful to individual teachers only to the extent that they follow the Unit Plan. Few teachers will be able to use it without making alterations to suit the unique aspects of their own in-car programs.

An educational tool   A road test should be an integral part of the educational process. Too often teachers regard tests as devices for arriving at grades and disregard their value as educational tools. Several procedures connected with the development and administration of road tests can enhance their educational value. First, the test can be developed to serve as a diagnostic tool. In this respect test items should be designed to identify the strengths and weaknesses in student performance. Second, the teacher can make certain that whatever information the test yields about the student's strengths and weaknesses is made available to the student. Only under such conditions can a test serve as a basis for future improvement. Third, the teacher together with the student can use test results to plan and conduct subsequent practice. The aim of such practice, of course, would be to correct the student's

---

* All good rating procedures attempt to reduce the amount of subjectivity involved in arriving at an evaluation. The degree to which they are successful in doing so varies.
† "Weighting" items refers to assigning more or less value to an item in the scoring procedure on the basis of its relative importance.

weakness. With this aim in mind it is usually advisable to plan for at least two road tests per pupil during an in-car program. Unit 15 of the Unit Plan incorporates these and other procedures designed to enhance the educational value of the road test.

Reduced subjectivity   Every possible precaution should be taken to reduce the subjectivity of the road-test rating procedures. This problem of subjectivity is common to most rating procedures. It reflects the fact that the teacher must make immediate judgments about the student's performance, and that these judgments may tend to be based on vacillating subjective standards instead of on objective standards that should be universally applied to all students at all times. As a result, rating procedures in general suffer from a lack of reliability and validity. In the development and administration of a road test the following procedures might help to reduce the problem of subjectivity.

1. *Make each item on the rating form as specific as possible.*   Rating on the basis of specific actions calls for less subjective judgment than does rating on general capabilities or general aspects of performance. For example, an item such as "checks blind spot before changing lanes" is more likely to lead to an objective and reliable judgment than an item like "exhibits smooth control of vehicle's speed."

2. *The scoring of each item should avoid calling for broad and general qualitative judgments.*   For example, the rating of a student's performance of a skill on the basis of whether it was "excellent," "good," "average," or "poor" is not advisable because the teacher's concept of what is "good" or "average" is bound to change from time to time. A more desirable alternative (particularly applicable to road tests) is to have the teacher indicate the presence or absence of a specific driver action. The teacher might check ($\checkmark$) an item each time the action occurs or fails to occur, such as "Fails to signal before turn $\underline{\checkmark}$."

3. *Compare rating judgments against those of another trained driver education teacher by simultaneously rating the performance of a few students.*   This enables both teachers to review and compare their judgments and revise those aspects of their rating procedure that reflect their own personal biases or limitations.

4. *Recognize the possible influence of the "halo" effect and take precautions to avoid it.*   The halo effect refers to the teacher's tendency to make favorable judgments about particular students for reasons other than the quality of the students' test performances. In some cases teachers make such judgments because they like the student, in others their past judgments about a student's performance may prejudice their evaluation of the student's test performance. The halo effect is a common problem in most ratings—especially in those situations where the teacher has had prior contact with the student. Avoiding its influence is not easy. Following the procedures outlined above can help reduce the problem. In addition, the teacher's conscious efforts to avoid the problem by judging performance, and not people, should be helpful.

Guide 43   *The road test should assess the student's progress in relation to the objectives and content of the course.*

Guide 44   *The road test should serve as an educational tool. It should assess student strengths and weaknesses and provide a basis for planning for further improvement.*

Guide 45   *All possible precautions should be taken to ensure the objectivity of the road test.*

THE DRIVING GROUP

In driver education programs students are divided into driving groups for in-car instruction. Normally the groups range in size from two to four students. In many cases the teacher will have to make important decisions about the size and composition of these groups.*

Size   There is no evidence to support either two, three, or four students as the optimal number for a driving group. The more common practice is to work with groups of four, but this may be the result of administrative exigencies rather than educational desirability. Both the larger (four) and smaller (two) groups have assets and liabilities. The larger group lends itself to greater efficiency with respect to some instructional practices. For example, when the teacher demonstrates a maneuver or when he explains what to do on a particular roadway, he instructs four students at once—instead of two. In addition, each student has an opportunity to observe (and hopefully to learn from) the performance of three other students. Scheduling large driving groups also provides for more total observation time per student during the course. On the other hand, the larger group increases the likelihood of distracting conversation or interaction occurring among the three students in the back seat. Also, since most teachers attempt to give each student an opportunity to drive during each period, driving practice is segmented into very short periods (perhaps ten minutes per student), which may be less than adequate at several stages of the learning process.

The final decision about the size of driving groups should be based on the effectiveness of observation time. Larger driving groups are desirable only in those situations where the considerable time spent observing (three-quarters of a student's in-car time) is put to good use. Based on my own experience with various sized driving groups, the educational advantages of working with small groups (two or three) outweigh the disadvantages.

Composition   There seem to be several advantages to grouping students in terms of their capabilities and past experience in driving. Such grouping leads to more uniform progress among the members of a group and thus helps to ensure mutual interest in what other members of the group are learning. For example, when all members of a group progress at a relatively uniform rate, they are likely to start practicing advanced maneuvers and techniques at approximately the same stage of the course. When the teacher demonstrates a maneuver, he can do so with the expectation that all students in the group will be performing it in the near future. Furthermore, when the first group member practices the maneuver, other members will be motivated to observe his performance closely because they will soon be practicing the same maneuver. This is not true for driving groups that include students with divergent capabilities. The advanced student will be practicing skills and techniques that are not of immediate interest to the slow student who will not be practicing these techniques for several weeks. Also, the teacher's instructions to one student are not likely to have immediate relevance for the others.

One method for achieving homogeneity of driving groups is to place all students with prior driving experience in the same group. In addition, those students who will practice at home during the course might be placed in separate groups. Finally, the teacher might establish tentative driving groups for the first two or three weeks of the course. During these

---

* In some schools teachers are allowed to design their schedules for in-car instruction and to determine the composition of driving groups. In other schools all this is done for the teacher, in advance, by administrators or guidance personnel.

first few weeks he can assess the basic capabilities of students and then reassign them to driving groups on the basis of their early performance. (Differences among students usually are evident early in their practice of basic skills and provide a reasonable basis for classification.) Of course, flexible scheduling practices of this type will require cooperation from school administrators. In schools where the scheduling of students for classroom and in-car phases of driver education is done without consulting the driver education teacher, homogeneous grouping is not likely to be possible.

Effective use of observation time   One of the more challenging aspects of in-car instruction is the task of making certain that observation time—that is, the in-car time spent by students while they are not driving—is well spent. In the absence of a planned involvement of student observers, they are likely to spend the time in idle daydreaming or in disruptive activities. Several techniques might be used to maintain the interest of student observers and to make observation time a valuable learning experience.

First, the teacher should take every opportunity to make instruction applicable to all members of the driving group. Obviously, there are many occasions when the problems of the student driver are unique and thus have no relation to the problems of other group members. On such occasions the teacher's instruction may not have general applicability. On the other hand, whenever the student driver's problems correspond to the problems of other members of the group, the teacher's explanations, comments on performance, corrections, and so on should be directed to the entire group. In addition, many "teachable moments" arise when the student driver faces an unusual emergency, when another driver commits a hazardous violation, or when unusual traffic problems are encountered. The teacher can use such moments to provide a valuable lesson for all members of the group.

Some teachers use a variety of special techniques to achieve increased involvement on the part of student observers. One relatively common procedure.is to have student observers rate the performance of the student driver. Another method is to have observers imagine that they are driving and analyze the differences between what they would do and what the student driver actually does. Still another approach assigns student observers certain teaching functions, such as monitoring the student driver's use of mirrors, obedience of traffic laws, speed control, and so forth.

Guide 46   *Group students homogeneously for in-car instruction.*

Guide 47   *Use a variety of techniques to enhance the value of student observation time.*

4

MULTIPLE-CAR METHODS*

INTRODUCTION

The multiple-car method provides simultaneous practice driving instruction to several students in separate automobiles. Instead of the teacher being in a single car with one student in the driver's seat, several student drivers independently drive vehicles on a multiple-car range while the teacher guides their practice *from outside the vehicles* using radio communication.† The method was introduced to enhance the efficiency of in-car instruction by increasing the student/teacher ratios, and to augment program effectiveness by increasing the amount and kinds of practice driving available to students. While the method has been in use for many years in certain programs, its popularity has grown recently. Approximately 560,000 (B 141) high-school students now receive part of their in-car training on multiple-car ranges, and the number is growing at an annual rate of 13 percent.

Multiple-car instruction is unquestionably one of the most challenging educational settings facing any teacher. As in most other formal educational settings, the teacher has to guide the learning experiences of several students at once. But unlike in most other settings, students on the multiple-car range, in effect, operate their own mobile miniclassrooms, which constantly change location within a very sizeable instructional area. Effectively controlling, monitoring, and evaluating student performance under such conditions are not easy tasks. Furthermore, although the collision experience on effectively managed driving ranges is apparently quite low (B 132), providing for the safety of several inexperienced drivers operating in a confined area is yet another dimension of the challenge facing the teacher who uses the multiple-car method.

Although the results of research on the effectiveness of the multiple-car method have been inconclusive, most studies indicate that students experiencing some combination of multiple-car and single-car instruction do as well or better on driving tests when compared to

---

* This chapter was written with the assistance of Professor Richard Ellis, The State University of New York, at Albany. Many of the ideas are based on his extensive experience with the multiple-car method.

† Normally one teacher is assigned to supervise a multiple-car session on a moderate-sized facility. On larger facilities with large numbers of cars (perhaps fifteen or more), more than one teacher may be needed.

students who experience standard amounts of single-car instruction only (B 145). Clearly, however, the multiple-car method does allow teachers to provide more practice time for greater numbers of students, and thus increases program efficiency (B 132).

On the other hand, the method is not without its limitations. Practice on a controlled multiple-car facility is useful only to the extent that (1) what is learned is positively transferred to performance in on-street settings (B 146), and (2) students are prepared for the full spectrum of driving tasks required in the on-street setting. While practice on most ranges does provide for the acquisition of basic control skills (speed control and tracking) and for initial practice of scanning and decision-making techniques, it cannot fully prepare students for many of the multidimensional variations in traffic and roadway characteristics that typify the on-street setting (B 145). In addition, while some professionals see virtue in a setting that allows students to develop independence and self-confidence by driving on their own (B 141), others see the instructional limitations imposed by a setting that does not permit the teacher to closely monitor and control various elements of student performance (B 145). Obviously, then, the challenge facing the teacher is to identify an optimal mix of range and on-street practice that uses each instructional setting to its best advantage.

MULTIPLE-CAR FACILITIES

The methods used and the content covered in the multiple-car phase of instruction will depend in part on the nature of the facility available. Authorities (B 132) distinguish between three types of facilities. The first, *basic skills facilities,* are comparatively small (less than two hundred by four hundred feet), paved areas designed to provide practice in skill exercises and maneuvers. Cones, stanchions, and some lane markings are used to mark off areas for practice. The variety of different kinds of practice on such facilities is restricted. Thus, most students can profit from only a limited amount of such range practice and need comparatively larger amounts of on-street practice. The second, *traffic-mix facilities,* are somewhat larger facilities (minimum two hundred by four hundred feet) designed around the principle of "traffic mix"— that is, providing opportunities for drivers to interact with other vehicles at intersections, merges, entrance and exit points, and so forth. On such facilities, in addition to practicing basic skills and maneuvers, students engage in initial practice of scanning, decision making, and communicating in traffic-mix situations. The third type, *advanced driver training facilities,* are much more elaborate facilities that permit the kinds of experiences mentioned earlier and, in addition, provide for such training exercises as off-road recovery, blowout simulation, skidding, and so on. These ranges are much larger than two hundred by four hundred feet and include such things as a full set of traffic control signs and signals, hills, banked curves, long straightways for higher speed driving, and so on.

At present, most authorities (B 146) recommend the development of traffic-mix facilities for driver education programs. They argue that such facilities promote the improvement of perception, judgment, and decision-making abilities that are most crucial to safe performance. While such facilities also provide "exercise" areas that are used to practice selected basic skills and maneuvers, much of the student's time on these ranges can be spent in traffic-mix situations similar to those experienced on-street. A prototype facility recommended by the Maryland State Department of Education (B 136) appears in Fig. 4.1, together with a description of key design characteristics. This type of facility would provide substantial opportunities for traffic mix as well as for isolated skill practice.

The equipment needed to operate a range facility includes (1) an appropriate number of dual-control vehicles equipped with rooftop car number signs and other standard dual-control

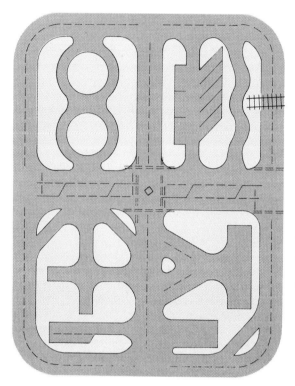

Components of the MULTIPLE-CAR Driver Education Range Facility

A. Physical Requirements of a Driver Education Range
1. Road surfaces wide enough for two-way traffic
2. Four-way and "T" inter-sections, and curves
3. Lane markings and signs
4. Space for development of fundamental skills
   a. Right angle and off-set backing
   b. Turning practice
   c. Turning around
   d. Diagonal, perpendicular, and parallel parking
   e. Lane changing
5. Arrangement for basic traffic experiences
   a. Two-way traffic
   b. One-way street
   c. Multi-lane roads
   d. Use of traffic controls
   e. Intersection approaches and turns
   f. Railroad crossing and crosswalk approaches
   g. Passing or overtaking
6. Range area should be large enough so that *all* skill areas and traffic experiences may be utilized at the same time, allowing student freedom of choice in a realistic situation

B. Specific Functions (Areas) of a Driver Education Range
1. Standard road markings, including right and left turn lanes, merging and diverging traffic
2. Standard highway signs either permanently mounted on posts, portable, or both
3. A perimeter road with two 12-foot lanes. Some portions of this road should have three-lane sections or should be designed as a divided highway with a median strip
4. Cross roads designed to include one major four-way intersection and at least one "T" intersection
5. A straight section of road long enough to practice the fundamental steps in safe overtaking and passing
6. An area for the "X" exercise for practice in forward and reverse driving and turning
7. An area or street for practicing the "Y" turn (or turning around on a dead-end street)
8. An area for entering and leaving a simulated two-car garage with a single-lane driveway intersecting at the street (or similar offset practice area)
9. An area or areas that can be designated as a one-way street
10. Provision for parallel and angle parking
11. Pedestrian crosswalks, simu-lated railroad crossing, etc.

C. Other Areas Recommended But Not Deemed Absolutely Necessary
1. A standard operational traffic light
2. A raised or "hill" section, preferably at one outside corner
3. An area for the "T" exercise for practice in forward and reverse driving
4. A "Figure 8" exercise for practice in steering — a serpentine exercise for prac-tice in forward and reverse driving which will develop steering control

Fig. 4.1   Source: Driver Education Unit, Maryland State Department of Education.

equipment so that the cars can be used for on-street instruction as well (at least one "reserve vehicle" should be available so that repair and maintenance can be accomplished without disrupting instruction); (2) portable or permanently located traffic signs; (3) traffic cones, flags and poles, and barricades to delineate practice areas, exercise areas, and restricted areas; (4) lane markings painted on permanently or "taped on" to allow for flexibility in marking the area; and (5) a radio communication system with an instructor's FM transmitter tuned into the cars' FM radios or to AM radios equipped with citizens' band (CB) converters.

Clearly, multiple-car ranges can differ substantially in size, cost, available practice areas, and the functional role they play in the overall program. Teachers who are contemplating the development of a multiple-car range should review appropriate resources (B 122, B 132, B 145) and consult state and local authorities who are in a position to offer expert advice. Of course, the decision to build and equip a multiple-car facility, as well as the type of facility required, should be based on a careful assessment of the peculiar needs and capabilities of the particular school district.

METHODS

Since the objectives of multiple-car instruction are similar to those of single-car instruction, many of the basic methodological principles discussed in Chapter 3 are applicable here. For example, teachers should (1) be cognizant of the potential dangers in the environment and implement appropriate controls, (2) arrange learning experiences to suit individual student needs and capabilities, and (3) provide for appropriate amounts and distribution of practice. On the other hand, the distinctive features of the multiple-car setting necessitate the adoption of special methods designed to cope with those features. The following sections examine these distinctive methods.

Instructional patterns and sequence

Two distinguishable instructional patterns are used on ranges: *group* and *individualized*. *Group instruction* occurs when all (or many) students are being taught the same task, either simultaneously or in sequence. For example, the teacher might give instruction in starting the engine by "talking all students through" the procedures at once. Later on all students might be instructed to drive around the perimeter of the range, starting with the first car, followed by the second, and the third, and so on. The *individualized instructional pattern* is characterized by instructing students who are practicing different skills and exercises at different locations on the range. For example, the teacher might alternate her attention among two students practicing forward driving on the perimeter road, two others practicing figure eights in a separate area, and two others practicing Y turns in yet another area.

There is a commonly recommended way of apportioning group and individualized instructional patterns over the span of a multiple-car program. In the first lesson or two, group instruction is carried out in the following way: (1) have the cars lined up side by side and six to eight feet apart; (2) talk the students through the procedures (simultaneously) for entering the vehicle, executing preparatory steps, and starting the engine; (3) guide the students (simultaneously) through moving the vehicle forward and stopping, several times; and (4) direct the students to drive forward around the range leaving appropriate spaces between vehicles. In each subsequent lesson a new skill, maneuver, or exercise is introduced using similar group instruction techniques. For example, in a later lesson the cars might be placed in various sections of the facility and all students simultaneously guided through the steps in parallel parking. Normally, during these later lessons, time is provided for each student to practice the new skill and to review skills introduced in earlier lessons. As students move from one lesson to the next, they build up a repertoire of skills, and an increasing variety of practice areas are made available to them. So, after the first lesson or two, group instruction is replaced by a combination of group and individualized instruction, with group instruction used to introduced new tasks and individualized instruction used during the remainder of the period when students are engaged in reviewing earlier skills as well as practicing the new one.

In general, the individualized instructional pattern is in operation most of the time in multiple-car programs. It permits "differentiated practice," which enables students to work at their own rate on the skills and maneuvers they need to attend to. In addition, it allows for efficient use of the range because each range area is used for the skills, maneuvers, and traffic-mix responses for which it was designed. Group instruction should be used only on those occasions when teachers and students need to focus on a common task, such as introducing new skills or showing students how to use a new area of the range.

Each of these instructional patterns places somewhat distinct demands on the teacher. Group instruction may appear to be less challenging because the teacher and students all focus on a common task. Yet this type of instruction is complicated by the fact that students possess different capabilities and do not always perform in the uniform manner anticipated by teachers. For example, there is the common problem of trying to talk eight or ten drivers through a multistaged maneuver, such as a Y turn, only to find that when most drivers have completed stages one and two, one driver has yet to successfully start the engine, and another is unable to move forward because he forgot to release the parking brake. Group instruction involves the constant challenge of trying to keep together a group of potentially variable performers.

On the other hand, in the individualized instructional setting the teacher has to contend with the many different tasks being practiced in different areas of the range by students who vary in their capabilities for performing those tasks. Indeed, at any moment in time, eight or ten different maneuvers may be in progress; each driver might be at a different stage in his maneuver, and a whole array of errors may be occurring. To effectively monitor student performance and provide appropriate instruction in such settings, the teacher must know where all the students are, what they are doing, and when to intervene to assist them. But realistically, no matter how experienced and skillful the teacher is, she can only attend to a portion of the ongoing activity and can only assist one learner at a time. Clearly, if these individualized settings are to be productive, student practice must be structured in such a way as to enable the students to improve on their own.

Guide 1   *Use group instruction during the first few multiple-car lessons and to introduce new skills and exercises during subsequent lessons.*

Guide 2   *Use individualized instruction on all other occasions when it is needed to provide differentiated practice experiences for students.*

Shifting responsibility and structuring practice

From the perspective of each student, most of the time in the multiple-car program is spent practicing on his or her own—that is, most of the time the teacher is not communicating directly with the student. If the program is to succeed, this independent practice time has to be utilized effectively. For this to be possible, much of the responsibility of learning and improving must be shifted to the student. In effect, this means that each student has to accept more responsibility for being his or her own teacher, and has to be equipped to carry out that responsibility. The teacher's corresponding responsibility is to structure the setting to provide for effective independent practice.

Practice involves repeating the performance of a skill or activity with the intent of improving in it. *Effective practice* yields those improvements. When the teacher is in the car with students (single-car method), she guides effective practice by prescribing tasks, observing and analyzing student performance, providing feedback, indicating corrective actions, and prescribing subsequent practice (see Chapter 3). In the multiple-car method, the same sort of guidance is needed, but most of the time the teacher is not there to give it. So the students have to provide it themselves.

To structure effective independent practice, teachers follow many of the guides mentioned in Chapter 3 (see Guides 11–15). In addition, however, they must provide students with the knowledge required to analyze and correct their own performance. Not only do students have to know how a skill or maneuver is "supposed to be performed," but they also have to know common errors that occur, how to use available feedback, how to diagnose the causes of their errors, and how to make appropriate corrections. In the absence of such knowledge they are likely to go on repeating the same errors over and over again. For instance, in practicing parallel parking the student should know the prescribed method of performance, the various errors that are likely to occur, and how to correct them. This would mean, for example, that when the rear tire contacts the curb in the midst of the maneuver the student can use this feedback (curb contact) to identify the faulty position of the car, assess the possible reasons for the position (steering and/or speed control errors), decide what corrections need to be made, and then employ those corrections in the next trial. If the student cannot do this, the next trial is likely to produce the same faulty result.

Obviously, beginning drivers cannot be fully equipped to be their own teachers. If they were, there would be no need for any kind of in-car instruction and supervision by the teacher—it could all be done in the classroom. Nevertheless, the *extent* to which students can be prepared to guide their own improvement will determine, in large part, the extent to which the multiple-car program succeeds. With this in mind, the student's advance preparation for multiple-car lessons takes on added significance (see the next section).

One additional technique for ensuring effective independent practice is to use "reciprocal teaching" at appropriate stages of the program. Reciprocal teaching simply refers to using one student to teach another. In the multiple-car setting, student partners can be encouraged to assist each other in the identification, diagnosis, and correction of errors. Of course, the process has to be carefully controlled by the teacher. For example, using the parallel parking illustration cited above, the teacher might provide the student driver's partner with a checklist of key elements of performance to watch for during execution of the maneuver. When an error occurs, this "extra pair of eyes" may detect a mistake the driver was unaware of.

Guide 3   *Develop and use a variety of techniques that equip students to guide their own practice and improvement.*

Preparing students for in-car sessions

Adequate student preparation for multiple-car lessons is extremely crucial. Unlike in the single-car setting, where the teacher is immediately available to give directions, review procedures, provide instruction, and so forth, on the range students cannot rely on the teacher's constant availability. There are two basic requirements that must be met in the advance preparation of students. First, the students have to know where to go and what to do (the procedures) so that confusion, delay, and dangerous mistakes are avoided. Second, they have to know enough about the content of the lesson to intelligently guide their own practice.

To meet the first requirement, students should know the *general rules* regarding the use of the facility. These rules should clearly define such things as:

1. Procedures for reporting to and leaving the facility
2. Procedures for entering, storing, and leaving the vehicles
3. The areas of the facility that may and may not be used at different stages in the program
4. What to do if you do not understand a procedure, or if you need the teacher's assistance
5. Rules governing pedestrian behavior on the facility
6. Directions for using the radio communication system
7. Special traffic rules related to following distances, speed limits, passing, and the like
8. The number of cars allowed in specific areas, and any special rules governing practice in those areas

The rules, together with a diagram of the facilities, should be printed and a copy distributed to each student. Prior to the first multiple-car lesson, the rules should be discussed fully in a classroom session.

Beyond this general preparation, students should be prepared specifically for *each* instructional session. *In advance* they should know (1) the content of the lesson (that is, how to perform the skill or exercise, common errors, how to identify and correct errors, and so on), (2) why the skill or maneuver is important in relation to safe driver performance, (3) where the skill or maneuver is to be practiced, and (4) the sequence and organization of instructional procedures for the period (such as who will do what, where, and for how long). To accomplish these purposes, three instructional modes are normally used: (1) independent study of printed materials, (2) classroom presentations, and (3) demonstrations on the facility.

Independent study   Printed materials that outline the objectives, content, and procedures for each lesson should be distributed to and studied by each student prior to range sessions. Diagrams of the maneuvers and exercises might be a part of these materials. In fact, some programs find it convenient to develop a complete student handbook of such materials. In addition, appropriate textbook chapters that emphasize the relevance of the content of the lesson for on-street driving might be assigned.

Classroom presentations   A variety of visual materials can be used in the classroom to clarify the lesson content and the specific range procedures to be used. Diagrams of the range on overhead transparencies, a magnetic traffic board containing a replica of the range, or actual videotapes or motion pictures of the range in operation might be used by the teacher to indicate precisely what should happen. Time should be devoted to answering any questions raised by students so that issues can be resolved before moving to the range.

Demonstrations on the facility   Demonstrations of the maneuvers, exercises, and procedures may also occur on the facility itself—although if the classroom preparation was thorough, these demonstrations should be short and to the point. The teacher, or a selected student who has been briefed in advance, might do the demonstrating. Other students should be grouped at convenient vantage points for viewing the critical elements of the demonstration. In many instances it is more advisable to have a student do the demonstrating so the teacher can more easily point out important features of the performance to the group of observers.

Guide 4   *Prepare students for using the facility by developing, distributing, and discussing general rules.*

Guide 5   *Use independent study of printed materials, classroom visual presentations and discussions, and demonstrations on the facility to prepare students to carry out procedures and guide their own improvement during each multiple-car session.*

The driving group

Most authorities recommend scheduling two students for each vehicle on the range. This enables all vehicles to be used each period despite student absences. Furthermore, when two students share the driving during a normal period (forty-five minutes) on the range, each student can practice for twenty to twenty-five minutes—which is sufficient for adequate practice of most new tasks and yet not long enough to produce boredom. Also, the nondriving student may be assigned some reciprocal teaching functions and may even be asked to use the dual-control brake when the occasion warrants it.

As with single-car methods, homogeneous ability grouping works well on the range. It allows more advanced students to move ahead at their own rate to practice higher-level tasks and not be held back by a slower partner. On the other hand, there are many occasions when it is advisable to place an advanced student with a slower student so the advanced student can provide special help.

Perhaps the best rule to follow here is to *remain flexible*; do not get locked into a particular grouping or allotment of driving time. The teacher should use the flexibility the range provides in ways that are best suited to accomplishing instructional objectives. For example, members of driving groups might be rotated from one session to the next so that those who have failed to master a particular exercise can be grouped together for intensive practice in it, while those who have mastered it may be allowed to travel freely through designated traffic-mix areas. Or there may be occasions when a certain student really needs an opportunity to develop complete independence and thus should be the only occupant assigned to a vehicle. Or on occasion it may make sense for three students to be assigned to one vehicle so that each can practice a new skill for fifteen minutes while a fourth student is assigned to another vehicle and drives for forty-five minutes reviewing several previously learned skills. Also, teachers should be alert to the possibility that members of a group may not get along with each other, or on the contrary may get along so well that they constantly engage in distracting personal conversation, in which case a rotation in group assignments is called for.

There is some professional disagreement with respect to the proper role of the nondriving student in the car. Some persons believe that the paramount advantage of multiple-car instruction is that it encourages student independence and responsibility, and that this objective is undermined by having the nondriving student provide instruction or use the dual-control brake. Others believe that having the nondriving students ready to use the dual-control brake enhances the safety of the range, and that these students can play an important instructional role in helping their partners progress. Both positions have validity. I favor a limited version of the latter position. Nondriving students should be taught to use the dual-control brake, but should be instructed to use it "only when necessary to prevent contact with persons or property." Further, partners should engage in reciprocal instruction on selected occasions that are carefully planned and controlled by the teacher (see example in previous section). Obviously the teacher should monitor the students' performance of these roles to be certain that they do not overplay their parts.

Guide 6   *Schedule at least two students per vehicle for each multiple-car session.*

Guide 7   *Remain flexible with respect to the assignment of specific students to specific vehicles for a lesson or lesson segment. Rotate group memberships, vary the number of students per car, and alter the time allotments per driver in ways that best suit the instructional objectives of each session and the needs of individual students.*

Guide 8   *Teach nondriving students to use the dual-control brake, but instruct them to use it only when necessary to prevent contact with persons and property.*

Guide 9   *On selected occasions, have student partners engage in reciprocal teaching.*

Teacher location and observation

On the multiple-car facility, teachers have to manage or regulate the position and movement of all vehicles to make certain the drivers are operating in assigned areas and the areas are being used appropriately. In addition, they have to provide instruction for individuals and groups of students at various times. In order to carry out these managerial and instructional functions, teachers have to see what is happening on the facility as a whole, and detect specific features of the performance of individual drivers. To some extent these are conflicting demands; teachers cannot attend to the problems of a single student and scan the entire facility at the same time. So from one moment to the next they have to decide where to look and what to look for. Their decisions should be based on a careful appraisal of the particular skills being practiced, the levels of student performance, the characteristics of the facility, and so forth.

As a general rule, teachers should position themselves so that they (1) have an un-obstructed view of the entire facility, (2) are closest to "critical instructional areas" or "potential points of conflict," and (3) can move quickly and freely to any point on the facility where they are needed.

Whenever several practice areas are being utilized simultaneously, the teacher should be in a position to periodically scan all areas and regulate the movement and position of vehicles as necessary. Potential obstructions to vision such as trees, large vehicles, fences, buildings, and so on should be considered in selecting a location. A position toward the center of the facility requires scanning a 360° radius and means the teacher will have to turn around frequently to monitor all areas; a position off to the side of the facility reduces the scanning radius (perhaps to 180° or less) and allows the teacher to observe all events without altering her directional orientation. On the other hand, a centralized location puts the teacher in closer proximity to all parts of the range.

To provide instruction to individual drivers on the multiple-car facility the teacher has to be close enough to carefully monitor student performance. While the teacher can detect gross elements of student performance at distances of one hundred to two hundred feet (such as the spacing between vehicles, use of directional signals, and vehicle speed), close-up observation is required to detect such things as steering movements, the checking of blind spots, use of mirrors, and exact vehicle position. Therefore, whenever possible teachers should position themselves in "critical instructional areas"—that is, areas where they can provide the most help to students who most need help. For example, if most of the students in the class are making right turns for the first time, the teacher should position herself close to the point of execution of the turn so she can observe performance and provide instruction to students as they pass the point. In addition, points of potential conflict often require close-up monitoring.

For example, the teacher might station herself at a four-way intersection being used by students for the first time, and provide directions as necessary to ensure safety.

While a good teacher should know the students' capabilities and be able to anticipate those places on the range where she will be needed, it is impossible to anticipate all of the problem situations that arise. Therefore, the teacher should be in a position to move quickly to those locations where she is needed. Among other things, this suggests that a teacher should enter a vehicle to give instruction, or otherwise tie herself to a specific location, only when it is absolutely necessary to do so.

Guide 10   *Position yourself to obtain an unobstructed view of the entire facility and, when appropriate, periodically scan the entire facility.*

Guide 11   *Whenever possible, position yourself close to critical instructional areas and potential points of conflict so that you can adequately monitor, instruct, and direct student performance at those locations.*

Guide 12   *Position yourself so you can move quickly and freely to any point on the facility where you might be needed.*

Communication

Communications from teacher to students on the range occur primarily through the radio system that carries the instructor's voice to each car radio. Understandably, then, the teacher's first responsibility with respect to communication is to make sure that the system is working. In part this can be accomplished prior to class sessions by going around to each car and testing the voice reception. In addition, a routine procedure for checking out reception should be carried out at the beginning of each lesson. For example, when the students first enter the cars, the teacher might count off each car number and have students respond in turn by sounding the horn to indicate they hear her voice.

Since all radios are tuned in all the time, the teacher has to clearly distinguish which driver she is addressing. This can be done by prefacing all communications with "all drivers," or giving the driver number, to clearly designate the target of the communication. Some teachers prefer to address the drivers directly by name (instead of by number) in an effort to personalize instruction.

One of the more pervasive problems on the range is that all drivers are normally tuned in to all of the teacher's remarks coming over the radio system. So even in those settings where the teacher limits the amount of commentary directed to each student, the total amount of commentary to which each student is exposed may be quite substantial. Certainly a constant stream of chatter on the radio can be disconcerting to beginning drivers. When this happens the students' only recourse is to try not to attend to the communications so they can concentrate on what they are doing. Of course this only enhances the possibility that students will miss some of the messages directed at them personally.

While there is no easy solution to this problem, the teacher might start by trying to follow the basic rule that applies to all in-car instruction; *don't talk too much*. Understandably it is especially difficult to follow this rule in multiple-car instruction (as compared to single-car instruction) because the teacher is confronted with several drivers and so many events that might elicit her reaction. Perhaps the best way to avoid the need for excessive communications during student practice is to make sure that students are well prepared for the lesson beforehand. If the students know where to go and what to do in advance, the need for teacher directions during practice is substantially reduced. When the need for giving directions does arise, the teacher should give a concise sequence of directions whenever possible (see Chapter 3). Also, it is probably wise to limit extensive use of verbal cues, or "talking students through" a maneuver, to group instruction settings where all students are performing the same maneuver. Finally, the volume of talk coming over the radio can be reduced by turning off the microphone at appropriate times and speaking directly to students—particularly on those occasions when an extended discussion with one student is in order.

In addition to teacher-to-student communication, provision needs to be made for student-to-teacher communication. A routine procedure should be established to cover those situations where students want to obtain the teacher's assistance. One convenient procedure in such situations is for the student to pull over to the curb, stop the vehicle, and sound the horn once or twice. Also, the teacher should be able to recognize those situations that will require two-way communication, such as when a student is making a serious error that the teacher wants to question him about. In these instances the teacher has to move to a point where she can hear what the student has to say.

Guide 13   *Check to see that the communication system is working in each car.*

Guide 14   *When using the radio system, preface all remarks by indicating who you are talking to—all drivers or a specific driver (give the driver number or name).*

Guide 15   *Do not allow too much talk to be conveyed over the radio system.*

Guide 16   *Provide ways for students to communicate with you.*

Evaluation and record keeping

Most of the basic principles and procedures relative to evaluation and record keeping covered in Chapter 3 are applicable to multiple-car instruction.

In well-organized multiple-car programs, learning tasks are arranged sequentially in order of their level of difficulty. In such programs students are often required to "test out" on subordinate tasks before being allowed to move on to more difficult ones. In addition, before students are permitted to proceed to on-street practice, they should be tested out on selected elements of performance on the range. Fortunately, multiple-car ranges are excellent settings for evaluating or testing out various features of student performance. The areas designed for practice of each skill and maneuver serve equally well as test areas. For example, the figure-eight area can be used as one test of the students' forward tracking ability. In addition, traffic-mix areas can be used to test the students' initial capability to scan for and respond to obstacles. Evaluation of most all elements of performance can be accomplished by the teacher from a vantage point outside the vehicle. Accurate tracking, speed control, positioning, and the like can all be judged by the movement of the vehicle in relation to the carefully delineated practice area. The students' proficiency in scanning and responding to obstacles can be judged by their reactions to the various traffic situations encountered. Carefully developed checklists or rating scales similar to those used in single-car evaluation may be used to guide the assessment.

Given the comparatively large number of students encountered by a single teacher using a multiple-car facility, accurate record keeping takes on added significance. Without adequate records, teachers cannot realistically hope to recall what all the students have been doing and how well they have performed. Thus students should be required to keep a record of each practice session and teachers should keep cumulative records of student evaluations. These records should provide the basis for making decisions about who should practice what in each upcoming multiple-car session.

Guide 17   *Design and use performance tests to evaluate the students' readiness to move on to more difficult tasks, and to engage in on-street practice.*

Guide 18   *Keep records of practice sessions and test scores; use them to plan subsequent practice.*

part II

THE UNIT PLAN
FOR IN-CAR INSTRUCTION

USING THE UNIT PLAN

Scope of the plan

The Unit Plan is a teacher's guide for planning and conducting that portion of the driver education program devoted to instruction in in-car tasks (see Fig. 2.1, p. 11). It focuses on content and methods for the in-car phase of instruction, where students learn to *perform* in-car tasks. The plan also outlines classroom and independent study experiences that enable students to learn the concepts and information that are prerequisite to effective performance of those in-car tasks.

There are fifteen units in the plan (see Fig. 2.3, p. 20). Each unit contains a description of the objectives for students; the concepts, skills, maneuvers, and strategies to be learned; common errors in student performance; an instructional or practice plan; a classroom guide; an in-car guide; and preparatory reading for students.

The plan *does not deal with all of the content of a comprehensive driver education program*. A complete driver education program should encompass readiness tasks (see Fig. 2.1, p. 11) as well as in-car tasks. Therefore, to supplement the Unit Plan, classroom sessions, films, and independent study experiences should be used to provide instruction in (1) knowledge of the highway transportation system, including the accident problem, licensing, law enforcement, and engineering; (2) operator fitness and its relationship to safe driving, including the effect of alcohol, drugs, emotions, fatigue, and carbon monoxide; (3) vehicle readiness, including mechanical operation and maintenance; and (4) trip planning.

Instructional pattern

Since effective learning and performance during in-car instruction is partially dependent on the student's prior understanding of related concepts and information, the basic instructional pattern recommended for each unit is (1) independent study of related concepts and information by students, (2) classroom review and discussion, (3) in-car practice, and (4) record keeping and evaluation of performance. Thus, for example, in a unit on changing lanes, the student first reads material on the risks involved in lane changes, the laws governing the maneuver, and the ways of performing the maneuver; then is exposed to a classroom session that clarifies and expands these concepts; and then practices changing lanes during an in-car lesson. Finally, either teacher or student (or both) keeps a record of the student's performance and evaluates it.

Written materials for students

A text and a laboratory manual for student drivers have been developed for use with the Unit Plan: *Learning to Drive: Skills, Concepts, and Strategies,* and *Laboratory Manual for Learning to Drive* (Addison-Wesley Publishing Company). The chapters of the text are coordinated with the Unit Plan and cover the basic concepts and information that students should know prior to in-car practice. The manual contains in-car practice guides for each unit, practice record forms, self-evaluation forms, and driving strategy forms—all of which are designed for use in connection with in-car instructional units.

Teachers who choose to use other high-school texts should review them carefully and determine which chapters or sections contain information related to the units of instruction in the Unit Plan. Appropriate sections from these texts should be assigned as preparatory reading for in-car sessions. In addition, the Unit Plan assumes that students will have access to a State Driver's Manual containing rules of the road, and a copy of the owner's manual for the driver education car.

Adapting the plan to program facilities

Single-car off-street area   The Unit Plan is designed directly for use in schools with minimal facilities—an off-street area available for single-car instruction, and on-street areas. The first three in-car units in basic procedures and skills (Units 2, 3, and 4) are designed for single-car off-street practice. Subsequent units take place on-street, with the exception of Unit 14, which is also an off-street unit (see table below).

FACILITIES AVAILABLE

Unit	Single-Car Off-Street Area (Only) or Multiple-Car Basic Skills Facility	Multiple-Car Traffic-Mix Facility (Vary Sequence as Necessary)
1. Orientation to task	Classroom (only)	Classroom (only)
2. Orientation to vehicle	Off-street	Off-street
3. Basic skills: forward	Off-street	Off-street
4. Basic skills: backward	Off-street	Off-street
5. Initial scanning, evaluating, responding	On-street (off-street if facility provides some traffic mix)	Off-street/on-street
6. Turns	On-street	Off-street/on-street
7. Changing lanes (and passing)	On-street	Off-street/on-street
8. Strategies for roadway and traffic characteristics	On-street	On-street
9. Backing maneuvers	On-street	Off-street/on-street
10. Turning around	On-Street	Off-street/on-street
11. Limited-access highways	On-street	On-street
12. Driving at night	On-street	Off-street/on-street
13. Special conditions	Off-street/on-street	Off-street/on-street
14. Emergencies	Off-street	Off-street
15. Evaluation	On-street	On-street

Multiple-car basic skills facility   With minor adaptations, the plan is equally applicable to programs using a multiple-car, basic-skills facility together with on-street practice. Basic procedures and skills (Units 2, 3, and 4) will take place on the range, although the specific sequence and types of practice will have to be varied to suit the unique characteristics and practice areas available on the facility. Of course, the instructional techniques employed also will have to be adapted to the range setting, using the methods suggested in Chapter 4. In addition, if the facility permits at least a minimal degree of traffic mix, initial instruction in scanning, evaluating, and responding (Unit 5) should take place on the range. The remaining units can be used directly to guide the on-street phase of the program.

Multiple-car traffic-mix facilities   The essential elements of content of the Unit Plan are applicable to programs that combine on-street practice with practice on a multiple-car traffic-mix facility. However, the sequence of the content will have to be adjusted to suit the unique characteristics of the range, and of course multiple-car methods will have to be used (Chapter 4).

As a general rule the basic procedures and skills (Units 2, 3, and 4) should be covered during the early stages of the range program, before the student practices on-street. Thereafter the range should be used for *introductory practice* of subsequent tasks, and this introductory practice should be integrated with on-street practice of those tasks. Thus, introductory practice in scanning, evaluating, and responding (Unit 5), reduced-risk turns (Unit 6), changing lanes (Unit 7), passing (Unit 7S), backing maneuvers (Unit 9), and turning around (Unit 10) should take place on the range and be followed up by on-street applications of these tasks. In the same way, when conditions permit, introductory practice in night driving (Unit 12) and driving under special conditions (Unit 13) might take place on the range first, and then be followed up by on-street practice (see the table).

On the other hand, strategies for roadway and traffic characteristics (Unit 8) and for limited-access highways (Unit 11) are primarily designed as on-street lessons and most multiple-car facilities can be used to provide only limited instruction in these tasks.

Simulators   The Unit Plan was not designed to coincide specifically with existing simulator programs. While much of the content of the plan is similar to the content of simulator programs, there are also some discontinuities between the two. Teachers who use simulation instruction should carefully examine the content of the simulator program and the Unit Plan, as well as the time available for each; then decide which tasks should be taught on simulators, which should be taught in-car, and which should be taught both ways; and then modify the content of either or both programs as necessary to ensure consistency between them. As a convenience for teachers, simulator lessons that are broadly related to in-car lessons are listed at the end of each unit in the plan.

Guides for using the unit plan

The following suggestions should help the teacher utilize the Unit Plan effectively.

1. Read through the entire series of units before attempting to use any single unit to guide in-car instruction. Since the units are closely related to one another, the effective conduct of each unit depends on the teacher's understanding of its relationship to the total plan.

2. A thorough familiarization with the text of each unit is a prerequisite to the effective use of the in-car guide during the actual conduct of an in-car period. The teacher who attempts to use the in-car guide without having carefully read the text will be unable to decipher the meaning or intent of most items included.

3. Treat the entire Unit Plan as a general guide. Be ready to make adjustments in content, sequence, and methods whenever it seems appropriate to do so. Deletions, additions, and alterations of suggested content and methods should be made whenever the proposed plan (1) does not suit the local teaching situation, (2) does not meet the needs and capacities of individual students, (3) is not consistent with the instructional style or capabilities of the individual teacher, or (4) is less desirable than an alternative plan available to the teacher. In particular, teachers should adopt an experimental attitude toward the total plan and toward each separate unit. They should be ready to make changes based on evidence accumulated

from past experience, to retain those portions of the plan that worked, and to discard or change those parts that did not work.

4. Each unit is treated as a distinct area of content with the understanding that the teacher will include reviews of prior units whenever such a review is appropriate. As a general rule, each driving period should begin with a brief review of the material covered during the previous period. This review may consist of a few well-chosen comments by the teacher or it may consist of student practice of skills.

5. Elements of content (driving skills, concepts, actions, and so on) are grouped into units on the basis of the similarity of the elements rather than the time required to cover the content. *In no case should the term "unit" be confused with a driving period.* Some units will require three practice periods in the car, others may require one, and others may require less than a period.

References and notations section

At various points in the Unit Plan, bracketed numbers appear, such as [1], [2], and so on, that refer the reader to appropriate portions of the References and Notations section at the end of the plan. This section contains a summary of some of the background research and data used in developing the plan. The section is intended to improve the reader's understanding of some of the bases for decisions regarding content selection, and to augment the information contained in the plan itself.

ORIENTATION TO THE DRIVING TASK AND TO IN-CAR INSTRUCTION

INTRODUCTION

This classroom unit deals with information and concepts to which students should be exposed prior to in-car instruction. The unit is designed for the classroom because the material covered lends itself to classroom presentation and discussion, and because the classroom offers the most efficient opportunity for reaching all students in a relatively short period of time. However, in spite of the fact that this is a classroom unit, it should be regarded as an integral part of the in-car program.

Phase 1 introduces concepts related to the driving task and the purposes of in-car instruction. Phase 2 familiarizes the student with the content of the entire in-car program. Phase 3 acquaints the student with the procedures that will apply during subsequent in-car lessons.

In this unit the objectives for students are:

1. *To identify the major components of the driving task and assess their relationship to safe driver performance*

2. *To identify the major features of the process of learning to drive, including the major features of the instructional program they will follow*

3. *To assess their own purposes for wanting to learn how to drive and to compare these purposes with the purposes of the instructional program (and/or the teacher)*

4. *To know the instructional procedures to be used during in-car instruction*

PHASE 1: THE DRIVING TASK AND THE PURPOSES OF IN-CAR INSTRUCTION

The concepts described below are intended to serve as discussion topics for orienting the student to the nature of the driving task and to the purposes of in-car instruction. The concepts should serve as focal points for an interchange of ideas between student and teacher, the outcome of which should be a better understanding of course objectives on the part of students. The classroom guide at the end of this unit outlines an approach to handling the

67

discussion of the concepts. The particular group of concepts included is an illustration of what might be discussed, and teachers should feel free to add or delete concepts that will better enable them to achieve their purpose.

Concept 1   *Learning to drive involves learning to perform the driving task.*

Driving task is the term used to identify the job a person performs when he drives an automobile. The task (or job) includes all those things a person has to do when he drives from one place to another.

Learning to drive is really a matter of understanding and developing the skills necessary to perform the driving task well. Just as job training in any field requires training in all the important aspects of the job itself, learning to drive requires training in all the important aspects of the driving task.

In recent years, research studies and expert analyses have helped us to get a clearer understanding of the driving task. Although authorities do not as yet fully understand many parts of the task, one thing is clear: driving is a very complicated and demanding activity. It requires a great many specialized skills and abilities. The old idea that driving is simple and that virtually anyone can learn to do it well is no longer acceptable.

Concept 2   *Safe driving is a complex and challenging task.*

The objective of driving is to transport oneself (and others) from one place to another in an efficient and safe manner. As the driver moves his vehicle towards its destination, the conditions facing him continuously change. The position of the car in relation to the roadway changes. The size and curvature of the road ahead change. The position and movement of other vehicles change. Traffic signals and signs change. And a variety of other conditions change. Facing these changing conditions is like moving through a whole series of situations—each one of which is slightly different from the one before.

The essential job of the driver is to move through these situations safely and efficiently. To do so, he must do the following:

1. *See all important elements in the situation.*   In any driving situation, various elements in different places have an important bearing on what the driver should do. The driver has to look in the right places to see the important elements and at the same time be able to distinguish the important from the unimportant.

2. *Understand what is seen.*   To see is not enough. The driver must understand what he sees. For example, he must understand the meaning of traffic signs and signals, and he must understand the relationship between other vehicles, pedestrians, and his own path of travel.

3. *Predict what will happen.*   A driver constantly has to think ahead because in a moment his car will be in a different place under a different set of circumstances. All driving situations contain things that move, such as other cars and pedestrians. The driver must predict what position they will be in as he nears them. Will other cars enter his path? In which direction will each of the cars go, and how fast? Are they likely to stop or slow down? Will a pedestrian step out into his path? Will the traffic lights change?

4. *Evaluate alternatives and make decisions.*   In most driving situations, the driver has a variety of alternatives from which to choose as he moves through the situation. Should he slow down? Stop? Speed up? Move to the right? Signal? He has to evaluate the situation and select the combination of actions that is best for each particular situation.

5. *Control the movement of the car.*   Having decided which actions to perform, the driver must carry them out correctly. To do this he uses his skills in braking, steering, speed control, and so on to move the car through the situation.

This process of seeing-understanding-predicting-evaluating-deciding-acting must be carried out in each situation. This alone makes driving a challenging task. The whole task is made even more difficult by the fact that new situations follow right on the heels of old ones, and so new decisions and actions are called for continually. Also, since the vehicle is often moving at high speeds, decisions must be made and actions taken very quickly—often within fractions of a second. Finally, a variety of unexpected events can happen in the middle of a situation, requiring the driver to change his entire plan of action.

Concept 3   *Driver errors cause accidents*

Faced with this kind of demanding task, it is no wonder that drivers make errors. Errors come in a variety of forms, such as failing to see an important element in a driving situation, incorrectly predicting the actions of another driver, choosing an unsafe alternative, or failing to control the movement of the vehicle effectively. Driving errors occur quite frequently, even among experienced drivers. A recent research study [1]* showed that experienced drivers made an average of more than *nine* errors for every *five* minutes of driving—and this study counted only the most noticeable errors (see Fig. 1.1).

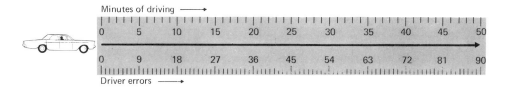

Fig. 1.1

As might be imagined, there are no perfect drivers. All drivers make errors. The difference between good and poor drivers is that good drivers make fewer errors, and their errors are less serious.

Driving errors are a major cause of traffic accidents [2]. Fortunately, only a small fraction of all errors result in accidents. Many errors are small enough, or are corrected quickly enough, so that accidents are avoided. Nevertheless, the driver who makes fewer errors, and whose errors are less serious, is less likely to get into trouble (see Fig. 1.2).

The picture of the driving task is not complete without an appreciation of the frequency and the consequences of accidents. Unfortunately, traffic accidents are commonplace. Approximately 15 million occur in this country every year. The consequences are serious: 1,200,000 people are injured and 45,000–50,000 are killed. The average accident frequency is estimated at approximately two accidents per driver in a five-year period (B 46). When drivers do their jobs poorly, they risk injury and death—for themselves and for others. At one moment in time a driver may be facing a difficult situation and make a serious error. The next moment he may be lying in his wrecked automobile, seriously injured or dying.

---

* The numbers in brackets [ ] refer to notations that appear in the References and Notations section at the back of this book.

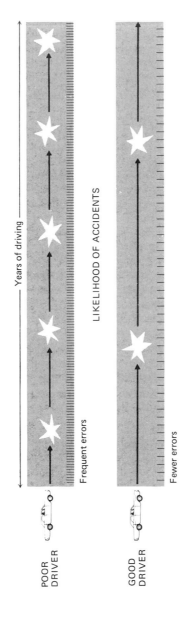

Fig. 1.2

What does all this mean in regard to the driving task? Above all, it means that unlike many other tasks we perform, driving is a very serious matter. From day to day we can afford to make many mistakes in most things we do, because the consequences are not really very serious. The same cannot be said for driving.

Concept 4   *Learning to drive is a complex process.*

Learning to drive not only involves learning to use controls skillfully (such as steering and braking), but requires extensive training and practice in all the other important aspects of the driving task. For example, students will have to practice *scanning* (looking) techniques until they are able to see all the important elements in all kinds of situations, study the actions of other drivers and pedestrians until they can accurately *predict* what they may do, practice *evaluating* a great variety of driving situations until they are able to consistently make the correct decisions in all situations, and acquire the specialized knowledge and skill required to meet many unusual driving conditions.

Concept 5   *Driver education is basic preparation for accident avoidance in the years ahead.*

A person who learns to drive at age sixteen or seventeen in a high-school driver education course is preparing for the many years of driving that lie ahead—perhaps as many as forty-five or fifty (Fig. 1.3). The real significance of the learning experience lies in its relationship to these many years of future driving performance.

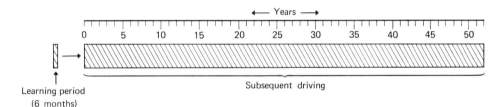

Fig. 1.3

The course succeeds to the extent that it develops the capability of each student to reduce his accident involvement in the future. It fails to the extent that it does not materially affect this capability (Fig. 1.4).*

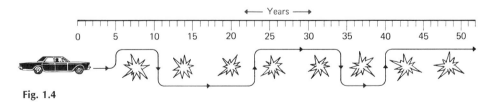

Fig. 1.4

---

* Of course, the actual accident experience of students who graduate from driver education courses will depend on other factors in addition to the quality of their experience in the course—for example, individual differences in basic capabilities, differences in driving exposure, and elements of chance which are beyond the driver's control.

Developing one's capability for safe driver performance is a formidable challenge. It involves more than most beginning drivers would suspect. For example, there is the difficult problem of reducing one's own errors. In view of the number of decisions the driver is called upon to make under normal conditions—a reasonable estimate is twenty major decisions for every mile traveled (B 63)—the likelihood of committing errors is substantial. Added to this is the problem of making driving adjustments that guard against the frequent errors made by other drivers.

The course is viewed as basic preparation, which means that the student is expected to continue to develop his ability for safe performance after he completes the course. The course should provide the student with an attitude toward the driving task and with an ability to examine his own performance that will enable him to continue to improve when he is on his own.

Concept 6   *A student's attitude toward learning to drive influences the quality of his learning and the extent to which he applies what he learns in the years ahead.*

The student who recognizes that learning to drive is a serious undertaking and decides that he *wants* to develop an ability to drive safely is in a favorable position to learn what is going to be taught. If, on the other hand, the student is more concerned with achieving some other objectives, he is not likely to profit fully from the course.

For example, many students are concerned exclusively with obtaining a driver's license so that they can enjoy the privileges that go with it. This kind of attitude leads to an inability to see beyond the driver's license test, and a tendency to want to learn only those things that will enable them to pass the test. Students with this outlook are not likely to be interested in learning those elements of safe driver performance that do not relate directly to passing the test. (Any one of the several examples from subsequent units might be cited to illustrate this point, such as performance in simulated emergencies.) Even more important is the fact that students with this attitude may learn things so that they can pass the test and may promptly disregard what they have learned once the test is passed. (Again, any one of several examples from subsequent units might be used to illustrate this point, such as selecting reduced-risk alternatives.) In such cases, the driver education experience has failed because it has not effectively influenced the students' future driving performance.

As a consequence of this discussion, students should at least recognize the significance of their own intentions as a potential influence on their learning experience. Hopefully, most students will begin to adopt the point of view that they are here to learn to drive safely. However, it is probably unrealistic to expect those students who come equipped with poor attitudes to change their outlook immediately—the remainder of the course should attend to this problem.

PHASE 2: CONTENT OF THE IN-CAR PROGRAM

Part of a classroom period should be used to present an overview of the content of the in-car program. The purpose of the overview is to enable students to appreciate the total scope of the program so that they will be in a position to better understand each element of instruction as they encounter it. Since each of the elements of content will be covered in detail in subsequent stages of the course, this initial review should be concise. It should acquaint students with the major areas of content and the relevance of each area to developing an ability to drive safely. It would be advisable to relate this discussion of content to the major elements of the driving task covered in Phase 1 of this unit.

Teachers should develop their own outlines for guiding classroom presentations. The classroom guide should be based on the teachers' own reviews of the content of Units 2–14 and on the unique elements of content that they intend to introduce in their own in-car programs.

PHASE 3: IN-CAR PROCEDURES

A portion of a classroom period should be devoted to those in-car procedures that students should be acquainted with in advance. An adequate review of these procedures in the classroom should negate the necessity for reviewing them with each driving group in the car.

An outline of some of the procedures that might be discussed appears below. No attempt is made to describe these procedures in detail because of the substantial differences that are likely to exist between the operation of one driver education program and another.

To add to the efficiency of this phase of instruction the teacher might have a list of procedures reproduced and distributed to students. Then students might review them at home and classroom time might be used more profitably to clarify selected procedures.

1. *The in-car schedule for driving groups and individuals.*

2. *Reporting for the in-car lesson.* The meeting place; what to bring wih you—learner's permits, glasses, notebook, and so forth; what to do in case of lateness; and so on.

3. *Practice time behind the wheel.* Students should understand the policies that affect the amount of practice driving they will do.

4. *The use of observation time.* Students should understand what is expected of them during the period when they are observing another student perform and how this relates to their total in-car experience.

5. *Individual differences in rate of progress.* The likelihood of different rates of progress among students should be discussed. The teacher should make certain that students understand why they will not be allowed to move on to more advanced maneuvers and skills before they master the more basic elements of performance.

6. *Evaluation of student performance.* The teacher should outline the procedures and standards that will be used to evaluate driving performance so that students will understand— from the beginning—what is expected of them.

7. *The teacher's role during in-car instruction.* The teacher should explain her role as the person responsible for the safety of car occupants, as well as her role as instructor. Special attention might be given to the presence of the dual-control brake and the conditions under which it will be used.

8. *Preparation for the in-car lesson.* Students should understand the importance of the classroom work and homework to their successful performance in the car.

9. *Outside practice.* If the teacher is going to permit and encourage outside practice during the period of the student's enrollment in the driver education course, she should thoroughly review the policies relating to this practice.

CLASSROOM GUIDE FOR UNIT 1
Orientation to the Driving Task and to In-Car Instruction

Topics	Instructional Plan

Phase 1. The Driving Task and The Purposes of In-Car Instruction

Illustrative concepts:

1. Learning to drive involves learning to perform the driving task.

2. Safe driving is a complex and challenging task.

3. Driver errors cause accidents.

4. Learning to drive is a complex and difficult process.

5. Driver education is basic preparation for accident avoidance in the years ahead.

6. A student's attitude toward learning to drive influences the quality of his learning and the extent to which he applies what he learns in the years ahead.

Procedural guides:

1. Use appropriate questions to introduce discussion of basic concepts.

2. Allow students to present and discuss their own ideas before presenting your own.

3. Document and support your point of view with statistics and specific examples.

4. Use diagrams for clarification of concepts.

Illustrative questions:

1. What do you suppose is the primary reason for offering this course?

2. Do you think that driving an automobile is a dangerous undertaking?

3. To what extent will your own actions as a driver (in the years to come) affect your chances of being involved in an accident?

4. How should in-car instruction prepare you for what lies ahead?

5. Why did you enroll in this course? And how will your reasons for enrolling affect what you learn?

Phase 2: Content of the In-Car Program

See Units 2 through 14.

Procedural guides:

1. Present brief summary of in-car units.

2. Use specific examples wherever appropriate.

3. Relate each major element of content to safe driver performance.

4. Organize content to fit the unique aspects of your own program.

CLASSROOM GUIDE FOR UNIT 1 (cont.)

Topics	Instructional Plan

Phase 3: In-Car Procedures

Illustrative topics:

1. In-car schedule.
2. Reporting for in-car lesson.
3. Practice time behind the wheel.
4. Use of observation time.
5. Individual differences in rate of progress.
6. Evaluation of student performance.
7. Teacher's role during in-car instruction.
8. Preparation for in-car lesson.
9. Outside practice.

Procedural guides:

1. Briefly present each procedure.
2. Allow for discussion and clarification.
3. Present rationale for procedures wherever necessary.
4. Reproduce and distribute procedures to students—if possible.

PREPARATORY READING FOR STUDENTS

1. *Learning to Drive: Skills, Concepts, and Strategies.* Chapter 1, "Introduction: Using This Book," pp. 1–2; Chapter 2, "The Driving Task and the Process of Learning to Drive," pp. 3–15; Chapter 3, "Instructional Procedures in the Car," pp. 16–18. Also have students skim over the Practice Guides at the end of Chapters 4 through 16 to get an idea of the content of the instructional program.

   —or appropriate sections from another high-school text.

2. *Accident Facts* (or other appropriate resource). Assign sections that provide an overview of the accident problem.

unit 2

ORIENTATION TO INSTRUMENTS AND DEVICES, AND PREPARING TO MOVE THE VEHICLE

INTRODUCTION

The content in this unit is divided into two phases. Phase 1 deals with the information about instruments and devices that is prerequisite to their intelligent use. It also provides the student with an opportunity to operate various instruments that will be used during subsequent in-car practice. Phase 2 focuses on the performance of the sequence of steps preparatory to moving the car [1]. In-car practice takes place in an off-street area. However, the objectives of this unit can be accomplished with minimal time spent in the car, provided the teacher carefully prepares the student in the classroom.

PHASE 1: ORIENTATION TO INSTRUMENTS AND DEVICES

The objectives for students are to locate, operate, and understand the function of:
1. Control instruments: *steering wheel, selector lever, accelerator pedal, service brake, parking brake, ignition switch*
2. Monitoring devices: *gasoline gauge, water temperature gauge, oil pressure gauge, speedometer, odometer, ammeter or generator charge light*
3. Communication instruments: *horn, directional signal lever, hazard warning signal, brake lights*
4. Devices for visibility: *rearview and sideview mirrors, headlights, windshield wipers and washers, defroster, sun visors*
5. Protective devices: *safety belts, door locks, head restraints*
6. Other devices: *heater, seat adjustment mechanism, interior lights, and other devices available on the car being used*

For a detailed description of these instruments and their function the teacher should consult the owner's manual for the driver education car and, if need be, a standard high-school textbook.

Instructional Plan

Classroom

A significant part of this orientation should take place in the classroom prior to the student's first lesson in the car. The teacher should discuss the purpose and operation of all gauges and instruments accessible to the driver, emphasizing their importance to safe and economical driving. A special effort should be made to relate the use of these instruments to successful performance of the key elements of the driving task discussed in Unit 1. The teacher might use a blackboard drawing or a wood or cardboard mock-up of the interior of the driver education car to explain the specific operation and location of gauges and instruments. The teacher's objective should be to use the classroom time to cover as much of the explanatory material as possible, so that the in-car lesson can be devoted to student practice in identifying and operating the instruments.

In-car identification and operation

Assuming that the student has been exposed to a prior classroom orientation, the in-car lesson may concentrate on identifying and operating the instruments and devices.

The student should have an opportunity to identify the gasoline gauge, oil pressure gauge, ammeter, speedometer, and odometer, and briefly indicate the important information provided by each.

In addition, the student should operate selected instruments. Special emphasis should be placed on those instruments she may *not* have a chance to use later on in this unit, including light switches, horn, directional signals, and windshield wipers. (Practice in using seat belts, mirrors, parking brake, and so on will occur in Phase 2 of this unit and, therefore, need not be done at this point.) Having the students actually operate these devices can be important. It is not uncommon for a student in the later stages of her training to find herself in a situation that requires using the horn, only to discover that she is not sure how to use it because she has had no previous opportunity to do so.

During this phase of instruction it is usually appropriate to introduce practice in selector lever positioning. Since proper use of the lever entails a simultaneous application of the foot brake, selector lever positioning might be viewed as a somewhat complex skill. Certainly, from the standpoint of safety, it is most important that the student develop an automatic and coordinated hand-foot response whenever she uses the lever. It would be wise, therefore, to provide the student with several opportunities to practice this coordinated response. The student should start with her foot on the floor and hands on the steering wheel; each time she uses the lever her foot should move from the floor to the brake and back to the floor. In addition to providing practice in selector lever positioning, this drill familiarizes the student with the position and feel of the foot brake. During or before practice the teacher should emphasize the safety value connected with making certain the brake is applied when using the selector lever.

PHASE 2: PREPARATION TO MOVE THE VEHICLE

The objectives for students are to correctly execute the steps in preparing to move the vehicle, in parking the vehicle, and in entering and leaving the vehicle; and to identify the relationship between these steps and safe driving.

Actions to Be Learned

To provide a frame of reference that will facilitate student learning, the steps are organized into three categories: (1) preparing myself to drive, (2) preparing the vehicle to be driven, and (3) determining whether the roadway is ready for my vehicle.

Preparing myself to drive   In determining her own readiness to drive, the student asks herself: (1) Can I reach and operate the controls? (2) Can I see? (3) Am I (we) secure? The initials C (controls), S (see), and S (secure) provide a convenient device for remembering the questions.

1. *Can I reach and operate the controls?*

   (a) The student checks to see that her foot is within easy reach of the accelerator pedal and brake pedal. The heel of the foot should rest comfortably on the floor at a point approximately one inch from the base of the accelerator pedal. (b) She checks to see that she is a comfortable distance from the steering wheel and that her position permits freedom of arm movement in steering; she places her hand in a reasonably comfortable and balanced position (at approximately 9 o'clock and 3 o'clock) on the steering wheel [2]. (c) She adjusts the seat as necessary to improve her position.

2. *Can I see?*

   (a) The student checks to see that her head is sufficiently elevated to permit an adequate view of the road ahead. In most vehicles she should be able to see the front fenders. (b) A readjustment of the seat may be necessary or, in the case of smaller students, it may be advisable to provide a seat cushion. (c) The student determines her visibility to the rear. (d) She adjusts the rearview and sideview mirrors as necessary. Mirror adjustment should provide the driver with the most complete view of conditions to the rear. The rearview mirror should provide a view directly to the rear, and the sideview mirror should eliminate (as much as possible) the blind spots on the left side and left rear of the vehicle. Both mirrors should be adjusted to the driver's normal head position so that she need not move her head when using the mirrors (Fig. 2.1).

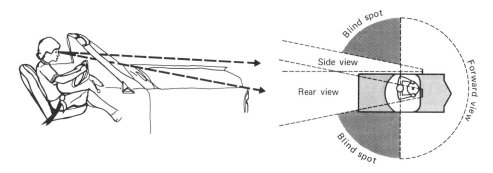

Fig. 2.1

3. *Am I (we) secure?*

   (a) The driver checks to see that *all* the doors are securely closed and locked. (b) She fastens her seat belt to secure her position in case of a collision. (c) She checks to see that the seat belts of other car occupants are fastened to secure their position in case of an accident [3]. She should be certain that the seat belts are properly adjusted—the lap belt should fit snugly and pass across the body at the hip joint; the shoulder belt should be less snug, there should be enough slack in the belt to allow the driver to fit a fist between her chest and the belt (Fig. 2.2).

Fig. 2.2

Students should understand some of the reasons for the sequence of steps described above. Seat adjustment must precede mirror adjustment because if mirror adjustment came first the subsequent adjustment of the seat would mean that the mirrors would need to be readjusted to suit the new seat position. For the same reason, fastening the seat belt must come after seat adjustment, otherwise seat belts would have to be readjusted to suit the new seat position.

Preparing the vehicle to be driven   In order for the vehicle to be ready to be moved, the engine must be running; there needs to be an adequate supply of gas, oil, and electricity; the transmission must be in Drive; and the parking brake must be off. To achieve these conditions the driver performs the following sequence of steps:

1. Places key in ignition
2. Checks parking brake to see that it is applied
3. Starts engine by first applying service brake and placing selector lever at N or P, and second, turning on (and releasing) ignition switch
4. Checks gauges
5. Applies service brake and moves selector lever to D
6. Releases parking brake

Determining whether the roadway is ready for my vehicle   To determine whether the roadway is ready the student performs a thorough check of conditions in the vicinity of the vehicle and decides when conditions are sufficiently safe to permit her vehicle to move [4]. Since the locale for this practice session is an off-street area that is relatively traffic free, a careful check of traffic conditions may not seem necessary. It is advisable, however, to include this as one of the steps so that the student incorporates it into her habitual sequence of actions at the very beginning of her driving experience. The exact nature of the check of conditions to be made is up to the discretion of the teacher and should depend on the unique aspects of the off-street environment. The teacher might have the student assume that she is parked by the curb at the side of a road, or emerging from a driveway, and perform her check of conditions accordingly. If possible it would be advisable to use the procedures for checking conditions presented in Unit 5.

Parking the vehicle   The steps involved in parking the vehicle are:

1. Apply service brake
2. Move selector lever to P
3. Apply parking brake
4. Turn off ignition
5. Remove keys

Entering and exiting from the vehicle   At some stage during this phase of in-car instruction the teacher should review procedures for entering and exiting from the vehicle. The procedures established should encourage students to enter and exit from the curb side of the vehicle. However, since it may be necessary to use the traffic side for entering and exiting at certain times during the in-car program, and since entering and exiting from the traffic side are common practices among experienced drivers, the teacher should emphasize the necessity for checking traffic conditions *before opening the door* to leave the vehicle on the traffic side. All students should develop the habit of turning completely around and thoroughly checking for traffic before the door is opened (Fig. 2.3).

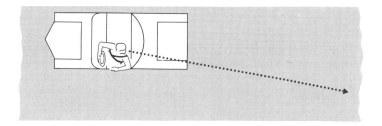

Fig. 2.3

Common Errors in Student Performance

Improper driver's position   Teachers should be alert to the fact that beginning drivers (especially the nervous ones) have a tendency to want to sit too close to the steering wheel. This can result in increasing the student's sense of discomfort as well as in restricting the freedom of arm movement used in steering. The teacher can discourage this tendency simply by having the student sit back and relax. However, in the case of smaller students, sitting back and relaxing may severely limit their ability to see the road ahead and to reach the accelerator and brake pedals. Seat cushions should be provided for these students.

Mirror adjustment—head position   In the process of adjusting mirrors, students have a tendency to move their heads to the right as they adjust the rearview mirror and to the left as they adjust the sideview mirror. This results in neither mirror's being adjusted properly once the driver returns to the driving position. Teachers can help to overcome this tendency by having students check the mirror adjustment by glancing from one mirror to the other—only a slight movement of the head and eyes should be necessary.

Starting the engine   Students may not recognize the point at which the engine starts, and as a result may tend to hold the key in the starting position too long. This rather costly error can be reduced by having the student focus her attention on the different sounds made by the engine and the starter motor, and by having her release the key just after the change in sound occurs. The teacher should recognize that in this situation the use of phrases like "release the key when the engine turns over" may be relatively meaningless to the beginning driver.

Omitting a step   In view of the relatively large number of steps involved, it is not uncommon for students to forget one (or more). Failing to release the parking brake and to move the selector lever to "Drive" are among the most common omissions. At this stage of instruction, it is probably wise for the teacher to provide the student with as much assistance as necessary in remembering the sequence of steps—the teacher might use a series of verbal cues that identify the steps for the student.

Instructional Plan

Classroom

A classroom lesson should acquaint students with all the steps in preparing to move the vehicle and in parking it before they are asked to practice them in the car. Particular attention should be given to the reasons for the *sequence* of steps and the relevance of each of the more important steps for safe driver performance. In addition, to avoid the necessity for lengthy explanations in the car, the more complex elements of performance that require advance knowledge (like mirror adjustment or checking traffic conditions) should be covered in detail in the classroom.

In-Car

In-car practice may be conducted in an off-street area. Each student should have an opportunity to go through the entire series of steps a few times. Since the total number of steps is quite extensive, it is usually advisable to break down the total sequence into meaningful parts during the student's initial trials. A convenient way to do this is to tell the student first "Prepare yourself to drive," then "Prepare the vehicle," and finally "Check conditions." When the student completes each segment of the sequence, she might report "I'm ready," "The car is ready," and "Conditions are clear." This procedure enables the student to work with manageable units of performace; it helps to emphasize the three important segments of the total sequence; and it provides the teacher with an opportunity to correct mistakes soon after they occur instead of having to wait until the end of the total sequence. As the student's ability to perform the total sequence improves, this "part" procedure may be discarded in favor of a "whole" approach.

Although the emphasis during the first in-car practice session is on *preparing* to move the vehicle, students should if possible be given some opportunity to move the vehicle. After practicing the preparatory steps a few times, students should be allowed to engage in initial practice of gradual acceleration, speed control, and gradual braking (Unit 3, Phase 1). Otherwise the artificiality of merely going through preparatory steps and the steps in parking may be both frustrating and disappointing to students who are anxious to "drive."

Mirror adjustment is the one relatively complex performance skill that deserves special attention during this phase of instruction. The teacher should be certain that the student understands (1) how the mirrors should be adjusted, (2) what she should be able to see by looking in the mirrors, and (3) what she cannot see by looking in the mirrors (blind spots). Since it is difficult for teachers (from their front-seat position) to know whether the student has adjusted the mirrors correctly, they might utilize any one of several methods for checking the adjustment. One popular method is to have another student stand at various points behind and to the side of the car while the student driver uses the mirrors to locate her. This also is a useful method for demonstrating to the student what she can and cannot see by using the mirrors.

Related Concepts and Information

Many of the steps involved in getting ready to move the vehicle (Phase 2) have a direct and rather obvious bearing on safe driver performance. In particular, the following relationships should be brought to the attention of students during either the in-car or classroom phase of instruction:

1. Proper mirror adjustment is indispensable to the safe performance of several driving maneuvers including changing lanes, passing, pulling out into traffic, and so on. Improper adjustment may lead to a failure to see other vehicles or obstacles at a critical moment in the performance of any one of these maneuvers. Furthermore, the habit of adjusting mirrors properly *before* moving the vehicle as opposed to doing it while the vehicle is in motion (which is not an uncommon practice among some experienced drivers) has an obvious relevance for safe performance.

2. Wearing a seat belt provides a significant degree of protection against injury in case an accident occurs. (This topic and the research evidence related to it deserves extensive discussion at some point in the classroom phase of the course.)

3. Checking to see that other occupants have their seat belts fastened is a responsibility that should be assumed by every driver. In the event of an accident (even one that is caused by someone else), the driver is ultimately responsible for the protection of passengers in her vehicle; that is, protection that was available.

4. Checking to see that the parking brake is applied before starting the engine and not releasing it until just before the vehicle is moved provides insurance against the possibility of having the vehicle move before the driver is ready.

5. Applying the service brake with each movement of the selector lever affords the same kind of insurance against unintentional movement of the vehicle.

6. Making an *especially thorough* check of conditions in preparing to move the vehicle is a crucial step because the vehicle is about to change its status from a stationary object to a moving vehicle. In on-street driving this change of status may very likely (and often does) come as a surprise to other drivers and pedestrians. As a consequence, they may not be in a position to avoid colliding with the now-moving object.

7. In parking the vehicle, making certain that the selector lever is on P, that the parking brake is *fully* applied, and that the engine is off are important practices in any situation where the driver is about to leave her position behind the wheel. These practices have special significance, however, in the driver education setting where there is a frequent change of drivers. If student drivers do not get in the habit of fully parking the vehicle prior to exchanging positions (to allow another student to drive), the consequences can be serious. For example, leaving the selector lever in "Drive" and the engine running, followed by an accidental depression of the accelerator pedal while exchanging positions, can produce a sudden acceleration at a time when three or four people are in the process of entering or leaving the car.

CLASSROOM GUIDE FOR UNIT 2

Orientation to Instruments and Devices, and Preparing to Move the Vehicle

Topics	Instructional Plan

Phase 1: Orientation to Instruments and Devices

1. Importance of being familiar with devices and instruments and their relationship to subsequent driving performance.

Discuss specific illustrations such as value of defroster in cold weather and water temperature gauge as a danger signal.

2. *Control instruments:*

   Steering wheel
   Selector lever
   Accelerator pedal
   Service brake
   Parking brake
   Ignition switch

Discuss:

1. How they operate
2. Their specific operation and appearance in driver education vehicle (use diagrams when necessary)

3. *Monitoring devices:*

   Gasoline gauge
   Water temperature gauge
   Oil pressure gauge
   Speedometer
   Odometer
   Ammeter or generator charge light

Review:

1. How they operate
2. Information they provide to driver
3. The importance of "monitoring the car's condition" as a feature of the driving task
4. Their location and appearance on driver education vehicle (use diagram or mock-up)

4. *Communication instruments:*

   Horn
   Directional signal lever
   Hazard warning signal
   Brake lights

Review:

1. How they are used to communicate information to other drivers and pedestrians
2. The role of communication in safe driving

5. *Devices for visibility:*

   Rearview and sideview mirrors
   Headlights
   Windshield wipers and washers
   Defroster
   Sun visors

Discuss:

1. Relationship between visibility and accident avoidance
2. When to use these devices

6. *Protective devices:*

   Safety belts
   Head restraints

Present and discuss data on value of seat belts in accidents

7. *Other devices:*

   Seat adjustment
   Interior lights
   Heater
   Other

Discuss only as necessary

CLASSROOM GUIDE FOR UNIT 2 *(cont.)*

Topics	Instructional Plan

Phase 2: Preparation to Move the Vehicle

1. Safe driving begins as soon as you enter the car.

Discuss concept; have students provide illustrations of relationships between preparatory steps and subsequent performance.

2. *Preparing myself to drive:*

   (C) Can I reach and operate *controls?*

   a) Brake, accelerator
   b) Distance from steering wheel
   c) Adjust seat (if necessary)

   (S) Can I *see?*

   a) Road ahead
   b) Readjust position (if necessary)
   c) To the rear
   d) Adjust mirrors (if necessary)

   (S) Am I *secure?*

   a) Check doors
   b) Fasten seat belt
   c) Check occupants' seat belts

1. Present total sequence of steps.
2. Discuss three major segments—driver, vehicle, roadway—and relate them to safe driving.
3. Discuss reasons for sequential arrangement.
4. Discuss how to adjust mirrors properly (use diagram).
5. Have students review steps before reporting for in-car lesson.

3. *Preparing the vehicle:*

   Key in ignition.
   Check parking brake.
   Start engine.
   Check gauges.
   Move selector lever to D.
   Release parking brake.

4. *Determining roadway ready:*

   Thoroughly check conditions.
   Decide when safe to move.

5. *Parking the vehicle:*

   Apply service brake.
   Move selector lever to P.
   Apply parking brake.
   Turn off ignition.
   Remove keys.

1. Present steps.
2. Discuss relevance to safety.

CLASSROOM GUIDE FOR UNIT 2 *(cont.)*

PREPARATORY READING FOR STUDENTS

1. *Learning to Drive: Skills, Concepts, and Strategies.* Chapter 4, "Orientation to Instruments and Devices, and Preparing to Move the Vehicle."

   —or appropriate sections from another high-school text.

2. Owner's manual for the driver education car. Sections dealing with instruments and devices.

RELATED SIMULATOR LESSONS

1. Aetna Drivotrainer System: "A Drive in an Automatic Shift Car."
2. Link Simulator System: "You Take the Wheel."

IN-CAR GUIDE FOR UNIT 2

Orientation to Instruments and Devices, and Preparing to Move the Vehicle

Teacher	Student

Phase 1: Orientation to Instruments and Devices

1. Ask student to identify:	Points to gauge and briefly indicates its function.
Gasoline gauge Water temperature gauge Oil pressure gauge Ammeter Speedometer Odometer	
2. Have student operate:	Operates each device once or twice.
Light switches Windshield wipers Horn Directional signals Parking brake	
3. Have student practice selector lever positioning. Emphasize: service brake on when using selector lever.	Performs several practice trials moving lever to different positions. After each trial, foot returns to floor.

Phase 2: Preparation to Move the Vehicle

Ask student to get ready to move car.	Performs sequence of steps.
Watch for seat position too close to wheel.	
Watch for head movement during mirror adjustment.	1. *Preparing myself:*
	(C) Can I reach and operate *controls?*
Emphasize and check accuracy of mirror adjustment.	Reaches brake and accelerator Distance from steering wheel Adjusts seat (if necessary)
	(S) Can I *see?*
	Road ahead Readjusts position (if necessary) To the rear Adjusts mirrors (if necessary)
	(S) Am I (we) *secure?*
	Checks doors Fastens seat belt Checks occupants' seat belts
	Reports, "I am ready."

IN-CAR GUIDE FOR UNIT 2 (*cont.*)

Teacher	Student
Supplementary cue, "Prepare the vehicle."	2. *Preparing the vehicle:*
Watch for delayed release of ignition switch.	Key in ignition
Emphasize applying service brake when using selector lever.	Checks parking brake
	Starts engine
	a) Selector lever at *N* or *P*
	b) Turns on (and releases) ignition switch
	Checks gauges
	Moves selector lever to D (service brake applied)
	Reports, "The car is ready."
Supplementary cue, "Check conditions."	3. *Determines roadway ready:*
	Thoroughly checks roadway conditions
	Decides when safe to move
	Reports, "Conditions are clear."
Ask student to "Park the car."	4. *Performs sequence of steps:*
	Applies foot brake
	Moves selector lever to P
	Applies parking brake
	Turns off ignition
	Removes keys

After several practice attempts, allow student some opportunity to move the vehicle (see skills in Unit 3, Phase 1). When appropriate, review and practice procedures for entering and exiting from the vehicle.

BASIC SKILLS IN
SPEED CONTROL
AND TRACKING
ON FORWARD PATHS

INTRODUCTION

Content   This initial unit in practice driving is divided into six phases:

Phase 1. Gradual acceleration, speed control, and gradual braking
Phase 2. Gradual stopping and positioning
Phase 3. Tracking* on a straight path
Phase 4. Tracking on turning paths
Phase 5. Quick braking
Phase 6. Checking to the rear and signaling for a stop

The unit is designed for use in an off-street area.

The major portion of the unit (Phases 1–5) is devoted to the development of basic skills in controlling the movement of the vehicle. Off-street practice of these skills should equip students with the basic tools necessary for coping with on-street driving in later practice sessions. Students should emerge from practice sessions in Unit 3 with a reasonable capability to accurately guide the direction, speed, and positioning of the vehicle.

The unit is divided into several phases principally because the total task of controlling the movement of the vehicle is too complex to be learned all at once. The division into phases permits the student to concentrate on mastering one major element of performance at a time. The sequence of phases is arranged so that the skills acquired in later phases build upon the skills acquired in earlier phases.

Adequate practice   Learning the basic skills in Unit 3 appears to depend heavily on the amounts of actual practice engaged in. Student progress frequently depends on trial and error learning that comes with repeated practice. The teacher, therefore, should plan to *provide as many practice trials as possible* for each student in the performance of each type of basic skill. For example, if the student is to drive for a specified period of time and if the teacher wants the student to concentrate on gradual acceleration and braking, the teacher may simply have the student stop and go as many times as possible during the practice period.

---

* *Tracking* refers to the ability of the driver to keep the vehicle on an intended path.

Preparation for on-street driving   One of the dangers that can arise in connection with utilizing off-street areas for practice driving is that both teacher and student can lose sight of its relevance to driving on public streets. It is not uncommon for off-street areas to be used for drills that are conveniently structured to suit the off-street environment, but have little relationship to the kinds of driving tasks the student will be called upon to perform later when operating the vehicle on public streets. Off-street practice should be conducted in a way that provides for transfer of training to on-street driving. Whenever possible, the off-street practice session or drill should be similar to on-street driving from the standpoint of the structure of the environment and the tasks performed by the student.

Emphasis on safety   Although this unit deals with the development of basic skills in an off-street area, the relevance for safe driver performance of what is learned should not be overlooked [1]. The teacher should be certain that each student understand the relationship between what is learned and the ultimate task of safe on-street driving. Emphasizing this relationship should help to make off-street practice more meaningful and to enhance the proper use of these skills in later on-street practice. The section entitled "Related Concepts and Information" identifies some of the relationships between the skills to be learned and safe driver performance. The *classroom* phase of instruction provides a most convenient and efficient opportunity to discuss these relationships.

PHASE 1: GRADUAL ACCELERATION, SPEED CONTROL, AND GRADUAL BRAKING

The objective for students is to move the vehicle from a stationary position to a traveling speed at a gradually increasing rate of speed, maintain an appropriate traveling speed, and then bring the vehicle back to a stationary position at a gradually decreasing rate of speed [2] (see Fig. 3.1); and to be able to identify the relationship between these skills and safe driving.

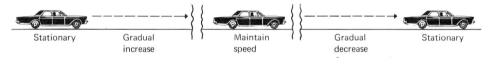

| Stationary | Gradual increase | Maintain speed | Gradual decrease | Stationary |

Fig. 3.1

Driving Skills to Be Learned   *[handwritten annotations: between the time you press on the accelerator and the car actually moves; gap between; feet on floor; too pressing down on accelerator]*

Gradual acceleration   Gradual acceleration involves slowly depressing the accelerator to move the car from a stationary position to an appropriate traveling speed. The key to correct performance is to depress the accelerator pedal gradually. Students should recognize that it takes time for the movement of the accelerator pedal to have its full effect on the speed of the car; the driver must allow for this delayed effect.

Speed control   Speed control is accomplished by adjusting the position of the accelerator pedal to increase speed or to reduce speed and holding the pedal more or less steady to maintain a constant speed.

From the student's standpoint, learning to control speed involves (1) *knowing* the speed at which he wants to travel, (2) *judging* whether the actual speed of the car is too fast, too slow, or just right, and (3) when the speed is too fast or too slow, *adjusting* the position of the accelerator until the desired speed is attained.

Students can check their speed judgment by glancing briefly at the speedometer. However, when they do so, they should make certain that their eyes return to the road ahead immediately.

Gradual braking Gradual braking involves gradually depressing the brake pedal to bring the car to a smooth stop. Students should understand that most brake pedals can be depressed one inch or more before the braking point is reached (the point at which the brakes in the wheels begin to take hold) and that therefore the first inch or so of movement of the brake pedal has little or no effect in stopping the car.

Right versus left foot braking At this stage in the student's practice, it is advisable to concentrate on right foot braking. Although there is some controversy with respect to whether left foot braking should be used in vehicles with automatic transmissions, most professionals agree that right foot braking is easier for beginners to master and better prepares them to drive all vehicles (standard or automatic).

Common Errors in Student Performance

Most beginning drivers have little difficulty with gradual acceleration; on the other hand, many have difficulty in bringing the car to a gradual stop. The most common error involves depressing the brake too fast and too hard—this tendency is especially noticeable when the vehicle is equipped with power brakes. In some cases the difficulty appears to be due to a failure on the part of the student to recognize that the brake pedal must reach the braking point before the brakes take hold. He begins to depress the brake gradually—notices that the car is not slowing down—and increases the rate of depression, which results in an abrupt stop.

One method for overcoming (or avoiding) this error is to have the student practice braking in stages (Fig. 3.2):

Stage 1 *Caution position*—foot on brake pedal.

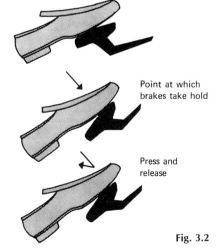

Point at which brakes take hold

Stage 2 *Slow—depress brake to braking point.*

Press and release

Stage 3 *Stop—increase pressure on pedal —release pressure just before stopping.*

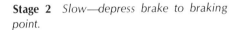

Fig. 3.2

* The names given to each stage might be used as verbal cues by the teacher to guide student performance.

Practice Plan

The student should be given several practice trials in gradual acceleration and g,. braking. In a suitably large off-street area with a relatively long straightaway path, the studen should be able to complete twenty or thirty practice trials in the space of a few minutes. Initial attempts should be performed at very slow speeds (5–10 mph) and at somewhat faster speeds as student competence increases (Fig. 3.3).

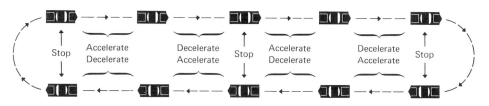

Fig. 3.3

During this stage of practice the teacher may or may not wish to give attention to steering—it will depend on the capabilities of the student driver. In most cases it seems wise to overlook initial errors in steering until the student gains a reasonable degree of control over the brake and accelerator. In fact, the teacher may wish to *manually assist* the student in steering so that the student is free to concentrate on accelerating and braking.

During the later stages of practice more attention should be given to speed control. Teachers should establish a target speed (perhaps 10–20 mph) that is appropriate for the size and layout of the off-street area, and then use verbal cues to assist the student in reaching and maintaining the target speed. Initially students may check their speed judgment by briefly glancing at the speedometer; eventually, however, they should be able to maintain the target speed by accurately sensing the speed of the vehicle.

Be careful not to overdo the practice of glancing at the speedometer. It takes approximately 1.4 seconds to move the eyes from the visual scene to the speedometer and then back to the scene (B 46). If the car is traveling at 35 mph, for example, it will travel 70 feet during this interval. Thus excessive glances at the speedometer can result in extended periods of potentially dangerous inattention to the road ahead.

Related Concepts and Information

Students should understand the relationship of gradual acceleration and braking to safe driver performance. In most driving situations (excluding emergencies) where the vehicle must be moved from a stationary position or brought to a stop from a traveling speed, gradual increases and decreases in the rate of speed are likely to incur less risk than would be the case with more abrupt changes in speed. Perhaps the most important advantage of gradual changes in speed is that they provide other drivers (or pedestrians) with an early warning that your vehicle is either starting to move or about to come to a stop. In particular, students should be aware of the advance warning provided by the brake lights in gradual braking. By contrast, they should appreciate the danger involved in abrupt braking (Fig. 3.4).

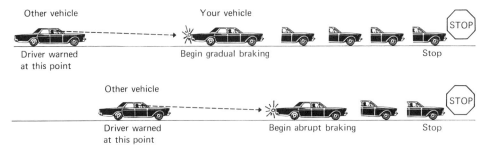

Fig. 3.4

At the same time, excessively early or gradual braking has its disadvantages, particularly in terms of its effects on other drivers. For example, if a driver begins braking one-half block before reaching a stop sign (at the corner), another driver (to the rear) may not expect the early reduction in speed and fail to slow down in time, or he may think that the first car intends to stop mid-block and attempt to pass it. With this in mind, the teacher should encourage the student to get into the habit of bringing the vehicle to an appropriately gradual stop—avoiding excesses in either direction.

Students should recognize the difference between learning the skill of speed control and learning how to drive at appropriate (and safe) speeds. Learning the skill of speed control allows the driver to drive the car at the speed he wants it to travel. Learning to drive at appropriate speeds involves judging the great variety of traffic and roadway conditions, deciding on a speed that is appropriate and safe for the conditions, and then using speed control skill to keep the car at the appropriate speed. While the student may achieve skill in speed control during his first few driving lessons, it will require a great many lessons under a great variety of conditions before he learns to drive at appropriate and safe speeds.

PHASE 2: GRADUAL STOPPING AND POSITIONING

The objective for students is to bring the car to a gradual stop at a designated position [3] (Fig. 3.5), and to identify the relationship between this skill and safe driving.

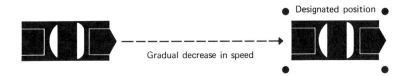

Fig. 3.5

The gradual stopping distance (the distance traveled from initial brake application until the vehicle is stopped) will vary depending on the speed at which the vehicle is traveling. What constitutes an appropriate gradual stopping distance (from a given speed) will depend on the judgment of the instructor. The distance should approximate the distance covered in making a safe stop under normal on-street driving conditions—it should be gradual enough to provide adequate warning to drivers to the rear but not so gradual as to confuse other drivers and pedestrians.

Driving Skills to Be Learned

Judging required stopping distance   This phase of the lesson requires the student to use the skill of gradual braking (practiced in Phase 1) to bring the vehicle to a stop at a specified position. This means that he will have to choose the appropriate moment to begin braking and will have to gauge the rate of decrease in speed more carefully. This should lead to the development of an appreciation for the distances required to bring the vehicle to a gradual stop and the consequent need to begin braking at appropriate points in advance of the intended stopping position.

Judging vehicle position   In addition, to stop the vehicle at the indicated position, the student will have to develop an awareness of the dimensions of his vehicle and the space it occupies on the roadway. This means that from his position in the driver's seat he must become familiar with the space to the front, rear, left, and right occupied by his automobile. As obvious as this awareness might seem to the experienced driver, beginning drivers do not necessarily develop it automatically—it is not uncommon for student drivers to progress through several lessons without developing an appreciation for the space occupied by the machine they are operating.

Common Errors in Student Performance

The most common errors made in gradual stopping and positioning involve choosing when to begin braking. Some drivers tend to begin braking too soon, with the result that they either stop too gradually or stop before the designated position. Other drivers tend to begin braking too late, with the result that they either stop too abruptly or stop beyond the designated position. This error is not easy to eliminate because the task involves a relatively complex set of judgments on the student's part. In cases where this error occurs consistently, the teacher might aid the student by providing a simple verbal cue ("begin braking") at the appropriate distance from the stopping position.

Some students will have difficulty judging the immediate position of the vehicle. For example, having brought the car to a stop the student might *think* it occupies the designated position when in actuality it is off-position. (This error is to be distinguished from an error in control: the student attempts to move the car into position but fails to do so because of an error in steering or braking and *knows* that his vehicle is not in position.) For students having difficulty in judging the immediate position of the vehicle, the teacher might design several practice trials in which the student is required to make repeated judgments about his vehicle's position. Smaller students who cannot easily see the front and rear fenders are especially prone to this error.

Practice Plan

Practice in gradual stopping and positioning is an extension of practice in acceleration and braking (Phase 1). The same layout and area may be used. The teacher merely needs to add designated stopping positions (Fig. 3.6).

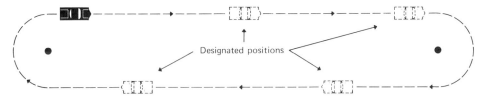

Fig. 3.6

It is usually desirable to mark both sides of the position with stanchions or some other objects that can be seen continuously from the driver's position (as opposed to street markings). This provides the beginner with needed reference points to make immediate judgments about his car's position.

During this stage of practice it is advisable to give the student ample opportunity to make judgments about the vehicle's position by *asking* him whether he thinks the vehicle is in position. This technique should be helpful in determining whether the student is having difficulty in judging the immediate position of the car or in controlling its movement.

During the later stages of practice the student should increase the speed of his approach to the stopping position and begin braking at appropriately earlier points as required by the increase in speed. The teacher should use this stage of practice to emphasize the need for early braking in most driving situations and its relevance for safe driver performance.

PHASE 3: TRACKING ON A STRAIGHT PATH

The objective for students is to keep the car on a straight path [4]. *Accurate tracking keeps the car on its intended path. Errors in tracking occur when the car moves off the path (Fig. 3.7). As the students progress they should reduce both the size and frequency of their tracking errors. Students should also be able to identify the relationship between accurate tracking and safe driving.*

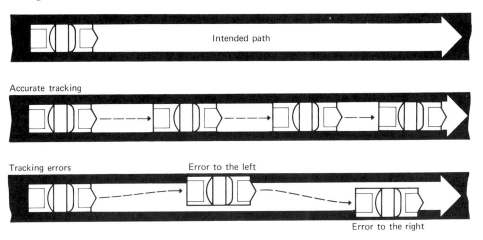

Fig. 3.7

Driving Skills to Be Learned

Learning to keep the car on an intended path (tracking) involves the development and coordination of several skills, including skills in steering, acceleration, perception, and judgment. Present knowledge of the driving task does not permit a precise description of the *tracking* process. Nevertheless, some of the basic elements of performance appear to include the following:

1. *Having a clear idea of the intended path over which the vehicle is to travel.* In most off-street practice areas this path should be a center path between pavement markings or stanchions (Fig. 3.8).

Fig. 3.8

2. *Looking ahead along the intended path and aiming the car for a point in the middle of the path.*   With beginning drivers it is usually helpful to encourage them to aim the car for a point in the middle of the intended path and well out ahead of the vehicle. In addition, students will probably have to periodically shift their visual focus to points close to the vehicle in order to make judgments about the vehicle's alignment in relation to lane markings [5] (Fig. 3.9).

Fig. 3.9

3. *Recognizing when the car begins to deviate from the intended path and making the necessary steering corrections* (Fig. 3.10).   The steering corrections required to keep the car on a straight path are relatively small (perhaps an inch or two) and are usually performed without changing the points at which the hands contact the steering wheel. It is helpful for the beginner to understand that a steering correction normally involves turning the wheel slightly in one direction, followed by a reversal that straightens out the wheels (Fig. 3.11).

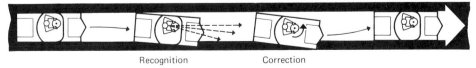

Recognition   Correction

Fig. 3.10

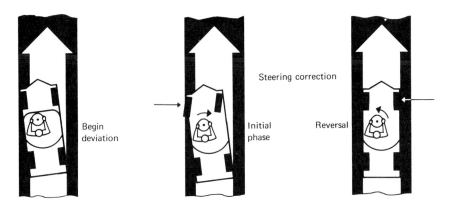

Fig. 3.11

Common Errors in Student Performance

Drifting   One of the most common errors among beginners is to allow the car to drift gradually to one side of the intended path or the other. This error may be due to any one of several factors. Very often beginning drivers focus their attention on one edge of the intended path and watch the movement of their front fender in relation to that edge. This practice frequently results in a tendency to steer in the direction in which the student's attention is focused (Fig. 3.12).

Fig. 3.12

Overcorrecting   Another common error among beginners is a tendency to *overcorrect* in steering when they notice the vehicle moving off its path. The error may involve turning the steering wheel further than is necessary to move the car back on the path or it may involve failing to straighten out the wheels once the car is back in the center of its path. Some times this error is compounded when an overcorrection in one direction is followed by an overcorrection in the opposite direction—this results in a weaving pattern (Fig. 3.13).

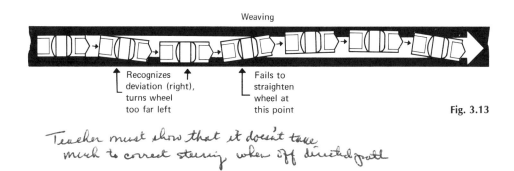

Fig. 3.13

Teacher must show that it doesn't take
much to correct steering when off directed path

Some beginning drivers overcorrect because they fail to realize that *small* corrections will *gradually* bring the car back on its path. As a result, when they deviate from a path they make a small correction, then because the car does not *immediately* return to its path, they increase the size of the correction and find themselves going off to the opposite side of the path.

To correct this error the teacher might emphasize the *smallness* of the steering corrections necessary to keep the car on a straight path and the need to *wait* for the vehicle to gradually return to its path. This can be accomplished most efficiently by *manually assisting* the student in making corrections.

Off-center path   Some drivers are able to maintain a relatively straight path but are inclined to stay on the right or left of the intended path (Fig. 3.14). This problem reflects an inability to judge the lateral position of the car in relation to the roadway—the driver thinks his car is in the center of the lane when in reality it is not.*

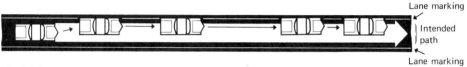

Fig. 3.14

It may be helpful in correcting this tendency to be certain that the student understands that the driver's position is on the left side of the vehicle, and when the vehicle is centered on its path the driver is slightly off center (to the left). As a consequence, in order to keep the vehicle centered on its path, the driver must keep his own position slightly to the left of center (Fig. 3.15).

Fig. 3.15

Practice Plan

The practice should be arranged to provide a long straightaway and the area should be marked to provide a clear indication of the intended path. The importance of clearly defining the intended path should not be underestimated. The objective of this lesson is accurate tracking. The student cannot attempt accurate tracking nor can the teacher make judgments about the accuracy of student performance unless the path is clearly marked.

The area should be marked to resemble on-street conditions—painted lane markings are most appropriate. The intended path should be a centered path between the lane markings.

---

*There is a natural tendency for most drivers to maintain a position slightly to the left of a centered lane position. One study (B-94) found that drivers, on the average, maintained a position five inches to the left of center on a straightaway.

Before the student attempts to perform he should be given clear directions regarding the intended path—otherwise the student's failure to follow the intended path may be misinterpreted as a tracking error.

An obvious problem connected with this phase of the unit is that when the vehicle reaches the end of the straightaway it must be turned around (or partly around) and redirected on another straight path. Some teachers find it most convenient, therefore, to combine this phase of the unit with the next phase, "tracking on turning paths." In this case they give simultaneous and equal attention to the skills involved in accurate guidance on both straight and turning paths. Other teachers may prefer to emphasize accurate guidance on a straight path before encouraging the student to concentrate on the skills in Phase 4. Using this approach the teacher may allow the student to turn the vehicle around at the end of the straightaway but does not concentrate on accuracy in turning until the student can accurately guide the car on a straight path.

Related Concepts and Information

The student should recognize that safe driving is very often a matter of inches. The driver is continually faced with the problem of guiding a car along a relatively narrow path in situations where a small tracking error to either side can result in a serious collision, in running off the roadway, or in some other kind of accident. Therefore, the student's ability to reduce to a minimum the size and frequency of his tracking errors during in-car instruction should be vital to his future as a safe driver.

In addition, the student should understand the importance of maintaining a centered lane position. Under most circumstances the centered position increases the space cushion between the vehicle and obstacles (abutments, curbs, road shoulders, other vehicles, and so forth) that frequently are at the edges of the lane. This increased space cushion affords the driver a greater margin of error, which can be crucial to avoiding an accident. For example, when a person drives to the right of center in a lane bounded on the right by a soft shoulder, a slight steering error might cause the front wheels to go off the pavement, causing an accident. Another driver who maintains a centered lane position could make the same error in the same situation, but his car would not leave the road because his centered position afforded a greater initial distance (space cushion) between his right wheels and the edge of the pavement. This principle applies in numerous other situations where the driver must avoid colliding with obstacles that are positioned (or moving) at the edge of his lane (Fig. 3.16).

Maintaining the centered lane position is valuable as a *general* rule. It does not apply, however, to all situations. There are many times when the driver must move off the centered lane position to avoid colliding with an obstacle (such as another vehicle) that is moving into, or is already within, his lane.

Driver 1 (drives right of center)

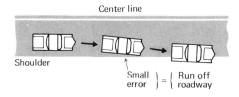

Driver 2 (drives in centered lane position)

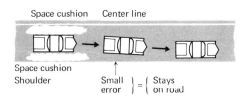

Fig. 3.16

PHASE 4: TRACKING ON TURNING PATHS (TO THE RIGHT AND TO THE LEFT)

The objective for students is to keep the car on an intended turning path (accurate tracking) to the right and to the left (Fig. 3.17). Errors in tracking occur when the car moves off the intended path. As the students progress they can be expected to reduce the size and frequency of their tracking errors. Students should also be able to identify the relationship between these skills and safe driving.

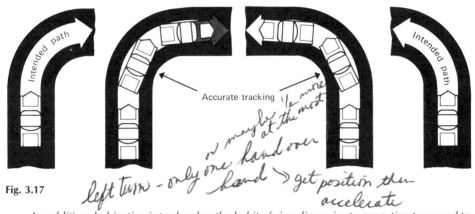

Accurate tracking

left turn - only one hand or maybe 1/2 more at the most hand over hand → get position then accelerate

Fig. 3.17

An additional objective is to develop the habit of signaling prior to executing turns and to understand its relationship to safe driving.

right hand turn - 2 hand over hand

Driving Skills to Be Learned

Teaching accurate tracking on a turning path will depend, in part, on the angle and sharpness of the turn. It would not be feasible to attempt to describe the learner's task in terms of the infinite variety of possible turning paths. Therefore, the description of the driver's task (below) is in terms of the actions required in performing *standard right and left turns* (turns of approximately 90° performed in a space roughly equivalent to that available when making a right or left turn from one street onto an intersecting street (see Fig. 3.18)). Major adjustments in driver performance necessitated by variations in the sharpness of the turning path are discussed in a subsequent section.

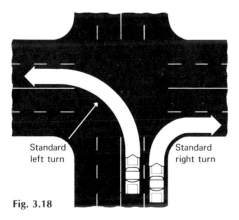

Standard left turn

Standard right turn

Fig. 3.18

Fig. 3–18

Learning to keep the car on an intended turning path involves the development and coordination of several skills, including perception and judgment skills, speed control skills, and special steering skills. Although these skills are performed more or less simultaneously as the driver negotiates the turn, for the sake of clarity they are separately described below. (As in the case of tracking on a straight path, the following descriptions attempt to emphasize some of the basic elements of an exceedingly complex human performance task.)

Perception and judgment skills   The task of tracking on a turning path involves (1) having a clear idea of the intended path over which the vehicle is to travel, (2) scanning ahead along the intended path and aiming the car for the center of the path, and (3) recognizing when the car begins to deviate from the intended path and making appropriate steering and/or speed adjustments (Fig. 3.19).

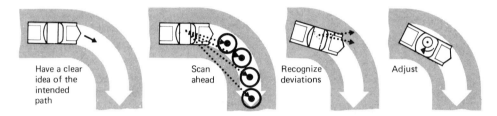

Have a clear idea of the intended path

Scan ahead

Recognize deviations

Adjust

Fig. 3.19

Speed control skills   Speed control skills include (1) decelerating and employing gradual braking to achieve an appropriately reduced speed (approximately 3–5 mph) as the vehicle enters the turn, (2) maintaining an appropriate turning speed during the turn by using the brake or accelerator pedal when necessary, and (3) gradually accelerating as the vehicle completes the turn (Fig. 3.20).

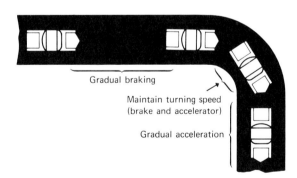

Gradual braking

Maintain turning speed (brake and accelerator)

Gradual acceleration

Fig. 3.20

Steering skills   The steering techniques used in performing a turn consist of two major phases: (1) initial (hand-over-hand) steering, and (2) recovery.

Initial (hand-over hand) steering is the first part of the steering control and redirects the vehicle toward its new path [6]. The accepted technique for performing the initial steering is referred to as hand-over-hand steering. Although professionals differ somewhat in describing the details of the hand-over-hand technique, the general principles involved are similar.* The procedure for a right turn is shown in Fig. 3.21.

Fig. 3.21

1. Right hand starts near the top of the wheel and pulls down and to the right.

2. As the right hand approaches a position at the bottom-right of the wheel, the left hand grasps the wheel close to the top and continues to turn the wheel as the right hand releases the wheel.

3. The right hand then crosses over the left and grasps the wheel as the left hand continues to turn the wheel.

4. The right hand continues to turn the wheel (as in Step 1) as the left hand releases the wheel and is brought back to a position at the left-top of the wheel.

5. Both hands are on the wheel in position to start the recovery.

The total procedure might be varied somewhat by beginning to turn the wheel with the left hand and then continuing with Steps 3, 4, and 5.

The hand-over-hand technique for turning to the left is similar to the technique for turning right—with the exception that the wheel is turned in the opposite direction. (For a description

---

* Differences in the capacities of the learner, steering-wheel radius, steering ratio, speed of the vehicle, and the precise angle of the turn may necessitate variations in the specific application of hand-over-hand steering in the teaching situation. As a consequence, the hand-over-hand technique should not be viewed as a precise formula for steering control. The teacher should approach hand-over-hand steering in a way that permits individual variations in technique and should not attempt to teach it as a rigid set of steps that must be performed by all students. In general, the student should be encouraged to adopt a method of steering that results in the most efficient control over the vehicle.

of the steps in turning left merely interchange the words "left" and "right" in the description of turning right.)

The hand-over-hand technique is intended to provide smooth, continuous steering control in turning. It is considered to be superior to the method of "walking" the wheel (pushing with one hand and pulling with the other without crossing hands), which tends to produce a jerky turn comprised of several small readjustments.

Recovery is the technique used to return the wheel to the straight ahead position. Recovery begins just *prior* to the point in the turn where the car first faces in its new direction. Recovery can be accomplished using one or a combination of two methods: (1) controlled slipping or (2) reversed steering (Fig. 3.22). In general, some degree of reversed steering is necessary in slow turns and, in most cases (for beginners), some form of the combined method will be required to complete the turn successfully.

Fig. 3.22

1. *Controlled slipping* allows the steering wheel to return to its original position by reducing hand pressure on the wheel and controlling its return movement by adjusting the amount of pressure applied. The hands remain in the same relative position in space and never lose contact with the wheel.

2. *Reversed steering* is the active turning of the wheel in the opposite direction (for right turns this would mean turning back to the left). This can be accomplished by using one of several modified versions of the hand-over-hand method described earlier.

3. *The combined method* utilizes both of the previous methods by first reducing the hand pressure on the wheel to allow the wheel to begin to return on its own, and then applying reversed steering as necessary to return the wheel to the proper position.

Differences in performance with variations in the sharpness of the turning path   Performance of the skills involved in turning the vehicle changes to some degree with the sharpness of the turning path. It is most important for the beginning driver to recognize the critical differences in performance required by variations in the sharpness of the turning path.

1. *As the sharpness of the turning path increases, the speed at which the turn is made should decrease.*   This reduces the possibility of moving or skidding to the outside of the turning path caused by the combination of high speed and sharpness of the turn. It also provides the driver with more time to perform the extensive hand-over-hand movements required in sharp turns.

2. *As the sharpness of the turn increases, the speed and extent of initial steering and recovery are increased.*   In the sharpest turns the steering wheel may have to be turned completely in the direction of the turn using rapid hand-over-hand steering movements. In a very gradual turn it may be necessary to use only a large steering correction (maintaining the point of contact between the hands and the steering wheel) in place of using hand-over-hand stering.

3. *On more gradual turning paths, traveled at higher speeds, the driver will need to look and aim further ahead along the turning path.*   This need to look further ahead when driving at higher speeds is necessary for achieving accuracy in tracking as well as for safety purposes.

4. *In performing most sharp turns the driver will need to turn his head in the direction of the turn in order to see far enough along the intended path.*

As obvious as these variations in performance might appear to be to the experienced driver, they are emphasized at this point because they are not equally obvious to the beginning driver. It is not uncommon for the beginning driver to attempt to negotiate a very sharp turn at a speed that is appropriate for a more gradual turn, or to decelerate to an unreasonably slow speed when approaching a gradual curve.

Relationship between tracking and steering techniques   The previous sections have attempted to describe the relationship between steering techniques and the ability to accurately guide a car through a turning maneuver (tracking). In effect, the steering technique employed is only one of many skills the driver uses to enable him to guide the car through a turn. The total tracking process is a complex task involving the interaction and coordination of perceptual as well as performance skills.

This distinction has been emphasized because of the tendency on the part of drivers (and teachers) to regard turning the vehicle as being synonymous with steering control. It is not uncommon for people to think, once they have mastered hand-over-hand steering and recovery, that they have simultaneously mastered the art of tracking a vehicle on a turning path. This assumption is not valid. A driver may acquire considerable facility in the execution of hand-over-hand steering movements and yet be unable to apply this steering control in a way that keeps the car on the intended path—this is particularly true for beginning drivers who sometimes rigidly apply steering techniques irrespective of their contribution to keeping the car on the intended path.

Common Errors in Student Performance

Speed too fast   Students often attempt to perform turns at the same speed used by more experienced drivers. In many cases, the student does not have sufficient control in steering and braking to accommodate this normal turning speed. The most common results are excessively wide turns, overcorrections in steering, or late recoveries (Figs. 3.23, 3.24, and 3.25). The teacher can help alleviate this problem by insisting that initial attempts at turning be made at especially slow speeds. Then increased speed can be allowed as the student's ability to control steering and braking improves.

Rigid use of hand-over-hand technique   Some students tend to rigidly perform the hand-over-hand steering movements irrespective of the car's speed and position—with the result that the car digresses from the intended path. For example, the student may perform the first two hand-over-hand movements relatively quickly when the car is traveling at a very slow speed that requires a slower steering rate (Fig. 3.26). The result, of course, is an excessively sharp and early turn. This error is frequently caused by the student's inclination to focus on the steering movements and not on tracking. For problems of this sort, the teacher might simply encourage the student to concentrate on tracking and not to worry about employing a precise sequence of hand-over-hand movements.

Late recovery   Some students tend to hold the steering wheel in a turned position until the vehicle is facing in the direction of its new path and then begin the recovery. As a consequence, the vehicle continues to turn beyond its intended new path before the student can recover the steering wheel (Fig. 3.27). This tendency may be caused by a failure to understand the necessity for beginning the recovery just prior to the point at which the vehicle is facing in its new direction. The teacher can help to avoid this error by emphasizing early recovery in her demonstration and by giving well-timed verbal cues ("Begin recovery") during the student's initial performance (Fig. 3.28).

Practice Plan

Initial practice on standard turning paths   During the initial stages of practice in turning, it is usually advisable to arrange the practice area so that the student can perform a consecutive series of standard right turns and then left turns. The markings should clearly define the turning path; it is advisable to have road markings or stanchions that indicate the lane from which and into which the car is to travel (Fig. 3.29). The straightaway between turns should be sufficiently long to provide the student with enough time to prepare for each maneuver.

There are several advantages in using standard turning paths during the *initial* stages of practice in turning. First, turning paths are identical to one another (that is, they are all 90°), eliminating the necessity for the student to readjust his performance at each turn. Second, having made a mistake on one turn, the student is in a favorable position to correct the mistake on the subsequent turn because it involves identical performance conditions. Third, using standard turning paths that simulate a most common type of on-street maneuver helps to make the off-street practice more meaningful (and useful) for the student.

During their initial attempts to perform accurate right and left turns, many students are prone to commit a combination of steering, speed control, and judgmental errors. Recognizing this possibility, the teacher should provide for a concentrated initial practice session in turning on standard paths for each student—a minimum of ten to fifteen minutes during which both teacher and student will have an opportunity to identify, analyze, and correct basic errors in performance.

At some point in this phase of instruction, particular attention should be given to the path of the rear end and sides of the car. The teacher should point out the fact that the rear end and

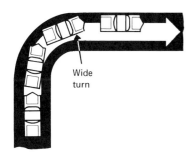

Wide
turn

Fig. 3.23

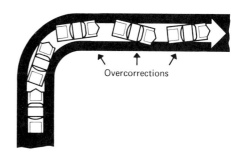

Overcorrections

Fig. 3.24

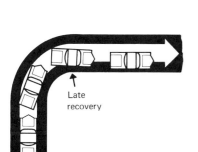

Late
recovery

Fig. 3.25

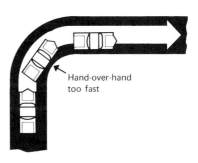

Hand-over-hand
too fast

Fig. 3.26

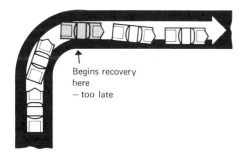

Begins recovery
here
— too late

Fig. 3.27

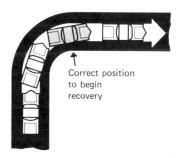

Correct position
to begin
recovery

Fig. 3.28

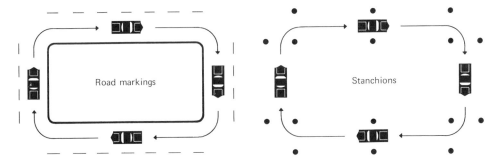

Fig. 3.29

side of the car do not follow the same turning path as the front end. For example, in making a right turn, the right side and rear end of the car traverse a path to the right of the path traveled by the front end (Fig. 3.30).

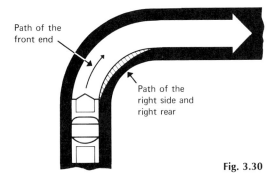

Path of the front end

Path of the right side and right rear

Fig. 3.30

Introducing the turn signal   At an appropriate stage in this phase of instruction it is advisable to have the student develop the habit of signaling prior to turning. A reasonable time to introduce signaling is immediately after the student has gained some initial competence in steering techniques and tracking. This means that the introduction of signaling would be somewhat delayed for slower students.

The teacher might introduce signaling by explaining that almost all on-street turning maneuvers require a signal and therefore it is wise to develop the habit of automatically signaling prior to making a turn. From that point on, she might require a signal prior to every turn (including off-street as well as on-street turns). The significance of the turn signal as a means of communication between drivers is discussed in future units—it is sufficient at this stage of instruction to develop the habitual response.

Varying the angle of the turning path   Once the student gains a reasonable degree of competence in tracking on standard turning paths, he should practice tracking on turning paths with different angles.

The teacher might design any one of several drills involving practice on different turning paths. These variations in turning should help the student recognize the need to adjust his steering techniques, speed control, and so on to meet the unique demands of the driving situation, and simultaneously discourage the adoption of rigid techniques that cannot be applied in various on-street situations. The diagram in Fig. 3.31 illustrates one of many possible ways of designing practice in tracking on varied-angle turning paths.

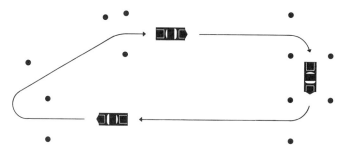

Fig. 3.31

During this stage of instruction some drills should be designed to enable the student to *explore the limits of steering control.* The student should be given the opportunity to make the sharpest possible turns and recoveries within a limited space. Practice in this kind of steering control should equip the student to perform advanced maneuvers like parking and turning around, and should improve his ability to estimate which turning maneuvers are required in various situations and how much clearance is necessary to perform a sharp turning maneuver. Once again, any number of drills might be designed by the teacher to accomplish this purpose—some examples appear in Fig. 3.32.

Driver makes sharpest possible turn

Driver makes sharpest possible figure 8

Fig. 3.32

Related Concepts and Information

As in the case of tracking on a straight path, developing the ability to accurately guide the car along a turning path is fundamental to safe driving. In particular, students should recognize that on-street turning maneuvers frequently require considerable accuracy in tracking because of the many obstacles adjacent to the turning path. They should fully understand the risks involved in making wide turns, short turns, late steering recoveries, and high-speed turns (Fig. 3.33).

In addition, students should be aware of the need to develop their skills in tracking on turning paths to the point where accuracy in performance becomes more or less automatic

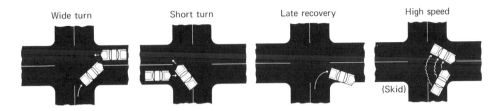

(Skid)

Fig. 3.33

(without the need for concentrating on hand-over-hand steering, speed control, or on some other element of skill performance). Then when students perform on-street turning maneuvers they will be free to concentrate on other vehicles, pedestrians, and so forth.

PHASE 5: QUICK BRAKING

The objective for students is to bring the vehicle to a quick, controlled stop in a short distance [7]. The student should also be able to identify the relationship between this skill and safe driving.

Driving Skills to Be Learned

Acquiring skill in quick braking involves learning to move the foot from the accelerato pedal to the brake pedal *as rapidly as possible,* and then depressing the brake pedal quickly and firmly. Quick braking entails a more controlled effort than all-out emergency braking, which usually involves a maximal application of force to the brake pedal that produces skidding even at slow speeds. Quick braking involves a less than maximal application of force that should produce little or no skidding. On the other hand, quick braking is considerably different from gradual braking with respect to the speed of the foot movement, the application of force, and the intent of the action.

Common Errors in Student Performance

Many beginning drivers who have acquired facility in gradual braking (Phase 1) have difficulty in mastering quick braking. For this reason a teacher should not assume that because a student is able to bring the vehicle to a gradual stop he will be equally capable of bringing it to a quick stop.

Reluctance to brake firmly A quick stop is an uncomfortable experience; it jostles passengers, it puts a stress on the vehicle, and it produces an abrupt stop that the student has learned to avoid in an earlier phase of practice. For all these reasons (and others), beginning drivers sometimes are reluctant to press down firmly on the brake. On the road this can be a dangerous reluctance that may result in not bringing the car to a stop in time to avoid colliding with an obstacle. Perhaps the best way to overcome this reluctance is to explain to the student that many driving situations require a quick stop to avoid an accident, and that reluctance to apply the brake quickly may result in an accident—in such cases the comfort of passengers takes second place.

Practice Plan

The student should be given several opportunities to brake quickly. The sk ll should first be performed while the car is traveling at low speeds (10–15 mph). The decision to have the students practice at higher speeds is up to the discretion of the teacher. Recognize, however, that the danger of skidding, upsetting car occupants, disturbing other drivers, an so on increases as the speed of the car increases.

The teacher might have the student respond to the one-word cue, "Brake!" The cue should be given in a firm manner that denotes a sense of urgency—and should be clearly distinguishable from the cue that calls for a smooth, gradual braking action.

Before practicing quick braking the teacher should be certain that all passengers (including herself) are ready for the quick stop. All seat belts should be fastened, and all passengers should brace themselves (with arms and legs) for the quick stop. If the braking action is properly controlled and the car is moving at low speeds, the stopping forces involved should pose a minimal threat to the safety of the passengers.

Related Concepts and Information

Students should recognize that quick braking is of value in all those situations where a more gradual application of the brake would not bring the vehicle to a stop in time to avoid an accident. At the same time, however, a quick braking action entails some inherent dangers. For example, on slippery roads, or when other vehicles are traveling close behind, quick braking may precipitate an accident. Therefore, as an element of safe driver performance, quick braking is to be used only in those situations where the risk of colliding with an object immediately in front takes precedence over the other risks that might be connected with the action.

PHASE 6: CHECKING TO THE REAR AND SIGNALING FOR A STOP

The objective for students is to become proficient in using techniques for checking traffic to the rear, and for providing an early warning to other drivers to the rear that their vehicle is about to slow down or stop (Fig. 3.34). Students should also be able to identify the relationship between these techniques and safe driving.

Fig. 3.34

Driving Skills to Be Learned

Checking traffic to the rear involves a *very brief* glance in the rearview mirror in order to determine whether or not any vehicles are following to the rear. Immediately after the glance the driver's attention returns to the road ahead. If the driver is unable to determine the nature of conditions to the rear with the first glance, he should repeat the action (Fig. 3.35).

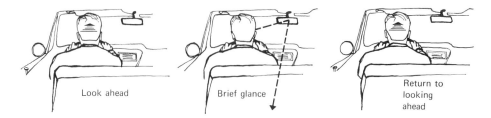

Look ahead   Brief glance   Return to looking ahead

Fig. 3.35

Hand signaling for a stop involves holding the steering wheel firmly in the right hand and extending the left arm out and down with the palm facing the rear (Fig. 3.36).

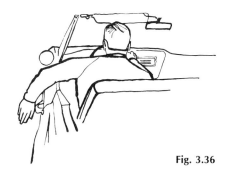

Fig. 3.36

Flashing the brake lights involves depressing the brake pedal until it reaches the braking point, then letting up slightly on the brake pedal and repeating the action. The pressure on the brake pedal should be just enough to cause the brake lights to go on, while at the same time causing a minimal reduction in speed.

Practice Plan

Practice in checking to the rear should be done to acquaint the student with the technique of using a *brief glance,* as well as to get the student into the *habit* of checking the mirror prior to stopping or slowing down. It is much easier to develop this habit and technique during the off-street practice than during on-street driving when the student has many other things to concentrate on.

Practice in using the mirror to scan the rear might be combined with the drills used in earlier phases of this unit. For example, once the student has gained reasonable proficiency in tracking on a turning path (Phase 4), he might be asked to check conditions to the rear on each approach to a turn.

Obviously, when driving in an off-street area, practice in using the rearview mirror is somewhat unrealistic since, ordinarily, there are no other vehicles following the driver education car. As a consequence, the student does not have an opportunity to realistically assess traffic conditions to the rear. It is up to the teacher to make this practice meaningful by explaining the importance of checking conditions to the rear, as well as the importance of mastering the technique *prior* to driving in traffic.

It is advisable to combine practice in hand signaling for a stop and in flashing the brake lights with practice in checking to the rear since these elements of performance normally occur together in on-street driving. The teacher might have the student follow a prescribed driving course stopping at prearranged locations and instruct the student to (1) "Check conditions to the rear prior to beginning the stop," (2) "Assume that a car is following you," and (3) "Provide a signal to the car behind that you intend to stop, use a hand signal, flashing brake lights, or both."

Related Concepts and Information

Students should understand that one of the most prevalent dangers in driving is the risk of being involved in a collision where their vehicle is struck from the rear. Although in many situations the driver in front will not be able to avoid the collision, there are occasions when he *will* be in a position to reduce the risk of being hit from behind by adjusting his own position or by signaling. Only those drivers who develop the *habit* of checking the rearview mirror at appropriate times are likely to be aware of the danger to the rear, and thus take steps to avoid it. (The importance of checking traffic conditions to the rear is discussed further in several subsequent sections of this text.)

The hand signal has considerable value as a safety meaure in situations where there is a possibility of being hit from the rear. For example, when a driver is about to stop in mid-block preparatory to parallel parking, the hand signal may be used well in advance of the stop and thus provide a warning to drivers to the rear who otherwise have no reason to expect a stop mid-block. Or when a driver is traveling on an expressway and notices an obstacle well ahead in his lane, he might use the hand signal to warn drivers to the rear. One of the most obvious advantages of the hand signal in situations of this kind is that it can be given well in advance of deceleration; this same advantage does not accompany the use of brake lights as a warning device.

As in the case of the hand signal for a stop, tapping the brakes is essentially a device for warning drivers to the rear that a stop is imminent. It should be used in situations where the warning is needed but where a hand signal is not feasible—when the windows are closed, or when there is not sufficient time to give a hand signal. The principal advantage of tapping the brakes is that it enables the driver to give an earlier warning than would otherwise be the case if he used more normal braking procedures.

CLASSROOM GUIDE FOR UNIT 3
Basic Skills in Speed Control and Tracking on Forward Paths

Unit 3 deals primarily with the acquisition of fundamental performance skills. Only a limited amount of realistic advance preparations for these fundamentals can be effectively carried out in the classroom (unless simulators are available). As mentioned previously, the learning of these basic skills will depend almost entirely on the actual practice which takes place in the car. However, classroom time could be used profitably to stress the relationship between the mastery of these fundamental skills and safe (on-street) driving.

Topics	Instructional Plan
1. Gradual acceleration, speed control, and gradual braking	1. Briefly describe (or diagram) objective of phase in terms of how vehicle should move (see "Objective").
2. Gradual stopping and positioning	
3. Tracking on a straight path	2. Briefly discuss skills to be learned (see "Driving Skills to Be Learned").
4. Tracking on turning paths	
5. Quick braking	3. Discuss and emphasize relationship between skills to be learned and safe driving (see "Related Concepts and Information"). Teacher might cite (or ask students to cite) examples of how errors in performance can produce hazardous situations.
6. Checking to rear and signaling for stop	
	4. Briefly discuss layout of practice area and other elements relating to in-car practice session that students should be aware of in advance.

PREPARATORY READING FOR STUDENTS

1. *Learning to Drive: Skills, Concepts, and Strategies.* Chapter 5, "Basic Skills in Moving the Vehicle Forward," pp. 39–63.

   —or appropriate sections in another high-school text.

RELATED SIMULATOR LESSONS

1. Aetna Drivotrainer System: "Angle Parking and Turning Maneuvers."
2. Link Simulator System: "The Art of Turning."

IN-CAR GUIDE FOR UNIT 3
Basic Skills in Speed Control and Tracking on Forward Paths

DEMONSTRATION

The teacher should briefly demonstrate the sklls involved in each of the six phases of the unit. The more elementary skills (Phases 1, 2, 3, and 6) should require only one demonstration trial; the more advanced skills (Phases 4 and 5) may require more attention. The demonstration should be conducted so that the student clearly understands the *objective* of each phase of the unit (that is, he should know how "gradual" a gradual stop should be, he should know where the intended path is and what constitutes accurate tracking, and so on). For the sake of efficiency, a capable student might serve as the demonstrator. The demonstration might be grouped as follows:

1. Demonstrate skills in Phases 1, 2, and 3 prior to all student practice.

2. Demonstrate skills in Phases 4, 5, and 6 before first student attempts Phase 4.

GUIDING STUDENT PRACTICE

Teacher	Student
Phase 1: Gradual Acceleration, Speed Control, and Gradual Braking	
Emphasize gradual movement of accelerator and brake pedals. If necessary use *three-stage braking:*	Performs several gradual accelerations and gradual stops. Concentrates on gradual acceleration and gradual braking.
1. Caution position 2. Slow (braking point) 3. Stop (release pressure just before stop)	Performs initial trials at very slow speeds (5–10 mph).
Watch for failure to develop awareness of braking point.	Later concentrates on maintaining target speed.
Be ready to assist student with steering if necessary.	
Evaluate progress on basis of ability to gradually increase and decrease the rate of speed, and to stop smoothly.	
Phase 2: Gradual Stopping and Positioning	
Prior to student performance:	
1. Be certain stopping position is clearly marked.	
2. Be certain that student knows precisely where to stop (give clear directions).	
Emphasize:	Performs several gradual stops.
1. Choosing appropriate moment to begin braking	As competence increases, drives at higher speeds and begins braking sooner.
2. Developing awareness of required stopping distance—need for early braking	
3. Developing awareness of car's position	

IN-CAR GUIDE FOR UNIT 3 (*cont.*)

Teacher	Student

Watch for:

1. Braking started too early or too late

2. Failure to be aware of immediate position of car (use questions)

Evaluate progress on basis of ability to stop within an appropriate distance and to position vehicle accurately.

Phase 3: Tracking on a Straight Path

Prior to student performance:

1. Be certain the intended path is clearly marked.

2. Be certain student knows precise location of path (specify centered lane position).

Emphasize:

1. Maintaining centered lane position

2. Looking well ahead—aiming for center of path

3. Recognizing deviations early

4. Making small, gradual steering corrections

Drives for long intervals without stopping.

Concentrates on keeping vehicle in centered lane position.

Watch for:

1. Drifting

2. Overcorrecting

3. Off-center path

Be ready to assist student in turning car at end of straightaway.

Evaluate progress on basis of size and frequency of tracking errors.

Phase 4: Tracking on Turning Paths

Prior to student performance:

1. Be certain the intended turning paths are clearly marked.

2. Be certain student knows precise location of turning paths (give clear instructions).

IN-CAR GUIDE FOR UNIT 3 (*cont.*)

Teacher	Student

Stage 1: Practice on standard (90 degree) turning paths (right and left)

Emphasize:	Practices series of turning maneuvers (right and left), concentrates on combining skills to achieve accuracy in tracking.
1. *Speed control:*	

Emphasize:

1. *Speed control:*

   Gradual braking
   Slow speed
   Gradual acceleration

2. *Steering:*

   Initial hand-over-hand
   Recovery (early)

3. *Perception and judgment:*

   Having clear idea of intended path
   Scanning ahead along turning path
   Recognizing deviations and correcting

4. *Awareness of path* traveled by rear end and sides of car.

After initial practice trials, introduce turn signaling habit.

Watch for:

1. Speed too fast

2. Rigid hand-over-hand

3. Late recovery

Be ready to:

1. Use verbal cues to indicate tracking errors (when students are unaware of them)

2. Diagnose underlying cause of tracking error

Evaluate progress on basis of size and frequency of tracking errors and speed of turn.

Stage 2: Practice on varied-angle turning paths (sharp and gradual)

Emphasize same elements as mentioned above (Stage 2). In addition:

1. Sharp turn—slow speed

2. Sharp turn—quick steering

3. Sharp turn—turn head to see path

4. Gradual turn—scan further ahead

Provide opportunity to explore limits of steering control (sharpest possible turns and recoveries).

Practices turns with different angles. Concentrates on adjustments in speed control and steering techniques required on different turns.

IN-CAR GUIDE FOR UNIT 3 (cont.)

Teacher	Student

Phase 5: Quick Braking

Prior to student performance:

1. Be certain that student understands what is expected (requires teacher demonstration).

2. Be certain car occupants are ready for abrupt stop and area is clear of traffic.

Emphasize:

1. Quick foot-movement to brake

2. Firm pressure on pedal

3. Controlled stop

Use cue "Brake!"

Performs a few quick braking drills from a relatively slow traveling speed (10–15 mph).

Phase 6: Checking to the Rear and Signaling for a Stop

Stage 1: Checking to the rear

Emphasize:

1. Brief glance technique

2. Developing habit of using glance before slowing down

Performs any one (or several) of the drills from previous phases—includes check of mirrors prior to each stop or slow down.

Stage 2: Hand signaling and tapping brakes

Emphasize:

1. Depressing pedal to braking point and release

2. Signaling well in advance

Performs each skill a few times. Understands on-street conditions during which they should be used.

BASIC SKILLS IN SPEED CONTROL AND TRACKING ON BACKWARD PATHS

INTRODUCTION

This unit of practice driving is divided into three phases:

Phase 1. Speed control and tracking on a straight path (backward)
Phase 2. Tracking on turning paths (backward)
Phase 3. Backing and positioning

It is designed for use in an off-street area.

The content involves the application of basic skills learned in Unit 2 to a new dimension of the driving task, moving the car backward [1]. The student driver has already acquired considerable skill in accelerating, braking, positioning, and tracking in connection with moving the car forward. This unit deals with these same skills as they apply to moving the car backward. Students who have mastered the basic skills in earlier lessons should be able to transfer much of their prior learning to the performance of backing maneuvers. On the other hand, the teacher should recognize that backing the car involves a substantial reorientation to the driving task. The driver must get used to steering the car with the front wheels while moving backward, manipulating the steering wheel while looking to the rear, operating the car from a turned driver's position, and so on. Some drivers have difficulty in reorienting themselves and as a consequence make rudimentary errors.

Beyond the problems of initial reorientation, the teacher should recognize that driving backward is an inherently more difficult task than driving forward. Motor vehicles are primarily designed to be driven forward, and many of the design features act as impediments to backing the car (front wheel steering, reduced visibility, and so forth).

PHASE 1: SPEED CONTROL AND TRACKING ON A STRAIGHT PATH (BACKWARD)

The objective for students is to move the car backward at an appropriately slow speed and to keep it on its intended path. Accurate tracking keeps the car on its intended path. Errors in tracking occur when the car moves off-path to one side or the other. As the students progress,

117

they should reduce the size and frequency of their tracking errors (Fig. 4.1). They should also be able to identify the relationship between this skill and safe driving.

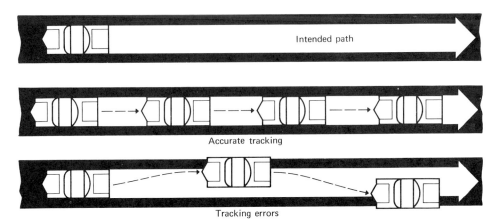

Fig. 4.1

Driving Skills to Be Learned

Steps preparatory to backing the car   The student should develop the habit of performing the following sequence of steps prior to moving the car backward; these apply to backing on straight paths (Phase 1) as well as to backing on turning paths (Phase 2):

1. Bring the car to a complete stop.
2. Depress the brake pedal to hold the car firmly in position.
3. Move the selector lever to the R position.
4. Assume the appropriate driver's position.
5. Check road and traffic conditions to be certain that they will permit the *safe* completion of the backing maneuver. Be ready to delay or postpone the maneuver when necessary.

Assuming the appropriate driver's position   The student should assume a driver's position that best enables her to (1) maintain control of the vehicle, (2) accurately guide it on the intended path, and (3) observe events on both sides of the intended straight path. Although there is no one precise position that suits all drivers equally well, the position described below may be used as a guide.

The driver turns her body slightly to the right (which may involve a slight shift of the hips on the driver's seat) and turns her head all the way around so that it faces directly to the rear. Whenever possible her head and eyes should be sufficiently elevated to permit her to see the rear fenders of the vehicle; this is an invaluable aid in tracking. The right foot remains on the brake—the turned position should not interfere with the driver's ability to reach the brake and accelerator. (Short drivers may have to restrict the degree to which they turn their bodies in order to stay within reach of the brake and accelerator pedals.) The left hand grasps the steering wheel at approximately the 12 o'clock position. The right hand and arm may be placed on top of the backrest—this is recommended to make the position reasonably comfortable (Fig. 4.2). (The teacher may wish to have the student keep her right hand on the steering wheel, provided it does not restrict her ability to assume the turned position.)

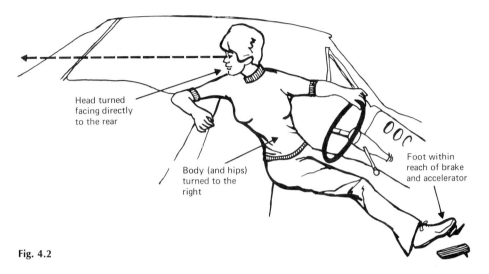

Head turned
facing directly
to the rear

Body (and hips)
turned to the
right

Foot within
reach of brake
and accelerator

Fig. 4.2

Speed control skills   Learning to control the speed of a vehicle while it is moving backward is primarily a matter of learning to keep it moving at *very slow* speeds. The student should be able to achieve the necessary control by utilizing the following techniques:

1. Gradually depress the accelerator pedal to put the car in motion (2–3 mph). Only a very small movement is necessary (in fact, some cars will move backward without any movement of the accelerator pedal).

2. Immediately move foot to brake pedal and control speed through gradual application and release of pedal.

3. Thereafter, use accelerator only as necessary to maintain the car's momentum.

Tracking skills   As in the case of tracking on a straight forward path, learning to keep the vehicle on an intended backward path involves the coordination of several skills in steering, acceleration, perception, and judgment. Some of the major elements of performance include:

1. Having a clear idea of the intended path over which the vehicle is to travel.

2. Looking along the intended path and aiming the car for a point in the middle of the path. (In backing, since the speed of the vehicle will be quite slow, it is not necessary to look as far along the path as in the case of forward driving.)

3. Recognizing when the car begins to deviate from the intended path and making the necessary steering corrections.

It is ordinarily advisable for beginners to use the left hand at top of wheel, the 12 o'clock position, as a guide to making steering corrections. Only small movements to either side of the position should be necessary to keep the vehicle on path.

Related Concepts and Information

Students should understand the following concepts related to the performance of the driving skills in Phase 1:

Preparatory steps   The preparatory steps relate to the safe performance of backing maneuvers in several ways. First, bringing the car to a complete stop and holding it *firmly* in place prior to moving the lever to the reverse position provides protection against the possibility of the car's moving backward before the driver intends it to move. Secondly, although the actual shift of the lever to reverse is a rudimentary skill, its omission can be a source of trouble. It is not uncommon for beginning drivers to bring the vehicle to a stop with the intention of backing up, to scan traffic conditions to the rear, and then to accelerate, only to discover that the car moves forward because they forgot to move the selector level to reverse. Finally, the initial check of traffic conditions prior to initiating the backing maneuver is most crucial for several reasons related to the movement of other vehicles and the expectations of other drivers (see discussion in Unit 9).

Driver's position   The turned position enables the driver to see to the rear as well as possible. Since the intended path of the vehicle is straight backward, it is most important for the driver to have a clear view of that path and to the sides of the path—especially to the right side. When compared with using a more restricted head turn to scan the intended path, the practice of turning the head to look directly to the rear has significant advantages. First, it enables the driver to get a better view of the path and the vehicle's position in relation to it and therefore should aid in tracking. Second, it permits her to observe better those events to the right rear adjacent to the intended path that will be important to the safe performance of on-street backing maneuvers (Fig. 4.3).

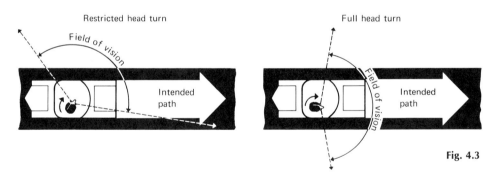

Fig. 4.3

Speed control   Since most backing maneuvers cover short distances and involve maneuvering in tight spaces, it is wise to perform them at especially slow speeds. Controlling speed primarily through brake application enables the driver to achieve greater speed control at the especially slow speeds used in backing. In addition, it places her in a constant position of being ready to stop in response to the frequent obstacles that arise in connection with on-street backing maneuvers.

Tracking   The beginning driver should understand how steering adjustments affect the backward movement of the car. An explanation suitable for beginning drivers appears in Fig. 4.4. It is usually helpful to remember that the *rear end of the vehicle moves in the same direction as the top of the steering wheel.*

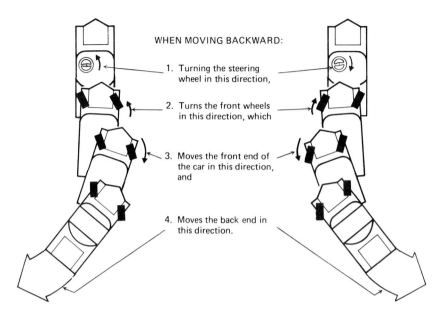

WHEN MOVING BACKWARD:

1. Turning the steering wheel in this direction,

2. Turns the front wheels in this direction, which

3. Moves the front end of the car in this direction, and

4. Moves the back end in this direction.

Fig. 4.4

Common Errors in Student Performance

Wheel corrections—wrong direction   Perhaps the most common problem during the early stages of backing is the tendency of students to become confused as to which way to turn the steering wheel. It is not unusual for a student to recognize that the vehicle is moving off-path, make a small steering correction in the wrong direction, recognize an increase in the movement off-path, increase the size of the erroneous correction, and end up in a position at right angles to the intended path (Fig. 4.5). This kind of gross error can be avoided by using any one of several techniques, including (1) having the student rehearse the direction of wheel correction while the car is in a stationary position, (2) manually assisting the student with steering until she gets the "feel" of the proper direction for wheel corrections, or (3) having the student stop the car when she *begins* to make the erroneous steering correction, identifying her error, and having her make the necessary adjustment.

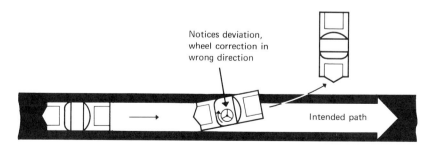

Notices deviation, wheel correction in wrong direction

Intended path

Fig. 4.5

Loss of speed control   It is frequently difficult for the beginning driver to exercise precise control over the accelerator pedal and brake pedal from the turned driver's position. More often than not this lack of control leads to a tendency to drive too fast and magnifies the size of the tracking errors. In some cases this difficulty arises because the student has turned her body too far, and her foot is not within easy reach of the brake pedal (this is particularly prevalent with short drivers). In other cases, the student may attempt to control the speed of the vehicle by using the accelerator pedal instead of the brake pedal. The teacher will need to take careful note of the student's driving position and foot movements in order to correct the error.

Using mirrors   Some students will have a tendency to use the rearview mirror while backing instead of turning their heads to the rear. The tendency is usually most noticeable during the initial and final stages of a backing maneuver (when the car starts to move backward and just before it comes to a stop). The teacher can discourage this tendency by insisting that the student assume the proper driving position *before* she moves the car backward, and by periodically checking the student's head position while the car is moving backward.

Restricted attention to one side   During the initial stages of tracking on a backward path, some students tend to concentrate on the movement of one or the other back fenders of the vehicle in relation to the edge of the intended path. (This is similar to the problem encountered during the early stages of forward driving.) As a consequence, the student is not in a position to recognize potential obstacles in the vicinity and, in addition, may tend to veer in the direction in which she is looking. The teacher may help overcome this difficulty by encouraging the student to *concentrate on the movement of the entire rear end of the vehicle, and on keeping the whole vehicle in a centered lane position.*

Practice Plan

Initial emphasis: speed control and steering corrections   During the initial stages of Phase 1 the emphasis should be on speed control and on adjusting to steering while backing. Once the student has assumed the proper driver's position for backing on a straight path, she should be given several opportunities to back the car on a relatively straight path while concentrating on keeping the car at low speeds through controlled application and release of the brake pedal. During these initial practice trials the student should be encouraged to practice gradual wheel corrections that move the vehicle to the left and to the right (Fig. 4.6).

The objectives of this drill are (1) to allow the student to concentrate on speed control through brake application, and (2) to familiarize the student with the relationship between the direction of steering wheel correction and its effect on the direction of the vehicle's movement. The teacher may guide the student's performance by providing appropriately timed verbal cues that indicate when to turn in one direction or the other.

In some cases it might even be advisable to have students *rehearse* steering corrections while the car is in a stationary position.

Practice gradual
steering correction

Fig. 4.6

Problem: terminology The teacher should recognize that when the driver is in a turned position (head facing the rear) the words "right" and "left" do not provide the same clear indication of direction that they provide for forward driving. For the student driver, the cue, "Move right," means to move in one direction based on the student's head position (facing the rear), but it means to move in the opposite direction based on the student's body position and the position of the vehicle.

To avoid the confusion that results from using the cues "right" and "left" to indicate direction in backing, the teacher should adopt more meaningful substitutes. For example, the teacher might simply say "turn" and at the same time point in the direction of the turn. Or, if the backing maneuver takes place in a lane adjacent to a curb, the teacher might use "turn in," meaning to turn in the direction of the curb, or "turn out," meaning to turn away from the curb. Whichever method the teacher uses to indicate direction in backing, he should be careful to standardize the terminology and explain it to students in advance.

Emphasis: accurate tracking Once the student can control the speed of the vehicle and make steering corrections in the proper direction, she is ready to concentrate on accurate tracking on a straight path. To encourage accurate tracking and to enable the teacher to make judgments about student performance, the intended path should be clearly defined (stanchions or painted road markings may be used to define the intended path). As the student gains competence in tracking, the path might be made narrower in order to make the task more challenging.

PHASE 2: TRACKING ON TURNING PATHS (BACKWARD)

The objective for students is to keep the car on an intended turning path (Fig. 4.7). Errors in tracking occur when the car moves off the intended path. As the students progress they should reduce the size and frequency of their tracking errors. Students should also be able to identify the relationship between this skill and safe driving.

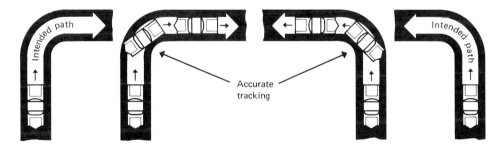

Fig. 4.7

Driving Skills to Be Learned

Assuming the appropriate driver's position The student should turn her head and shoulders in the direction in which the rear end of the car is to move; that is, to the right when backing to the right, and to the left when backing to the left. The extent of the head turn should be sufficient to allow the driver to see directly to the rear and to the side rear (either left or right side depending upon the direction of the turning maneuver). However, the extent of the head and shoulder turn is limited enough to permit the driver to keep both hands on the steering wheel (Fig. 4.8).

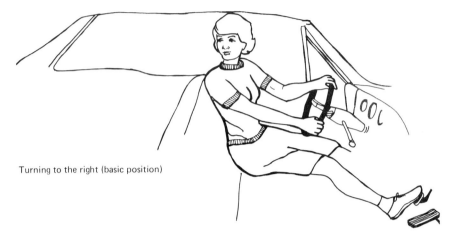

Turning to the right (basic position)

Fig. 4.8

The driver's position described above should be considered a *basic* position for backing and turning, but the driver will have to change her head and body position from time to time as the need arises to scan in different directions. For example, when the driver is backing and turning to the right she will periodically need to turn her head to the left to check the blind spot on that side of the car (Fig. 4.9).

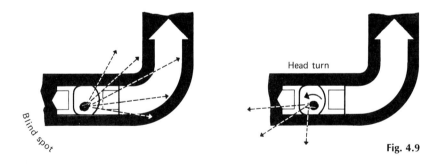

Fig. 4.9

The turned position of head and shoulders helps the beginning driver turn the steering wheel in the correct direction. For example, in backing and turning to the left the driver's head and shoulders are turned to the left—this body position facilitates turning the steering wheel to the left and inhibits any tendency to turn the wheel to the right.

Speed control skills   The techniques for controlling speed while backing and turning are the same as for backing on a straight path. The driver controls speed, as much as possible, through the application and release of the brake pedal.

Tracking skills   Perhaps the most distinctive feature of tracking on a backward turning path is the steering technique employed. The hand-over-hand technique recommended for use in backing the car is similar to the steering techniques used in turning while moving forward (see Unit 3). The major difference is that the hand-over-hand movements used in backing normally are restricted to the side of the steering wheel closest to the direction in which the vehicle is turning. For example, in backing and turning to the right, the hand-over-hand movements occur primarily in the upper right-hand quadrant of the steering wheel—between 12 o'clock and 3 o'clock. (Utilizing one side of the steering wheel enables the driver to maintain the turned body position, see Fig. 4.10.)

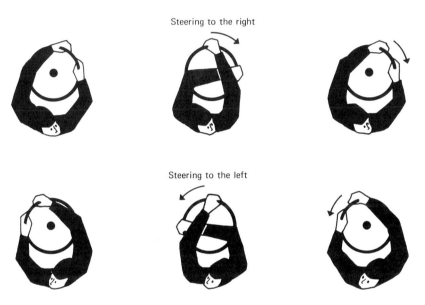

Fig. 4.10

Related Concepts and Information

Students should understand that in tracking on a backward turning path the lateral movement of the front end of the vehicle is in the opposite direction from the rear end (Fig. 4.11).

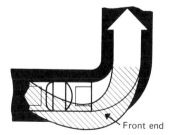

Front end

Fig. 4.11

They should also understand the significance of this movement to the safe performance of a variety of backing maneuvers. For example, when a driver backs into a driveway from a parking lane, it is most important for her to recognize that the front end of her vehicle extends into the traffic lane during the course of the maneuver (Fig. 4.12).

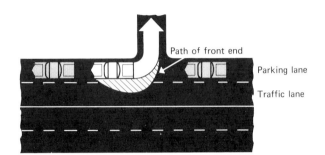

Fig. 4.12

Common Errors in Student Performance

Speed control   Some students who acquire skills in speed control while moving backward on a straight path (Phase 1) tend to lose some of this control when they attempt to guide the vehicle on a backward turning path. This frequently involves allowing the vehicle to travel at higher speeds than are appropriate for backing and turning maneuvers. The speed leads to tracking errors as well as to a general loss of control. Apparently the combination of skills required (including speed control, hand-over-hand steering, and tracking) often proves to be too difficult for the beginner. Difficulties can be avoided if the teacher emphasizes the need to maintain *very slow* speeds (2–5 mph) during the student's initial practice trials.

Oversteering   There is a decided tendency on the part of beginning drivers to steer too quickly (and extensively) during the initial stages of backing and turning maneuvers, causing the vehicle to move to the inside of the intended path (Fig. 4.13). In some cases, this error is the result of steering at the same rate as was used in forward turning maneuvers (when the vehicle was traveling at higher speeds). In such cases, students should understand that the very slow speeds used in backing and turning maneuvers require the use of relatively gradual hand-over-hand steering techniques.

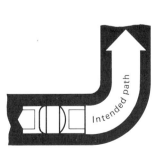 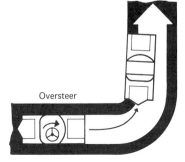

Fig. 4.13

Practice Plan

The student should be afforded several practice trials in backing on a turning path to allow her to become accustomed to using hand-over-hand steering while backing, and at the same time to emphasize the maintenance of very low speeds. The teacher might design any one of a number of drills to accomplish the purpose of this phase of the lesson. The drills shown in Fig. 4.14 are illustrative of what might be done. It would seem advisable to include turns in both directions and turns with varying degrees of sharpness.

Once the student has gained some proficiency in using hand-over-hand steering and speed control skills, she should be encouraged to concentrate on accurate tracking. The same drills shown in Fig. 4.14 might be used here with the addition of a clearly marked path.

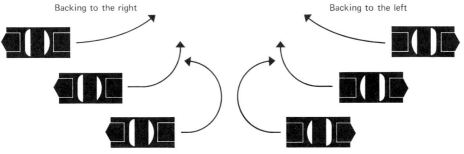

Backing to the right   Backing to the left

Fig. 4.14

During this phase of the lesson the teacher should place special emphasis on the movement of the front end of the vehicle and on the need to be aware of its position in relation to the turning path.

PHASE 3: BACKING AND POSITIONING

The objective for students is to back the car into a variety of positions with maximum accuracy and efficiency (Fig. 4.15), and to be able to identify the relationship between these skills and safe driving. Errors in accuracy occur when the student fails to place the vehicle in the designated position. Errors in efficiency occur when the student requires more than one maneuver to achieve the position (Fig. 4.16).

Driving Skills to Be Learned

This phase of practice in backing requires the student to utilize all the skills in backing acquired during previous phases, including:

1. Assuming the appropriate driver's position (and varying it in accordance with the unique aspects of the maneuver)
2. Using speed control skills to maintain slow speeds
3. Using tracking skills (including hand-over-hand steering) to guide the vehicle toward the position

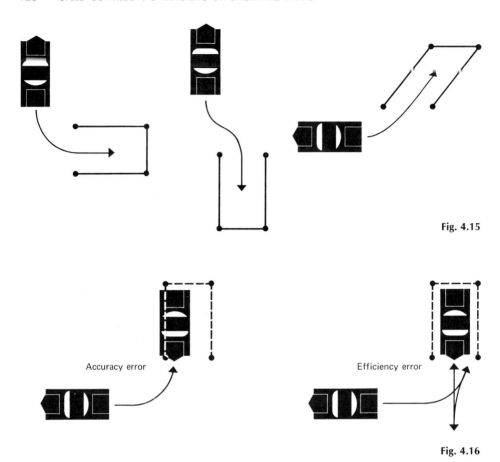

Fig. 4.15

Accuracy error

Efficiency error

Fig. 4.16

In addition, the student will need to use her ability in judging the immediate position of the vehicle (Unit 3, Phase 2).

The distinctive feature of this phase of the unit is that the student must now combine these skills in the most efficient way to achieve a predetermined position. In particular, she will have to select an appropriate starting position from which to begin the maneuver, guide the vehicle toward the position, and stop at the point when the position is reached. The proper selection of the starting position can lead to the easy completion of the maneuver; improper selection can doom the driver to failure before she begins. Two important rules to use in selecting a starting position are (1) *leave enough distance to complete the turn,* and (2) *provide for a wide enough turning angle* (Fig. 4.17).

Related Concepts and Information

Backing a vehicle into a predetermined position is characteristic of most on-street backing maneuvers, including backing into a parking space, backing into and out of a driveway, and backing during a Y turn. The development of *accuracy* in backing and positioning enables the driver to avoid the dented bumpers and fenders that might otherwise result.

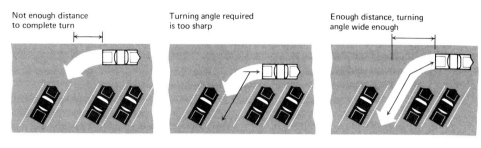

Fig. 4.17

The development of efficiency in backing and positioning should help avoid the increased exposure to accidents that so often accompanies inefficient performance. For example, the driver who moves her vehicle into a parking space in one efficient movement incurs less exposure to moving traffic than the driver who requires several maneuvers to park (Fig. 4.18).

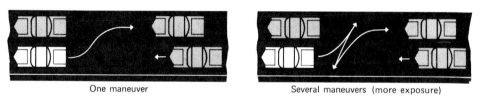

Fig. 4.18

Common Errors in Student Performance

Backing maneuvers that move the vehicle into a predetermined position are perhaps the most demanding of all driving maneuvers in terms of the judgmental and control skills required for successful performance. Students are likely to commit any one or a combination of the common errors mentioned earlier (Phases 1 and 2), in addition to several other unique errors that arise in connection with the specific backing and positioning maneuver being practiced. In fact, the variety of errors that arise is so numerous that it seems inadvisable to attempt to identify one or two of the "most common" errors.

In attempting to correct student errors, teachers should take special precautions to analyze student performance and identify the underlying (or basic) errors before suggesting corrective measures. Teachers should attempt to correct the basic errors before treating the more superficial ones. Perhaps the most common mistake made by teachers during this phase of instruction is to attempt to correct all errors at once, confusing and ultimately frustrating the student.

Practice Plan

The teacher should design several drills that resemble the kinds of backing and positioning maneuvers that students will be called upon to perform in on-street driving. The drills should include the task of driving forward to an appropriate position from which to begin the backing maneuver. The drills in Fig. 4.19 are illustrative of what might be done.

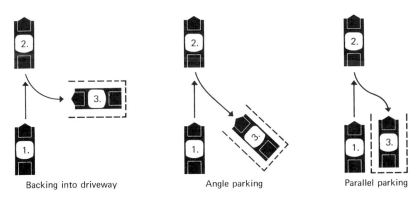

| Backing into driveway | Angle parking | Parallel parking |

Fig. 4.19

During practice the teacher should emphasize the importance of achieving a suitable starting position prior to moving backward. In fact, it is usually not wise to allow the student to proceed with the backing maneuver until she has achieved an appropriate starting position. Otherwise she starts backing with two strikes against her and is bound to fail.

In view of the level of difficulty involved in performing backing and positioning maneuvers and the limited experience of the student, the teacher should avoid using drills that exceed the student's capabilities. The final position should not be so narrow, or require such a high degree of steering control and judgment, that most students will continually fail. On the other hand, the drills should not be so easy that they do not resemble the requirements of similar on-street maneuvers.

CLASSROOM GUIDE FOR UNIT 4
Basic Skills in Speed Control and Tracking on Backward Paths

As in the case of the material covered in Unit 3, the basic skills involved in this unit are learned primarily through actual practice in the car. As a consequence, only a limited amount of realistic advance preparation can take place in the classroom.

Topics	Instructional Plan
1. *Unique aspects of backing car:* Need for reduced speed Steering with front wheels Reduced visibility	1. Contrast general elements of performance while moving forward.
2. *Backing on a straight path:* Steps preparatory to backing Driver's position Speed control skills Tracking skills	1. Briefly describe actions and skills involved. 2. Discuss relevance for safe driving (see "Related Concepts and Information"). 3. Emphasize movement of front and rear of vehicle in relation to movement of steering wheel (use diagram or model).
3. *Tracking on turning paths (backward):* Driver's position Tracking skills	1. Briefly describe skills. 2. Emphasize path of front end of car in relation to path of rear end (use diagram or model).
4. *Backing and positioning:* Importance of starting position	1. Discuss need for accuracy and efficiency. 2. Describe (diagram) drills to be used during in-car lesson.

PREPARATORY READING FOR STUDENTS

1. *Learning to Drive: Skills, Concepts, and Strategies.* Chapter 6, "Basic Skills in Moving the Vehicle Backward."

   —or appropriate sections in another high-school text.

IN-CAR GUIDE FOR UNIT 4
Basic Skills in Speed Control and Tracking on Backward Paths

DEMONSTRATION

The teacher or a capable student should briefly demonstrate the skills involved in each of the three phases of the lesson. The emphasis should be on (1) preparatory steps, (2) driver's position, (3) speed control skills, and (4) tracking skills. The drills should be performed precisely as students are expected to perform them.

GUIDING STUDENT PRACTICE

Teacher	Student
Phase 1: Speed Control and Tracking on a Straight Path (Backward)	

Prior to student performance:

1. Be certain intended path is clearly marked.
2. Be certain student knows precise location of path.

Teacher	Student
Steering rehearsal, emphasize:	Rehearses steering corrections, points in direction of turn (vehicle stationary)
1. "Turn top of wheel in direction in which you want the rear end of the car to go."	
2. Left hand at 12 o'clock position.	
Preparatory steps, emphasize:	Performs preparatory steps:
1. Early shift to R	1. Stops car
2. Thorough check of conditions	2. Depresses brake
	3. Moves selector lever to reverse
Driver's position, emphasize:	4. Assumes turned position—head faces directly to the rear, left hand at top of wheel
1. Seeing to both sides of intended path	
2. Foot within reach of accelerator and brake	5. Checks conditions
Practice speed control and steering corrections, emphasize:	Backs car at slow speed, practices turning it gradually in one direction, then in the other
1. Controlling speed with brake—very slow	
2. Making small, gradual steering corrections	
Practice accuracy in tracking, emphasize:	Backs car, concentrates on keeping it on path
1. Aiming car for center of path	
2. Recognizing deviations	
3. Making early, small steering corrections	

IN-CAR GUIDE FOR UNIT 4 (*cont.*)

Teacher	Student

Watch for:

1. Tendency to correct in wrong direction
2. Loss of speed control
3. Attention to one side

Evaluate progress on basis of ability to control speed and on size and frequency of tracking errors.

Phase 2: Tracking on Turning Paths (Backward)

Prior to student performance:

1. Be certain intended paths are clearly marked.
2. Be certain student knows precise location of paths.

Teacher	Student
Preparatory steps (see Phase 1):	Performs preparatory steps
Driver's position, emphasize:	Assumes turned position

1. Both hands on wheel
2. Ability to see to rear in direction of turn
3. Varying position when necessary to check blind spots

Practice accurate tracking, emphasize:	Practices backing on variety of turning paths, to the right and left, concentrates on accurate tracking

1. Scanning ahead along turning path
2. Aiming for center of path
3. Maintaining slow speed
4. Hand-over-hand steering
5. Awareness of movement of front end

Watch for:

1. Speed too fast
2. Oversteering

Evaluate progress on basis of size and frequency of tracking errors.

IN-CAR GUIDE FOR UNIT 4 (cont.)

Teacher	Student

Phase 3: Backing and Positioning

Prior to student performance:

1. Be certain position is clearly marked.

2. Be certain student knows precisely where and how she is expected to position her vehicle (need for clear directions).

Preparatory steps and driver's position, emphasize:

1. Assuming basic position appropriate for maneuver

2. Varying position to check blind spot

3. Awareness of movement of front end

Performs preparatory steps and assumes position

Practice backing into position. Utilize several drills designed to simulate on-street backing maneuvers. *Emphasize:*

Performs several drills concentrating on achieving accuracy in positioning

1. Moving car into appropriate starting position: leave enough distance, provide wide enough turning angle

2. Being continuously alert to make steering corrections as maneuver progresses

Be ready for occurrence of several errors—identify basic cause of difficulty.

Evaluate progress on basis of accuracy in positioning and efficiency (maneuvers required to achieve position).

ORIENTATION TO ON-STREET DRIVING, AND INITIAL TECHNIQUES IN SCANNING FOR, EVALUATING, AND RESPONDING TO OBSTACLES

INTRODUCTION

Practice driving in this unit constitutes the student's first experience in *on-street* driving. In contrast to her earlier off-street experience, the student must now contend with numerous events and elements that were not present in the off-street area, including other moving objects (vehicles, pedestrians, and so on), traffic signs and signals, and special features of the roadway. The techniques developed in this unit are designed to provide the student with an initial capability for coping with these new (on-street) elements. At the same time, the unit emphasizes the application of basic skills in speed control and tracking (Unit 3) to the on-street setting. In-car practice is divided into Phase 1, "Orientation to On-Street Driving," and Phase 2, "Initial Techniques in Scanning for, Evaluating, and Responding to Obstacles." The skills developed in scanning for and responding to obstacles and potential obstacles are *basic skills* in the sense that they form the foundation for the development of more advanced techniques covered in later units.

A substantial portion of the unit deals with the learning of tasks (scanning and recognizing) that are not easily observed and evaluated by the teacher. For example, it is usually difficult for the teacher, at a given moment, to know where the student is looking and whether or not she recognizes a particular object in the environment. In an effort to overcome the difficulties caused by the covertness of these tasks, the instructional plan uses the technique of "limited commentary driving." In essence, it involves having the students use one-word or two-word phrases to identify obstacles in the driving environment. This teaching technique itself constitutes an important part of the total instructional content of this unit, and it is used again in later units.

Related Concepts and Information

A considerable amount of related material needs to be covered (in the classroom) prior to the student's initial on-street driving (Phase 1) and her practice of scanning techniques (Phase 2). Most of the concepts and information are described in subsequent sections of this unit. In addition, the important rules of the road that apply to initial on-street practice deserve attention, including the regulations related to (1) right-of-way, (2) speed, (3) traffic signs and signals, and (4) road markings.

The vehicle and traffic laws of the state should be used as a reference. An attempt should be made to explain and discuss the laws in relation to their intended role in accident prevention—as opposed to simply having students memorize the regulations. It is also helpful to discuss the laws in relation to the specific driving route and traffic conditions that students will encounter during their initial on-street practice.

The Classroom Guide for Unit 5 outlines the related concepts and information to be covered prior to on-street practice.

PHASE 1: ORIENTATION TO ON-STREET DRIVING

The objectives for students are:

1. *To identify the key actions required in entering traffic, and in applying speed control and tracking skills to on-street driving*
2. *To identify all of the rules of the road that will apply during initial on-street driving— especially right-of-way rules, speed regulations, traffic signs and signals, and road markings*
3. *To be able to explain how these rules should be applied in a variety of driving situations and locations*
4. *To correctly execute the actions required in entering and leaving traffic*
5. *To effectively apply basic skills in speed control and tracking to the on-street situations encountered*
6. *To effectively apply appropriate rules of the road to the on-street situations encountered*

This phase of instruction emphasizes *established path driving,* where the driver moves the vehicle forward from a position within a traffic lane to subsequent positions within the same lane, changing speed and stopping when necessary for traffic signals, other vehicles, and so on (Fig. 5.1).

Fig. 5.1

Guides for Initial On-Street Performance

Listed below are several guides for initial on-street performance. For the most part they relate to the application of the basic skills acquired in Unit 3 and to driving in accordance with rules of the road. The number of guides has been kept to a minimum so that the student has a manageable group of things to concentrate on. In addition, they have been carefully selected to provide a meaningful transition between what was previously learned in the off-street setting and what will be learned in subsequent on-street lessons. Of course, the extent to which these guides will be applicable to conditions in a particular driver education program will vary. Teachers may have to add to (or delete from) the list in accordance with the unique requirements of their own on-street setting.

Entering traffic*

Guide 1 *Check conditions thoroughly before entering the roadway. Yield the right of way to vehicles already in the traffic lane.*

The student will probably enter the roadway from a driveway or from a parked position at the curb. In either case, she should ask the following questions:

1. Is my path clear?
2. Will it remain clear? (See Fig. 5.2.)

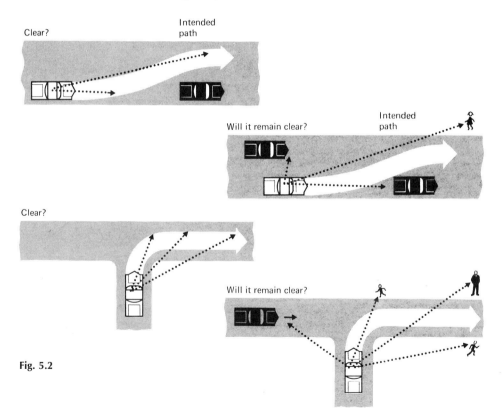

Fig. 5.2

---

* Unquestionably, entering traffic is one of the most critical features of the driving task (B 45–B 66). National accident statistics indicate that 5.1 percent of all accidents occur when one vehicle is either leaving a parked position (1.4 percent) or leaving a driveway (3.7 percent).

In response to these questions the student should scan along her intended path and in adjacent areas that might contain potential obstacles. This amounts to an introduction to scanning procedures, which will be covered more systematically in Phase 2 of this unit.

Whenever the student is about to enter a traffic lane, she should be encouraged to check well along the lane in the direction of approaching traffic (Fig. 5.3). The student should recognize that as she enters the lane, it will take time for her car to reach the normal speed of traffic. During this time, the gap will rapidly close between her car and other vehicles approaching in the lane. So she has to make certain that the approaching lane is clear for a considerable distance before moving into it.

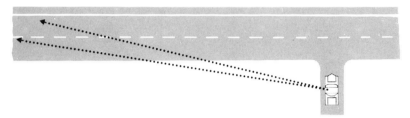

Fig. 5.3

When entering a traffic lane from a parked position at the curb the student should:

1. Turn completely around and check conditions by looking directly along the approaching lane. She should not depend on the mirrors.
2. Signal her intentions, using the mechanical and/or a hand signal. It is usually advisable to give a hand signal in addition to a mechanical signal because the visibility of the mechanical signal may be blocked by other vehicles parked behind her vehicle.

Applying speed control and tracking skills

Guide 2   *Use gradual acceleration when moving from a stationary position and gradual braking when coming to a stop.*

(Unit 3 describes the techniques involved and the reasons why gradual acceleration and braking are advisable.)

Guide 3   *Adjust speed to the normal speed of traffic, and stay within the speed limits.*

Students should understand that adjusting speed to the normal (or average) speed of other traffic is important for safety. Research studies indicate that the more a driver's speed varies from the average speed of all traffic, the more chance she has of being involved in an accident. This means that going too slowly as well as going too fast can be dangerous [1].

Since most beginners will tend to drive at slower than normal speeds, they should be encouraged to use the lane closest to the right-hand edge of the roadway.

Guide 4   *Whenever possible, stay within a single lane of traffic and maintain a centered-lane position.*

Students should be aware of the fact that on roads that have clearly marked traffic lanes, they are required to drive within a single lane and to move out of the lane only when they are sure it can be done safely (check state traffic laws).

Guide 5 *Maintain a space cushion on both sides of your vehicle.*

The student should keep a safe distance between the sides of her vehicle and all nearby obstacles, including other vehicles, pedestrians, abutments, and so forth (Fig. 5.4). At times, this will mean that she has to move off of the centered-lane position in order to provide an adequate space cushion on one side or the other (Fig. 5.5).

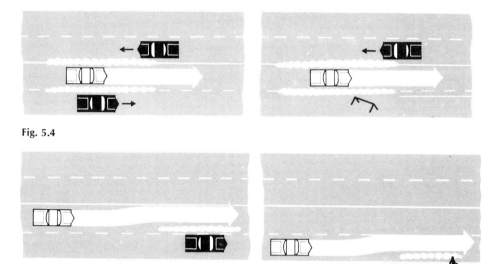

Fig. 5.4

Fig. 5.5

Guide 6 *Maintain a space cushion between your vehicle and other vehicles ahead.*

The general rule to follow is to allow at least a two- to three-second gap between your car and the vehicle ahead. This can be done by identifying a point on the roadside next to the car ahead (such as a pole or tree) and then counting off the seconds it takes you to reach this point (Fig. 5.6). To help students time the distance, have them say "Keep a safe distance" for each elapsed second.

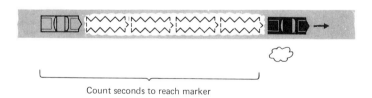

Count seconds to reach marker

Fig. 5.6

Applying Rules of the Road

"Applying a rule" simply means that when the student encounters a situation she uses her knowledge of the rule to guide her actions. In some situations, more than one rule may have to be applied. Students should know and be ready to apply all the rules of the road before driving on a public street. They may meet any number of unexpected and special situations that require the application of special rules. There are certain types of rules, however, that will probably have to be applied quite frequently during initial on-street lessons. Guides 1–6 refer to some of these rules, such as those relating to speed limits, staying within lanes, and so forth. Guides 7 and 8, which follow, remind the student to apply two types of rules that are especially important in the first on-street lessons.

Guide 7   *Be ready to yield the right of way to other vehicles and pedestrians.*

To understand right-of-way rules, the student should first understand one rather simple concept. Certain portions of most roads must be used by different vehicles (and pedestrians) at different times, for travel in different directions—in other words, their paths conflict (Fig. 5.7). When two vehicles (or a vehicle and a pedestrian) arrive at a conflicting point *at the same time,* an accident occurs. Obviously some rules are needed to make clear who has the right to go first and who must yield the right of way. Many traffic control signs and signals serve the same purpose.

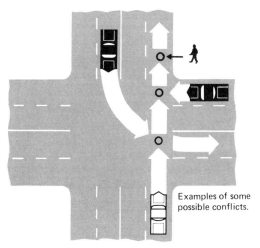

Examples of some possible conflicts.

Fig. 5.7

Four common situations in which drivers are required to yield are pictured in Figs. 5.8–5.11. (Check state traffic laws for these and other right-of-way rules.) First, when approaching an intersection, yield to a vehicle already in the intersection (Fig. 5.8). Second, yield to the vehicle on the right when it approaches an uncontrolled intersection at the same time you do (Fig. 5.9). Third, yield to pedestrians at intersections or in crosswalks between intersections (Fig. 5.10). Fourth, when turning left, yield to the vehicle approaching from the opposite direction if it is close enough to be a hazard (Fig. 5.11).

Guide 8   *Look for traffic signs and signals, and be ready to respond well in advance of reaching them.*

To follow this guide, students have to know all the laws relating to signs and signals, and the specific meanings attached to each. Sometimes these meanings are not so simple as they first appear to be to students. For example, the rules relating to a stop sign indicate not only that the driver should stop, but where to stop and how long she is required to stay stopped.

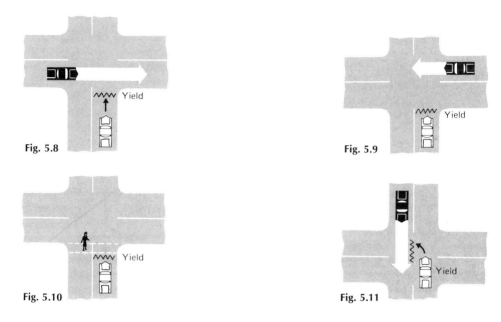

Fig. 5.8

Fig. 5.9

Fig. 5.10

Fig. 5.11

The purpose of this guide is not only to get the student to obey traffic signs and signals, but to encourage her to *look for them in advance*. Obviously she cannot obey them if she does not notice them, or if she cannot see them until it is too late (see "Common Errors in Student Performance").

Leaving traffic

Guide 9   *When leaving traffic, warn other drivers to the rear and completely leave the traffic lane as promptly as possible.*

Students should be alerted to the possibility of obstructing traffic and perhaps causing a rear-end collision as they slow down to leave traffic—especially since they may be slowing down at mid-block or at other points where other drivers may not expect them to reduce speed. In preparing to leave a traffic lane students should routinely check traffic to the rear and signal well in advance, using a hand signal for a stop if necessary. After slowing to an appropriate speed, they should concentrate on getting completely out of the traffic lane (or completely off the road) without delay.

Common Errors in Student Performance

Slow speeds   Some students will tend to drive at especially slow speeds in comparison to the prevailing speed of other vehicles. This may be a reflection of the slower traveling speeds to which they have become accustomed in their off-street driving, or it may simply reflect a natural cautiousness characteristic of initial on-street driving. Despite the fact that the slow speeds may impede the flow of traffic and cause other drivers to pass the driver education vehicle, it is usually unwise to urge such students to attain normal speeds during their first few on-street experiences. Students who are forced to drive at uncomfortably fast speeds (for them) may become quite anxious and indeed may not have sufficient skill to cope with the higher speeds. It is usually advisable to allow these students to drive at speeds that are comfortable (for them) during the first few on-street lessons. Then, after pointing out the dangers involved in traveling at excessively slow speeds, encourage them to gradually increase their speed. In any case, most students display a natural tendency, without the teacher's help, to increase their normal speed of travel as they become acclimated to on-street driving.

The "shy-away" response   Some students may over-respond to the presence of other vehicles, pedestrians, and objects adjacent to their traffic lane by moving off-path to the opposite side. Perhaps the two most common responses are to move too far right in response to oncoming vehicles, and to stay too far left in response to the presence of parked vehicles on the right. Since the student is very often unaware of the fact that she is over-responding, the teacher's first responsibility is simply to bring the error to the student's attention. If the tendency persists, the teacher should encourage the student to concentrate on maintaining a centered lane position and should manually assist the student in steering at appropriate moments

Failing to respond to traffic signs and signals   As a general rule, beginning drivers respond surprisingly well to the substantial variety of new elements they encounter in the on-street setting. For some reason, however, they are prone to an occasional failure to see or respond to traffic signs and signals. Although these errors are more likely to occur during the first few on-street lessons, they may also occur during the later stages of training.

In such instances the teacher has to be especially alert to the acceleration-deceleration pattern employed by the student on her approach to the sign or signal. The best tip-off to the likelihood that a student driver is about to go through a red light or stop sign is that she continues to accelerate beyond the point at which she normally takes her foot off the accelerator and places it over the brake. At that moment the teacher's immediate action should be to announce "red light" or "stop sign"—or, when there is not sufficient time for such cues, to use the dual brake.

Recurrence of speed control and tracking errors   It is not unusual for previous errors in tracking and speed control (which had apparently been overcome during off-street practice) to recur during initial on-street performance. Indeed, some students will commit errors they never made before. In most instances these errors are merely symptoms of the anxiety produced by the on-street setting. They normally disappear rather quickly once the student calms down. In some cases, however, they may be indicative of the student's failure to have mastered the basic skills, and the teacher may wish to consider having the student return to the off-street area for more concentrated practice.

Instructional Plan

Classroom   Considerable classroom preparation is required prior to the student's initial on-street experience (see "Classroom Guide" in Unit 5).

Selection of driving area   Since this unit deals primarily with established path driving, the route should permit as much uninterrupted straight forward driving as possible. There should be a minimal need for changing lanes and turning corners, which require somewhat more advanced skills in scanning and judgment. In addition, it is advisable to select a route that is not heavily traveled and does not require high-speed driving. A typical residential area is usually a suitable environment.

Demonstration and familiarization with route   It is usually advisable for the teacher to drive over the route prior to the practice of the first student in the driving group. The teacher can use this occasion to demonstrate the application of "Guides for Initial On-Street Performance" as well as to familiarize the students with the outstanding features of the route such as signs, signals, traffic patterns, visibility factors, and so forth.

Student practice   The student should be allotted a reasonable period of time for her first on-street practice session—perhaps a minimum of fifteen or twenty minutes. This helps ensure that she will become acclimated to the on-street setting and develop a reasonable degree of confidence. The student should concentrate on applying "Guides for Initial On-Street Performance." Whenever necessary, the teacher might use brief verbal cues to remind the student of critical elements of performance (such as "centered lane" or "signal light ahead"). For the most part, however, it seems wise to talk to the student as little as possible during this period when she will need to devote her full attention to the new demands placed on her by the on-street setting.

PHASE 2: INITIAL TECHNIQUES IN SCANNING FOR, EVALUATING, AND RESPONDING TO OBSTACLES

The objectives for students are:

1. *To define the concepts of* obstacle *and* potential obstacle, *and to identify common obstacles and potential obstacles in a variety of driving situations*

2. *To describe basic scanning techniques and explain why they are used*

3. *To define the process of* identifying, predicting, *and* deciding, *and to describe how it is used in a variety of driving situations*

4. *To successfully cope with a variety of on-street driving situations by:*
   a) *Correctly employing basic scanning techniques*
   b) *Accurately evaluating the situations*
   c) *Choosing and executing the appropriate speed control responses to obstacles and potential obstacles (Fig. 5.12)*

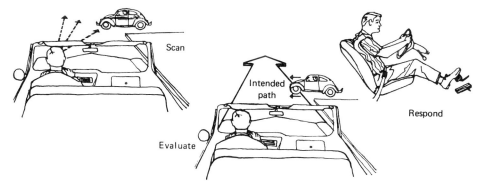

Fig. 5.12

An *obstacle* is any element *in the path* of the vehicle that would prevent it from safely continuing along the path (Fig 5.13).

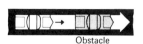
Obstacle

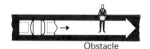
Obstacle

Obstacle

Fig. 5.13

A *potential obstacle* is any obstacle (not currently in the path of the vehicle) that has a reasonable chance of moving into that path (Fig. 5.14).

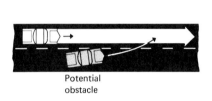
Potential
obstacle

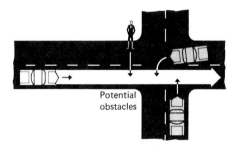
Potential
obstacles

Fig. 5.14

The techniques are initial ones because they are designed to meet the limited capabilities of students at this stage of instruction. The *scanning techniques* are designed for use in situations where the driver is moving in a forward direction on an established path with the intention of maintaining that path. *Responses* to obstacles and potential obstacles are limited to speed control responses and, in particular, to various degrees of speed reduction. More advanced scanning techniques and responses to obstacles are emphasized in subsequent units.

Elements of Performance to Be Learned

1. Scanning techniques [3]

The scanning* techniques described below should be viewed as *general rules* that can be applied in most driving situations and are suited to most drivers. There are exceptions to these rules, however, and as a consequence the techniques may not be applicable to all driving situations or to all drivers. For example, one of the techniques suggests that the driver "look ahead, well along the intended path and to the sides of the path." Under most circumstances

---

* The word *scanning* has various dictionary and technical definitions. It is used here, in its broadest sense, to refer to the act of *looking;* that is, to directing one's eyes in order to see or perceive. The term *perception* refers to the more complex process by which people select, organize, and interpret sensory stimulation into a meaningful and coherent picture of the world. Thus scanning is one part of the total process of perception. Here the term *scanning procedures or techniques* refers to methods for looking designed to enhance effective perception while driving.

this rule is appropriate for determining a clear path, but there are many occasions when it is not. For example, when a driver approaches a blind intersection she may find it necessary to look carefully from side to side and to disregard temporarily the projected path of the vehicle because she cannot adequately see vehicles approaching on the intersecting roadway unless she devotes her full attention to looking from side to side. Therefore, the teacher should not attempt to force the student to use all the techniques, or any one technique, at all times.

Technique 1   *Look for obstacles and potential obstacles along the intended path* [4] (see Fig. 5.15).

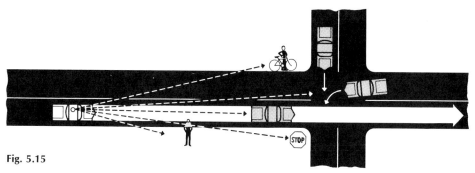

Fig. 5.15

Actions involved: The driver knows, in advance, the intended path of the vehicle. With this intended path in mind, she actively looks for obstacles and potential obstacles along the path; that is, her scanning has a purpose: to locate any object in the path, or approaching the path, that might influence the continued safe travel of her vehicle. As she encounters different driving situations, she *varies* her scanning procedures in search of the obstacles and potential obstacles in the particular situation. For example, as she approaches an intersection she looks for cars on the intersecting roadway, or as she is driving in a stream of traffic she carefully watches the movement of the car ahead.

Teachers should encourage students to scan particularly for those obstacles and potential obstacles that are frequently associated with accidents. The following types of obstacles have been shown to be associated with 44 percent of all traffic accidents (B 46):

1. Laterally moving vehicle—other vehicles approaching from cross streets or from another lateral approach (20.5 percent of all accidents)

2. Vehicle ahead—other vehicle in the driver's intended path, which may be stopped, traveling in same direction at constant speed, or decelerating (12 percent of all accidents)

3. Laterally moving object—pedestrian, child, cyclist, and so on, moving laterally toward or into the intended path (6.5 percent of all accidents)

4. Intruding approach—vehicle coming from opposite direction, which may be turning left, passing, drifting over center line, and so forth (5.5 percent of all accidents)

Technique 2   *Shift your eyes frequently over the intended path and to the sides of it—and occasionally to the rear* [5] (see Fig. 5.16).

Actions involved: The driver shifts her eyes frequently (every few seconds) to various points along the vehicle's path and to the sides of the path. In addition, she periodically checks to the rear using a "brief glance technique"—particularly before coming to a stop. She avoids

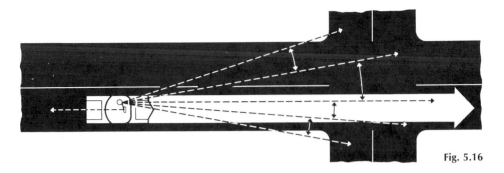

Fig. 5.16

concentrating her vision (and attention) on one object or event for an extended period of time. However, she does not shift fixations simply for the sake of shifting. She does so in order to see all objects and events that might influence the continued safe movement of her vehicle. (In this respect, Technique 2 is reciprocally related to Technique 1; the fact that the driver shifts her eyes influences her ability to see obstacles and potential obstacles, and her intent to search for obstacles and potential obstacles influences where she looks when she shifts her eyes.)

Technique 3   *Look ahead, well along the intended path and to the sides of it* [6] (see Fig. 5.17).

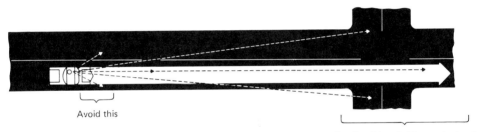

Avoid this

Practice this — 8-12 seconds ahead

Fig. 5.17

Actions involved: The driver habitually looks well ahead down the path of the vehicle and to the sides of the path. She avoids continuously focusing her vision (and attention) on the ground immediately in front of the vehicle and on other events close to the present position of the vehicle that do not have a bearing on its movement—however, she may periodically need to shift her focus to near points in order to check on the alignment of the vehicle in relation to the roadway.

Precisely how far ahead the driver should look will depend on the driving situation. However, in most situations, a good rule to follow is to search ahead to the point where your vehicle will be in eight to twelve seconds (B 138). Of course this rule has to be applied flexibly—there may be many instances where events closer to the vehicle prevent the driver from scanning too far ahead (for example, a nearby vehicle or pedestrian). In the driver education car the teacher will have to utilize his professional judgment in deciding whether an individual student is looking far enough ahead (or perhaps too far).

Coordinating the techniques   The student should notice that these three techniques are closely related. Technique 3 determines where she looks, Technique 2 determines how she looks, and Technique 1 determines what she looks for; the techniques must be coordinated and applied all at once by shifting the eyes to look for obstacles and potential obstacles ahead.

2. Evaluating [6]

Actions involved: Having seen objects or events in the vicinity of her vehicle, the driver evaluates the situation by:

1. *Identifying* obstacles in her path and potential obstacles that might move into the path
2. When potential obstacles are present, *predicting* whether or not they will move into the path
3. *Deciding* whether or not the path is clear enough and will remain clear enough to allow her to continue on the path at the present speed, or whether a change in speed or direction is required (Fig. 5.18)

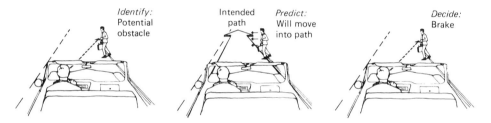

Fig. 5.18

    What constitutes an obstacle or potential obstacle or an appropriate decision at any given moment will depend on the unique characteristics of the particular driving situation. For practical purposes in the driver education car it will be the teacher's judgment that determines what is, and what is not, an obstacle or potential obstacle and what decision is called for. The accuracy of the student's judgments will depend on the degree to which they correspond with the teacher's judgments.
    The situations encountered can be classified into three general types:

1. *Situations in which there is reasonable certainty that the path is clear and will remain clear.*   In these situations the driver can see that there are no obstacles in the path for a safe distance ahead and that there are no potential obstacles present that could enter the path. Normally, in these situations the decision is to continue along the path at the present speed.

2. *Situations in which it is certain that the path is not clear or will not remain clear.*   In these situations the driver identifies obstacles in the path or identifies potential obstacles and predicts that they will move into the path. Normally in these situations the decision is to slow down, stop, or alter the path to avoid a collision.

3. *Situations in which it is not certain whether the path is clear or will remain clear.*   Students will encounter a great variety of these uncertain situations. For example, in some situations they will not be certain as to whether potential obstacles will move into their path; in others, they will not be able to see the path for a safe distance ahead; and in others, they may be unable to see potential obstacles approaching their path (Fig. 5.19). In these uncertain situations they will have to choose the safest response alternative for the particular situation. Deciding which response is safest in these uncertain situations is not easy. In many instances the safest alternative may be to slow down or stop. In other settings where there are following vehicles, slowing down may seriously increase the risk of a rear-end collision. And in some situations, slowing down may confuse other drivers and pedestrians who are expecting the student to continue. Guides for responding in uncertain situations appear in the following section.

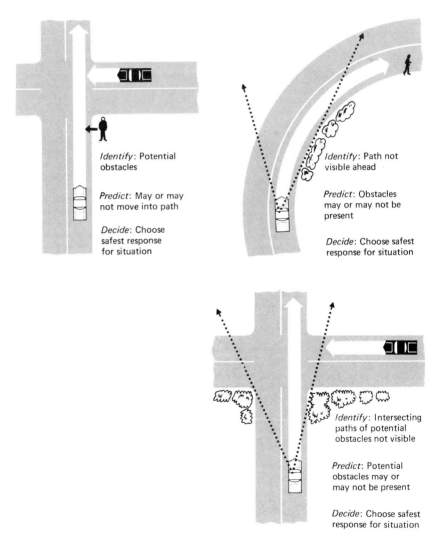

Identify: Potential obstacles

Predict: May or may not move into path

Decide: Choose safest response for situation

Identify: Path not visible ahead

Predict: Obstacles may or may not be present

Decide: Choose safest response for situation

Identify: Intersecting paths of potential obstacles not visible

Predict: Potential obstacles may or may not be present

Decide: Choose safest response for situation

Fig. 5.19

3. Speed control responses to obstacles and potential obstacles

Actions involved: In view of the student's limited on-street driving experience at this stage of instruction, it seems wise to concentrate on the development of appropriate speed control responses to obstacles and potential obstacles. These responses would include:

1. Continue at present speed (with accelerator at a constant position)
2. "Decelerate" (release accelerator)
3. "Caution" position (foot touching brake)
4. "Slow" (gradual brake application)
5. "Stop" (gradual stop)
6. "STOP" (quick stop)
7. An appropriate combination of some of the above: 2 and 3; or 2, 3, 4, and 5

The beginning driver may encounter obstacles or potential obstacles to which a more experienced driver might react by swerving from her established path or by accelerating. Such responses are too advanced for the beginner at this stage of learning. In later units the more advanced responses will be considered.

The appropriateness of a response in a given driving situation will depend on the unique characteristics of that situation. Once again, it will be up to the teacher to make judgments about which response is appropriate in a particular situation. The following guides for determining appropriate actions are provided to aid the teacher in making these judgments:

Guide 1   *Begin decelerating early in response to obstacles and potential obstacles well ahead along the intended path.*

For example, when a car is stopping for a traffic light well ahead and is likely to remain stopped or when a vehicle is turning into the lane ahead and is likely to move slowly within the lane, begin to decelerate early (Fig. 5.20). Reducing speed means that a shorter stopping distance is necessary, and prepares the student to deal with the situation as she gets closer to it. Decelerating also helps prevent the necessity for abrupt last-minute braking that can result in a rear-end collision or skidding. In addition, in many situations early deceleration allows more time for obstacles to clear out of the path ahead so that the driver can resume normal speed without having to brake or stop. For example, when vehicles ahead are turning into cross streets or crossing the path, early deceleration by the student gives them time to get out of the path before the student reaches the intersection (Fig. 5.21).

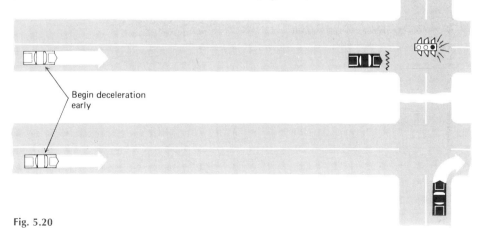

Begin deceleration
early

Fig. 5.20

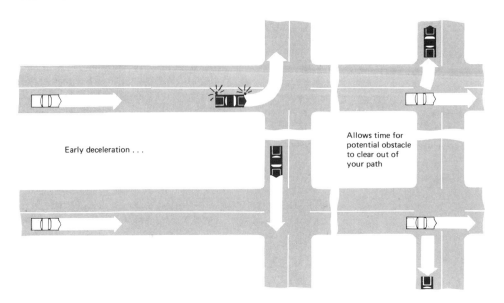

Fig. 5.21

Guide 2   *Use caution position* in response to the more critical potential obstacles.*

When a potential obstacle poses a very likely threat to the path of the vehicle, the caution position should be used. For example, a car traveling in an adjacent lane in the same direction is a potential obstacle that should be recognized, but it may not require the caution position. However, when that car begins to move laterally toward the student's path, the caution position should be used (Fig. 5.22). A car stopped on a minor intersecting roadway waiting for the driver education vehicle to pass on the main thoroughfare is a potential obstacle that should be recognized, but again a caution response may not be called for. However, should the car on the intersecting roadway begin to move toward the student's path, the caution position should be used (Fig. 5.23).

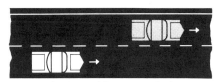

Caution position not required

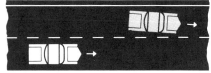

Caution position required

Fig. 5.22

---

* The caution position refers to the placement of the foot over the brake pedal without the actual application of the brake.

In such situations the caution position has the advantage of making the driver physically and psychologically ready to stop, while at the same time avoiding the more rapid deceleration involved in braking, which may create a hazard to other drivers following behind the driver education vehicle.

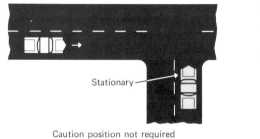
Caution position not required

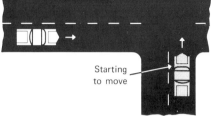
Caution position required

Fig. 5.23

Guide 3   *Decelerate, slow down, or stop as necessary when the path is not visible for a safe distance ahead or when the paths of intersecting vehicles and pedestrians are not visible.*

The amount of speed reduction required in these situations will depend on the amount of reduced visibility. For example, at a blind uncontrolled intersection where the visibility along intersecting paths is sharply reduced, it may be necessary to come to a complete stop and determine that the intersecting lanes are clear before proceeding. At an intersection where visibility is not so sharply reduced, the driver can decelerate and determine the clearance along intersecting lanes as she approaches, and then continue through the intersection without stopping (Fig. 5.24).

Guide 4   *Avoid the overuse of "decelerate," "slow," and "stop" to the point where such changes in acceleration would confuse and obstruct other drivers and the pedestrians* [7].

Beginning drivers should understand that they can become overcautious to the point where they create hazards. For example, when approaching an intersection where another vehicle is waiting for the student's vehicle to pass in order to make a left turn across its path, it is important to recognize the other vehicle as a potential obstacle. It might be advisable to use the caution position (which would involve slight deceleration), but it is probably unwise to apply the brake and slow down to the extent that the driver of the other vehicle is led to believe that the student driver intends to stop. Such overcautious behavior might very well encourage the other driver to turn in front of the driver education vehicle, causing the hazardous situation that the student was attempting to avoid (Fig. 5.25).

The overcautious response can create special hazards for vehicles to the rear of the car. For example, if a student is driving between intersections with other vehicles following and a pedestrian, standing at a point adjacent to the intended path, is waiting to cross the street, it is important to recognize the pedestrian as a potential obstacle and perhaps to use the caution position. On the other hand, it is probably unwise to slow down considerably, or to stop and encourage the pedestrian to cross, because this action will come as a surprise to the vehicles following and may precipitate a rear-end collision. Of course, this whole situation would change if the pedestrian, instead of waiting for the vehicle to pass, were actually moving toward its path.

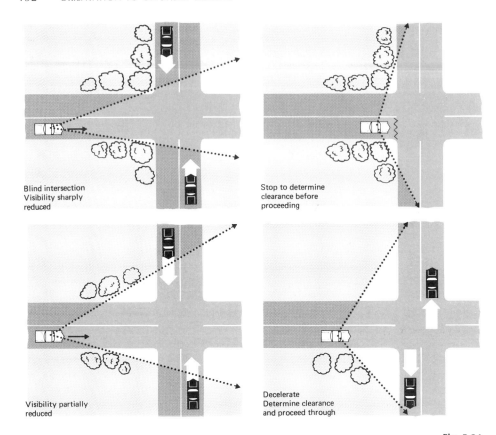

Blind intersection
Visibility sharply
reduced

Stop to determine
clearance before
proceeding

Visibility partially
reduced

Decelerate
Determine clearance
and proceed through

Fig. 5.24

Overuse of slowdown and its consequence

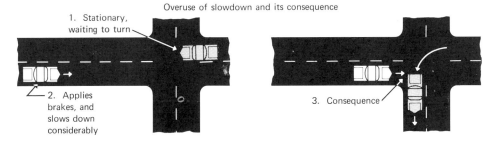

1. Stationary,
waiting to turn

2. Applies
brakes, and
slows down
considerably

3. Consequence

Fig. 5.25

Instructional Plan

Classroom

Extensive classroom preparation is required to ensure effective in-car practice in this phase of instruction. Concepts like obstacle and potential obstacle will have to be carefully discussed and illustrated. In addition, the technique of limited commentary driving has to be thoroughly reviewed (see "Classroom Guide" for Unit 5).

Selection of driving area

It is advisable to use the same route as was used in Phase I of this unit for the student's initial practice of the techniques covered in this phase. The student's familiarity with the route should make it easier for her to concentrate on scanning for, recognizing, and responding to obstacles. As the student's capability increases, other routes should provide for extensive established path driving and should contain enough obstacles and potential obstacles to challenge the student's capacities for scanning and responding.

In-car demonstration and explanation

More than in any previous unit, the teacher's demonstration is crucial to effective instruction and practice. His demonstration will set specific standards for applying the general principles and concepts discussed in the classroom. For example, the student may have a general idea of what constitutes a potential obstacle as a consequence of prior classroom discussion. But it is not until the teacher identifies potential obstacles (using commentary driving) that the student has specific models of performance upon which to base her own performance. In the same way, the teacher's use of scanning procedures, and his selection of appropriate responses, will establish specific standards of performance that students may be expected to emulate.

Student practice

Student practice is divided into two stages:

Stage 1   *Practice initial scanning techniques.*

During this stage of instruction the student should have an opportunity to concentrate on employing the appropriate scanning techniques. It will probably be necessary to use verbal cues to remind students of the techniques both prior to and during their performance. It will be difficult at this point in the practice period to make judgments about *what* the student sees. However, it should be possible to watch the student's eye movements and detect any consistent errors in performance such as "staring," "looking directly over the fender," "failing to use the mirrors," and so forth.

Stage 2   *Practice evaluating and responding.*

During this stage of practice the student should concentrate on evaluating and responding to obstacles and potential obstacles. The scanning techniques developed in Stage 1 should be an integral part of performance. The technique of limited commentary driving is particularly appropriate for use here.

Limited commentary driving   The term *commentary driving* is normally used in a rather general way to refer to any continuous commentary on the part of the driver describing what she sees as she drives. The technique of limited commentary driving is a simplified variation of commentary driving adopted for use with beginning drivers. In essence, this technique has the student use one-word or two-word phrases to identify important obstacles and potential obstacles as she drives along an established path. A typical example of limited commentary driving appears in Fig. 5.26, with some general rules describing the technique.*

---

* Field tests of Unit 5 have demonstrated that it is advisable for teachers to practice commentary driving on their own before they attempt to use the technique with students.

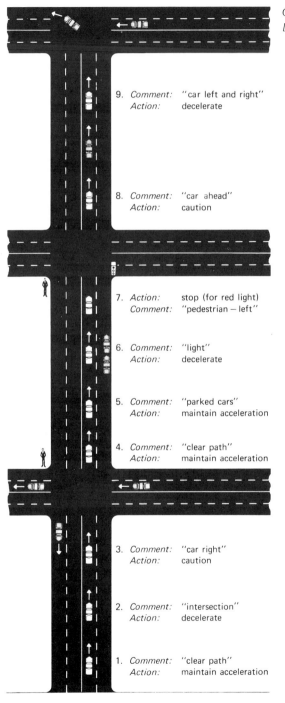

9. *Comment:* "car left and right"
   Action: decelerate

8. *Comment:* "car ahead"
   Action: caution

7. *Action:* stop (for red light)
   Comment: "pedestrian — left"

6. *Comment:* "light"
   Action: decelerate

5. *Comment:* "parked cars"
   Action: maintain acceleration

4. *Comment:* "clear path"
   Action: maintain acceleration

3. *Comment:* "car right"
   Action: caution

2. *Comment:* "intersection"
   Action: decelerate

1. *Comment:* "clear path"
   Action: maintain acceleration

General Rules for Limited Commentary Driving

1. The comment "clear path" should be used when there are no obstacles or potential obstacles for a safe distance ahead. (Use "clear path" periodically, not continuously.)

2. When there is an obstacle(s) or *important* potential obstacle(s) ahead, identify it out loud using *one* or *two* words.

3. Identify only the *most important* potential obstacles. (Recognize that it is impossible to identify all the potential obstacles that you see.)

4. Limit the total number of comments (perhaps three to five per block as a maximum).

5. Simply *identify* the obstacle or potential obstacle; do not attempt to *explain* anything about it.

6. Obstacles and potential obstacles should be identified *well in advance* of the point at which the vehicle reaches them.

Fig. 5.26

Advantages and limitations of commentary driving [8]   The most important advantage gained from the use of this technique is that it provides the teacher with additional feedback (in addition to the student's physical performance), which can be most valuable to the instructional process. The teacher can use the student's comments as evidence of where the student is looking, what she sees, and how she interprets what she sees. This evidence can form the basis for refining and correcting student performance.

In addition, it provides a framework for maintaining student attention to relevant events. A student who knows that she is supposed to verbally identify obstacles is not likely to allow her mind to wander. Also, a student who must constantly look for and identify obstacles is likely to begin to view the driving task as a problem in safe movement and not merely as a problem in manipulative skill. (In other words, this technique would seem to have an inherently desirable effect on attitude development.)

The teacher should recognize, however, that although commentary driving has some distinct advantages, it also has some important limitations. First, the student's verbalization of what she sees will be only a rough estimate of what she actually sees. Just as there is difficulty judging a driver's thoughts on the basis of her physical actions, there will be difficulty judging what she sees and thinks on the basis of what she says. (In fact, the very act of attempting to tell someone what you see has inherent limitations because of the qualitative differences between visual images and words.) Thus, the information provided by student comments is, at best, a rough indication of her observations.

A second limitation in using commentary driving relates to the limited capabilities of some students at this stage of their driving experience. Students who are still in the process of acquiring the basic motor skills involved in operating an automobile may experience difficulty in attempting to talk about what they are doing at the same time they are doing it. This can be a serious problem and teachers are urged to make allowances for student capabilities.

Finally, commentary driving is limited by the fact that if it is used improperly, it can result in a distortion of driver performance. For example, the student can get so wrapped up in playing the word game that she fails to make the appropriate physical responses. Or she can become so involved in verbalizing one element in the environment that she neglects others. Hopefully, these dangers can be reduced by careful planning and skillful application of the technique on the part of the teacher.

Conducting practice   During the initial stages of the student's commentary driving,* the teacher should remain relatively quiet and allow the student to adjust to the task. Once the student begins to adjust, the teacher may use verbal cues to assist and correct the student. For example, if the student fails to identify major obstacles, the teacher may identify some of them for her; if the student is identifying potential obstacles too close to the car or too far ahead, or if the student tries to identify too many potential obstacles, the teacher should suggest appropriate corrective measures.

In addition, the teacher should be ready to assist the student in selecting appropriate responses through the use of verbal cues. For example, if the student approaches a dangerous potential obstacle and fails to use the caution position, the teacher may simply say "caution," indicating the appropriate response at the moment.

The major concern of the teacher during this phase of the unit should be: (1) *Does the student recognize the critical potential obstacles far enough in advance?* and (2) *Does the*

---

* Some teachers have found it advantageous to have students practice the initial commentary while the teacher drives the vehicle.

student begin to respond in advance of these obstacles? The teacher should not expect the student to become an immediate expert in commentary driving. The student is likely to make many mistakes—the teacher should expect such mistakes and make allowances for them.

As the student carries on commentary driving, the teacher should check periodically to see how the student is coping with the task. The teacher might ask questions such as, "Do you find it difficult to make the comments?" "Do the comments tend to distract you from your driving?" If the student reports that the commentary is too difficult or distracting, then the teacher might suggest some alternatives. Perhaps the student should reduce the number of comments, or perhaps for the time being she should discontinue the commentary.

Restricting the duration of commentary driving   Commentary driving is a teaching technique for use during the student's initial experiences in this phase of instruction. *It should not be carried on indefinitely.* Once the student has developed a reasonable initial competence in scanning, evaluating, and responding, the practice of commentary driving should be discontinued. One or two on-street practice sessions should be sufficient for most students.

CLASSROOM GUIDE FOR UNIT 5

*Orientation to On-Street Driving, and Initial Techniques in
Scanning for, Recognizing, and Responding to Obstacles*

Topics	Instructional Plan
1. *Driving route(s)* to be used during the in-car practice session(s).	1. Diagram route(s). 2. Discuss outstanding features of route that students should be aware of in advance.
2. *Rules of the road* (applicable to initial on-street driving): a) Right-of-way b) Speed c) Traffic signs and signals d) Road markings	1. Review important regulations. 2. Discuss relevance for accident prevention. 3. Provide illustrations of how regulations apply to practice driving route.
3. *Guides for initial on-street performance:* Entering traffic: a) Check conditions before entering roadway: Is my path clear? Will it remain clear? Applying speed control and tracking skills: b) Use gradual acceleration and braking. c) Adjust to normal speed of traffic. d) Stay within single lane, maintain centered lane position. e) Maintain space cushion ahead and to sides. Applying rules of the road: f) Be ready to yield right-of-way. g) Look for traffic signs and signals. Leaving traffic: h) Warn others and leave promptly.	1. Discuss each guide. 2. Provide illustrations of how each guide might apply to practice driving route.
4. *Understanding the concepts:* a) Path of vehicle b) Obstacle c) Potential obstacle	1. Use blackboard, traffic board, to illustrate concepts.
5. *Initial scanning techniques:* a) "Look for obstacles and potential obstacles." b) "Shift eyes frequently." c) "Look ahead." d) Combine and vary techniques to meet needs of situation.	1. Describe each technique—illustrate using blackboard, slide film, etc. 2. Emphasize importance of varying techniques to meet situation—use examples from route to be used during in-car lesson.

CLASSROOM GUIDE FOR UNIT 5 (*cont.*)

Topics	Instructional Plan
6. *Evaluation and response:*	1. Discuss each concept.
a) Difference between seeing an obstacle and identifying it as a potential hazard.	2. Illustrate each concept using examples from on-street driving route to be used during in-car lesson.
b) Identifying, predicting, deciding.	
c) When to use caution position.	
d) When to slow down or stop.	
e) Avoiding overuse of "slow down" and "stop."	
7. *Limited commentary driving.*	1. Explain purpose of technique.
	2. Review general rules governing technique.
	3. If possible, practice commentary driving using motion pictures.

PREPARATORY READING FOR STUDENTS

1. *Learning to Drive: Skills, Concepts, and Strategies.* Chapter 7, "Orientation to On-Street Driving"; and Chapter 8, "Scanning for, Evaluating, and Responding to Obstacles."

   —or appropriate sections from another high-school text.

2. *State Driver's Manual.* Thoroughly study all "rules of the road" that might apply during on-street lesson(s).

RELATED SIMULATOR LESSONS

1. Aetna Drivotrainer System: "Blending in Traffic," "Introduction to IPDE."

2. Link Simulator System: "Perceptive Driving," "Moderate Traffic," "Control."

IN-CAR GUIDE FOR UNIT 5

*Orientation to On-Street Driving, and Initial Techniques in
Scanning for, Recognizing, and Responding to Obstacles*

Phase 1: Orientation to On-Street Driving

DEMONSTRATION

Drive over route to be used by students:

1. Point out important features of environment.

2. Demonstrate application of "Guides for Initial On-Street Performance."

GUIDING STUDENT PRACTICE

Teacher	Student
Emphasize:	Drives over route and concentrates on:
1. Guides for initial on-street performance	1. Checking conditions before entering roadway, determining
2. Driving in accordance with rules of the road	a) path is clear
	b) will remain clear
Watch for:	2. Using gradual acceleration and braking
1. Excessively slow speeds	3. Adjusting to normal speed
2. The shy-away response	4. Maintaining centered lane position
3. Student awareness of traffic signs and signals	5. Maintaining space cushion
4. Errors in speed control and tracking	6. Being ready to yield
	7. Looking for traffic signs and signals
	8. Leaving traffic safely

Phase 2: Initial Techniques in Scanning for, Evaluating, and Responding to Obstacles

DEMONSTRATION

Demonstrate initial scanning techniques, calling attention to:

1. Looking for obstacles and potential obstacles

2. Keeping eyes moving

3. Looking ahead

Demonstrate limited commentary driving:

1. Using "clear path"

2. Naming obstacles

3. Naming most important potential obstacles

4. Calling attention to selection of appropriate responses to obstacles and potential obstacles: "Decelerate," "caution" position, "slow," "stop".

IN-CAR GUIDE FOR UNIT 5 *(cont.)*

GUIDING STUDENT PRACTICE

Teacher	Student

Stage 1: Practice Initial Scanning Techniques

Emphasize initial scanning techniques.	Drives, concentrating on:
Watch eye movements.	1. Looking for obstacles and *important* potential obstacles
Correct any consistent errors in eye movements.	
Emphasize varying techniques to suit the situation.	2. Shifting eyes frequently
	3. Looking ahead

Stage 2: Practice Evaluating and Responding

Have student use limited commentary driving and practice speed control responses.	Drives using limited commentary driving; also concentrates on selecting appropriate speed control responses.
Review general rules for commentary driving before student begins:	

1. Use "clear path."

2. Use one or two words to identify obstacles.

3. Identify only most important potential obstacles.

4. Limit total number of comments.

5. Identify, do not explain.

6. Identify in advance.

Emphasize selecting appropriate speed control responses:

1. "Decelerate"	2. "Caution"
3. "Slow"	4. "Gradual stop"
5. "STOP"	

At first keep quiet; let student adjust to task.

Later use verbal cues as necessary to help student select appropriate responses.

Periodically check student capacities for commentary driving: "Are you distracted by comments?" and so on.

INTRODUCTION TO
REDUCED-RISK PERFORMANCE

INTRODUCTION

Subsequent units deal with reduced-risk performance of driving maneuvers. Prior understanding of the concept of reduced risk [1] is important to the successful conduct of these units.

The objective for students is to identify the major features of reduced-risk performance and the ways in which they apply to a variety of on-street driving maneuvers.

The following description of the concept is taken directly from the high-school text, *Learning to Drive: Skills, Concepts, and Strategies,* and thus is in a form suitable for communication to high-school students.

REDUCED-RISK PERFORMANCE

Whenever you are about to perform a driving maneuver, you are actually faced with a variety of ways of executing it. For example, in changing lanes you can start the maneuver early, signal early, move at high speeds, and turn gradually—or you can start later, signal later, move at slower speeds, and turn sharply—or you can use any one of several other ways of performing it (Fig. A). All the possible ways of performing the maneuver are *alternatives* from which you must choose.

In reduced-risk performance, your objective is to choose the alternative that involves the least chance of getting you into an accident. For example, in changing lanes in a traffic situation such as the one pictured in Fig. B, you might cut directly in front of the faster moving vehicle in the left lane (Alternative 1), or you might accelerate and try to squeeze between vehicles No. 1 and No. 2 (Alternative 2), or you might maintain your speed and allow the vehicle on the left to pass before beginning to change lanes (Alternative 3). Alternative 1 involves the substantial risk of being hit by vehicle No. 1. Alternative 2 involves the risks of being hit by vehicle No. 1 or hitting the rear of vehicle No. 2. Alternative 3 involves the least risk of an accident and therefore is the reduced-risk alternative in this situation.

It is not always easy to choose the reduced-risk alternative. One problem is that there are often several kinds of risks in a driving situation: a driver action that reduces one type of risk can increase another type of risk and result in an overall increase in the *total risk*. For example,

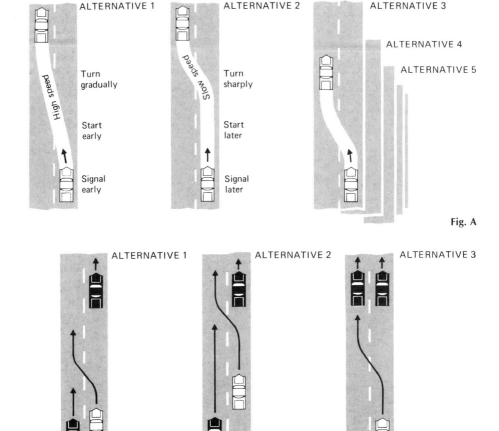

in making a left turn, suppose that instead of turning at a normal speed you decide to turn at a very slow speed to reduce the risk of making tracking errors; in doing so, however, you substantially increase the risk of being hit by oncoming vehicles (Fig. C). Although you reduced one kind of risk, you created a more serious one and thus increased the total risk involved. In such multiple-risk situations, you should always choose the alternative with the least total risk.

The problem is further complicated by the fact that if you perform the same maneuver in the same way in two different situations, it may be the reduced-risk alternative in one situation, but it may not be the reduced-risk alternative in the other situation. For example, in most situations when you make a right turn, the reduced-risk alternative includes moving from the

NORMAL TURNING SPEED   VERY SLOW TURNING SPEED

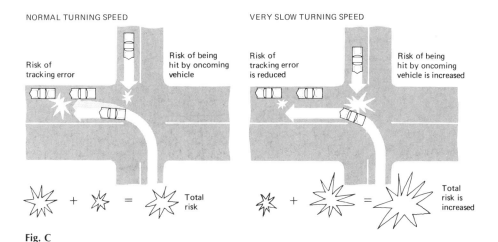

Fig. C

center of the right lane on the approach street to the center of the right lane on the intersecting street (Fig. D). But there are other situations in which this path is not part of the reduced-risk alternative (Fig. E). The selection of the reduced-risk alternative always depends on the conditions present in the particular situation. Therefore, your job is to *evaluate each situation and choose the alternative that involves the least risk of an accident for that particular situation.*

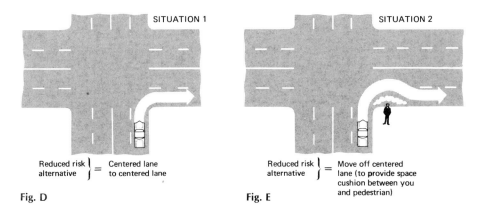

Fig. D   **Fig. E**

Of course, in addition to selecting the reduced-risk alternative, you must be able to carry it out. You must be able to use your skills in speed control, tracking, and positioning so that you move your car on the path you have selected and at the speed you have chosen. Also, if signaling is required, you will have to use the appropriate signals. For example, in parallel parking, once you have selected the reduced-risk alternative, you then have to apply your skills in speed control, tracking, and positioning to move your car into position (Fig. F).

One last complicating factor needs to be mentioned. Often, in the midst of a maneuver, conditions in the driving situation change and you will have to change your plans to suit the

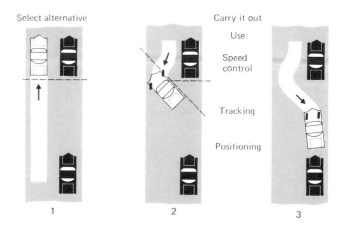

Fig. F

change in conditions. For example, in making a left turn, suppose you evaluate the situation and decide that the safest procedure is to slow down and make the turn without stopping because oncoming traffic is far enough away (Fig. G). But at the last moment, children enter the crosswalk and block your path. You must, of course, change your plans and wait for both the children and the oncoming vehicle to pass (Fig. H).

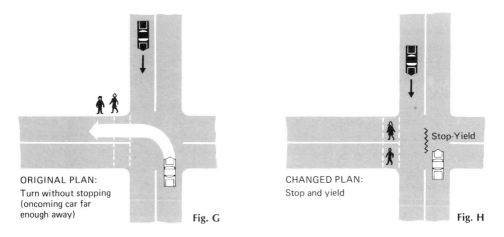

The performance of reduced-risk maneuvers is a complicated business. It involves the use of several different types of skills:

1. Scanning and evaluating
2. Communicating intentions (signaling) [2]
3. Selecting the reduced-risk alternative
4. Controlling the car's movement (speed control, tracking, and positioning)

The driver must perform some of these skills continuously throughout the maneuver, and frequently has to perform several different skills at once. For example, Fig. I pictures the skills used in changing lanes.

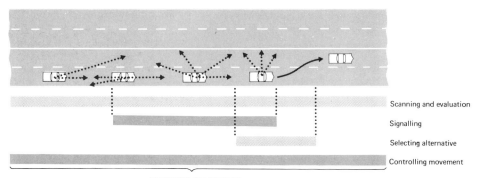

Scanning and evaluation

Signalling

Selecting alternative

Controlling movement

DURATION OF ACTIONS

Fig. I

During future on-street driving lessons, you will be practicing reduced-risk maneuvers. As you practice, keep in mind that for each maneuver you will have to master all four types of skills (scanning and evaluating, communicating, selecting alternatives, and controlling movement), and that your *overall objective is to develop those skills to the point where you consistently choose reduced-risk alternatives and carry them out effectively.*

Summary of the Major Aspects of Reduced-Risk Performance

1. Whenever you are about to perform a maneuver, you actually have a variety of alternatives to choose from.
2. The risk in a situation always depends on the particular conditions in that situation. You must evaluate each situation intelligently, and choose the alternative with the least risk for that particular situation.
3. Your objective should be to choose the reduced-risk alternative, the one that reduces the *total risk* of an accident to a minimum.
4. Keep in mind that if conditions in the driving situation change in the middle of a maneuver, your plans may have to change to suit the changed conditions.
5. Reduced-risk performance involves the use of several different types of skills including *scanning and evaluating, selecting* the reduced-risk alternative, *communicating* intentions, and *controlling* the car's movement.

In effect then, reduced-risk performance recognizes that there is no *one standard way* of performing a given maneuver. Instead, it implies that a maneuver may be performed in a variety of ways and whether or not it was performed "correctly" depends primarily on the driver's selection and execution of risk-reducing alternatives in relation to prevailing conditions. This point of view does not negate the fact that there are *general rules* that should govern the performance of maneuvers—especially legal restrictions and requirements. It simply focuses on the driver's need to remain flexible in his application of general rules and in the performance of the many aspects of a maneuver that are not governed by general rules. The reduced-risk approach to instruction in driving maneuvers is an attempt to emphasize those elements of driver performance that are most crucial to the *safe* completion of the maneuver. Hopefully, as a consequence of this approach to instruction, students will view driving maneuvers as *problems in safe performance* and will be trained to select those alternatives that lead to the safest solution.

There is an important distinction here between the reduced-risk approach and teaching a *standard* method for performing maneuvers. Many teachers give instruction in maneuvers in a way that leads students to adopt a standard and relatively inflexible approach to the performance of a specific maneuver. As a consequence, students are usually equipped to perform the maneuver under relatively ideal conditions (that is, no obstacles or potential obstacles), but when they are confronted with a variation in conditions that calls for a variation in execution, they are reluctant to change their standard method of performance. This is especially true when students know that they will be evaluated on the extent to which their performance resembles the standard model.

REDUCED-RISK TURNS

INTRODUCTION

This unit deals with the on-street maneuvers of turning right and turning left [1]. It emphasizes reduced-risk elements of performance including (1) early entry into the approach lane, (2) communicating intentions, (3) speed control and tracking, (4) scanning and evaluating, and (5) selecting reduced-risk alternatives.

Student practice is organized into three phases: (1) successive right turns, (2) successive left turns, and (3) right and left turns (at high-risk locations). Practice in turning right precedes practice in turning left because of the more demanding assessment procedures called for in making left turns.

As a consequence of earlier off-street and on-street experiences, students should be equipped to perform many of the basic elements of reduced-risk turns. They should have acquired competence in accurate tracking, signaling, and speed control on turning paths (Unit 3, Phase 4) and should have acquired basic skills in scanning and evaluating (Unit 5). Assuming that the student has learned these skills well, the teacher should be able to concentrate on the unique elements of content in this unit: scanning and evaluating procedures used in turning maneuvers and selecting reduced-risk alternatives in performing turns.

In this unit the objectives for students are:

1. *To identify the common risks involved in the various stages of right turns and left turns*

2. *To identify the kinds of driver actions required to reduce those risks, including appropriate techniques in scanning and evaluating, communicating intentions, selecting alternatives, and controlling the car's movement*

3. *To demonstrate knowledge of all of the "rules of the road" related to performing turns and to be able to apply those rules to a broad variety of turning situations*

4. *To execute reduced-risk right and left turns consistently in a broad variety of driving situations*

Related Concepts and Information

Common risks in turning   On-street turning maneuvers can be particularly difficult because several types of risk can occur and the types of risk can change dramatically from one stage of a maneuver to the next. *As you approach the turn,* there are the risks of being hit from the rear as you reduce your speed, hitting another vehicle in front that stops unexpectedly, or hitting

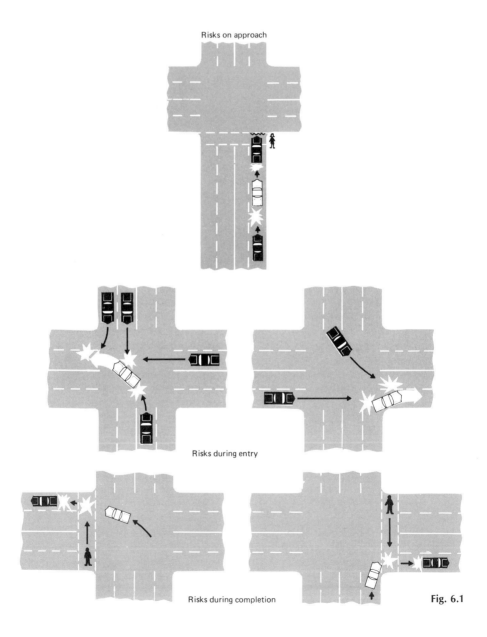

Risks on approach

Risks during entry

Risks during completion

Fig. 6.1

pedestrians in the near crosswalk. *As you enter the turn* there are the risks of colliding with vehicles in cross traffic, vehicles turning into the same street, vehicles passing you, and, in left turns, oncoming traffic. *As you complete the turn* there are the risks of hitting pedestrians in the other crosswalk and colliding with other obstacles that may be present on the street into which you turn (Fig. 6.1).

Legal requirements   Prior to practicing on-street turning maneuvers, students should be familiar with the legal requirements governing the performance of turns. The requirements described below are based on the Uniform Vehicle Code (B 139). (Teachers should review the traffic laws for their state, and where differences exist, they should be certain that their students know the state laws.)

Lanes used in right turns   The approach for a right turn and the turn itself should be made as close as practicable to the right-hand curb or edge of the roadway. When cars are parked along the right-hand curb, the lanes next to the parking lanes are used. When there is no parking lane, the lanes adjacent to the curb are used. Following this rule helps avoid several conflicts for the right-of-way that might otherwise occur (Fig. 6.2).

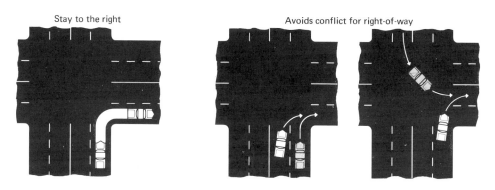

Fig. 6.2

Lanes used in left turns   On two-way roadways the approach for a left turn is made in the extreme left-hand lane available to traffic. The turning path passes to the left of the center of the intersection and enters the intersecting roadway in the extreme left-hand lane available to traffic. Following this path also helps avoid several conflicts for the right-of-way that might otherwise occur (Fig. 6.3). At intersections where traffic is restricted to one direction on one or more of the roadways, the approach and the completion of the turn are made in the extreme left-hand lane lawfully available to traffic (Fig. 6.4).

Signaling for turns   A signal for a turn must be given continuously during not less than the last 100 feet traveled by the vehicle before turning.

Required path   Avoids conflict for right-of-way

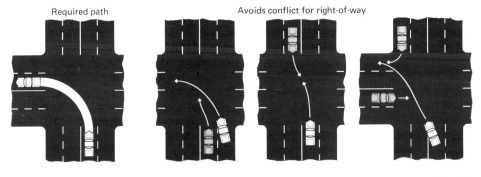

Fig. 6.3

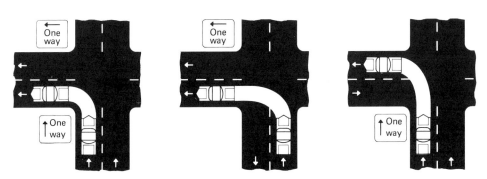

Fig. 6.4

Yielding to oncoming traffic when turning left   The driver of a vehicle entering an intersection with the intention of turning left should yield the right-of-way to any vehicle approaching from the opposite direction that is within the intersection or close enough to constitute an immediate hazard (Fig. 6.5). (This problem of coping with oncoming traffic in turning left is one of the crucial aspects of the maneuver and is discussed further in subsequent sections of this unit.)

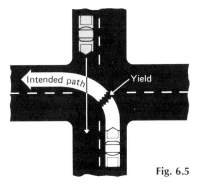

Fig. 6.5

Elements of Reduced-Risk Performance

Preparatory phase

Early entry into the approach lane   The approach lane for a right turn is the extreme right lane—excluding an occupied parking lane. The approach lane for a left turn is the left lane. An early entry into the approach lane reduces the possibility of having to make a "last minute" lane change (see discussion in Unit 7) just prior to reaching the intersection.

When it is necessary to change lanes to enter the approach lane, all the elements of performance in changing lanes will need to be carried out (see Unit 7).*

Communicating intentions   The signal for a turn should be given well in advance of reaching the intersection (at least 100 feet). The signal should provide advance information of the driver's intentions to other people in the vicinity—the earlier the signal is given, the more time these other people will have to adjust their behavior accordingly (Fig. 6.6).

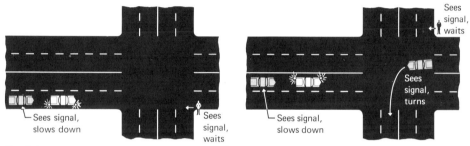

Fig. 6.6

On the other hand, the signal should not be given so far in advance that other drivers and pedestrians are led to believe that the driver intends to turn at an earlier point (perhaps into a side street or driveway) or that he has inadvertently forgotten to turn off his signal.

Since turning maneuvers involve slowing down (and sometimes stopping) in a traffic lane, it is occasionally advisable to provide drivers to the rear with an added warning of the intention to slow down, in the form of a hand signal. This added warning is particularly appropriate in those situations where the driver has reason to believe that other drivers may not expect him to slow down (Fig. 6.7).

Finally, it is important to recognize that the *presence* or *absence* of a signal will cause other drivers and pedestrians to behave accordingly. If there is a disparity between the driver's use of signals and the actual movement of his vehicle, it can cause considerable difficulty (Fig. 6.8).

Speed control   All turns are made at slow speeds, and in many situations the driver has to come to a complete stop before completing the turn. In order to be certain that the students enter the turn at an appropriately slow speed and are ready to stop when necessary during the turn, they should *begin gradual deceleration early and approach the intersection at a slow speed with their foot in the caution position.*

---

* Since systematic practice in changing lanes is covered in a subsequent unit (Unit 7), initial on-street practice of turning maneuvers should occur in settings that require few, if any, lane changes prior to turning (see "Instructional Plan").

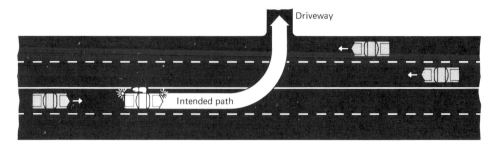

Fig. 6.7

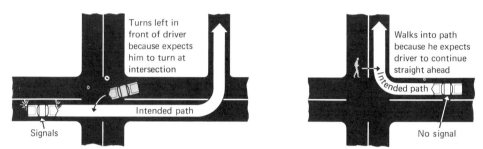

Fig. 6.8

Scanning and evaluating   The driver can gather important information about conditions existing at the intersection well before he reaches it. The beginning driver is frequently guilty of not attending to these conditions until he reaches the point at which he is to make the turn. It seems advisable, therefore, to encourage the student to begin *to size up conditions early* (at least one-half block from the intersection) *by scanning for obstacles and potential obstacles as he approaches the turn.* Also, during the approach to the intersection, the driver should glance briefly in the rearview mirror to check for following vehicles. If they are following too closely, or if there is reason to believe they do not expect him to slow down for a turn, a hand signal for a stop should be used.

The final evaluation before turning left   Perhaps the most critical distinction between right and left turns is that (under most circumstances) the left turn is made across an oncoming lane of traffic. This distinction makes the left turn a potentially more dangerous undertaking. In turning left the driver must determine that oncoming traffic is far enough away and/or traveling at a slow enough speed to permit him to complete his turn safely. Moreover, at the same time he makes this judgment, he must be sure that his turning path is clear enough to permit him to complete the turn. Once he initiates the turn, if an obstacle moves into his turning path (like a pedestrian in the crosswalk) and he is forced to stop in the middle of the turn, his vehicle is exposed to substantial danger from oncoming traffic (Fig. 6.9).

In effect, this means that the *decision* to initiate a left turn is quite crucial because once the decision is made and the turn is initiated, any interruption of the maneuver or any hesitancy on the part of the driver may prove hazardous.

The right turn does not involve the same kind of risk since it is not made across an oncoming lane of traffic. Once a driver initiates a right turn, a subsequent decision to interrupt the turn usually does not produce the same degree of risk.

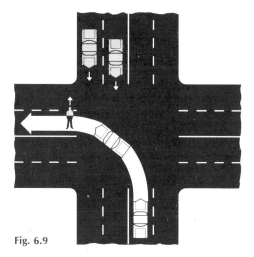

Fig. 6.9

This critical distinction between right and left turns suggests that in turning left the driver should give special attention to the *final evaluation* prior to initiating the turn. The decision to turn should be based on a simultaneous evaluation of the turning path and the oncoming traffic lanes. A serious obstacle in either place should result in postponing the initiation of the turn (Fig. 6.10). (In the instructional setting the teacher should encourage the student to be ready to stop prior to initiating the turn.)

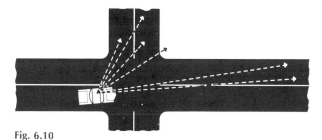

Fig. 6.10

Execution phase: when intersection and path are clear

Speed control and tracking   When scanning and evaluating procedures determine that the intersection and the turning path are clear of obstacles and potential obstacles, the driver should select a standard turning path and should guide the car over the turning path at an appropriately reduced speed. In a right turn, the standard turning path is from the center of the right lane to the center of the right lane on the intersecting street. In a left turn, the standard path is from the center of the left lane to the center of the left lane on the intersecting street, and the path passes just to the left of the center of the intersection (Fig. 6.11). To keep the car on path, the driver applies skills in "tracking on turning paths" learned earlier. In particular, he concentrates on applying hand-over-hand steering and recovery techniques.

Right turn standard path

Left turn standard path

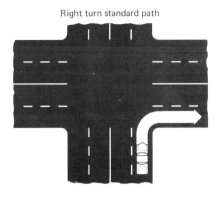 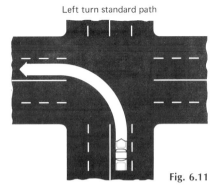

Fig. 6.11

Scanning and evaluating   Since obstacles and potential obstacles may arise at various stages during the turning maneuver, the driver should *continuously scan for obstacles and potential obstacles along the intended turning path*. The emphasis here is on *continuous*; at no point in the turning maneuver can the driver afford to relax his search for obstacles. In addition, it is most important that the scanning is done in relation to the *intended turning path*; that is, the driver must anticipate the future position of his vehicle on the turning path and conduct his scanning procedures accordingly. This has special significance for beginners who may have a tendency to limit their attention to events immediately in front of the vehicle (Fig. 6.12).

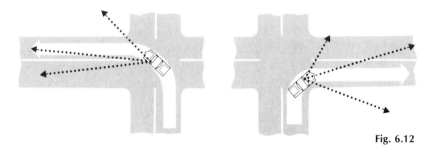

Fig. 6.12

Execution phase: when obstacles or potential obstacles are present

When any one or a combination of obstacles arises, the driver may find it necessary to select an alternative to the standard path and acceleration pattern in order to reduce the risk of being involved in an accident during the maneuver. Since the variety of situations the driver might encounter in turning is virtually limitless, the variety of possible alternatives is also limitless.* For purposes of illustration, a few typical situations and alternatives are described below.

Examples of reduced-risk alternatives in right turns   A driver might make a wide turn to increase the space cushion between his vehicle and a pedestrian (or other obstacle) on the right side of his turning path (Fig. 6.13).

---

* In the driver education car, whether or not the student correctly assesses the situation and selects the appropriate reduced-risk alternative will depend on the unique aspects of the situation and on the *teacher's judgment* with respect to which alternative was called for.

Previously intended path

Adjusted path

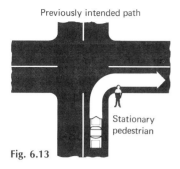
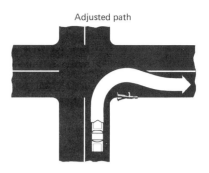

Stationary
pedestrian

Fig. 6.13

A driver might make a sharp turn to increase the space cushion between his vehicle and another vehicle or obstacle on the left side of his turning path (Fig. 6.14).

Previously intended path

Adjusted path

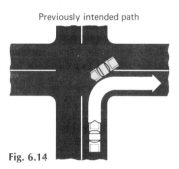

Fig. 6.14

A driver might reduce the speed of the turn (or possibly stop) to reduce the likelihood of colliding with a pedestrian or other obstacle (Fig. 6.15).

Previously intended speed

Adjusted (reduced) speed

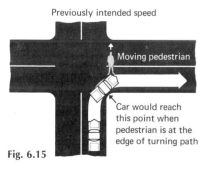
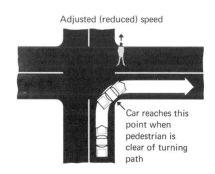

Moving pedestrian

Car would reach
this point when
pedestrian is at the
edge of turning path

Car reaches this
point when
pedestrian is
clear of turning
path

Fig. 6.15

A driver might accelerate at an early point in the turn to reduce the danger of being hit from the rear (Fig. 6.16).

A driver might choose to postpone the turn (by driving ahead for another block) in order to avoid the risks involved (Fig. 6.17).

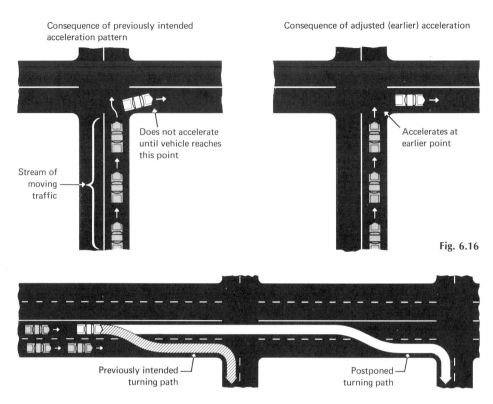

Consequence of previously intended
acceleration pattern

Consequence of adjusted (earlier) acceleration

Does not accelerate
until vehicle reaches
this point

Accelerates at
earlier point

Stream of
moving
traffic

Fig. 6.16

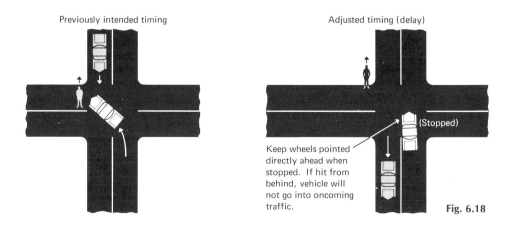

Previously intended
turning path

Postponed
turning path

Fig. 6.17

Examples of reduced-risk alternatives in left turns A driver might stop prior to initiating the turn and delay the performance of the maneuver to reduce the potential hazard posed by oncoming traffic and pedestrian traffic (Fig. 6.18).

Previously intended timing

Adjusted timing (delay)

(Stopped)

Keep wheels pointed
directly ahead when
stopped. If hit from
behind, vehicle will
not go into oncoming
traffic.

Fig. 6.18

A driver might turn into the left-most portion of the new lane to increase the space cushion between his vehicle and another vehicle making a right turn (Fig. 6.19).

Previously intended path

Adjusted path

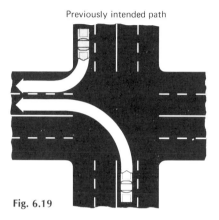
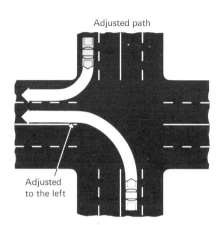

Adjusted
to the left

Fig. 6.19

A driver might accelerate at an earlier point in the turn to reduce the risk of a collision from the rear. Of course, this earlier acceleration would be performed only after a careful check of oncoming traffic and of obstacles in the turning path (Fig. 6.20).

Consequence of previously intended
acceleration pattern

Consequence of adjusted (earlier) acceleration

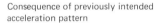
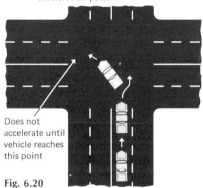
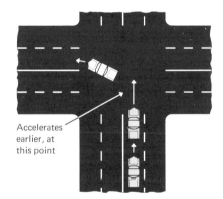

Does not
accelerate until
vehicle reaches
this point

Accelerates
earlier, at
this point

Fig. 6.20

A driver might adjust his turning path to increase the space cushion between his vehicle and a vehicle making a left turn from the opposite direction (Fig. 6.21).

Of course, alternatives should be selected with the objective of reducing the *total* risk involved. A driver should not select an alternative that reduces one risk only to create another, more serious, risk in the process. For example, accelerating at an earlier point in the turn to reduce the possibility of being hit from the rear may not be advisable if there are pedestrians or other cars ahead on the intended turning path. In this sense, reduced-risk turns should always involve the evaluation of competing risks and the selection of the safest alternative.

Previously intended path

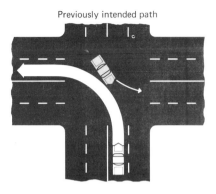

Adjusted path

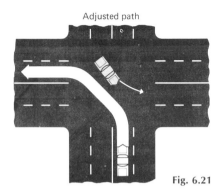

Fig. 6.21

Common Errors in Student Performance

Recurrence of earlier problems   Any one of the several problems connected with accurate tracking on a turning path (Unit 3, Phase 4) may recur during on-street practice of turning maneuvers. In particular, the problems of excessive speed, rigid use of hand-over-hand technique, and late recovery may reappear (see descriptions in Unit 3, Phase 4). Even those students who had gained a reasonable amount of skill in tracking on turning paths in the off-street area may commit some basic tracking errors during their initial practice of on-street turns. Apparently, the more complex nature of the on-street environment, which calls for continuous scanning and assessment, makes it more difficult for the student to concentrate on and apply the tracking skills learned earlier.

Limited scanning   Some beginning drivers encounter difficulty in scanning ahead along a turning path. Instead, they tend to scan directly in front of the vehicle and are aware only of obstacles found there. Consequently, in turning right or left, it is not uncommon for such drivers to move two-thirds of the way through a turn before recognizing the presence of an obstacle five or ten feet ahead on the turning path. The teacher can help to counteract this limited scanning by emphasizing the need to scan along the *intended turning path* and by providing some well-timed verbal cues that encourage students to do so (Fig. 6.22).

Avoid this

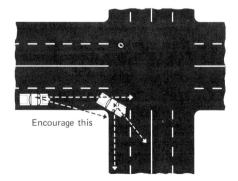

Encourage this

Fig. 6.22

Exposure to oncoming traffic—turning left   The left turn, when made across the path of oncoming traffic, can be one of the most dangerous maneuvers performed in the driver education car. The reason for the danger lies in the fact that a poorly timed decision to turn on the part of the student may place the car in a hazardous position before the teacher has an opportunity to assume control. For example, a student driver might have the vehicle in a stationary position waiting for a gap in oncoming traffic before he initiates the turn. He may start to turn, moving the vehicle only a few feet, before realizing that the gap in oncoming traffic is not sufficient to permit a safe turn (see Fig. 6.23). The serious problem at this point is that the vehicle is *exposed* to oncoming traffic, and there is little the teacher can do about it. Even if she uses the dual-control brake, the two or three feet of movement have already placed the driver education vehicle in the path of oncoming traffic.

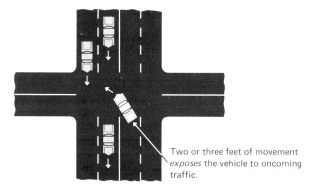

Two or three feet of movement *exposes* the vehicle to oncoming traffic.

Fig. 6.23

It is up to the teacher to prevent such exposure by not permitting the turn to be *initiated* unless the path is clear. In situations where oncoming traffic is present, the teacher should be ready to instantly use the dual-control brake at the moment a poorly timed turn is initiated. Or she might have the student announce his intention to turn by saying "clear" before actually initiating the turn. This will provide the teacher with enough time to assume control in the case of an incorrect decision by the student.

Judging the intended turning path to the left   Under most circumstances, the appropriate path for a left turn is from left lane to left lane and passes just to the left of the center point of the intersection. Many beginning drivers have difficulty tracking along this path—probably because there are no reference points out in the center of the intersection that can be used to aid the driver in visualizing the path. The consequence of this difficulty is usually an early or a late left turn. Both of these errors constitute hazards for other drivers (Fig. 6.24).

The teacher should be alert to such tracking errors, and to a certain extent should expect them to occur during the early stages of learning. One of the best ways to reduce this type of error is to simply provide immediate feedback for the student by indicating that the turn was "early" or "late," and then having the student repeat the maneuver while concentrating on making the appropriate correction.

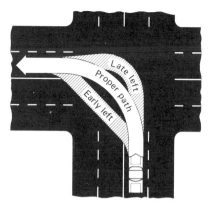

Fig. 6.24

Instructional Plan

Classroom   Considerable attention should be devoted to a discussion of the special problems connected with making reduced-risk right and left turns, prior to on-street performance. Students should be especially cognizant of the more common obstacles and potential obstacles to turning maneuvers so that they are in a position to adopt appropriate scanning and evaluation procedures. (See "Classroom Guide" in this unit for an outline of the content.)

Selection of driving area   The driving area should provide the opportunity for making a series of successive right turns and/or left turns. A "square block" provides this opportunity; a driver may perform four successive right or left turns in driving around the block. During the initial stages of the lesson an area relatively free of obstacles and potential obstacles is desirable; that is, an area relatively free of pedestrian and vehicular traffic, blind corners, steep grades, signs and signals, and so on. Also, since the students have yet to systematically practice changing lanes (Unit 7), it is desirable to conduct practice on two-lane streets (one lane in each direction) so that students don't have to change lanes in their approach to turns. As the student progresses in his capacity to perform turns, he should be allowed to practice in areas that contain progressively more obstacles. In particular, when the student is ready to concentrate on scanning and evaluation procedures (see "In-Car Guide" for this unit, Phase 3), the driving area should be selected to challenge his capacity for safe performance without exposing him to unreasonable risks.

In-car demonstration and explanation   A brief demonstration of right and left turns by the teacher or a capable student should be helpful. The demonstration should emphasize evaluation of obstacles and potential obstacles and the risk-reducing elements of performance. However, be careful to avoid the rather common tendency to *overdemonstrate* turning maneuvers. Instead, analyze the right turn and the left turn, identify the two, three, or four most critical elements of performance for beginners in each maneuver, and emphasize these elements of performance in the demonstration.

Student practice   Student practice is organized into three phases: successive right turns, successive left turns, and right and left turns (at higher-risk locations). In Phase 1, the student performs a continuous series of right turns by driving around a block. This continuous series permits the student to concentrate on the unique elements of performing right turns, and to correct errors immediately after they are committed. (For example, a student who makes a wide right turn at one corner has an immediate opportunity to correct the error at the next corner.) For the same reasons, Phase 2 allows the student to perform a continuous series of left turns. This concentrated practice in left turns should provide the teacher with an opportunity to emphasize the distinctive features of the left turn—particularly the problem of oncoming traffic. Phase 1 precedes Phase 2 because of the normally greater demands placed on drivers in performing left turns.

Since Phase 1 and Phase 2 constitute the student's initial (systematic) exposure to on-street turning maneuvers, they should take place in a relatively traffic-free environment that permits the student to gain some competence without being exposed to unreasonable risk.

In Phase 3, the students perform several right- and left-turn maneuvers on busy streets and intersections that expose them to the variety of complex situations they are likely to encounter as licensed drivers. Of course, students should not be permitted to progress to Phase 3 until they have achieved considerable competence in all elements of reduced-risk performance.

The provision for an alternating pattern of right and left turns is likely to necessitate some lane changes and thus provides a convenient opportunity to introduce changing lanes (Unit 7).

Analysis of performance   Periodically during practice, the teacher might help the student to analyze his own performance. After the student completes a turn (or series of turns) in which several obstacles were present, the teacher might ask: "What (potential) obstacles did you see?" and "What adjustments did you make to reduce the risk?" The student's response should be indicative of his level of awareness of obstacles and potential obstacles. When appropriate, the teacher should point out elements in the situation that were overlooked by the student.

CLASSROOM GUIDE FOR UNIT 6
Reduced-Risk Turns

Topics	Instructional Plan
1. The reduced-risk concept: a) Choice of alternatives b) Risks in various situations c) Choosing reduced-risk alternatives d) Skills involved	1. Present overall concept. 2. Use illustrations from student's on-street experiences.
2. Related concepts and information: a) Common risks in turning b) Legal requirements: Lanes used in right turns Lanes used in left turns Signaling for turns Yielding to oncoming traffic when turning left	1. Discuss critical risks, using illustrations 2. Have students review appropriate state traffic laws. 3. Discuss reasons for each regulation.
3. Reduced-risk concept applied to turning maneuvers: a) Actions that reduce risk b) Actions that increase risk	1. Conduct general discussion of alternatives available to driver.
4. Elements of reduced-risk performance: a) Early entry into approach lane b) Communicating intentions c) Speed control and tracking d) Scanning and evaluating e) Final evaluation before turning left f) Selecting reduced-risk alternatives	1. Review each element of performance. 2. Discuss its relation to reducing risk. 3. Provide specific illustrations.
5. In-car procedures: a) Driving routes b) Organization of practice phases c) Commentary driving and analysis of performance	1. Briefly discuss procedures to be used during in-car lesson.

PREPARATORY READING FOR STUDENTS

1. *Learning to Drive: Skills, Concepts, and Strategies.* Chapter 11, "Right and Left Turns."

   —or appropriate sections of another high-school text.

2. *State Drivers Manual.* Review all rules of the road related to turning maneuvers.

3. *Accident Facts.* Sections dealing with turning maneuvers and accidents, and with directional analyses of intersection accidents.

IN-CAR GUIDE FOR UNIT 6
Reduced-Risk Turns
DEMONSTRATION AND EXPLANATION

Provide brief demonstration of right and left turn.

Emphasize reduced-risk elements of performance (see description of elements below).

Caution: select only most important elements for emphasis and explanation.

GUIDING STUDENT PRACTICE

Teacher	Student
Phase 1: Successive Right Turns	

Teacher	Student
Select relatively low-risk route (few obstacles).	Performs several successive right turns concentrates on reduced-risk elements of performance
Emphasize scanning and evaluation procedures.	
Instructional procedure:	*Preparatory phase:*
1. Use verbal cues to guide performance during initial trials (then reduce to minimum).	1. Enters approach lane early and reduces speed gradually
2. Have student correct errors on subsequent turns.	2. Signals (at least 100 feet before turn)
3. At appropriate times have student stop vehicle and analyze his assessment of previous situations.	3. Begins gradual deceleration (foot in caution position)
	4. Begins scanning and evaluation early. Looks for:
	Obstacles in turning path
	Potential obstacles approaching turning path
	Traffic signs and signals
	Following vehicles
	Execution phase:
	When intersection and path are clear:
	5. Uses tracking and speed control skills (including hand-over-hand steering and recovery) to control car on standard right-turn path
	6. Continuously scans ahead (in relation to turning path)
	When obstacles or potential obstacles are present:
	7. Chooses other reduced-risk alternative—
	Adjusts speed (or stops)
	Adjusts path
	Other

IN-CAR GUIDE FOR UNIT 6 (*cont.*)

Teacher	Student

Phase 2: Successive Left Turns

Select relatively low-risk route (few obstacles).

Emphasize:

1. Scanning and evaluating
2. Final evaluation prior to initiating turn
3. Being ready to stop and yield to oncoming traffic

Instructional procedure:

1. Use verbal cues to guide performance during initial trials.
2. Have student correct errors on subsequent turns.
3. At appropriate times have student stop vehicle and analyze his assessment of previous situations.

Watch for:

1. Improper initiation of turn that exposes vehicle to oncoming traffic (have student announce "clear" before initiating turn)
2. Difficulty in judging intended turning path

Performs several successive left turns, concentrates on reduced-risk elements of performance

Preparatory phase:

1. Enters approach lane early and reduces speed gradually
2. Signals (at least 100 feet before turns)
3. Begins gradual deceleration (foot in caution position)
4. Concentrates on final evaluation before turning
   Scans for oncoming traffic and clear turning path
   Begins turn only when path is clear and will remain clear
   Comments "clear"

Execution phase:

When intersection and path are clear:

5. Uses tracking and speed control skills (including hand-over-hand steering and recovery) to control car on standard left-turn path
6. Continuously scans ahead (in relation to turning path)

When obstacles or potential obstacles are present:

7. Chooses other reduced-risk alternative—

   Adjusts speed (or stops)
   Adjusts path
   Other

Phase 3: Right and Left Turns

Select relatively higher-risk locations (sufficient obstacles to challenge student's ability to perform safely).

Emphasize:

1. Scanning and evaluating
2. Selecting reduced-risk alternatives

Introduce lane changes (Unit 7) at appropriate time and integrate with practice of turns.

Performs several right and left turns, concentrating on reduced-risk elements of performance (see items above)

REDUCED-RISK LANE CHANGES

INTRODUCTION

This unit deals with the maneuver of changing lanes [3]. It emphasizes reduced-risk elements of performance, including (1) scanning and evaluating, (2) communicating intentions, (3) speed control and tracking, and (4) selecting the reduced-risk alternative. As a result of earlier practice, the student should have little difficulty with signaling and accurately guiding the vehicle on a change-of-lane path. On the other hand, the scanning and evaluation procedures and the selection of alternatives are new and require relatively advanced levels of performance. Instruction should focus on these more advanced elements of performance.

There are several reasons for emphasizing the change-of-lane maneuver at this early point in the on-street experience of the beginning driver. In the normal on-street lesson the beginning driver starts from a parallel position at the curb, pulls out into the traffic lanes, and then returns to the curb position, when it is time to exchange positions and allow the next student to drive. This procedure of pulling away from and then back to the curb is essentially a lane-change maneuver. In addition, the beginning driver may find a variety of obstacles in her path that she must go around; to go around is also to change lanes. Another reason for covering the change-of-lane maneuver at this point is that it is an important prerequisite to the performance of turning maneuvers on multiple-lane streets.

In this unit the objectives for students are:

1. *To identify the common risks involved in changing lanes and the actions required to reduce those risks*

2. *To describe how the rules of the road and the expectations of other drivers should influence the performance of a lane change*

3. *To execute reduced-risk lane changes consistently (to the left and to the right) in a broad variety of driving situations*

4. *To postpone the execution of lane changes in those situations where a lane change would increase the risk of an accident*

185

Related Concepts and Information

Prior to practicing on-street lane changes, students should be exposed to the following concepts, all of which should have a direct bearing on the performance of the maneuvers. (A portion of a classroom lesson might be devoted to these concepts.)

Responsibility for driving within a lane   Vehicles are required to be driven "as nearly as practicable" within a single lane and should not be moved from the lane until the driver has first determined that the "movement can be made with safety" (B 139). Therefore, the driver who intends to change lanes is responsible for first determining whether the change can be made safely, and she should *not* make the change when conditions are not safe.

Predicting the actions of other drivers   It is the normal expectation of most drivers that other vehicles will continue to occupy the lanes in which they are traveling. A change of lanes may very well come as an unexpected event to other drivers in the vicinity of the vehicle that is making the lane change. Therefore the driver making the lane change should predict that nearby drivers will not expect or allow for her change-of-lane maneuver (Fig. 7.1).

Predict others will not change speed or direction

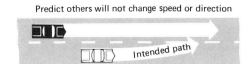

Fig. 7.1

Avoiding unnecessary lane changes   Changing lanes is a necessary part of driving. Very often drivers simply have to change lanes to get where they want to go. Nevertheless, because lane changes are inherently dangerous maneuvers, drivers who make many unnecessary lane changes increase their risk of an accident. Most unnecessary lane changes are made because drivers are trying to get ahead of other vehicles; they switch from one lane to another and back again in search of the quickest lane. The time they save is usually not worth the risks involved. As a general rule, risk can be reduced by using "established path driving" as much as possible and avoiding unnecessary lane changes.

Maintaining awareness to the front   Performing a moving lane change can be a dangerous task for any driver—but especially for the beginner. While the driver is using the mirrors to check conditions to the rear and side, her vehicle is *moving forward*. This means that if an obstacle moves into the path in front at a moment when the driver is checking conditions to the rear, the driver may not see it in time to react. In fact, beginning drivers, in their enthusiasm to check conditions to the rear thoroughly, often are guilty of prolonged inattention to the road ahead. It seems wise for all beginning drivers to be keenly aware of this danger, and to use scanning procedures that enable them to maintain a relatively constant awareness of the road ahead (Fig. 7.2).

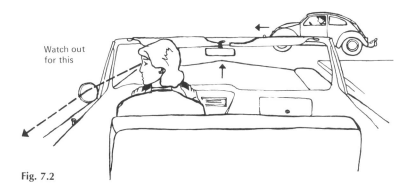

Watch out
for this

Fig. 7.2

Elements of Reduced-Risk Performance

Preparatory phase

Preparing in advance   In order to perform a safe lane change, a thorough check of traffic conditions to the rear, side rear, and side must be made first. This thorough check takes time. In addition, occasionally there are obstacles in the path of the intended lane change that force the driver to delay the start of the maneuver. These factors suggest that it is usually advisable to *begin to prepare for the lane change well in advance* of the point at which it has to be made. For example, if the driver must get into the left lane to make a left turn at an intersection, it is advisable to start to prepare for the lane change (by scanning to the rear and side, and signaling) well before reaching the intersection. In this way the driver will have ample time to evaluate conditions (and perhaps to allow another vehicle to pass) before reaching the intersection. When the preparation does not occur well in advance, the driver is often faced with having to make a last-minute lane change that does not allow time for a proper check of conditions, and that may necessitate cutting in front of another driver.

Scanning and evaluating   These procedures include the visual scanning techniques and evaluation process employed to determine whether existing conditions will permit a safe change of lanes. The suggested sequence of steps* involved in the scanning and evaluating procedures for changing lanes to the *left* are shown in Fig. 7.3. The head turn,† step 5, is optional.

---

* The steps for scanning and evaluating have been listed in logical sequence. In any given driving situation, however, it may be necessary to vary the sequence to obtain the best view of the critical area. The sequence itself would seem to be less important than the end product; that is, the determination that the critical area is clear.

† The head turn should be viewed as an optional step to be used when the driver is not certain (as a result of checking in the mirrors) that the left side is clear of obstacles. Because the head turn involves relatively prolonged inattention to the road ahead, it should not be used in situations where this inattention might substantially increase the risk.

1. Get set to scan for the obstacles and potential obstacles in the *critical area*. (The *critical area* in this case refers to the combined areas—front, front left, side left, and rear left.) In other words, the intent of the driver before she actually starts to scan is to check this critical area to see that it is free of obstacles and potential obstacles.

2. Scan *well ahead* to the front and front left of the vehicle to see that the current path and the intended change in path are clear of obstacles and potential obstacles (that is, driver checks for "clear path"—see Unit 5).

3. Glance in the rearview mirror to check for other vehicles directly behind vehicle. (Recheck in front.)

4. Glance in the sideview mirror to check for other vehicles to the left rear of vehicle. (Recheck in front.)

5. *Optional.* Turn head to the left (briefly) to check for other vehicles on the left side of the vehicle (blind spot) and to recheck for other vehicles to the left rear of the car. (In cases where the car is moving, the head turn is performed as quickly as possible so that the driver is immediately able to return her attention to the road ahead.) (Return to front scanning.)

6. Decide whether the critical area is *clear enough* of obstacles and potential obstacles to permit a safe change in lanes. (The actual decision to change lanes should be based on a reasonable degree of *certainty* that the critical area is clear of obstacles and potential obstacles. Certainty is crucial in view of the speed with which each scanning procedure must be performed and the consequent likelihood of error.)

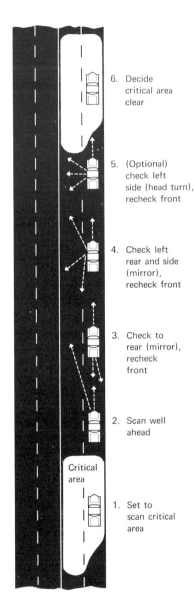

6. Decide critical area clear

5. (Optional) check left side (head turn), recheck front

4. Check left rear and side (mirror), recheck front

3. Check to rear (mirror), recheck front

2. Scan well ahead

1. Set to scan critical area

Fig. 7.3

Intermediate steps: Note that between steps 3, 4, and 5, the driver rechecks for obstacles and potential obstacles in front. In effect, there should be an almost continuous awareness of what is happening in front.

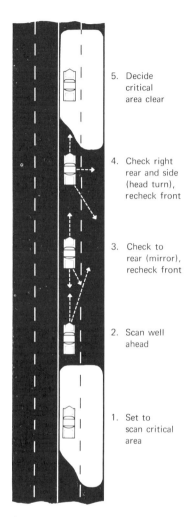

5. Decide
   critical
   area clear

4. Check right
   rear and side
   (head turn),
   recheck front

3. Check to
   rear (mirror),
   recheck front

2. Scan well
   ahead

1. Set to
   scan critical
   area

The steps involved in changing lanes to the *right* are quite similar to those employed in changing to the left. The major difference is that the head turn to the right becomes a mandatory part of the procedure; especially in vehicles which are not equipped with right side-view mirrors. In changing lanes to the *right*, the steps involved are shown in Fig. 7.4.

1. Get set to scan for obstacles and potential obstacles in the *critical area*. (The critical area in this case refers to the combined areas—front, front right, side right, and rear right.)

2. Scan *well ahead* to the front and the front right of the vehicle to see that the current path and the intended change in path are clear of obstacles and potential obstacles.

3. Glance in the rearview mirror to check for other vehicles directly to the rear and as far to the right rear as possible. (Recheck in front.)

4. Turn the head to the right to check for other vehicles on the right side and the right rear (brief turn).

5. Decide whether the critical area is *clear enough* of obstacles and potential obstacles to permit a safe change of lanes. (The actual decision to change lanes should be based on a reasonable degree of certainty that the critical area is clear.)

Fig. 7.4

Intermediate steps: Note that between steps 3 and 4, the driver will need to recheck for obstacles and potential obstacles in front.

The scanning procedures employed to check conditions to the rear and sides require the driver to look for other vehicles (see steps 3, 4, and 5 under the change to the left, and steps 3 and 4 under the change to the right), and the driver should not be concerned with most other events (pedestrians, roadway elements, and so forth). The reason for this type of scanning is that the only significant events (for the driver) in these sectors of the driving environment are the presence or absence of, and the movements of, other vehicles. Once the driver knows that she is looking for other vehicles, the task of checking to the rear and side is simplified. In this sense it is very different from forward scanning, which requires the driver to look for and recognize a great variety of obstacles and potential obstacles.

In addition, the first step in the scanning procedure suggests that the driver "scan *well ahead* to the front and to the front left (or right) . . . ." *Well ahead* is emphasized to point out the need for an extra amount of clearance to the front before the driver attempts to scan to the side and rear. Scanning to the rear and side (even though it is accomplished by brief glances) decreases the driver's capacity to see and evaluate events in front at the same time. Therefore, before undertaking rear and side scanning, the driver should assure herself that the road ahead is extra clear.

Execution phase: when critical area is clear

Communicating intentions   To communicate the intention to change lanes, a left-turn signal is given before moving from a right to a left lane, and a right-turn signal is given before moving from a left to a right lane. In most cases the signal will be given by using the mechanical directional signal. However, in situations where other drivers are not in a favorable position to see the mechanical signal, a hand signal may be necessary. The signal is given *well in advance* of the actual change of lanes. (*Well in advance* implies that there should be a sufficiently long interval between the initiation of the signal and the actual change in direction to enable other drivers to recognize the intention and to make adjustments in their own actions.) In addition, it is probably wise for beginning drivers to get into the habit of giving a lane-change signal irrespective of traffic conditions; in other words, the signal should be given even when no other vehicles are in the vicinity.

Speed control and tracking   The steering adjustments necessary for changing lanes are relatively simple. The steering wheel is turned gradually in the direction of the lane change and is followed by a gradual recovery. Normally, the adjustments are made without changing the point at which the hands contact the wheel. The total task of tracking while changing lanes amounts to nothing more than a large steering correction (see Unit 3, Phase 3) and should be well within the capabilities of the student at this stage of instruction.

Under most circumstances the change of lanes should involve a *gradual* adjustment in direction. A gradual adjustment should serve as insurance against other drivers who have failed to recognize the signal, and against the possibility that the driver has failed to recognize an obstacle in the adjacent lane into which she is moving. For example, when a driver is changing lanes to the left and has failed to recognize another vehicle in the left lane opposite her left rear fender (blind spot), a gradual change might permit the other driver to blow her horn or brake in time to avoid an accident; a quick change might not permit enough time for such evasive actions (Fig. 7.5).

Fig. 7.5

Execution phase: when obstacles are present

If, during the process of scanning and evaluating conditions, the driver detects the presence of obstacles, any one of several alternatives should be employed depending on the exact nature of the prevailing conditions. Some illustrations of typical driving conditions and the selection of reduced-risk alternatives are listed below.

1. A vehicle moving at a faster speed than the driver's might be passing on the left. In such cases the driver should simply maintain her speed and postpone the lane change until the vehicle has passed—at which time she will have to repeat the scanning and evaluation procedures (Fig. 7.6).

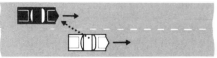

Sees overtaking vehicle, delays initiation of lane change

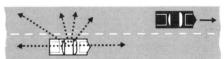

After vehicle passes, renews scanning and assessment procedures and changes lane

Fig. 7.6

2. Another vehicle in the same position as the one above (left rear) might be traveling at the same speed as the driver's vehicle, in which case it is usually advisable to slow down (provided a third vehicle is not immediately behind the driver's vehicle) and allow the vehicle to pass before initiating a lane change (Fig. 7.7).

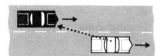

Sees vehicle to the rear (traveling at same speed)

Slows down (gradually)

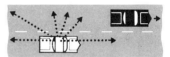

After vehicle passes, renews scanning and assessment procedures

Fig. 7.7

3. In a similar situation another vehicle might be to the left rear of the driver's vehicle, traveling at the same speed, but the situation might be complicated by the presence of other vehicles immediately behind the driver's vehicle—in which case a reduction in speed might cause a rear-end collision. In such a situation, the driver might postpone the lane change indefinitely (Fig. 7.8).

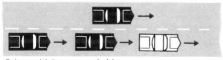

Other vehicles rear and side

Postpone lane change

Fig. 7.8

4. In the event that it might be necessary to change lanes (perhaps the driver was about to make a left turn at the next intersection), the safest alternative might be for the driver to increase her speed and initiate the lane change when she is a sufficiently safe distance from the other vehicles. Of course, the increase in speed should not exceed the speed limit or a safe speed for conditions, nor should it be done unless conditions in front are clear of obstacles (Fig. 7.9).

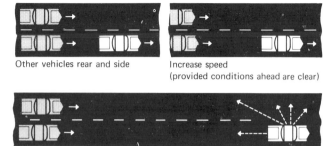

Other vehicles rear and side

Increase speed
(provided conditions ahead are clear)

Initiate lane change when distance is safe

Fig. 7.9

There are literally countless other situations and alternatives that might be examined, some of which are far more complex than the ones described above. Perhaps the most important point to be made about a lane change is that, under most circumstances, it can be performed at any one of a number of points along the roadway as opposed to (for example) a turn from one street onto another, which must occur at a relatively specific point on the roadway. Therefore the driver frequently has *considerable latitude in choosing the point* at which she will perform the lane change. Her choice of location for performing the maneuver should be made with due regard for the risks involved at that point.

Common Errors in Student Performance

Prolonged scanning to the rear and side   One of the major problems that arises during the performance of moving lane changes is the student's tendency to perform *prolonged* precautionary checks to the side and rear. Frequently, the result is that the car veers from its established path while the student is attending to the precautionary checks, or the student may fail to perceive obstacles in front (traffic lights, other cars, and so on). This problem may be avoided if the teacher stresses the necessity for making *brief* checks (brief glances in the mirror and a brief head turn). If the brief glance does not enable the student to determine whether conditions are clear enough to permit a change of lane, then another brief glance is called for. In between glances the driver's attention should return to the road ahead. In spite of this advance warning, however, the student may persist in committing steering errors while scanning to the side and rear. In such cases the teacher should be ready to manually assist with steering control at appropriate moments or to warn the student about events in the forward sector.

Instructional Plan

Classroom   Prior to in-car practice, a classroom period should be devoted to a thorough discussion and analysis of changing lanes. Particular attention should be given to related concepts, and to the *reasons* underlying elements of reduced-risk performance.

Selection of driving area   The initial portion of this lesson is best conducted on a wide street with little or no traffic. The choice of a relatively traffic-free environment is most important since the student is inexperienced and will need to devote her full attention to a difficult maneuver. Once the student has gained some proficiency in the maneuver, it might be advisable to allow her to drive in areas with a moderate traffic flow.

If possible, the street should have multiple lanes to allow for movement to the left and back to the right traffic lane. Since it may be difficult to find a traffic-free, multiple-lane street, the teacher may need to use a narrower street and simulate lane changes by having the student move from the left side to the right side of a single wide traffic lane.

In-car demonstration and explanation   Provided the teacher has given ample attention to changing lanes during a prior classroom session, only a *very brief* demonstration and explanation is called for before the student practices the maneuver. During the demonstration the teacher might use the form of commentary driving designed for this unit.

Student practice   Several practice trials should be planned. However, since the maneuver can be dangerous and complex, it probably is not wise to plan for more than one or two lane changes per block. The teacher should avoid placing the student in a situation where she is forced to change lanes under difficult traffic conditions, or where the constant changing of lanes will constitute an obstruction for other drivers. In addition, it is advisable to allow the student some latitude in choosing where to change lanes instead of directing her to change lanes at a given moment. (For example, the teacher might direct the student to "change lanes to the left at some point in the block ahead.") After initial practice trials on selected streets, subsequent practice in changing lanes can easily be combined with further practice in right and left turns (see Unit 6, Phase 3).

Use of commentary driving   A special (and very limited) form of commentary driving is suggested for use in connection with practicing lane changes. The commentary is limited to prevent it from interfering with performance. The commentary consists of (1) saying "check critical area" before beginning the scanning and evaluation procedures, (2) saying "clear" when the driver is certain that conditions are clear enough to permit a safe change of lanes, and (3) when appropriate, using a one-word cue to identify obstacles to the lane change. Two examples of a driver's actions and commentary in changing lanes appear in Figs. 7.10 and 7.11.

Note that the commentary is quite restricted in that the driver comments only once at the beginning and once at the end of the scanning procedure. Each of these comments, however, should serve a valuable purpose. The first comment, "check critical area," is a device for reinforcing the student's intent to scan the appropriate areas. It also serves to inform the teacher that the student remembers that she is supposed to scan the critical area. Any subsequent student comment that identifies an obstacle provides valuable information for the teacher with respect to what the student sees. (For example, if the student checks her mirrors and fails to see another car in the left-rear blind spot, her failure to comment will inform the teacher that the student has not seen it. The teacher would therefore be in a better position to act appropriately.) Finally, the last comment, "clear," is a device for emphasizing the need to be reasonably certain that the critical area is clear. It also provides the teacher with the information that the student has made her decision and is about to turn the steering wheel. This can be an important warning for the teacher, especially when the student has made an erroneous judgment about clearance—for example, in the event that the path is not clear, it may provide the teacher with enough time to veto the lane change by simply saying "No!"

NO OBSTACLES

Actions	Commentary	
1. Signal		
2. Continue driving	"Check critical area"	
3. Scan ahead		
4. Scan rear (use mirror)		
5. Scan left rear (use mirror)		
6. Scan side (turn head if necessary)		
7. Total evaluation	"Clear"	
8. Make steering adjustments		

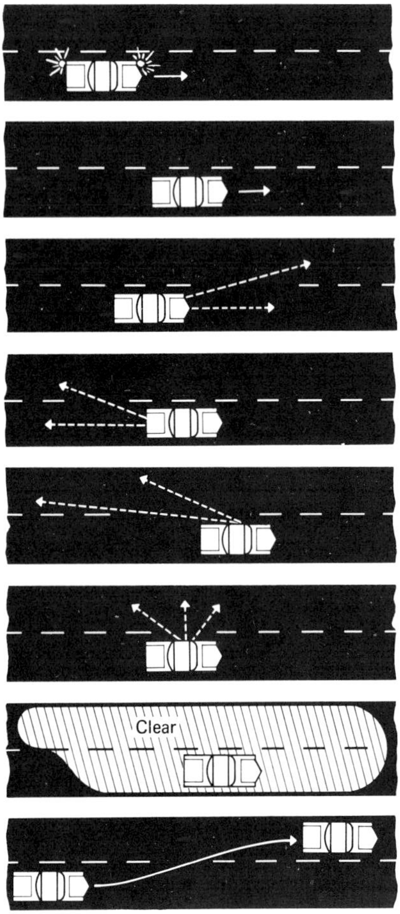

Fig. 7.10

AN OBSTACLE

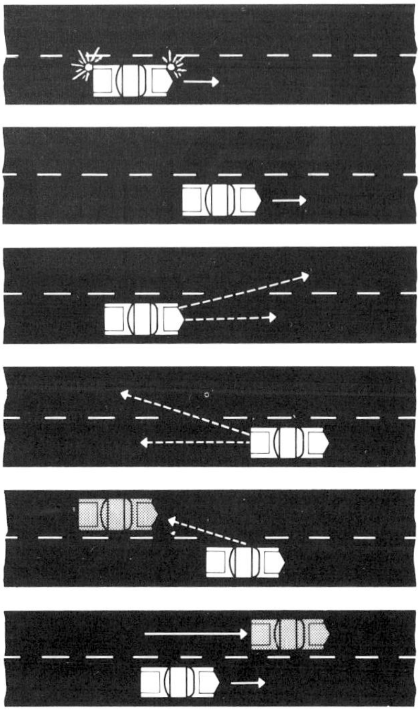

Actions	Commentary
1. Signal	
2. Continue driving	"Check critical area"
3. Scan ahead	
4. Scan rear (use mirror)	
5. Scan left rear (use mirror)	"Car"
6. Interrupt process and make necessary adjustments	

Fig. 7.11

CLASSROOM GUIDE FOR UNIT 7
Reduced-Risk Lane Changes

Topics	Instructional Plan
1. The variety of driving situations that require a lane change, the hazards involved, and related concepts: a) Right-of-way rules b) Normal expectations of other drivers c) Preparing for lane change in advance d) Checking to rear while driving forward	1. Discuss and give specific illustrations. 2. Point out the consequent need for careful execution of actions.
2. Reduced-risk concept applied to changing lanes: a) Actions that reduce risk b) Actions that increase risk	1. Conduct general discussion of alternatives available to driver.
3. Elements of reduced-risk performance: a) Communicating intentions b) Scanning and evaluation procedures c) Selecting reduced-risk alternative d) Accurate guidance on selected path	1. Describe each element of performance. 2. Discuss reasons for each element. 3. Discuss specific illustrations.
4. Commentary driving used in changing lanes: a) "Check critical area" b) "Clear" c) Name obstacle	1. Briefly discuss technique.
5. Driving route to be used for in-car practice.	1. Briefly discuss the route and procedures to be followed.

PREPARATORY READING FOR STUDENTS

1. *Learning to Drive: Skills, Concepts, and Strategies.* Chapter 9, "Reduced-Risk Performance"; and Chapter 10, "Changing Lanes."

   —or appropriate sections of another high-school text.

2. *State Driver's Manual.* Review rules of the road that apply to lane changes.

RELATED SIMULATOR LESSONS

1. Aetna Drivotrainer System: "Blending in Traffic," "Separating and Compromising Risk."

IN-CAR GUIDE FOR UNIT 7
Reduced-Risk Lane Changes

DEMONSTRATION AND EXPLANATION

Demonstrate lane change:

1. Changing lane: right lane to left lane
2. Changing lane: left lane to right lane

Include commentary driving.

Use cues:

"Check critical area"

"Clear"

Emphasize:

1. Critical area
2. Scanning well ahead
3. Continuous rechecking of front
4. Reasonable certainty before changing lanes
5. Selecting reduced-risk alternative

GUIDING STUDENT PRACTICE

Teacher	Student
Have students perform periodic lane changes—perhaps one per block.	Performs several lane changes to left and right, concentrating on reduced-risk elements of performance.
Emphasize:	Changes lanes, right to left:
1. Communicating intentions	*Preparatory phase:*
2. Scanning and evaluating	1. Begins preparation early Comments: "Check critical area"

3. Selecting reduced-risk alternatives (when necessary)	2. Scans and evaluates *critical area:*
	   a) Gets set to scan critical area
	   b) Scans well ahead (front and front left)
	   c) Glances in rearview mirror
	      (Rechecks in front)
	   d) Glances in sideview mirror
	      (Rechecks in front)
	   e) Turns head; checks blind spot
	      (Returns to front scanning)
	   f) Decides whether critical area is *clear enough*
	   g) Comments: "clear" or names obstacle

Watch for:	
1. Excessively long checks to side and rear	
2. Veering	
When appropriate, comment on student's selection of alternative. Indicate when a safer (less risky) alternative existed.	*Execution phase:* When critical area is clear: 3. Signals 4. Gradually moves car into new lane When obstacles or potential obstacles are present: 5. Chooses other reduced-risk alternative for situation

IN-CAR GUIDE FOR UNIT 7 *(cont.)*

Teacher	Student
	Changes lanes, left to right

Preparatory phase:

1. Begins preparation early
   Comments: "check critical area"

2. Scans and evaluates *critical area:*

   a) Gets set to scan critical area
   b) Scans well ahead (front and front right)
   c) Glances in rearview mirror
      (Rechecks front)
   d) Turns head; checks blind spot on right side
      and right rear
      (Returns to front scanning)
   e) Decides whether critical area is *clear enough*
   f) Comments: "clear" or names obstacle

Execution phase:

If critical area is clear:

3. Signals

4. Gradually moves car into new lane

If obstacles or potential obstacles are present:

5. Chooses reduced-risk alternative for situation

When appropriate, integrate practice in changing lanes with practice of right and left turns.

PASSING

INTRODUCTION

On-street passing maneuvers can be practiced only when existing roadway and traffic conditions are appropriate; in other words, the lead vehicle is traveling at an unusually slow speed, the roadway provides adequate space and sight distance, and there are sufficient gaps in traffic. Such conditions are not easily arranged and controlled by teachers.* Thus, for the most part, student practice of passing maneuvers will have to take place when the appropriate occasions arise. For this reason passing is a supplementary unit.

Instruction in passing should be provided during a classroom session so that students are prepared for those occasions in the car when a passing maneuver is required. Teachers should be familiar with the material in this unit so that they are equipped to guide student performance on those occasions.

In this supplementary unit the objectives for students are:

1. *To identify those situations in which passing maneuvers should not be performed because of excessive risk and/or legal restrictions*

2. *To identify the common risks involved in passing*

3. *To identify the driver actions required to reduce those risks, including appropriate techniques in scanning and evaluating, communicating intentions, selecting alternatives, and controlling the car's movement*

4. *To execute reduced-risk passing maneuvers in a broad variety of driving situations*

5. *To correctly determine when a situation will not permit a safe passing maneuver and to avoid passing maneuvers in these situations*

---

* There is the possibility of having two driver education vehicles engage in alternate passing maneuvers. However, unless the teaching procedure is very carefully planned it may result in obstructing traffic or in exposing both vehicles to unreasonable risk.

PASSING ON A MULTIPLE-LANE ROAD

Practicing reduced-risk lane changes (Unit 7) prepares the student to perform passing maneuvers on multiple-lane roadways (maneuvers that do not require crossing into an oncoming traffic lane). Such passing maneuvers simply require a combination of lane changes from right to left and then left to right (Fig. 7S.1).

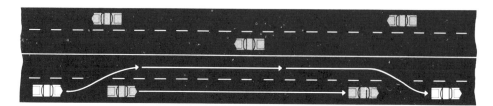

Fig. 7S.1

For the most part, the elements of performance involved in this type of passing maneuver are the same as for lane changes (see Unit 7). The major distinguishing feature of this maneuver is the initial determination of whether or not it is advisable to pass. As a general rule, students should be discouraged from engaging in unnecessary passing maneuvers. They should recognize that a passing maneuver requires an extensive series of driver actions and involves several possible conflicts for the right-of-way. These factors are likely to increase the possibility of driver error and/or the vehicle's exposure to risk in comparison to the alternative of remaining in a single lane behind the vehicle ahead.

PASSING ON LEFT OF CENTER OF ROADWAY

On roadways with a single traffic lane in each direction the oncoming lane must be utilized in passing another moving vehicle [1]. Regardless of who is driving, this is a comparatively dangerous maneuver. A recent study (B 46) indicates that 4.5 percent of all accidents occur in situations where a vehicle is passing left of center. It is especially demanding for the beginning driver. In many passing situations when an unforeseen obstacle appears in the oncoming lane at a point midway through the maneuver, the driver must make the critical decision to accelerate and continue on, or to brake and return to a position behind the vehicle being passed. This is a demanding decision and the execution of alternative actions requires considerable skill. It is not uncommon for this situation to cause beginners to "freeze." Moreover, unlike many other situations, the teacher may not be able to make up for a student's error by simply applying the dual-control brake. Such factors should be taken into consideration in deciding whether or not to encourage the student to practice this kind of passing maneuver. They should be weighed against the realization that students will be performing such maneuvers when they are licensed drivers and therefore should profit from supervised practice during driver education.

If the teacher decides to provide for on-street practice of the passing maneuver, it would be advisable to do so during the latter stages in a student's training and to restrict practice to those students who have developed sufficient capabilities in accurate tracking at high speeds. Of course, such practice should be encouraged only when conditions are suitable. Remember that conditions that allow an experienced driver to pass in safety may not be safe for student drivers.

On the other hand, if a sufficiently large off-street area is available, and if the teacher can control conditions in this area to provide for realism and safety, systematic practice in passing should be emphasized.

In any case, the passing maneuver should be thoroughly examined during classroom instruction. The discussion should focus on the demanding nature of the maneuver, the risks involved, and the elements of reduced-risk performance.

Related Concepts and Information

The risk of a head-on collision   Whenever a vehicle crosses the center lines and enters an oncoming traffic lane the risk of a head-on collision is increased. This type of collision is perhaps the most serious kind of accident in terms of its likelihood of producing injury or death.

The danger of not having a way out   One of the most dangerous aspects of a passing maneuver is that when an oncoming vehicle unexpectedly appears, the passing vehicle may be caught in a dangerous situation from which there is no escape. In effect, the passing vehicle is at the mercy of the drivers in the other two cars. Unless the oncoming car moves off the road, or the vehicle being passed gives way to the right and/or stops, the passing vehicle has no safe alternative paths (Fig. 7S.2).

Fig. 7S.2

Distance required to pass   To pass a vehicle moving in the same direction requires considerable time and distance. The situation in Fig. 7S.3 illustrates this point.

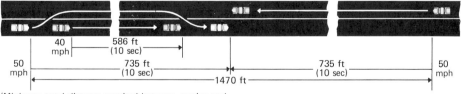

(Minimum total distance required between passing and oncoming vehicle: equivalent to approximately 5 football fields)

Fig. 7S.3

Legal restrictions against overtaking on the left   Because of the dangerous nature of the passing maneuver, the responsibility of avoiding possible conflicts with other vehicles is placed on the passing vehicle. The driver is prohibited from passing on the left side of the road unless "such left side is clearly visible and free of oncoming traffic for a sufficient distance ahead to permit such overtaking and passing to be completely made without interfering with the operation of any vehicle approaching from the opposite direction or any vehicle overtaken. In every event the overtaking vehicle must return to an authorized lane of travel . . . before coming within 200 ft. of any approaching vehicle" (B 139).

In addition, the law usually prohibits the use of the left side of a two-way roadway when approaching the crest of a grade or a curve, at intersections and railroad crossings, on approaches to bridges or tunnels, and within no passing zones.

The initial decision to pass   As a general rule, remaining on the right side of the road behind a moving vehicle involves less risk than moving across the center line and passing the vehicle ahead. Therefore the decision to pass should be made only when the reason for passing justifies the added risk. One reason for passing is to save time. Frequently this reason does not justify the risk involved. For example, suppose you are traveling at 50 mph (on a roadway with a 50 mph speed limit) and approach a vehicle traveling at 45 mph. You have five miles to go to reach your destination. You decide to pass the vehicle and maintain your 50 mph for the remaining five miles instead of following the lead vehicle at 45 mph. The amount of time you save is *forty seconds*. In many similar instances the amount of time saved by passing is so meager that it cannot be used to justify the assumption of any added risk.

Another reason for passing is that the lead vehicle is moving at an unreasonably slow speed and in doing so creates a hazardous situation. For example, a driver might travel 35 mph in a 50 mph zone, causing traffic to pile up behind her and encouraging other drivers to take unreasonable risks to pass her. In this case the risk involved in passing her may be less than the risk involved in staying to her rear (Fig. 7S.4). In this and similar instances, clearly the reasons for passing justify the decision to do so.

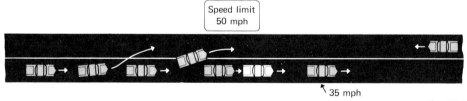

Fig. 7S.4

Elements of Reduced-Risk Performance

Preparatory phase

When approaching the vehicle ahead, the driver's first job is to decide whether it is really advisable or necessary to pass. If the reasons for passing justify the risks involved, then perform the maneuver; otherwise stay behind.

Scan ahead to see that the path is clear and will remain clear. It may be necessary to move to the left side of the lane to obtain an adequate view ahead. Also, glance in the sideview mirror and (if necessary) check the left side blind spot to see that no one is passing you (Fig. 7S.5).

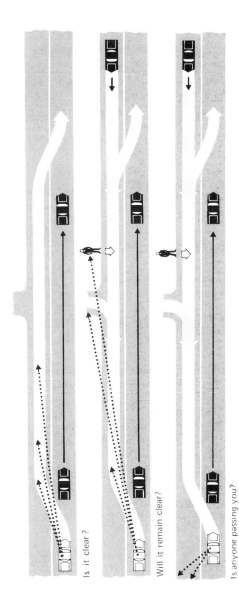

Is it clear?

Will it remain clear?

Is anyone passing you?

Fig. 7S.5

Decide to begin the maneuver only when the intended path is clear and will remain clear. Whenever there is any doubt about the present or continued clearance available, the reduced-risk alternative is to remain behind the lead vehicle on the right side of the road.

Communicate your intention to pass by signaling for a lane change. Also, in some situations it may be necessary to sound the horn to warn the driver ahead of your intentions, especially if the car ahead starts to drift to the left or accelerate.

During the performance of these preparatory procedures, maintain a space cushion between yourself and the vehicle ahead. Students should recognize that they can get so involved in scanning ahead and to the rear that they might run into the back end of the car they intend to pass (Fig. 7S.6).

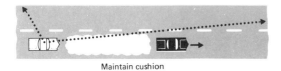 

Maintain cushion   Avoid this

Fig. 7S.6

Execution phase: when path is clear and remains clear

When pulling out and passing the vehicle, continuously scan ahead for unforeseen obstacles and maintain a space cushion between your vehicle and the car being passed (Fig. 7S.7).

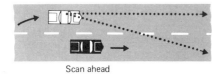 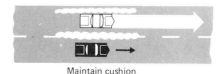

Scan ahead   Maintain cushion

Fig. 7S.7

Before returning to the right side of the road, (1) signal your intentions, (2) glance in the rearview mirror to check the position of the vehicle being passed, and (3) turn your head to check the right side blind spot. In returning to the right side of the road, leave an adequate space cushion between yourself and the vehicle you have passed (Fig. 7S.8).

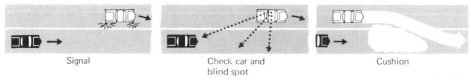

Signal   Check car and   Cushion
                               blind spot

Fig. 7S.8

Execution phase: when obstacles appear during maneuver

If, during the early stages of the maneuver, an unforeseen obstacle appears along the intended path, the reduced-risk alternative is to slow down and return to a position behind the lead vehicle (Fig. 7S.9).

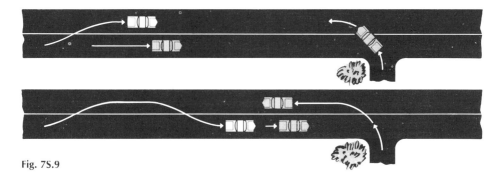

Fig. 7S.9

When obstacles arise during the later stages of the maneuver, there are several alternatives, *but they all involve considerable risk* (Fig. 7S.10). Of course, the object of learning to pass safely is to prevent such situations from arising.

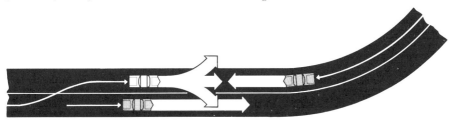

Instructional Plan

When suitable occasions arise (a slow lead vehicle, safe conditions, and a capable student) the teacher may decide to have the student perform a passing maneuver. If the maneuver takes place on a multiple lane street and does not require crossing into an oncoming traffic lane, then the procedure used in changing lanes is appropriate (see Unit 7).

When the passing maneuver involves crossing over into an oncoming traffic lane, the teacher will need to take special precautions to be certain that the intended path is clear, and that the student does not initiate or continue the maneuver when it is unsafe to do so. A special form of limited commentary driving might be used (Fig. 7S.11).

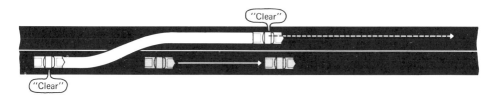

Fig. 7S.11

1. The student announces "clear" before starting the maneuver to indicate that she has scanned the intended path and judged it to be clear of obstacles.

2. During the early stages of the maneuver, the student announces "clear" again, to indicate that she is continuing to scan ahead and that the roadway is still clear.

At either of these points in the maneuver when the student comments, the teacher can veto the decision to initiate or continue the maneuver by saying "NO."

In practicing the passing maneuver, it is not uncommon for beginners to *be reluctant to accelerate* to the speed necessary to complete the maneuver within a reasonable distance. This is particularly true for students who have limited driving experience at higher speeds. The teacher will need to be alert to this tendency and be ready to give appropriate cues (such as "accelerate") to keep the student from dangerously prolonging the maneuver.

CLASSROOM GUIDE FOR UNIT 7 (SUPPLEMENT)

Passing

Topics	Instructional Plan
1. Passing on a multiple lane road, avoiding unnecessary passing maneuvers.	1. Discuss added risk connected with frequent passing.
2. Passing on left of center of roadway: a) Risk of head-on collision b) Danger of not having a way out c) Distance required to pass d) Legal restrictions against overtaking on the left e) Initial decision to pass	1. Discuss each concept and give specific illustrations.
3. Elements of reduced-risk performance: a) Communicating intentions b) Scanning and evaluation procedures c) Selecting reduced-risk alternatives d) Accurate guidance	1. Describe each element of performance. 2. Discuss reasons for each element. 3. Give specific examples.
4. Commentary driving used in changing lanes: a) "Clear" before initiating maneuver b) "Clear" in early stages of maneuver	1. Briefly discuss technique.

PREPARATORY READING FOR STUDENTS

1. *Learning to Drive: Skills, Concepts, and Strategies.* Chapter S10, "Passing."

    or appropriate sections of another high-school text.
2. *State Driver's Manual.* Review rules of the road that apply to passing.

RELATED SIMULATOR LESSONS

1. Aetna Drivotrainer System: "Perfect Passing."

IN-CAR GUIDE FOR UNIT 7 (SUPPLEMENT)

*Passing**

Teacher	Student
When the occasion arises requiring a passing maneuver (using oncoming traffic lane), instruct student to pass the vehicle ahead when it is safe to do so.	*Preparatory phase:*

	1. a) Maintains space cushion
	   b) Scans ahead:
	      Is path clear?
	      Will it remain clear?
	   c) Checks left side blind spot

Conditions required:	
1. Slow-moving vehicle ahead	If clear:
2. Safe road and traffic conditions	2. Comments: "clear"
3. Capable student	Signals left; if necessary, sounds horn; and begins maneuver
Watch for:	
1. Adequate clearance before allowing student to initiate maneuver	If not clear:
	3. Comments: "obstacle"
2. Student reluctance to accelerate	Stays behind lead vehicle
3. In early stages of maneuver be ready to order student to return to position behind lead vehicle when obstacle appears in oncoming lane	*Execution phase:*
	When path is clear and remains clear:

	4. In passing:
	   Continuously scans ahead
	   Maintains space cushion on sides
	   Maintains appropriately fast speed

	5. Before returning:
	   Signals intention to move right
	   Glances in rearview mirror to check position of vehicle passed
	   Turns head to check right blind spot
	   Leaves space cushion in returning

	When obstacles appear during maneuvers:
	6. During early stages of maneuver, slows down and returns to position behind lead vehicle
	7. During later stages, chooses best available alternative for situation (good luck)

* This in-car guide is for passing using an oncoming traffic lane. For passing maneuvers on multiple lane roads, see "In-Car Guide for Unit 7."

STRATEGIES FOR ROADWAY AND TRAFFIC CHARACTERISTICS

INTRODUCTION

This unit involves the development and application of driving strategies designed to meet the roadway and traffic conditions on specific routes of travel [1].

A strategy is a plan, developed in advance, for driving from one location (origin) to a subsequent location (destination) along an established route. The plan serves as a guide to safe performance in relation to the important roadway and traffic characteristics of the route. The strategies are developed in the classroom by students and teacher and are based on the student's (1) prior knowledge of recommended driving practices, and (2) familiarity with the important characteristics of the route. In-car instruction provides an opportunity for students to apply the strategies by driving over the routes and using the plan to guide their performance.

From the teacher's standpoint, the unit has several underlying purposes. One is to expose the students to a wide range of driving environments so that they have an opportunity to learn and apply the substantial variety of driving techniques required by these environments. Another purpose is to encourage the student to recognize that advance planning can play an important role in safe driver performance. A third important purpose is to develop a sensitivity on the part of students to the need for adjusting their driving to differences in roadway and traffic characteristics.

In this unit the specific objectives for students are:

1. *To identify a broad range of important roadway and traffic characteristics and to describe the types of driver actions that are most appropriate for dealing with those characteristics*

2. *For a given driving route, to be able to record its most important characteristics and to devise (in writing) an appropriate driving strategy*

3. *Having developed strategies for a variety of driving routes, to effectively apply those strategies while driving over the routes*

SELECTED CONCEPTS AND DRIVING PRACTICES FOR ROADWAY AND TRAFFIC CHARACTERISTICS

The concepts and practices identified below are intended as background information for teachers in helping students develop driving strategies. This section covers only *some* of the material that teachers will have to use in strategy development. *The concepts, skills, and techniques covered in Units 5, 6, 7, and 7S* are also applicable to the development of strategies. Teachers should also consult other sources of information, including the high-school textbook being used, state and local traffic laws, professional journals, and research reports.

Teachers should recognize, however, that all of these sources (including this book) deal with *general* aspects of driver performance that are *generally* appropriate for various kinds of roadway and traffic conditions. While they can provide the necessary background information for developing strategies, they cannot provide all the *specific* elements of a driving strategy that is designed for use on a *specific* route. In the last analysis the driver education teacher will have to serve as the resource person for the student's development of specific strategies. Although the teacher's judgments will be based in part on the information in the sources mentioned above, they also will be based on her ability to analyze a specific route and to select those elements of strategy that are uniquely suited to the specific conditions along the route.

Sight Distances

Sight distance is the distance the driver can see along the intended path. Whenever possible, sight distances should be greater than the car's stopping distance.

Accident data reveal that "where sight distances are short (less than eight hundred feet) accident rates are double those at locations where sight distance is not limited" (B 138). In one study of accidents, restricted sight distance was the single most frequent causal factor, and in one-half of the accidents involving restricted sight distances drivers were traveling at excessive speeds (B 9).

Curves and hills are common roadway characteristics that reduce sight distances. The appropriate strategy when approaching curves and hill crests is usually to stay to the right and reduce speed to bring the stopping distance within the sight distance.

Occasionally, large vehicles immediately in front of the driver reduce his sight distance. In this case the appropriate strategy is usually to (1) increase the space cushion between oneself and the vehicle ahead (to guard against an unexpected stop), and (2) when possible reposition the car by changing lanes or by passing.

When another car immediately ahead blocks sight distance, make a special effort to be aware of what is happening beyond the car ahead by scanning through its windshield and to the sides.

Sight distances along the intersecting paths of other vehicles are also important, especially in situations where intersecting vehicles have the right-of-way and are moving at high speeds. If vehicles, trees, or other obstructions limit sight distances along these intersecting paths, the appropriate strategy is usually to stop, then creep ahead gradually to a point where the driver can see along the intersecting path, and proceed only when the intersecting path is clear.

Curves

Curves are dangerous because of the limited sight distances involved and because centrifugal force tends to pull the car to the outside of the path. Excessive speed in entering curves and failure to maintain proper lane position while negotiating a curve are frequent causes of accidents (B 138).

The appropriate strategy for driving on most curves is to (1) reduce speed prior to entry, (2) watch for and obey signs indicating maximum speed for curve, (3) scan well ahead, (4) maintain lane position and do not cut across lanes, and (5) whenever necessary reduce speed during turn by decelerating or braking lightly, trying to avoid sudden hard braking that will increase the probability of a skid.

Hills

When driving up a hill, speed will decrease (due to the effect of gravity) if the accelerator pedal is kept in the same position as on the level part of the road. By itself there is nothing wrong with this. However, if other vehicles are following and the decrease in speed is substantial, the following vehicles may be tempted to try to pass on a dangerous part of the hill. In these situations, therefore, it is usually advisable to maintain a safe speed going uphill by accelerating slightly. On long steep hills it may be necessary to shift to a lower gear to maintain appropriate speeds.

Approaching the crest of the hill, stay far to the right and reduce speed to compensate for the reduced sight distance ahead.

Starting downhill, the pull of gravity will cause an increase in speed even though the driver does not accelerate. In addition, braking distance on a downgrade is much greater than it is on a level road because of the pull of gravity. Therefore, it is frequently advisable to test the brakes and slow down prior to beginning a steep downgrade. When going downhill, control speed to keep stopping distance within safe limits by decelerating. If necessary, apply continual light pressure on the brake or shift to a lower gear (which causes the engine to act as a braking force and saves brake wear). Also, periodically check to the rear to see whether following vehicles are accelerating excessively.

The importance of training students to cope with both curves and hills cannot be overemphasized. Together these features of roadway alignment contribute to a sizable proportion of all roadway accidents. For example, in a recent case study of serious accidents (B 31), 84 percent of all the accidents occurred on roadways with some degree of horizontal or vertical curvature.

Intersections*

Good driving strategy should consider the types of accidents that can occur at intersections and should enable the driver to avoid them. The most common types of intersection accidents are pictured in Fig. 8.1. However, the types of accidents that are most likely to occur at a given intersection will depend on the special characteristics of the intersection. Because of their special characteristics, one intersection may be the scene of more angle collisions; another, more rear-end collisions; and another, more pedestrian accidents.

The driver's job is to devise the best strategy for each intersection, one suited to the special characteristics of the particular location. Some examples of different strategies for specific types of intersections are given in Fig. 8.2. They may or may not be typical of any of the intersections through which you drive.

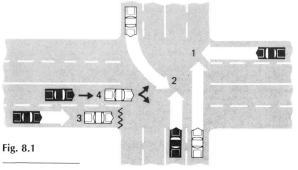

1. Two cars entering at an angle
2. One car turning left, other car entering from opposite direction
3. One car stopped, other car entering from behind
4. One car turning, other car entering from same direction

Fig. 8.1

* For other strategies and techniques for driving at intersections, review Units 5 and 6.

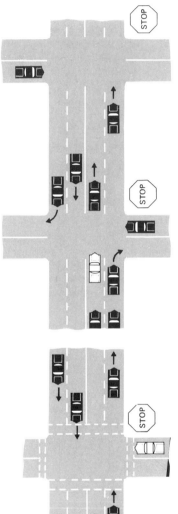

CHARACTERISTICS On main street, in heavy traffic. Intersects with several side streets. Side street traffic controlled by stop signs.

STRATEGY Maintain normal speed of traffic (avoid slowing down at each intersection because of increased risk of rear end collision). Maintain awareness of vehicles on side streets. Be ready to slow down or stop if they move toward your path.

CHARACTERISTICS On side street intersecting with main street. Heavy traffic on main street. Stop sign facing you.

STRATEGY Stop at crosswalk. Scan both ways: left, then right. Repeat scanning as necessary until intersecting lanes in both directions are clear. When clear, scan ahead, accelerate (move through intersection without delay).

Fig. 8.2

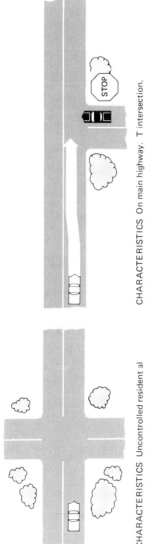

CHARACTERISTICS Uncontrolled residential intersection. Light traffic on both roads. Partially obstructed sight distances of intersecting roads.

STRATEGY Reduce speed on approach. Scan left and right before reaching intersection. If intersecting lanes are clear, scan ahead and resume speed as you enter intersection (move through intersection without delay).

CHARACTERISTICS On main highway. T intersection. Vehicles on side road face stop sign. Their view along highway is obstructed, and so they edge out to obtain view.

STRATEGY On approach, reduce speed slightly. Adjust lane position to provide space cushion. When you are sure they see you and will wait, resume speed.

Fig. 8.2 (cont.)

Lane Usage

As a general rule it is wise to use the far right lane (using the left lane to pass), maintain a centered-lane position, and stay within a single lane as much as possible. However, specific decisions about lane usage in specific situations will vary depending on the situation. On roads with more than one lane going in the same direction, the driver should choose the lane that involves the least risk of an accident and allows for efficient movement. Some of the factors to consider in making this choice are as follows:

1. In some areas and on some roads, the law requires the use of the right-hand lane except when passing.

2. Left lanes are closer to traffic moving in the opposite direction.

3. In busy districts, right lanes may be obstructed by double-parked cars and trucks.

4. In heavy traffic, left lanes may be obstructed by cars waiting to turn left.

5. A car traveling at slower speeds will obstruct moving traffic in the left lanes.

6. On approaches to special intersections, left or right lanes may be reserved for turning vehicles.

Parked Cars

Driving alongside parked vehicles can be dangerous. The most crucial potential obstacles in these settings are pedestrians or animals who may emerge from between parked vehicles, occupants who open the doors of parked cars on the traffic side, or the parked car itself that may suddenly move out into the traffic lane (B 138). Strategies for driving alongside parked cars should include the following:

1. Reduce speed.

2. Scan ahead for pedestrians between cars, indications that an occupant might be leaving, and indications that the car might be leaving (such as exhaust smoke, signals, back-up or brake lights on).

3. Leave a space cushion between yourself and parked cars (four feet if possible).

4. Use horn to warn occupants or pedestrians, but at the same time be ready to brake quickly.

Traffic Density, Flow, and Type

Heavy traffic   In heavy traffic, a large number of potential obstacles are in the vicinity of the driver's intended path, increasing the likelihood of an accident. The driver's responsibility is to use a strategy that prepares one for the possibility that one of these potential obstacles will move into the path. The best preparation is to drive at a sufficiently reduced speed so that the vehicle can be brought to a stop in time to avoid hitting other vehicles (or pedestrians) that do move into the path, and to leave a space cushion between oneself and the vehicle ahead in case it stops suddenly.

In addition, scanning techniques should be adjusted to meet the demands of heavy traffic. It is usually advisable for drivers to concentrate on keeping their eyes moving in a way that allows them to maintain an awareness of the several potential obstacles in the vicinity of the path. Since the car should be traveling at a slower speed and the driver concentrating on several nearby obstacles, it is usually not necessary (or possible) to scan as far ahead as would be required under other conditions.

Traffic flow   When traffic flows smoothly at a uniform speed and without a lot of lane changing, there is less likelihood of accidents, especially rear-end collosions. This is why it is usually advisable to adjust speed to the normal speed of traffic and avoid unnecessary lane changes. Drivers obstruct the smooth flow of traffic when they drive at slower than normal speeds, change speed frequently (and unnecessarily), or change lanes unnecessarily, instead of contributing to the safe flow of traffic. In heavy traffic, however, contributing to the safe flow of traffic is complicated. On the one hand, there is the need to reduce speed to compensate for the presence of many potential obstacles; on the other, there is the need to maintain the normal speed to contribute to safe traffic flow. This can lead to problems—especially when a safe speed (in terms of the potential obstacles present) should be slower than the normal speed of other vehicles (Fig. 8.3). It is difficult to suggest a strategy for such situations. Teachers will have to make decisions based on the specific characteristics of the situations encountered and the kinds of risks they prefer to take.

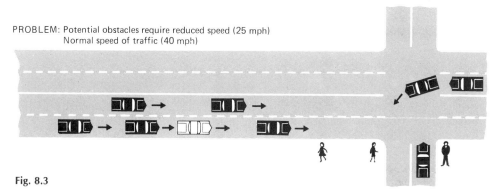

PROBLEM: Potential obstacles require reduced speed (25 mph)
            Normal speed of traffic (40 mph)

Fig. 8.3

Lighter traffic   Under light traffic conditions, there are fewer potential obstacles in the vicinity of the intended path. Drivers can usually be sure of a clear path for a greater distance ahead. They can, therefore, drive at higher speeds and use fewer eye movements, but will have to scan further ahead along the intended path to compensate for the increase in speed.

An important problem connected with lighter traffic conditions is that although there may be fewer potential obstacles in the vicinity, this does *not* necessarily mean that there is less chance a potential obstacle will move into the intended path. When traffic is light, other drivers and pedestrians are less likely to expect your presence and, therefore, more likely to move into your path. For example, a driver who would never back out of a driveway onto a heavily traveled street without checking conditions first, might do so onto a lightly traveled street. Or a child who would never run out into a main street after a ball, might do so on a lightly traveled residential street. So in lighter traffic be ready for unpredictable actions by any potential obstacles in the vicinity.

Being followed and passed   Under various traffic conditions the driver frequently has to cope with other drivers following or passing. To avoid being hit in the rear by a following vehicle the basic strategy should be to warn the following driver about any impending speed reduction or stop and to avoid abrupt or unexpected stops whenever possible. When a vehicle to the rear is tailgating, slow down very gradually, move to the right side of the lane and allow it to pass. When another vehicle is passing, maintain an awareness of the passing vehicle's position and the clearance ahead, watch for indications that the car might cut back sharply into your lane, if necessary slow down, and give way to the right to maintain an acceptable space cushion.

Oncoming vehicles   Drivers must be continuously alert to the possibility of oncoming vehicles crossing the center line and entering their path. A recent study indicates that 5.5 percent of all accidents involve vehicles entering a driver's path from the opposite direction (B 46). Early detection is an important feature of the strategy for coping with such situations. Scan far ahead along oncoming lanes and watch for indications that other vehicles might cross the center line (for example, directional signal indicating intent to pass, one vehicle tailgating another, a double-parked vehicle or roadway obstruction that might cause vehicles to swing around it, and so on). When an oncoming vehicle begins to cross the line, slow down by pumping the brake (to warn other drivers to the rear) and provide the oncoming driver with as large a space cushion as possible to complete the maneuver—give way to the right as necessary. In those instances where the oncoming car is close enough to cause a serious hazard, sound the horn and be ready to employ appropriate braking and steering responses (see Unit 11). Also, scan the space available on the right side of the roadway and be ready to take evasive action by driving onto the shoulder if it is necessary and safe to do so.

Pedestrians

In order to develop effective strategies for coping with pedestrians the teacher and the student must first have a reasonable understanding of the pedestrian accident problem. Much information is available on this topic in standard textbooks, professional journals, and research reports. Teachers should study the information and see to it that an appropriate amount of classroom time is devoted to discussing the various dimensions of the problem. A very brief overview of some of the important aspects of the problem is presented below.

The pedestrian accident problem is enormous. Over 130,000 pedestrian deaths and injuries result each year from traffic accidents (B 137). Unsafe behavior of pedestrians is responsible for a large proportion (45 percent) of the accidents—particularly failure to yield the right of way when required to. In one study of children (ages 0–14) involved in pedestrian accidents, 82 percent ran into the roadway and 59 percent were guilty of complete lack of attention to traffic (B 58). Most pedestrians killed were not licensed to drive or did not understand traffic problems. The proportion of pedestrian accidents that were caused in part by alcohol consumption on the part of the pedestrian is estimated at approximately 20 percent (B 26).

A study by the Department of Transportation (B 26) identified four common types of pedestrian accidents that account for the majority of all urban pedestrian accidents:

1. *Dartout*—pedestrian darts out between intersections, short exposure to driver (33 percent)

2. *Intersection dash*—a quick crossing attempt at or near an intersection (9 percent)

3. *Vehicle turn*—attention conflict: driver attempting to turn into traffic attends to traffic in one direction and strikes pedestrian in other direction (8 percent)

4. *Multiple threat*—pedestrian is struck after other cars, which blocked the vision of the striking driver, stopped to permit the pedestrian to cross (3 percent).

Table 8.1 describes some of the circumstances surrounding pedestrian accidents. Notice particularly the large proportion of accidents involving persons who are crossing or entering the roadway, and that entering between intersections seems to be a special problem with younger people while older people are especially prone to accidents at intersections.

Given the countless number of different situations drivers encounter that involve pedestrians, it is most important that each strategy adopted fit the unique (and often subtle) characteristics of the particular setting. Nevertheless, the following general elements of strategy may be applied in most settings.

Scanning and evaluating   Search for pedestrians about to enter the roadway. Predict that certain pedestrians are likely to enter your path—especially young children, elderly people, apparently intoxicated people, and all others who are not attentive to your car (for example, young people playing games, persons looking in other directions, and so on). In any event, *do not expect* pedestrians to obey right-of-way rules at intersections and elsewhere with the same frequency as drivers do.

Execution   At all times, when pedestrians are in your path or entering it, yield the right-of-way by stopping or taking evasive action. When there is a reasonable probability that a pedestrian might enter the intended path, (1) sound the horn, (2) slow down, keeping foot in the caution position, and (3) leave a space cushion between the vehicle and the pedestrian as you pass.

Bicyclists

The increasing use of bicycles for recreation and transportation has resulted in a dramatic increase of the motor vehicle–bicycle accident problem. The National Safety Council estimates that 100,000 motor vehicle–bicycle accidents occur each year, which results in approximately 1,100 fatalities. Bicyclists pose special problems for motorists because for the most part they are young, untrained, often violate the rules of the road, and are guilty of erratic behavior (B 26). Studies of motor vehicle–bicycle accidents reveal that the major accident-causing actions of bicyclists are cycling out of a driveway into path of vehicle, cycling out from between parked cars, entering an intersection without due care, disobeying traffic signs, changing direction in front of cars, and midblock crossing (B 18, B 26).

Strategies for driving in relation to bicyclists are similar to those used for pedestrians (see previous section). Perhaps the most important rule to follow in confronting bicyclists is *predict the unexpected*—that is, allow for the possibility that the cyclist will do the unexpected and select a strategy that reduces the risk in the event the possibility materializes.

Traffic Signs, Signals, and Regulations

When driving on any route, a driver's actions should be governed by (1) existing speed limits, (2) applicable right-of-way rules, (3) regulatory signs (such as Stop and Yield signs), (4) traffic signals, (5) roadway markings (such as lane markings, stop lines, and so forth), (6) regulations for special locations on the route (such as at railroad crossings and school zones), (7) regulations govering special vehicles such as school buses, emergency vehicles, and so on, and (8) any other regulations which apply to the particular route.

To develop strategies that are in accordance with these signs, signals, and regulations, students will have to be thoroughly familiar with the relevant information in their state driver's

Table 8.1 DEATHS AND INJURIES OF PEDESTRIANS BY AGE AND ACTION, STATEWIDE

Actions	All Ages		Age of Persons Killed and Injured							
	No.	%	0–4	5–9	10–14	15–19	20–24	25–44	45–64	65 and Over
Total Pedestrians	128,700	100.0%	100.0%	100.0%	100.0%	100.0%	100.0%	100.0%	100.0%	100.0%
Crossing or entering	90,100	70.0	71.0	76.4	70.0	59.6	58.6	59.8	69.6	79.2
—at intersection	39,300	30.5	12.7	22.8	28.0	33.6	32.5	34.8	43.9	50.3
—between intersection	50,800	39.5	58.3	53.6	42.0	26.0	26.1	25.0	25.7	28.9
Walking in roadway	7,800	6.1	2.1	2.7	7.4	13.4	10.4	7.9	7.2	6.8
—with traffic	4,500	3.5	1.0	1.3	4.4	8.9	6.7	4.3	4.4	3.7
—against traffic	3,300	2.6	1.1	1.4	3.0	4.5	3.7	3.6	2.8	3.1
Standing in roadway	5,300	4.1	1.2	0.8	2.7	7.7	9.7	9.1	6.0	3.9
Getting on or off vehicle	2,300	1.8	0.7	0.8	1.6	2.6	3.1	3.5	2.9	1.9
Pushing or working on vehicle in roadway	1,400	1.1	*	*	0.3	1.8	4.2	3.3	2.1	0.5
Other working in roadway	1,200	0.9	*	0.1	0.1	1.0	1.5	3.0	2.0	0.3
Playing in roadway	6,900	5.4	13.3	9.4	7.8	2.0	0.7	0.2	0.1	*
Other in roadway	7,900	6.1	8.9	8.2	6.0	5.4	5.3	5.0	3.5	2.3
Not in roadway	5,800	4.5	2.8	1.6	4.1	6.5	6.5	8.2	6.6	5.1

Source: *Accident Facts*, 1975, published by the National Safety Council.
* Less than 0.05%.

manual. If necessary, have them review these sections in the manual. Once they know the rules and regulations, have them study the driving route and determine where, when, and how the rules must be applied.

Students should recognize that applying the rules and regulations is not always easy. Often the specific characteristics of the route or existing traffic conditions affect the way in which rules are applied. For example, traffic laws require that drivers approaching a Yield sign at an intersection should "slow down to a speed reasonable for existing conditions" and "if required for safety, . . . stop" at a "stop line, but if none, before entering the crosswalk or, if none, at the point nearest the intersecting roadway," where they have a "view of approaching traffic on the intersecting roadway," and then to yield to traffic on the intersecting roadway. The way in which this rule is applied to a specific location will depend on the roadway and traffic characteristics of the location. How much to slow down, whether to stop, where to stop, and whether to yield will depend on sight distances along the intersecting road, roadway markings, and traffic conditions on the intersecting road. At different locations the law may have to be applied differently (Fig. 8.4).

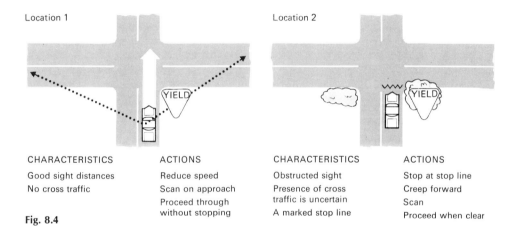

Location 1		Location 2	
CHARACTERISTICS	ACTIONS	CHARACTERISTICS	ACTIONS
Good sight distances	Reduce speed	Obstructed sight	Stop at stop line
No cross traffic	Scan on approach	Presence of cross traffic is uncertain	Creep forward
	Proceed through without stopping	A marked stop line	Scan
			Proceed when clear

Fig. 8.4

Railroad Crossings

Students should recognize that railroad crossings are among the most dangerous locations on the roadway. Approximately 1,300–1,500 persons are killed and 5,000 injured each year in collisions at railroad crossings (B 137), and surprisingly the drivers run into the train in one-third of these accidents (B 138). The normal strategy for approaching crossings is: (1) scan for signs or road markings warning that a crossing is immediately ahead; (2) slow down and prepare to stop unless a clear view of the tracks is available; (3) if the signal indicating the approach of a train is activated, or if a train is sighted, stop at the marked stop line or at a point well in advance of the crossing; (4) if necessary, warn traffic to the rear of the impending stop by pumping the brakes or using a hand signal for a stop; (5) proceed through the crossing only when you are *certain that the path is clear and will remain clear*; and (6) in crossing the tracks, maintain speed and take other preventive action against stalling. (Consult state regulations governing railroad crossings.)

Adjacent Areas

Adjacent areas are the areas alongside the road on which the car is traveling. To the driver, the most important feature of these areas is whether or not they contain potential obstacles. Do they contain people, animals, cars, bicycles, or other movable objects that might move into the car's path? Some areas are especially likely to contain potential obstacles, such as busy parking lots, school streets, playgrounds, and sidewalks in commercial districts. The most appropriate strategy to use when approaching these areas is simple:

1. Reduce speed.
2. Use scanning techniques that enable one to maintain an awareness of the potential obstacles.
3. When appropriate, maintain a space cushion between the car and the potential obstacles.

Road Surfaces

Students should be exposed to a reasonable variety of road-surface conditions and should develop a sensitivity to the need to adjust performance to such conditions as wet, icy, or snow-covered roads; sand or gravel-covered cement roads; dirt or gravel roads; surfaces with potholes or ruts; and so forth. Driving strategies for coping with these types of surface conditions normally involve slowing down and increasing following distances to compensate for reduced traction, and avoiding sharp turns, quick stops, and quick accelerations that might produce skids. (Unit 14 covers special strategies for wet, icy, and snow-covered roads in more detail.)

INSTRUCTIONAL PLAN

Knowledge of Recommended Driving Practices for Roadway and Traffic Characteristics

The development of effective strategies will depend in large part on the student's prior knowledge of what constitutes desirable driving practices under different roadway and traffic conditions. Classroom discussion periods and appropriate reading assignments should be used to familiarize students with these practices. In addition, several films are available that emphasize driving practices for different types of roadways and areas [2].

Selection of Routes

The teacher will have to decide in advance on the driving routes for which strategies are to be developed and applied. In all cases the teacher will be limited by the routes available for instruction within a reasonable distance of the school. Working within these limitations, however, the teacher should attempt to select a variety of routes that are representative of the diverse roadway and traffic conditions the student is likely to encounter during his future driving experience. It would seem advisable to select routes that expose students to (1) *heavy urban-commercial traffic conditions,* (2) *rural roadways with hills, curves, and limited sight distances,* and (3) *suburban streets.* In addition, routes should be selected keeping in mind the current level of the students' abilities. Beginning drivers should not be exposed to conditions with which they will be unable to cope.

Familiarization with Route

Before a strategy can be developed, students will need an opportunity to familiarize themselves with the route. Perhaps the best way to accomplish this is for each driving group to travel over the route. The teacher (or an advanced student) can do the driving while other members of the group record its characteristics. Another alternative is to use routes (or segments of routes) that the students have been exposed to during their prior lessons in the car. Guides for recording characteristics appear on p. 222.

Development of Strategies

The development of strategies should be a cooperative effort on the part of students and teacher. A classroom session might be used to identify and discuss the important characteristics of a route (based on prior familiarization with it), and to develop an appropriate strategy. Procedures for developing strategies are outlined below.

The teacher may decide that the entire class should arrive at a single strategy for a given route, or she may allow for some individual variations in strategy. This should depend on the quality of the variations—students should not, of course, be allowed to develop and apply strategies that are likely to result in unsafe performance.

Students should keep a written record of the strategies developed so that they can review and apply them during subsequent in-car lessons.

In-Car Application of Strategies

Students should drive over the routes for which they have developed strategies and use the strategies to guide their performance. Before starting on a route, students should have an opportunity to review the major elements of the strategy which they intend to employ. As the students drive along the route the teacher may provide a few verbal cues when necessary to remind them of the major elements of the strategy. However, for the most part students should be allowed to use their own recollection of the strategy to guide their performance.

At the completion of the drive the student (and the teacher) should evaluate the driving performance and make observations about the effectiveness of the strategy. Particular attention should be given to any alterations in strategy that were necessitated by unexpected events.

Procedures in the Development of Strategies

The following sequence is suggested for use in developing strategies.

Driving route The driving route for which the strategy is to be developed must be identified. The origin (starting point), the destination (end point), and the roadways leading from origin to destination should be clearly specified.

Recording characteristics Important characteristics of the route should be recorded. Emphasis should be placed on those characteristics that are most closely related to safe driver performance and that most need to be brought to the attention of the student drivers. No attempt should be made to record all of the features of a route—this would result in an excessively detailed record in which significant features would be lost in a maze of minor details and, eventually, in an excessively detailed strategy that students would be unable to utilize.

It is advisable to classify characteristics in a way that will facilitate the eventual development of a strategy. The following system for classification, based partly on (B 63) and (B 38), incorporates most important features of the roadway and traffic, and has been used effectively in the development of strategies for beginning drivers. Teachers might use the system as a guide for recording characteristics. It should be recognized, however, that all categories will not apply to a given route, and that the system does not itemize all possible characteristics that might be found on a route.

A. *Continuous and recurring characteristics* are present throughout most of the route (continuous) or occur at several points along the route (recurring). These characteristics can be classified as follows:

1. Roadway features:
   a) Traffic lanes: number, direction, markings, and so on
   b) Curves and grades
   c) Intersections: type, traffic patterns
   d) Obstructions to sight distance: hill crests, trees, parked vehicles, and so on
   e) Adjacent areas: road shoulders, abutments, parking lots, driveways, and so on

2. Traffic signs, signals, and regulations:
   a) Speed limits and speed zones
   b) Applicable right-of-way regulations—particularly at intersections
   c) Restrictions on passing and lane position
   d) Traffic signals
   e) Traffic signs: stop, yield, warning, and so on

3. Traffic conditions:
   a) Volume
   b) Normal speed
   c) Patterns of movement: intersecting, passing, headway, pulling out, lane changing and holding, and so on

4. Pedestrians:
   a) Normal pedestrian crossings
   b) Other patterns of pedestrian movement

5. Other characteristics include any other continuous or recurring features of the driving environment that are likely to have a significant influence on driver performance.

B. *Characteristics of specific locations* are those that are uniquely related to one location and that because of their special nature call for relatively unusual actions on the part of the driver—"unusual" in the sense that the actions are reasonably different from normal actions that occur at other points along the route. Some examples of such locations might include (1) merging traffic lanes, (2) an unusually sharp curve on a downgrade, which requires a substantial speed reduction, (3) a "blind" intersection, and (4) a main intersection with special turning lanes and traffic signal phases.

The strategy   The strategy should be based on the recorded characteristics of the roadway and traffic, and should constitute a plan for driver performance that meets the requirements of the characteristics of the route. Although the specific nature of the strategy that is developed will depend on the unique features of the route, the following major components of performance should be considered:

1. Speed control adjustments
2. Tracking and positioning
3. Scanning and evaluation procedures
4. Communicating intentions

In developing the strategy it is advisable to keep it as simple as possible in order to ensure the likelihood of its effective application. Beginning (and experienced) drivers are not likely to remember and apply strategies that are excessively detailed or complex.

All strategies should have two basic rules in common. One is: *Be flexible. Alter the strategy when unexpected events require it.* Since it is impossible to predict many events that will take place while driving over a particular route, the driver must be continuously ready for the occurrence of unexpected events that require an alteration in strategy. For example, a strategy might call for the maintenance of a particular speed that is consistent with the speed limits and with the normal speed of traffic for the route. Obviously, however, this element of strategy must be changed when traffic conditions are unexpectedly congested and the average speed of other vehicles is slower than normal. Using this basic rule as a guide, the student should be able to avoid the dangers involved in attempting to stay with a preplanned strategy in spite of its inappropriateness for the immediate situation.

A second basic rule is: *Be alert. Concentrate on what you are doing now.* The student should always give a sufficient amount of attention to what is happening at the moment so that he is ready to cope with the immediate situation. One of the dangers of attempting to employ a strategy is that the drivers might "overconcentrate" on certain elements of the strategy to the point where they are distracted from attending to what they are doing at the moment. For example, a driver might concentrate on a strategy that applies to the intersection a block ahead and fail to give sufficient attention to the car in his immediate path.

Illustrative Strategies

The strategies developed in a driver education class will be uniquely related to the specific driving routes for which they are designed. Therefore, it is not feasible to present (in this text) ready-made strategies that might simply be abstracted and applied in a driver education course.

The following strategies should serve merely as illustrations of what a driving strategy might entail. Two strategies are presented. One is for what might be considered a typical rural route and one is for a typical urban route. The strategies are designed for normal conditions (daytime, clear weather, dry roads).

DRIVING STRATEGY 1

Origin: School parking lot

Destination: Junction of Routes 35 and 26

Intermediate roadway(s): Route 35

Roadway and Traffic Characteristics	Driving Strategy
1. *Continuous and recurring characteristics:*	1. *Continuous and recurring actions:*
a) Area: rural	a) Basic rules: (1) be flexible, (2) be alert.
b) Two lanes: one in each direction	b) Maintain normal speed: 45 mph (when appropriate).
c) Solid center line, no other lane markings	c) Maintain centered position between center line and pavement edge.
d) Normal speed: 45 mph	d) Allow four-to-five car-length headway.
e) Traffic volume: moderate	e) Scan well ahead to allow for relatively high speed.
f) Speed limit: 50 mph	f) On curves: reduce speed before entering, signal vehicles to the rear if necessary, maintain centered lane position.
g) Frequent sharp curves, obstructed sight distance beyond curves	g) On approach to traffic signals be alert for change from green to yellow; use gradual braking when possible; check vehicles to the rear.
h) Several right-angle intersections with traffic signal controls	h) Be ready for slow acceleration of vehicles turning right into lane ahead of driver education vehicle (T intersections and driveways).
i) Several T intersections, entering traffic controlled by stop sign	i) Avoid passing unless vehicle ahead is traveling well below normal speed; pass only when sight distance ahead is very substantial.
j) Several private driveways	
k) Occasionally other vehicles pass from opposite direction and in same direction	
2. *Characteristics of specific locations:*	2. *Actions at specific locations:*
Location 1. Long steep upgrade, hill crest with reduced sight distance, followed by short steep downgrade	*Location 1.*
	a) Maintain speed on upgrade, especially when other vehicles are following (increase accelerator pressure as necessary).
	b) Gradually reduce speed on approach to crest to compensate for reduced sight distance; signal to following vehicles as necessary.
	c) Do not exceed safe speed on downgrade; let up on accelerator as necessary.
Location 2. Four-way intersection, traffic signal, cross-traffic volume heavy, view of intersecting traffic blocked by trees	*Location 2.*
	a) After stopping for red signal, when signal changes to green creep forward scanning to both sides for cross traffic while entering intersection.
	b) On approach to intersection, when signal is green, reduce speed provided other vehicles are not following close behind.

DRIVING STRATEGY 1 (cont.)

Roadway and Traffic Characteristics	*Driving Strategy*

Location 3. Point of entry onto Route 35 for vehicles leaving a superhighway, vehicles enter from access road that forms 30° angle with Route 35, entering vehicles have yield right-of-way sign, entering volume normally heavy (Fig. 8.5)

Location 3.

a) Scan for vehicles approaching on access road at earliest opportunity.
b) Be ready to reduce speed when vehicles are entering and gradually accelerating ahead.
c) Be ready to signal other vehicles to the rear when speed reduction is necessary.

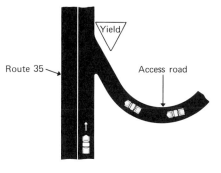

Fig. 8.5

DRIVING STRATEGY 2

Origin: Route 35 and Main Street

Destination: Broadway and Route 11

Intermediate roadway(s): Main Street and Broadway

Roadway and Traffic Characteristics	*Driving Strategy*
1. Continuous and recurring characteristics:	*1. Continuous and recurring actions:*
a) Area: urban, commercial	a) Basic rules: (1) be flexible, (2) be alert.
b) Four lanes: two in each direction, double center line, broken line divides lanes	b) Maintain consistent lane position (left or right)—whichever offers least obstruction (avoid frequent lane changes).
c) Traffic volume: heavy	c) Maintain normal speed, allowing adequate headway for vehicle in front (do not allow so much headway that other drivers are encouraged to pass or cut in front of car).
d) Normal speed: 25 mph	
e) Speed limit: 30 mph	
f) Parked cars along entire route	
g) Heavy pedestrian traffic at and between intersections	d) Note traffic signal placement and pattern; be able to anticipate likelihood of change in signal.
h) Busy four-way intersections, controlled by traffic signals, frequent left turns from same and opposite directions	e) Before moving forward from stopped position at intersection (light changes from red to green), check for cross traffic, pedestrians, and other vehicles turning left across path.
i) Sight distance at intersections reduced by presence of parked cars	f) Be ready to yield right-of-way to buses moving from curb out into lane of driver education car.
j) Frequent double-parked trucks in right lane	
k) Bus stops on every other corner, buses entering and leaving	g) Anticipate the need for lane changes in advance; be ready to yield to traffic in adjacent lane prior to changing lanes.
2. Characteristics of specific locations:	*2. Actions at specific locations:*
Location 1. Intersection of Main Street and Broadway, where driver education vehicle turns right onto Broadway, extremely busy intersection, other vehicles and pedestrians. Heavy pedestrian traffic across right turning path (i.e., pedestrians crossing Broadway when light is green for traffic on Main Street)	*Location 1.*
	a) Signal for turn early; gradually reduce speed on approach to intersection; entry into turn should be slow enought to permit immediate stop for pedestrians entering path.
	b) Stop at any point in the turn when there is a possibility that a pedestrian will enter vehicle path, remain stationary until pedestrian crosses path.
	c) Turn into right lane to avoid conflict with vehicles turning left from Main Street onto Broadway.

DRIVING STRATEGY 2 (cont.)

Roadway and Traffic Characteristics	*Driving Strategy*

Location 2. Driveway exit from large shopping center parking lot onto Broadway. Exit volume extremely heavy. Sight distance of exiting drivers is restricted by parked cars. They edge out into the traffic lane before stopping for oncoming vehicles (Fig. 8.6)

Location 2.

a) Scan for exiting vehicles well in advance.
b) When edging out pattern is apparent, reduce speed, signal drivers to the rear, be ready to yield to exiting vehicle (or when possible, change lanes to the left). In any case, avoid last minute emergencies when traveling at a relatively high speed with vehicles on the left and immediately to the rear, and with the right side of the path obstructed by an exiting vehicle.

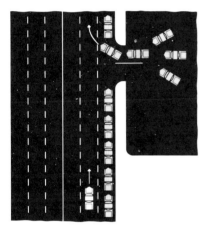

Fig. 8.6

CLASSROOM GUIDE FOR UNIT 8
Strategies for Roadway and Traffic Characteristics

Topics	Instructional Plan
1. *Safe driving practices:*	1. Discuss the variety of roadway and traffic characteristics in these areas.
a) Sight distances, curves, hills	
b) Intersections	2. Discuss and explain reasons for adopting practices for different characteristics.
c) Lane usage, parked cars	
d) Traffic density and flow	
e) Pedestrians	
f) Traffic signs, signals, and regulations	
g) Adjacent areas	
h) _____	
i) _____	
2. *Development of strategies:*	1. Discuss the procedures used in developing strategies.
a) Nature of strategies	
b) Recording characteristics of route	2. Explain the value of strategies to safe driver performance.
c) Relating strategies to characteristics	
3. *Strategy for Route 1:*	1. Specify the route.
a) *Roadway and traffic characteristics:* continuous and recurring, specific locations	2. Students and teacher record characteristics.
b) *Driving strategy:* continuous and recurring actions, actions at specific locations	3. Use class discussion to arrive at most important characteristics.
	4. Use class discussion to identify major elements of strategy.
4. *Strategy for Route 2* (same as above)	5. Have students keep record of strategy.
5. *Strategy for Route 3* (same as above)	

PREPARATORY READING FOR STUDENTS

1. *Learning to Drive: Skills, Concepts, and Strategies.* Chapter 14, "Strategies for Roadway and Traffic Characteristics."

   —or appropriate sections from another high-school text.

2. *Laboratory Manual for Learning to Drive.* Section III, "Driving Strategies."

3. *Accident Facts.* See those sections that describe accident frequencies and types for different areas (rural, urban, and so on) and different types of roads (highways, rural roads, and so on).

4. Other selected articles that provide useful background information about roadway and traffic characteristics.

RELATED SIMULATOR LESSONS

1. Aetna Drivotrainer System: "Safe Highway Driving," "Traffic Strategy."

2. Link Simulator System: "Intermediate Traffic," "Complex Traffic," "Hit the Highways," "A Formula for Traffic Survival."

IN-CAR GUIDE FOR UNIT 8
Strategies for Roadway and Traffic Characteristics

Teacher	Student

Phase 1: Strategy for Route 1

1. Prior to student performance, make certain route is clearly specified and understood.

1. Before starting to drive, briefly review major elements of strategy:

   a) Basic rules: (1) "Be flexible, alter the strategy when unexpected events require it"; (2) "Be alert, concentrate on what you are doing now."

   b) *Continuous and recurring actions:*

_____

_____

_____

_____

_____

_____

   c) *Actions at specific locations:*

_____

_____

_____

2. As student drives:

a) Allow student to concentrate—use verbal cues sparingly.

b) Use cues when necessary to help student remain flexible and alert.

2. Concentrates on applying the strategy. Also remains flexible (alters strategy when required) and alert (concentrates on what he is doing).

3. When trip is completed:

a) Guide student's evaluation of his performance.

b) Allow student to make observations about effectiveness of strategy.

c) Discuss briefly required alterations in strategy.

3. When trip is completed takes part in evaluation of:

a) His performance

b) Strategy

c) Alterations employed

Phase 2: Strategy for Route 2
(Same as Phase 1)

Phase 3: Strategy for Route 3
(Same as Phase 1)

unit 9

REDUCED-RISK
BACKING MANEUVERS

INTRODUCTION

This unit covers a variety of on-street backing maneuvers that are intended to be representative of the broad range of maneuvers the student will encounter during later driving experiences [1]. Four specific maneuvers are suggested in this unit (see "In-Car Guide"), including (1) backing along a curb, (2) backing into a driveway, (3) backing onto a street (from a driveway), and (4) parallel parking. However, teachers are encouraged to delete from or add to this group of maneuvers in keeping with the requirements of their course and the unique demands of local traffic conditions and regulations.

The student's ability to perform these maneuvers effectively will depend largely on her mastery of the basic skills covered in Unit 4, including (1) speed control and tracking on a straight path (backward), (2) tracking on turning paths (backward), and (3) backing and positioning. This unit assumes that the student has achieved a reasonable level of competence in these basic guidance skills and thus emphasizes additional elements of reduced-risk performance required for on-street driving, including (1) communicating intentions, and (2) scanning and evaluating.

One of the principal reasons for grouping these on-street maneuvers into a unit of instruction is that it provides a useful way of emphasizing the reduced-risk elements of performance that are common to all (or most) of the maneuvers. For example, all the maneuvers involve a relatively common set of scanning and evaluation procedures, which are performed prior to initiating the maneuver. In particular, three of the four maneuvers involve the evaluation of conditions on an intersecting traffic lane(s). Also, the reduced-risk alternative of delaying the start of the maneuver is common to all the maneuvers.

However, it is not the purpose of this unit to suggest that these maneuvers are identical. On the contrary, there are substantial differences between the maneuvers, particularly with respect to the application of tracking and positioning skills. Teachers are encouraged to be certain that students are aware of the distinctive features of each maneuver.

In this unit the objectives for students are:

1. To identify the common risks involved in performing on-street backing maneuvers

230

2. *To identify the driver actions required to reduce those risks, including appropriate techniques in scanning and evaluating, communicating intentions, selecting alternatives, and controlling the car's movement*

3. *To be able to explain how the rules of the road and the expectations of other drivers should influence the performance of backing maneuvers*

4. *To execute reduced-risk backing maneuvers in a variety of on-street settings, including backing along a curb, backing into a driveway, backing onto a street from a driveway, parallel parking, and other common backing maneuvers (selected by the instructor)*

Related Concepts and Information

Responsibility to yield the right-of-way   The driver of a vehicle that is moving backward has the legal responsibility not to perform the maneuver "unless such movement can be made with reasonable safety and without interfering with other traffic" (B 139). This regulation implies that the driver of the vehicle moving backward must take special precautions before initiating the maneuver and must be ready to yield the right-of-way to other vehicles utilizing the same portion of the roadway (Fig. 9.1).

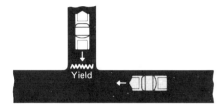

Fig. 9.1

Predicting the actions of others   Backing a vehicle involves moving it in a direction other than the normal direction of vehicular movement on a given piece of roadway. It also involves movement in a direction opposite to the direction in which the vehicle is faced. As a consequence, the backing maneuver may come as a surprise to other drivers and pedestrians in the vicinity, and they may not be ready to make the appropriate evasive adjustments. Even when other drivers know the vehicle is about to move backward, they expect the driver to yield the right-of-way before moving. So, when planning to move backward, the driver should predict that other drivers and pedestrians will not change direction or stop to allow her to do so. In many situations this prediction will result in delaying the start of the maneuver (Fig. 9.2).

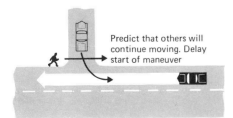

Predict that others will continue moving. Delay start of maneuver

Fig. 9.2

Obstacles to backing maneuvers   In moving forward, the driver is particularly concerned with the movement of obstacles and potential obstacles in relation to the projected path of her own vehicle; that is, she must be concerned with obstacles well ahead on her path because this is where her vehicle will be within a few moments. In backing the car, however, the vehicle normally is traveling at a much slower speed and the projected path of the vehicle is ordinarily much shorter. As a consequence, while backing, the driver is more concerned with the movement (or placement) of obstacles and potential obstacles in the *immediate vicinity* of the vehicle. In addition, however, she must be particularly aware of the projected path of other vehicles that are moving on a path that will intersect the path of the backing maneuver. For example, in backing out of a driveway onto a street, the driver must be concerned with the movement of pedestrians, the location of stationary objects, and so forth, that are in the immediate vicinity of her path. At the same time, however, she must realize that she will occupy a space in a traffic lane (on the roadway) for several seconds during the completion of the maneuver and so must scan well along the traffic lane in search of other vehicles whose projected paths may conflict with the space she will occupy (Fig. 9.3).

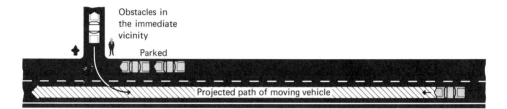

Fig. 9.3

Elements of Reduced-Risk Performance

The following discussion of reduced-risk elements of performance is intended to be generally applicable to the majority of on-street backing maneuvers. Each element of performance, however, may need to be adapted to meet the unique requirements of the specific driving situation.

Preparatory phase

Preparatory steps   Before backing, the driver brings the car to a complete stop; depresses the brake to hold the car firmly in position; moves the selector lever to R, and assumes the appropriate (turned) driver's position (see Unit 4). The ability to use appropriate scanning techniques during backing will depend on whether or not the correct driver's positions are chosen.

Scanning, evaluating, and communicating   The driver scans along the intended path and near the path, looking for any obstacles and potential obstacles that might prevent the safe completion of the maneuver (Fig. 9.4). When persons who might move into the path are unaware of the intention to move backward, a short signal on the horn is used to attract their attention.

The driver scans well along intersecting traffic lanes for approaching vehicles (Fig. 9.5). Whenever a traffic lane intersects the intended path, the driver determines that the lane is clear

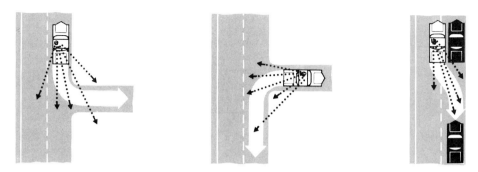

Fig. 9.4

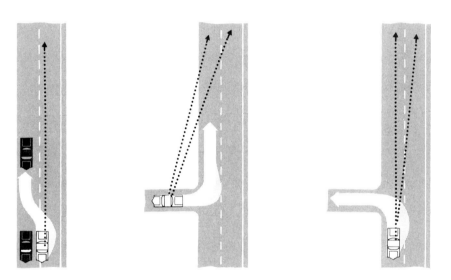

Fig. 9.5

before beginning the maneuver.* In this case, "clear" means that the lane is free of traffic for a sufficient distance to permit the completion of the maneuver without causing a conflict for the right-of-way. In situations where the car will temporarily occupy two traffic lanes, the driver scans for vehicles in both lanes. (In Fig. 9.5, notice particularly how the front end moves into the second lane.)

The decision to begin the maneuver is made only when the path is clear and will remain clear throughout the maneuver. When there is any doubt about present or continued clearance, the reduced-risk alternative is to delay the start of the maneuver (Fig. 9.6).

---

* During in-car instruction, the teacher might have the student comment "path clear" and "lane clear" prior to initiating the backing maneuver.

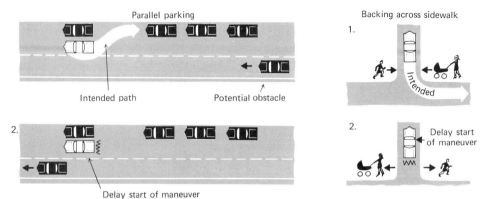

Fig. 9.6

Execution phase: when path is clear and remains clear

Speed control and tracking   The vehicle is moved backward at slow speeds and tracking skills are used to keep the car on path (see Unit 4). Also, a space cushion is maintained between the car and obstacles next to its path (Fig. 9.7).

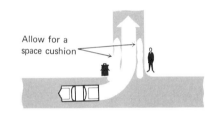

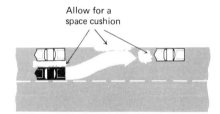

Fig. 9.7

Scanning and evaluating   The driver continuously scans along the intended path for obstacles and potential obstacles (Fig. 9.8). Since the vehicle is moving backward at slow speeds, pedestrians and other drivers may enter its path because they fail to detect the vehicle's movement. Continuous scanning helps to guard against this possibility. At critical points in the maneuver, a brief glance is used to check the movement of the front end (Fig. 9.9).

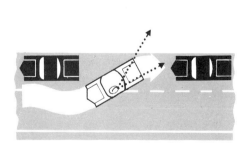

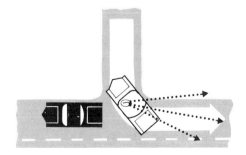

Fig. 9.8

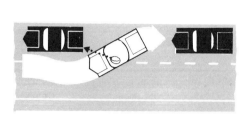
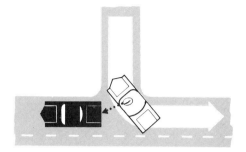

Fig. 9.9

In backing and turning maneuvers, the front end of the car follows a path that is quite different from the path followed by the rear end of the vehicle (see Unit 4). As a consequence, at critical points (Fig. 9.9) in several backing maneuvers when the front end moves close to nearby obstacles, the driver has to turn her head to see that there is sufficient clearance to proceed. A brief glance technique is used for checking on the position of the front end so that the driver's attention to the rear is not interrupted for an unreasonable length of time.

Execution phase: when obstacles appear during maneuver

Since backing maneuvers frequently take time to complete, it is not unusual for obstacles to enter the intended path while the maneuver is in progress. In such cases, the risk-reducing alternative is simple: Bring the car to an immediate stop. Unlike forward driving, an abrupt stop while backing does not involve the danger of being hit by a following vehicle.

Many backing maneuvers are performed in areas where several obstacles are next to the intended path. When performing in such areas, drivers continually face the possibility of misjudging the position of their vehicle and having a minor collision (a dented fender, perhaps). In situations of this kind, whenever there is a possibility of contact between the car and an obstacle, use the following procedure: (1) Stop. (2) Recheck the clearance between your vehicle and the obstacle. (3) If there is any doubt about hitting the obstacle, the driver should move forward and make the appropriate correction, allowing for an increased amount of clearance (Fig. 9.10).

Pole

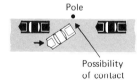

Possibility
of contact

Stop,
recheck clearance

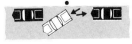

If necessary,
move forward
and correct   **Fig. 9.10**

Parallel parking

Unlike most other backing maneuvers, parallel parking lends itself to a relatively standardized sequence of steps, which (if followed properly) can help the beginner guide the car accurately into the parking space (Fig. 9.11).

1. *The approach.* Select the starting position and gradually guide car toward it. Use a hand signal for stop to warn drivers to the rear.
2. *Starting position.* Stop the car parallel to the car behind which you intend to park. Rear bumpers should be even, and cars should be two to three feet apart. Shift to reverse.
3. *Midpoint position.* Back slowly, turning the steering wheel to the right (at a moderate rate) until car is at a 45° angle to the curb. At this point the rear bumper of the car in front should be even with the middle of your right front door.

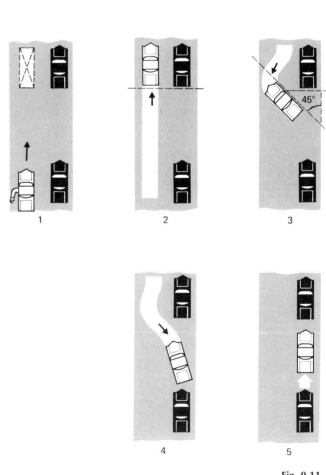

Fig. 9.11

4. *Curb position.* Continue backing slowly, turning steering wheel to the left (at moderate rate) until the car is in position parallel to the curb.

5. Move forward as necessary to center car in space, and bring it parallel to curb.

Note: It is usually helpful for the beginner to concentrate on reaching the three positions in sequence. When a major error in positioning is made on steps 1 or 2, it is usually advisable to start over again.

The teacher should recognize that these steps constitute only a part of reduced-risk parallel parking. Communicating intentions, scanning and evaluating procedures, and selecting the reduced-risk alternative are equally important features of the total reduced-risk performance.

Common Errors in Student Performance

Speed control and tracking errors   Many students, when faced with the problem of performing relatively difficult on-street backing maneuvers, make basic skill errors in speed control and tracking. The errors frequently represent a recurrence of errors made earlier during off-street practice in backing (Unit 4). It is not uncommon for students to make wheel corrections in the wrong direction, oversteer, and allow the vehicle to move too fast (see Unit 4). One of the reasons for the recurrence of these errors is that accurate guidance on backward paths apparently requires relatively high levels of skill development, and the limited amount of off-street practice in backing is not sufficient to permit many beginners to achieve adequate degrees of skill. The teacher should be alert to the recurrence of these earlier errors and should be ready to provide a brief review of basic skills prior to on-street practice. In some cases, where students have extreme difficulty in tracking, it may be advisable to return to the off-street area and review the drills performed in Unit 4.

Inattention—front or back   In the more complex backing maneuvers, the driver must maintain a relatively constant awareness of the movement of both the front and back ends of the vehicle. It is not unusual for beginners to have difficulty in appropriately dividing their attention between front and back. As a consequence, many beginners attend to the movement of one end of the vehicle at a time when they should be attending to the other end. For example, in parallel parking, when the car is moving from position 2 to position 3, many beginners tend to devote too much attention to the clearance between their right front fender and the vehicle in front, which results in prolonged inattention to the rear (Fig. 9.12). On the other hand, there are many situations where the beginner tends to devote her attention exclusively to the rear and forgets to check the front end at appropriate moments.

The teacher can help overcome this error by having the student analyze the maneuver beforehand and identify the *critical points* in the maneuver when she needs to check on the

Inattention to the rear

Fig. 9.12

movement of the front end. The student then carries out the maneuver devoting her attention primarily to the rear, but uses a brief glance to check on the movement of the front end at the critical points.

Overconcentration on accurate guidance and positioning   The task of accurately guiding and positioning a vehicle in an on-street backing maneuver is normally a very challenging undertaking for the beginning driver. This is particularly true for maneuvers that require relatively precise positioning, like parallel parking and angle parking. Faced with this challenging task, many beginners focus their attention exclusively on the problem of getting the car into position and devote less than an adequate amount of attention to scanning and evaluation procedures. For example, the student may approach a parallel-parking maneuver and completely forget to scan for obstacles before initiating the maneuver because she is so intent on getting the car to a position twelve inches from the curb. Hopefully, the teacher's entire approach to this unit of instruction will tend to reduce this kind of error.

Instructional Plan

Classroom   Elements of reduced-risk performance related to each backing maneuver should be discussed. Students should be alerted to the more common obstacles and potential obstacles that are likely to arise in connection with each maneuver. (See "Classroom Guide" for an outline of the content.)

Selection of maneuvers to be performed   Four maneuvers are suggested for inclusion in this unit: (1) backing along a curb, (2) backing into a driveway, (3) backing onto a street, and (4) parallel parking. However, the teacher should feel free to cover additional backing maneuvers that are in keeping with the context of his course, or to omit one or more of the suggested maneuvers which do not suit his teaching situation. The maneuvers covered should provide the student with a reasonable sampling of the kind of on-street backing maneuvers she will be called upon to perform in her later driving.

In-car   The student should have several opportunities to practice each backing maneuver. Emphasis should be placed on reduced-risk elements of performance. A limited form of commentary driving might be used in connection with carrying out the scanning and evaluation procedures. Prior to initiating each maneuver the student might be asked to comment (1) "path clear" when the intended backing path and areas adjacent to it are clear of obstacles and potential obstacles, and (2) "lane clear" when the traffic lane(s) intersecting the backing path is (are) sufficiently clear of oncoming traffic. This is one way of emphasizing the importance of the initial scanning procedures, and, in addition, provides the teacher with advance warning as to the accuracy of the student's assessment of the situation.

CLASSROOM GUIDE FOR UNIT 9
Reduced-Risk Backing Maneuvers

Topics	Instructional Plan
1. Related concepts and information:	1. Discuss each concept.
a) Responsibility to yield right-of-way b) Predicting actions of others c) Obstacles to backing	2. Have students present examples of how concepts apply to specific situations.
2. Reduced-risk concept applied to backing maneuvers:	1. Have students provide specific illustrations of each kind of action.
a) Actions that reduce risk b) Actions that increase risk	
3. Elements of reduced-risk performance:	1. Discuss all elements of performance for each maneuver to be covered:
a) Scanning and evaluating prior to maneuver and during maneuver (review driver's position) b) Communicating intentions c) Selecting reduced-risk alternatives d) Speed control and tracking (review material from Unit 4 as necessary)	a) Backing along curb b) Backing into driveway c) Backing onto street d) Parallel parking e) _____ f) _____
4. In-car procedures:	1. Briefly discuss procedures to be used during in-car lesson.
a) Locations for each maneuver and any special hazards present at location b) Commentary driving and analysis of performance	

PREPARATORY READING FOR STUDENTS

1. *Learning to Drive: Skills, Concepts, and Strategies.* Chapter 12, "Backing Maneuvers." Also review Chapter 6, "Basic Skills in Moving the Vehicle Backward."

   —or appropriate sections from another high-school text.

2. *State Driver's Manual.* Review rules of the road that apply to backing maneuvers.

RELATED SIMULATOR LESSONS

1. Aetna Drivotrainer System: "Backing Safely," "ABC's of Parallel Parking."

2. Link Simulator System: "Special Maneuvers."

IN-CAR GUIDE FOR UNIT 9
Reduced-Risk Backing Maneuvers

DEMONSTRATION AND EXPLANATION

Demonstrate each maneuver:

1. Backing along curb

2. Backing into driveway

3. Backing into street

4. Parallel parking

5. Other teacher-selected maneuvers

　　All maneuvers should not be demonstrated at one time. The teacher (or a selected student) should demonstrate one or two maneuvers, then allow for student practice.

Emphasize:

1. Elements of performance (see description of elements below)

2. Review techniques used in accurate guidance as necessary (see Unit 4)

3. Review commentary driving applied to backing maneuvers

GUIDING STUDENT PRACTICE

Teacher	Student

One outline of teacher and student actions is used for all three phases of instruction because of the considerable similarity among phases. Teachers should make the necessary adjustments in procedure to adapt the outline to the specific requirements of each maneuver.

Teacher	Student
Emphasize:	*Preparatory phase:*
1. Scanning path and intersecting traffic lane(s)	Before starting the maneuver:
2. Slow speed	1. Brings car to stop; depresses brake; moves selector lever to R; assumes appropriate (turned) driver's position
3. Being ready to delay or interrupt maneuver	2. Scans intended path (if necessary uses horn to attract attention)
Watch for:	3. Scans intersecting traffic lanes
1. Recurrence of speed control and tracking errors	4. Begins maneuver only when path is clear and will remain clear
2. Inattention front or back	If clear:
3. Overconcentration on tracking and positioning (neglecting scanning and evaluating)	Comments: "path clear," "lane clear" Begins maneuver
	If not clear:
	Delays start of maneuver

IN-CAR GUIDE FOR UNIT 9 (*cont.*)

Teacher	Student
	Execution phase:
	When path is clear and remains clear:
	1. Moves backward slowly, on path
	2. Maintains space cushion
	3. Scans continuously along path
	4. When necessary, checks movement of front end
	When obstacles appear during maneuver:
	1. Stops immediately when obstacle enters path
	2. When necessary, stops, rechecks clearance, and corrects
	3. Chooses other alternatives as necessary
	In *parallel parking:*
	1. Approach: signals for stop
	2. Stops in *starting position:*
	Parallel (in relation to car behind) Two to three feet away (in relation to car behind) Rear bumpers even (in relation to car behind)
	3. Moves to *midpoint position:*
	45° angle Right door even with rear bumper
	4. Moves to curb position
	5. Moves forward as necessary to center car in space and brings it parallel to curb

REDUCED-RISK
TURNING AROUND

INTRODUCTION

This unit deals with the general problem of turning the vehicle around (on-street) so that it faces in the opposite direction on the same roadway [1]. Particular emphasis is placed on two maneuvers: the U turn (Phase 1) and the Y turn (Phase 2). In addition, other maneuvers that accomplish the same purpose (going around the block) are brought to the attention of the student, and practice in selecting the safest maneuver for turning the car around is included (Phase 3).

One of the principal reasons for grouping the various methods for turning around into a single unit is to help students view these methods as alternatives for accomplishing the same purpose, instead of viewing each maneuver as an end in itself. For example, as a consequence of this unit students should view the Y turn as one of several maneuvers that turn the car around, to be used only when it represents the safest available alternative for turning around in a particular driving situation.

The successful performance of the maneuvers depends largely on the application of previously learned skills in speed control, tracking, and scanning. In particular, some of the scanning and assessment procedures developed in Unit 9 (backing maneuvers) are directly applicable to performing Y and U turns. There are, however, some unique elements of content in this unit, including (1) the problem of selecting the safest method for turning around, (2) the problem of selecting the safest location for performing a Y or U turn, and (3) the scanning and assessment procedures related to moving across two or more traffic lanes on which vehicles might approach from either direction.

In this unit, the objectives for students are:

1. *To identify the types of risks connected with the different methods of turning the car around*

2. *To identify the type of turning around maneuver that is safest for a given driving situation*

3. *To be able to identify safe and unsafe locations for turning around (including legally restricted locations)*

242

4. *To identify the driver actions required to reduce the risks involved in performing U turns and Y turns, including scanning and evaluating, communicating intentions, selecting alternatives, and controlling the car's movement*

5. *To choose the safest maneuver for turning around in a variety of on-street situations and to choose the safest location for performing the maneuver*

6. *To execute reduced-risk Y turns and U turns in a variety of on-street settings*

Related Concepts and Information

Choosing the safest method   In most situations, when the driver intends to maneuver his vehicle so that it faces in the opposite direction, he is in a position to select one of several alternatives for doing so. His responsibility is to select the safest maneuver with respect to existing conditions in the driving environment. Two of the more common maneuvers for turning the car around are U turns and Y turns; in addition, however, the driver might choose to go around the block or to use a driveway for turning, or some other method (Fig. 10.1).

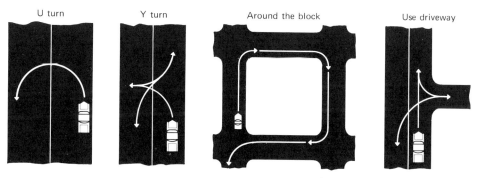

Fig. 10.1

In spite of the driver's ability to perform any one of the maneuvers, he may expose himself to unreasonable risk because he chooses to perform a turning around maneuver *at the wrong place or time.* For example, a driver may be especially skillful in performing a Y turn, but he may choose to do it on a busy roadway with the result that his vehicle is exposed to oncoming traffic from both directions during the completion of the maneuver. Thus the ability to turn the car around safely is dependent on the driver's selection of a maneuver as well as on his ability to perform it.

The relative risks   The choice of method for turning the car around should depend on the relative risk involved in each method. In most cases the risk attached to a particular maneuver will depend on unique elements of the driving situation. However, there are some more or less consistent risks related to each maneuver that should be taken into consideration in making the choice.

U turns, Y turns, and using a driveway involve moving across traffic lanes. This exposes the vehicle to oncoming traffic from both directions. In situations where oncoming traffic (in either or both directions) is excessively heavy, all three maneuvers are inappropriate and should be rejected in favor of going around the block or perhaps using a side street to turn around (Fig. 10.2).

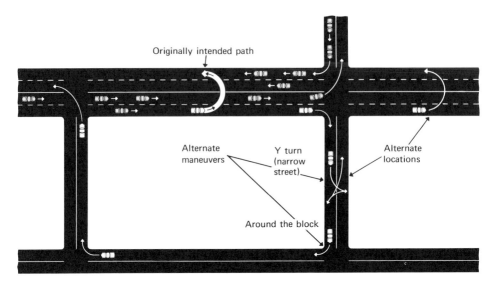

Originally intended path

Alternate maneuvers

Y turn (narrow street)

Alternate locations

Around the block

Fig. 10.2

The Y turn requires a longer time to complete and therefore involves a *longer* exposure to oncoming traffic than does the U turn. With this in mind it is usually advisable to choose the U turn. The choice of a U turn may involve the careful selection of a location that is wide enough to permit the turn, in addition to starting the maneuver from a "far right" position (Fig. 10.3).

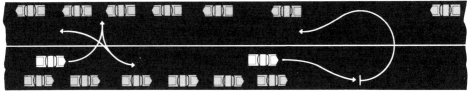

Y turn = longer exposure   U turn = shorter exposure

Fig. 10.3

The U turn, Y turn, and using the driveway involve a stationary starting position that is frequently located in a moving traffic lane. In many situations, bringing the car to a stop in a moving traffic lane may expose it to a rear-end collision, or may unreasonably obstruct the movement of other vehicles. All three maneuvers should be avoided in such situations (Fig. 10.4).

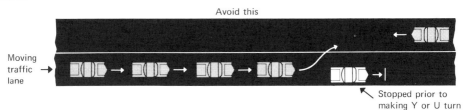

Avoid this

Moving traffic lane →

Stopped prior to making Y or U turn

Fig. 10.4

Going around the block by making three right turns and a left turn avoids most of the hazards mentioned above and therefore frequently represents the most appropriate method for turning the car around—especially when the street on which the vehicle is traveling is congested. Yet going around the block does not always involve the least risk. The driver who goes around the block must do considerably more driving to achieve the same objective and must cope with the risks involved in this extra driving—especially the risks involved in performing four separate turning maneuvers at four different intersections. In many cases the total risk of going around the block may exceed the risk involved in performing a Y or U turn.

(The above discussion of relative risks deals with some elements of performance. The teacher should explore other dimensions of the problem with students.)

Legal restrictions   Because of the potential dangers inherent in U turns and Y turns, state traffic laws and local traffic ordinances place restrictions on these maneuvers. Although the regulations may vary from locality to locality, U turns and Y turns are frequently prohibited in business districts, on curves, at or near the crest of a grade, across a double solid line, or on specific roadways. (Teachers should utilize classroom time to review state and local regulations that relate to the performance of U and Y turns.)

Elements of Reduced-Risk Performance

Preparatory phase

Choosing a location   A U or Y turn can be performed at any one of several points along a street. The driver's first responsibility is to select a location that offers the greatest advantages in terms of safely completing the maneuver.

The selected location should offer the widest possible area for maneuvering so that the turn can be accomplished as efficiently as possible, without the need for excessive maneuvering back and forth (see Fig. 10.5).

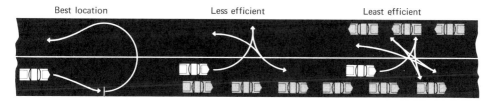

Best location   Less efficient   Least efficient

Fig. 10.5

The selected location should be removed as far as possible from busy intersections and other sources of potential obstacles (Fig. 10.6).

The selected location should afford a clear view of the roadway for a substantial distance in both directions so that the driver can see oncoming traffic and so that other drivers can see him (Fig. 10.7).

After choosing the location, the driver should bring the car to a full stop in the starting position for the maneuver. This position should be as far to the right edge of the road as possible to allow enough space to complete the maneuver efficiently. Since the starting position is normally in mid-block or at some point where other drivers might not expect a stop, a hand signal for a stop is used (when necessary) when approaching the position. Then a signal for a left turn is given (Fig. 10.8).

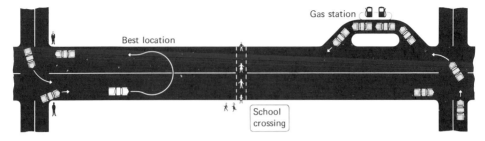

Fig. 10.6

Avoid these locations   **Fig. 10.7**

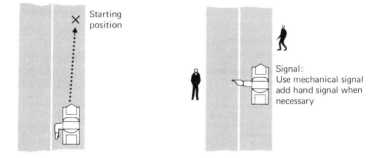

Fig. 10.8

Scanning, evaluating, and communicating   From the stationary position at the curb, the driver scans along the intended path and near the path, looking for any obstacles or potential obstacles that might prevent the safe completion of the maneuver (Fig. 10.9). When persons who might move into the path are unaware of the driver's intention to turn, a short signal with the horn should be used to attract their attention.

In addition, the driver scans well along both intersecting traffic lanes for approaching vehicles (Fig. 10.10). In most situations, the driver scans first to the front, then to the rear, then rechecks the front before moving. Of course this procedure may have to be repeated until the driver is certain that all approaching lanes are clear. In scanning the lanes to the rear, the driver turns his head around to secure the best possible view of conditions.

Students should recognize that they are required to yield the right of way to other vehicles traveling on these lanes and that other drivers will expect them to do so. *Thus* when *they* see other vehicles approaching, they should predict that the vehicles will not stop to allow them to proceed, and should delay the maneuver accordingly.

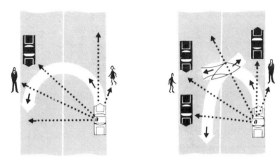

Fig. 10.9

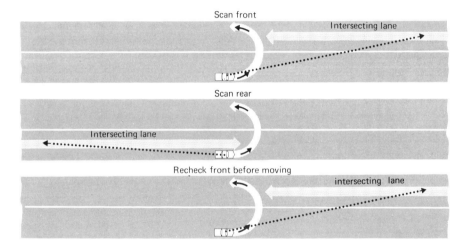

Fig. 10.10

The decision to begin the maneuver should be made only when the intended path is clear and will remain clear throughout the maneuver. When there is any doubt about the present or continued clearance, the reduced-risk alternative is to delay the start of the maneuver. During in-car instruction the teacher might have the student report "lanes clear" prior to starting the maneuver.

Execution phase for U turn

The driver proceeds at slow speeds and uses extensive hand-over-hand steering, turning the wheel fully and rapidly to achieve the shortest possible turning radius. When speed is too fast or steering is too slow, the student may be unable to complete the maneuver in one efficient turn (Fig. 10.11). A space cushion should be maintained between the car and obstacles next to the path (Fig. 10.12).

The driver continually scans along the path ahead throughout the maneuver and is ready to stop if obstacles enter it. Students should recognize that the path turns sharply and

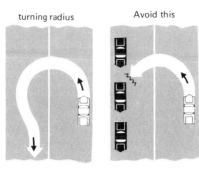

turning radius   Avoid this

Fig. 10.11

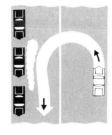

Fig. 10.12

completely, so to scan ahead they will have to turn their heads to the left to look (ahead) along the path (Fig. 10.13).

If the path crosses over the traffic lane into which the vehicle is turning, the driver should recheck the lane for approaching vehicles before entering it (Fig. 10.14).

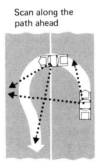

Scan along the
path ahead

Fig. 10.13

Recheck lane
before entering

Fig. 10.14

Execution phase for Y turn

Moving from position 1 to position 2, the driver:

1. Moves at slow speeds and uses extensive and rapid hand-over-hand steering to the left
2. Scans along intended path
3. Just before reaching position 2, turns steering wheel to the right to pre-aim wheels for next phase of maneuver
4. Stops, leaving a space cushion ahead
5. Holds brake firmly and shifts to R
6. Rescans both traffic lanes and assumes turned driver's position for backing
7. Delays maneuver if obstacles appear (Fig. 10.15)

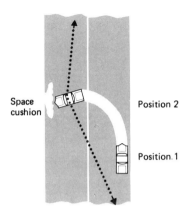

Fig. 10.15

Moving from position 2 to position 3, the driver:

1. Moves at slow speeds and uses hand-over-hand steering to the right
2. Scans along intended path
3. Just before reaching position 3, turns steering wheel to the left to pre-aim wheels for completion of maneuver
4. Stops, leaving a space cushion to the rear
5. Holds brake firmly and shifts to D; rescans both traffic lanes
6. Delays maneuver if obstacles appear (Fig. 10.16)

Moving from position 3 into new lane, the driver:

1. Accelerates and steers as necessary into traffic lane (Fig. 10.17)

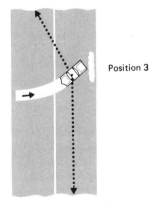

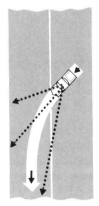

Fig. 10.16   **Fig. 10.17**

Common Errors in Student Performance

In performing these relatively advanced maneuvers, students are prone to commit any one of a great variety of errors. In particular, the teacher might expect errors similar to those described in Units 6 and 9. In addition, some unique errors tend to occur in connection with performing Y turns and U turns.

Failure to recheck oncoming traffic before starting   There are many situations in which the driver scans for traffic in oncoming lanes (front and rear), notices an approaching vehicle, waits for it to pass, and then starts the maneuver without rechecking in the opposite direction (Fig. 10.18).

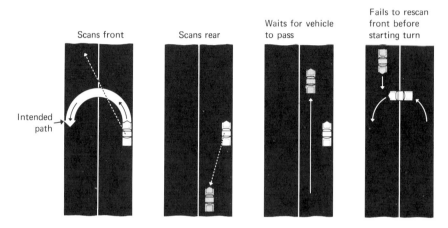

Fig. 10.18

Failure to move the selector lever   In performing Y turns, students frequently become so involved in scanning, assessment, and tracking procedures that they forget to move the selector lever to R in position 2 and to D in position 3, with the result that they accelerate with the intention of moving in one direction, but the vehicle moves in the opposite direction. This error can be avoided if the teacher emphasizes moving the selector lever as soon as the car reaches position 2 and position 3.

Hesitancy and delay   The Y turn can be an imposing challenge for many beginners, particularly because of the several elements of performance required at each of the three positions. In an effort to be thorough and careful, the student driver often becomes quite hesitant in his performance with the result that the total maneuver consumes an unreasonably long period of time during which the vehicle is exposed to oncoming traffic. In some cases, although traffic conditions may have been clear at the beginning of the maneuver, the student takes so long to complete the maneuver that he is bound to obstruct traffic in the process. The teacher can help avoid this development by providing well-timed verbal cues to guide student performance, and by emphasizing the risks involved in excessive delay.

Instructional Plan

Classroom A portion of a classroom period should be devoted to discussing "Related Concepts and Information" and reduced-risk elements of performance in Y and U turns. (See "Classroom Guide" for an outline of the content.)

In-car Student practice is divided into three phases: U turns, Y turns, and selecting a method for turning around.

Phases 1 and 2 emphasize reduced-risk performance of each maneuver, including the task of selecting a location. This means that students should be afforded an opportunity to practice not only the execution of each maneuver, but the selection of a safe location for its execution. Teachers can provide this kind of practice by simply asking students to perform a U or Y turn at the safest location on the next block instead of telling them precisely where to perform it. Initial practice in Y and U turns should take place on streets that are relatively free of traffic.

Phase 3 is intended to provide the student with practice in selecting the most appropriate method for turning the car around. A problem-solving approach is well suited to this phase of instruction. At preplanned locations the teacher should confront the student with the problem of having to turn the vehicle around, then allow the student to select one of several possible maneuvers for accomplishing the purpose. The student's solution (his selection of a maneuver) should be evaluated on the basis of its risk-reducing effect.

A limited form of commentary driving (used in Unit 9) is suggested for phases 1 and 2. When the vehicle is in the starting position for a U or Y turn, the student comments (1) "path clear" when the intended turning path and areas adjacent to it are clear of obstacles and potential obstacles, and (2) "lanes clear" when the intersecting traffic lanes (front and rear) are sufficiently clear of approaching vehicles.

CLASSROOM GUIDE FOR UNIT 10
Reduced-Risk Turning Around

Topics	Instructional Plan

1. Related concepts and information:
 	
  a) Choosing safest method for turning around
  b) Relative risks involved in each method
  c) Legal restrictions
	1. Discuss the alternative methods:
	
	  a) U turn
	  b) Y turn
	  c) Around the block
	  d) Use driveway
	  e) Other
	
	2. Discuss the risks attached to each method.
	
	3. Review state and local regulations related to turning around.

2. *Reduced-risk* concept applied to turning around:
 	
  a) Actions that reduce risk
  b) Actions that increase risk
	1. Have students provide illustrations of each kind of action.

3. Elements of reduced-risk performance:
 	
  a) Selecting location
  b) Communicating intentions
  c) Speed control and tracking
  d) Scanning and evaluating
  e) Selecting reduced-risk alternatives
	1. Discuss all elements of performance for each maneuver:
	
	  a) U turn
	  b) Y turn

4. In-car procedures:
 	
  a) Locations for each maneuver
  b) Commentary driving to be used
  c) Procedures for selecting safest method (phase 3)
	1. Briefly discuss the procedures to be used during the in-car lesson.

PREPARATORY READING FOR STUDENTS

1. *Learning to Drive: Skills, Concepts, and Strategies.* Chapter 13, "Turning Around."

  —or appropriate sections from another high-school text.

2. *State Driver's Manual.* Review rules of the road that apply to turning around.

IN-CAR GUIDE FOR UNIT 10
Reduced-Risk Turning Around
DEMONSTRATION AND EXPLANATION

Demonstrate each maneuver:

1. U turn

2. Y turn

Emphasize:

1. Reduced-risk elements of performance (see description below)

2. Commentary driving, "path clear" and "lane(s) clear"

GUIDING STUDENT PRACTICE

Teacher	Student
Phase 1: U Turns	

Teacher	Student
Direct student to "choose the safest location and perform U turn."	Performs U turns, concentrates on reduced-risk elements of performance.
Emphasize:	*Preparatory phase:*
1. Thorough scanning before starting maneuver	1. Chooses safest location, which provides for:
2. Delaying start until path and lanes are clear	Most efficient turn
3. Maintaining space cushion at all times	Distance from obstacles
	Adequate view of road in both directions
Watch for:	(Avoids locations where turning around is prohibited by law)
1. Recheck of lanes to front and rear when necessary	2. Comes to full stop (right edge of road)
2. Excessive hesitancy	Signals for stop if necessary
	Signals for left turn
	3. Scans intended path and nearby path (if necessary, uses horn to attract attention)
	4. Scans intersecting lanes
	5. Begins maneuver only when path is clear and will remain clear
	If clear:
	Comments: "path clear," "lanes clear"
	Begins maneuver
	If not clear:
	Delays start of maneuver
	Execution phase:
	6. Uses slow speed and extensive steering
	7. Maintains space cushion
	8. Continuously scans along path (if necessary, rechecks for approaching vehicles before entering new lane)

IN-CAR GUIDE FOR UNIT 10 (*cont.*)

Teacher	Student

Phase 2: Y Turns

Direct student to "choose the safest location and perform a Y turn."

Emphasize:

1. Thorough scanning before start of maneuver

2. Rescanning intersecting traffic lanes before moving from positions 2 and 3

3. Delaying moving from starting position, position 2, and position 3 until lanes are clear

4. Maintaining space cushion at all times

Watch for:

1. Failure to shift to R at position 2 and to D at position 3

2. Excessive hesitancy

Preparatory phase:

1. Chooses safest location, which provides for:

   Most efficient turn
   Distance from obstacles
   Adequate view of road in both directions
   (Avoids locations where turning around is prohibited by law)

2. Comes to full stop (right edge of road)

   Signals for stop if necessary
   Signals for left turn

3. Scans intended path and nearby path. (If necessary, uses horn to attract attention)

4. Scans intersecting lanes

5. Begins maneuver only when path is clear and will remain clear

   If clear:

   Begins maneuver

   If not clear:

   Delays start of maneuver

Execution phase:

6. *Position 1 to position 2*

   Slows speed, extensive steering to the left
   Turns wheels to right before stopping
   Stops, leaves space cushion
   Holds brake and shifts to R
   Rescans both lanes
   Assumes turned driver's position
   If obstacles appear, delays

7. *Position 2 to position 3*

   Slows speed, extensive steering to the right
   Turns wheels to left before stopping
   Stops, leaves space cushion
   Holds brake and shifts to D
   Rescans both lanes
   If obstacles appear, delays

8. *Position 3 to traffic lane*

   Accelerates and steers as necessary into lane

IN-CAR GUIDE FOR UNIT 10 (*cont.*)

Teacher	Student

Phase 3: Selecting a Method for Turning Around

Select locations that necessitate different methods for turning around.

Present student with the problem: "We are faced in a particular direction on this street. You want to reach destination X, which is on this street but in the opposite direction. Select the safest method for reaching the destination."

Give student reasonable amount of time to review alternatives before he starts.

After student completes maneuver, help him evaluate his selection.

Reviews alternatives and selects safest one:

1. U turn
2. Y turn
3. Going around block
4. Using driveway
5. Other

Concentrates on reduced-risk elements of maneuver selected.

EMERGENCIES: PERCEPTION AND RESPONSES

INTRODUCTION

Content

This unit deals with the responses of drivers to emergency situations [1]. The word "emergency" is used to denote those situations in which an accident is imminent and that require immediate and unusual driver actions to avoid the accident.

In a sense, the content of this unit is quite distinct from what has preceded it. Previous units have been concerned with driver actions that anticipate and thus avoid the onset of an emergency. This unit deals with actions that should be taken subsequent to the onset of the emergency in order to avert the actual accident. Hopefully, as a consequence of this unit, the student will acquire a repertoire of responses that will enable her to operate more effectively in emergency situations. In addition, as a result of experiencing emergencies the student should develop a better appreciation of the value of previously learned actions that avoid the onset of emergencies.

Selecting a Method

There is little doubt that special training to meet driving emergencies should constitute an important part of any program that attempts to develop the student's capabilities for safe performance. Several studies indicate that inadequate driver responses in emergency situations lead directly to accidents. In many cases the inadequacy of the response appears to be due to the fact that the driver has never before encountered the situation. Although the need for training to meet emergencies is apparent, the selection of methods for accomplishing it poses several problems. The problems arise out of a basic conflict between (1) the necessity to provide for the immediate safety of students by not exposing them to unreasonable risk, and (2) the need to make training as realistic as possible in order to provide for the transfer of learned responses to future emergency situations.

Alternative Methods

The teacher has to select from one of several alternatives. Those schools that have a driving simulator installation should be able to use it to good advantage in training students to meet emergencies (see simulator lessons listed under classroom guide). Another alternative is for teachers to create simulated emergencies through their own instructions to student drivers during an in-car lesson. These simulated emergencies might take place in an off-street practice area or in a relatively traffic-free on-street area. (The major disadvantage of conducting simulated emergencies on-street is that they constitute a potentially hazardous distraction to other drivers because of screeching brakes, and so on. This factor should be given serious consideration in deciding whether or not to use on-street simulation.) In addition, the teacher might use special techniques that more realistically simulate emergencies in off-street areas; for example, having an assistant move some kind of object into the path of the vehicle (perhaps a· cardboard box), or providing a slippery road surface that produces actual skids. Finally, several classroom techniques might be used to augment (or in some cases to substitute for) in-car training. Carefully selected films, filmstrips, and mimetic drills,* together with classroom discussion of basic concepts related to emergency performance, should prove of value.

Selecting Content

Ideally, a unit that trains drivers to meet emergencies should contain emergency situations that the driver is most likely to encounter in the future. The unit should also develop responses that will successfully avoid accidents in emergency situations. The accomplishment of this objective, however, is limited by a number of problems, some of which are as follows:

1. There is a limitless variety of emergency situations from which to choose, and a consequent limitless variety of possible responses that might be practiced in relation to each situation. The task of choosing an appropriately representative sample of situations and responses for inclusion in driver education programs is difficult in itself.

2. Existing information and data are of limited value as a basis for selecting and simulating the most common emergencies. For example, accident statistics may suggest that a particular type of accident is common, but normally they do not reveal the specific nature of the emergency situation that preceded the accident.

3. The emergency situation that turns out to be common for a particular driver may depend largely on the general pattern of behavior the driver exhibits. Therefore, an emergency situation that is common for one driver because it is an outgrowth of her tendency to drive in a certain way may not be common for another driver who tends to drive differently.

4. There is a danger in developing a "certain kind·of response" to meet a "certain kind of situation" because subtle differences among emergency situations may require substantially different responses. For example, a student might be trained to brake and steer right in response to another vehicle moving from right to left across her path (Fig. 11.1). As a consequence of this training, however, she might also tend to steer right and brake in situations that closely resemble the one above, but that actually call for a different response (Fig. 11.2).

---

* "Mimetic drills" refers to going through the motions or mimicking actions actually required in driving, such as moving one's foot from accelerator to brake pedal.

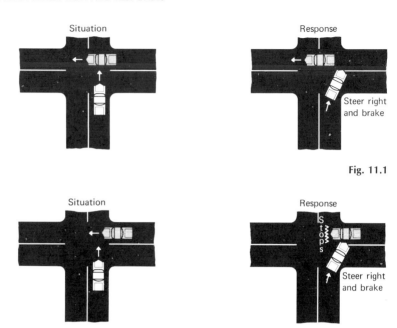

Fig. 11.1

Fig. 11.2

In a very practical sense, the teacher cannot hope to completely overcome these problems. He can, however, recognize the limitations they impose and make intelligent decisions in the selection of content by taking these limitations into consideration. For example, he can be careful not to devote his attention exclusively to the development of one specific series of responses to an emergency, when in fact slight variations in the emergency might require alternative responses. Students should be given an opportunity to discuss the alternative responses that might be required to meet subtle differences in the situation (and perhaps even to practice these alternatives).

Selecting the Method and Content for Unit 11

Unit 11 is divided into six phases. Phase 1, "Perception of Emergencies," is a classroom lesson devoted to the presentation of a variety of emergency situations using movies (or other visual materials). The purpose is to develop the student's ability to accurately perceive emergencies at the earliest possible moment. Movies are suggested for accomplishing this purpose because other methods of in-car simulation are either less realistic or too dangerous. Of course, if classroom driving simulators are available they provide an excellent method for training in this phase.

Phases 2–6 are devoted to in-car practice of common emergency responses, including quick braking responses, quick braking and steering responses, quick acceleration responses, skid-control responses, and other emergency responses. The purpose is to develop a repertoire of emergency responses, together with an understanding of the situations in which the responses are useful and the dangers that accompany their use. Practice takes place in off-street areas and alternative methods for simulating emergencies are suggested.

The unit is designed with the full realization of the limitations imposed by the problems discussed earlier. Noticeable limitations are the following:

1. The more realistic simulation of the perceptual elements in emergencies (Phase 1—films) is separated from the realistic application of emergency responses (Phases 2–6—in-car).

2. In some respects, the evidence to support the selection of the responses to be practiced (Phases 2–6) is weak.

3. In some cases, the safe methods suggested for simulating off-street emergencies provide a less than desirable degree of realism.

In spite of these limitations, however, the content should at least help the student avoid some of the blatant errors that seem to characterize driver behavior in emergency situations.

The design assumes that the school does not have a simulator installation available for use. Obviously, in schools where such installations are available they should be used to provide the major portion of the student's training for emergencies, together with supplementary in-car practice.

PHASE 1: PERCEPTION OF EMERGENCIES

The objectives for students are:

1. *When exposed to a variety of emergency situations (on film), to accurately identify the nature of the emergency at the earliest possible moment, and to select the appropriate response for the situation.*

2. *To identify the common types of emergency responses and, for each type of response, to be able to indicate (1) the types of situations in which the response is useful, and (2) the potential dangers that accompany its use.*

Content

The students should have an opportunity to view common emergency situations and to make decisions about which responses to employ to meet the emergency. Movies provide the most appropriate medium for presenting these emergency situations—particularly those films taken from the driver's position within the vehicle. Selected filmstrips also might prove valuable.

An attempt should be made to introduce visual materials depicting a reasonable variety of common emergency situations, such as:

1. Other vehicle enters path at intersection

2. Other vehicle stops in path ahead

3. Pedestrian enters path ahead

4. Vehicle coming from opposite direction enters path ahead

5. Other vehicle changes lanes (or swerves) into path

6. Other vehicle turns into path

7. Various situations involving skids on slippery surfaces

8. Various situations involving obstructed or reduced visibility

In addition to viewing the situations, students should be encouraged to respond actively to the emergency by using commentary driving to describe their immediate reactions, or by going through the motions of performing the responses.

PHASE 2: QUICK BRAKING RESPONSES

The objectives for students are:

1. *To demonstrate proficiency in quick braking (holding the wheel straight) in simulated situations that clearly call for the response*
2. *To identify the types of situations in which the response is useful and the potential dangers that accompany its use*

Illustrative Situations and Responses

The situations in Fig. 11.3 are illustrative of the type that might be simulated during in-car instruction.

In each case a quick braking response is called for. The advisability of veering to one side or the other in addition to braking is reduced because of the presence of other obstacles and because of the position of the obstacles in the immediate path.

Related Concepts

The following concepts are illustrative of what might be discussed in relation to the utility of and the dangers involved in quick braking:

1. Quick braking is useful in situations where obstacles are in the immediate path of the vehicle.
2. Situations requiring quick braking may arise because of an error on the driver's part (like inattention) or because of negligent behavior on the part of others.
3. Quick braking is used only when more gradual braking will not stop the vehicle in time to avoid a collision.
4. Quick braking increases the risk of being hit from the rear. Therefore, when it is used in situations where it is not needed it creates an unnecessary risk.
5. Quick braking increases the possibility of skidding—especially on slippery surfaces.

PHASE 3: QUICK BRAKING AND STEERING RESPONSES

The objectives for students are:

1. *To demonstrate proficiency in quick braking and steering in simulated situations that clearly call for the response*
2. *To identify the types of situations in which the response is useful and the potential dangers that accompany its use.*

Illustrative Situations and Responses

The situations in Figs. 11.4 and 11.5 are illustrative of the type that might be simulated during in-car instruction.

Other vehicle stops in path ahead, obstacles on both sides.

Other vehicle enters path from intersecting street.

Pedestrian enters turning path.

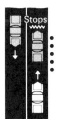

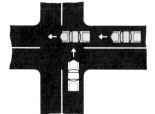

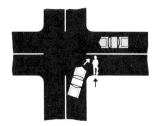

Fig. 11.3

Situation	Response

Other vehicle starts to turn left, stops in left side of driver's path.

Brake quickly and steer right. (Steering should be minimal to eliminate possibility of a roll-over.)

Fig. 11.4

Situation	Response

Approaching stop signal at intersection—vehicle on right swerves into driver's lane.

Brake quickly and steer left. (Steering should be minimal to eliminate possibility of a roll-over.)

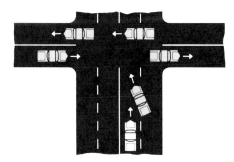

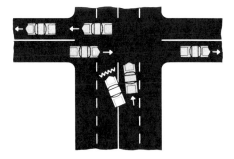

Fig. 11.5

Related Concepts

The following concepts are illustrative of what might be discussed in relation to the utility of and the dangers involved in quick braking and steering:

1. Quick braking and steering are useful in situations where quick braking alone would not avoid the collision, and where the steering adjustment helps to avoid the accident.

2. The addition of quick steering (to quick braking) is particularly helpful in situations where a portion of the path ahead is obstructed.

3. The addition of quick steering can be *especially dangerous* in situations where there are obstacles on either side of the path. (Particular attention should be given to the possibility of steering left into oncoming traffic. In fact, immediately after a student practices steering left and quick braking, the simulated situation might be changed to include oncoming traffic that would necessitate the avoidance of the steering left response.)

4. At relatively high speeds, quick steering increases the likelihood of lateral skidding and turning over.

PHASE 4: QUICK ACCELERATION RESPONSES

The objectives for students are:

1. *To demonstrate proficiency in quick acceleration in simulated situations that clearly call for the response*

2. *To identify the situations in which the response is useful and the potential dangers that accompany its use*

Illustrative Situations and Responses

The situations in Fig. 11.6 are illustrative of the type that might be simulated during in-car instruction.

Other vehicle entering intersection at angle aimed for the rear end of driver's vehicle.

Other vehicle entering highway—on collision course—a third vehicle following driver.

Driver has entered parkway—another vehicle is approaching at high speed.

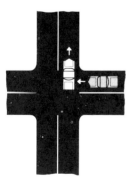  

Fig. 11.6

In each case a quick acceleration response is called for. It should be noted, however, that the appropriateness of the quick acceleration response is based on the assumption that the emergency situation is not perceived until it is too late to stop or to take some other evasive action.

Related Concepts

The following concepts are illustrative of what might be discussed in relation to the utility of and the dangers involved in quick acceleration:

1. Quick acceleration is generally useful in situations where other vehicles are moving toward the present position of your vehicle and where maintaining your speed or decelerating would increase the likelihood of an accident.

2. A poorly timed quick acceleration might cause the very accident that it attempts to avoid (for example, accelerating on an approach to an intersection to "beat" the other vehicle through, when in fact there was sufficient time to stop).

3. A sudden acceleration increases the likelihood of colliding with obstacles in (or entering) the path ahead.

4. The necessity for quick acceleration normally can be avoided by recognizing the emergency at an earlier point, as it is developing.

PHASE 5: SKID CONTROL RESPONSES

The objectives for students are:

1. To demonstrate proficiency in basic skid control responses in simulated situations

2. To identify the basic principles related to the causes, prevention, and control of skids

Related Concepts

Before a student attempts to practice skid control responses she should be exposed to the basic information related to the causes, prevention, and control of skids. The existing information in this area is extensive; it includes basic scientific principles as well as data accumulated from various testing grounds. The teacher should utilize a classroom lesson to cover this information. High-school textbooks and other professional literature might be used as guides (B 97–B 126). The lesson might include such basic considerations as:

1. The role of friction in starting and stopping

2. Road conditions that reduce friction

3. The differences between stationary friction, rolling friction, and sliding friction

4. The different types of skids and their causes

5. Driver actions that cause skids

6. Basic rules for responding to skids

7. Driver actions that intensify a skid

8. Skid prevention techniques

In addition, any one of several films could supplement the classroom lesson.

Illustrative Situations and Responses

Although the specific type of skid and the nature of conditions at the time of the skid will require appropriate variations in the driver's response, there are certain basic rules that apply to most skidding emergencies:

1. Steer gradually in the direction in which the rear end is skidding (countersteering)— steering in the opposite direction can cause your car to spin entirely around.
2. Gradually release pressure on the accelerator.
3. During the skid, avoid slamming on the brakes, oversteering, or accelerating. These actions would increase the severity of the skid.
4. Avoid using the brake until steering control is reestablished.
5. When or just before the car is properly aligned, apply brake pressure in a series of firm, gentle pumping motions.
6. Straighten the wheels gradually just prior to reaching the desired direction.

The student should have an opportunity to practice these basic responses during the in-car lesson. The situations in Figs. 11.7 and 11.8 are illustrative of the type that might be simulated.

Situation

Approaching intersection, apply brakes to stop, rear end starts skidding to the right.

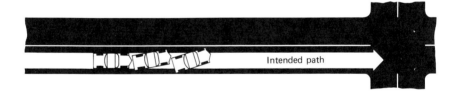

Intended path

Response

Release brake, countersteer to the right; when direction control is reestablished use gradual braking.*

Fig. 11.7

---

* Provided the car has reestablished a straight-line direction, "stab braking" (or pumping the brake) might be used to bring it to a stop.

Situation	Response
Rounding a curve, rear end starts to whip around to the left.	Gradually release accelerator, countersteer to the left until direction control is reestablished.

 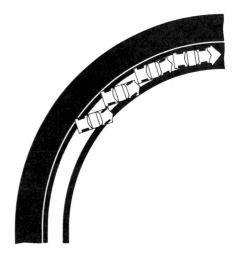

Fig. 11.8

PHASE 6: OTHER EMERGENCY RESPONSES

The objective for students is to effectively execute other emergency responses in simulated situations and to understand the reasons for these responses.

Illustrative Situations and Responses

Responses to blowouts, brake failure, stuck accelerator, and running off the pavement have been selected because there is reason to believe these events are reasonably common and because the responses involved are sufficiently different from other emergency responses to warrant practice (see Figs. 11.9 and 11.10).

1. Situation: Blowout	Response
While driving on a straight road, the right front tire blows out, car begins to veer to the right.	Hold steering wheel firmly, try to keep car on as straight a path as possible, let up on accelerator—do not brake until the car is under control.

Fig. 11.9

2. Situation: Brake Failure

Response

While driving on a straight road, driver depresses brake pedal, brakes do not respond.

Pump brake to restore pressure—if this doesn't work, gradually apply parking brake and at same time hold release lever in off position to reduce possibility of locking brakes, and downshift. If necessary sound horn and activate emergency flasher to warn others. If necessary, drive off road or choose a path that would involve the least chance of a severe accident.

3. Situation: Stuck Accelerator

Response

Driver accelerates on a roadway, pedal sticks in the down position, car continues to pick up speed.

In cars with power steering and power brakes, shift to neutral to cut off power to wheels, apply brakes and leave roadway at safe opportunity. In cars with no power steering or brakes, immediately turn off ignition. In any case, avoid reaching down to try to free the accelerator and thus diverting attention from roadway.

4. Situation: Run off Pavement Edge

Response

Driving at high speed on a straight roadway, the right wheels go off the pavement onto a soft shoulder.

Avoid slamming on the brakes and trying to steer back onto roadway at high speed. Hold steering wheel steady and allow the car to slow down gradually; pump brake if necessary. When a slow speed is reached, check traffic and turn wheels sharply to the left.

Fig. 11.10

Related Concepts

The following concepts are illustrative of what might be discussed in relation to these emergencies:

1. A blowout in a front tire produces veering in the direction of the blowout, while a blowout in a rear tire results in a swerving of the rear end from side to side.

2. When a blowout occurs, jamming on the brakes or oversteering can produce a skid and possibly a roll-over accident.

3. When brake failure occurs, pumping the brake may build up enough pressure in the brake lines to allow the driver to stop; downshifting will produce "engine drag" to slow down the car.

4. When the accelerator sticks, the main objective is to cut the power to the wheels, without reducing the control available (for example, power steering and power brakes), and then bring the car to a stop in a safe manner.

5. When the right wheels go off the road onto a soft shoulder, trying to steer back onto the road at high speeds or slamming on the brakes can produce a dangerous skid or a roll-over.

6. The precise responses in all these emergencies may have to be varied to meet special conditions of the environment, such as the presence of other vehicles or obstacles.

INSTRUCTIONAL PLAN

Classroom The classroom phase of instruction should be used to allow students to view common emergencies (Phase 1) and to discuss information and concepts related to the in-car performance of the emergency responses (Phases 2–6).

In-Car An off-street area should be used for practicing the emergency response. Careful precautions should be taken to be certain that the area is safe for the kind of practice intended. In particular, the surface of the area should be free of sand, gravel, and other elements that might produce a hazardous skid when quick braking is employed. In addition, the area should be clearly marked to depict lanes, intersections, roadway edges, and other elements important to the simulation of particular emergency situations.

All emergency responses should be practiced at *slow speeds* to eliminate the possibility of dangerous skids or roll-overs. The teacher should demonstrate each emergency response in the precise manner in which the student is expected to perform it. Prior to the student's performance, the teacher should provide instructions that clearly describe the nature of the emergency situation that will be encountered. That is, the instructions should effectively set the stage for the impending emergency. The teacher should encourage students to ask for clarification of the situation whenever they do not fully understand the instruction.

The method for simulating an emergency will vary with the precise nature of the situation and according to the preference of the teacher. Some suggestions for simulation are:

1. In most situations the teacher might use short, well-timed, verbal cues to indicate the onset of the emergency, for example, "car turning," "car crossing," "blowout," "skid-right," and so on. In each case the meaningfulness of the cues would depend on the prior instructions that set the stage for the emergency.

2. Other stationary (unoccupied) vehicles and/or pedestrians located adjacent to the intended path of the vehicle might be used as aids in simulating emergencies. For example, a stationary vehicle might be used to simulate an intersection emergency (Fig. 11.11).

 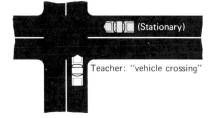

Fig. 11.11

When using this method of simulation, of course, the teacher should be certain that the other vehicle or pedestrian is far enough removed from the path of the driver education car to preclude the possibility of an actual collision.

3. In simulating front-wheel blowouts, the teacher might pull the steering wheel in the direction of the blowout.

4. In simulating running off the pavement, a suitable edge of the off-street area that closely resembles the edge of a roadway might be used. Or, if this is not possible, a long board (or series of boards) might be used to simulate the roadway edge, and to produce the sensation of having run off the pavement.

CLASSROOM GUIDE FOR UNIT 11
Emergencies: Perception and Responses

Topics	Instructional Plan
1. *Perception of emergencies—objective:* early and accurate detection. Utilize wide variety of common emergencies.	1. Present common emergency situations, preferably using films. 2. Have students respond to emergencies, verbally or physically. 3. Discuss appropriate responses for each situation.
2. *Quick braking responses:* a) Situations that require quick braking b) Causes and prevention of these emergencies c) Dangers involved in quick braking—rear-end collision, skidding	1. Present illustrative situations. 2. Discuss responses to each situation.
3. *Quick braking and steering responses:* a) Situations that require quick braking and steering b) Causes and prevention of these emergencies c) Dangers involved in quick steering responses—steering into oncoming traffic, skidding, overturning	1. Present illustrative situations. 2. Discuss responses to each situation.
4. *Quick acceleration responses:* a) Situations that require quick acceleration b) Causes and prevention of these emergencies c) Consequences of poorly timed acceleration responses d) Quick acceleration and other obstacles ahead	1. Present illustrative situations. 2. Discuss responses to each situation.
5. *Skid control responses:* a) Role of friction in vehicle control b) Road conditions and friction c) Stationary, rolling, and sliding friction d) Causes of skids—driver actions e) Basic rules for responding to skids; countersteering, avoiding brakes, oversteering, and accelerating f) Skid control responses to specific situations	1. Present basic information related to causes, prevention, and control of skids. 2. Present illustrative situations. 3. Discuss responses to each situation.

CLASSROOM GUIDE FOR UNIT 11 (cont.)

Topics	Instructional Plan

6. *Other emergency responses:*
  a) Blowouts
  b) Brake failure
  c) Stuck accelerator
  d) Run off pavement
  e) Others _____
  _____
  f) Concepts related to each type of
    emergency
	1. Discuss and illustrate nature of each type of emergency.
	2. Discuss appropriate responses to specific emergencies.

PREPARATORY READING FOR STUDENTS

1. *Learning to Drive: Skills, Concepts, and Strategies.* Chapter 18, "Emergencies: Perception and Responses."

   —or appropriate sections from another high-school text.

RELATED SIMULATOR LESSONS

1. Aetna Drivotrainer System: "Crash Avoidance," "Driving Emergencies."
2. Link Simulator System: "Hazardous Situations."

IN-CAR GUIDE FOR UNIT 11

Emergencies: Perception and Responses

DEMONSTRATION AND EXPLANATION

Demonstrate each type of emergency response:

1. Quick braking

2. Quick braking and steering

3. Quick acceleration

4. Skid control responses (right and left)

5. Other responses to blowout, run off roadway,
   brake failure, stuck accelerator

Emphasize:

1. Slow speed at which car will travel in simulated emergencies

2. Avoiding oversteering

GUIDING STUDENT PRACTICE

Teacher	Student
Phases 2–6: Quick Braking Responses, Quick Braking and Steering Responses, Quick Acceleration Responses, Skid Control Responses, and Other Responses	

(The teacher should design simulated emergency situations that require each different type of response. The following outline might be used to guide practice in Phases 2–6.)

Teacher	Student
Prior to student performance:	Carefully attends to instructions—asks for clarification whenever necessary.
1. Be certain that driving area is clearly marked.	
2. Check area for possible hazards (road surface, other obstacles).	
3. Be certain that accessory devices that simulate conditions are in place and ready (boxes, dummies, other cars, etc.).	
4. Provide instructions that clearly set the stage for the emergency.	
5. Specify speed at which car should travel (slow).	
During student performance:	Approaches emergency situation—responds to teacher's cue indicating onset of emergency.
1. Provide short, well-timed cues that indicate onset of the emergency.	
2. Perform auxiliary acts that help to simulate emergency (pulling on steering wheel).	
After student performance ask student to evaluate response and to comment on dangers imposed by response.	Comments on the adequacy of the response and assesses dangers imposed by the response.

unit 12

STRATEGIES FOR
LIMITED ACCESS HIGHWAYS

INTRODUCTION

This unit is an extension of Unit 8, "Strategies for Roadway and Traffic Characteristics." Here the strategies are designed for limited access highways. ("Limited access highways" refers to freeways, turnpikes, expressways and the like.) [1]

Since limited access highways have many features in common, it is possible to recommend some general driving practices (see "Characteristics of Limited Access Highways" in this unit) to be applied during practice on these highways. However it is the teacher's responsibility to revise these general guides as necessary to fit the unique aspects of the routes her students use. The procedures specified in Unit 8 for developing strategies may be used to develop specific strategies for continuous and recurring characteristics, and for characteristics of specific locations along the route.

Only advanced students who have demonstrated the skillful and error-free driving required to make them low-risk drivers on highways should be allowed to practice on limited access highways.

Check state and local traffic regulations regarding the permissibility of conducting practice driving lessons on limited access roadways in your area. Also, it would be wise to check with state and local police authorities regarding when and where it would be appropriate to conduct the practice.

Use the Instructional Plan in Unit 8 as a guide for planning this unit of instruction.

In this unit the objectives for students are:

1. *To identify the important characteristics of limited access highways and the common accident risks on these highways*
2. *To describe the driving practices designed to deal with these characteristics and reduce the risks*
3. *To develop driving strategies for given routes along limited access highways*
4. *To effectively apply the strategies while driving on the route*

272

SELECTED CONCEPTS AND DRIVING
PRACTICES FOR LIMITED ACCESS HIGHWAYS

Characteristics of Limited Access Highways

Students should be able to identify the distinctive roadway and traffic characteristics of the limited access highways on which they drive, and develop strategies for coping with those characteristics. While all highways are not the same, most good highways have several features in common: (1) on-ramps and acceleration lanes for entering, and off-ramps and deceleration lanes for exiting; (2) multiple lanes in each direction; (3) comparatively wide lanes; (4) relatively high traffic speeds and speed limits; (5) relatively gradual curves and grades; and (6) good sight distances. Driving strategies should be developed to fit both these characteristics and the special variations of these characteristics that may be encountered. For example, students may develop a general strategy for entering highways with long acceleration lanes, but should be encouraged to vary the strategy when they enter a highway with a very short acceleration lane. Obviously students should also continuously adjust their strategies to suit changing conditions of traffic flow and density.

The Accident Problem on Limited Access Highways

The traffic accident pattern on limited access highways differs from the patterns found elsewhere. The driving strategies developed should take into consideration the types of accidents that are common on such highways and should incorporate driving practices that help guard against these accidents. Some important features of the accident problem on highways are listed below.* Teachers should consult other resources for additional data—perhaps data on local and state highways are available.

1. Forty-five percent of limited access highway accidents involved cars moving too fast for conditions.
2. At least one-half of all freeway accidents were rear-end collisions. A large proportion of rear-end collisions involved cars that had stopped in the roadway.
3. Thirty-five percent of limited access highway accidents occurred on crests and sags. The rate of rear-end collisions was one and one-half times higher on crests and sags as on other sections of through lanes.
4. Eighteen percent of freeway accidents occurred on through lanes in the vicinity of ramps.
5. "Cutting in" contributed to 26 percent of urban expressway accidents.
6. A large proportion of turnpike accidents involve only one car that, for a variety of reasons, runs off the roadway.

Subsequent sections of this unit contain additional data on accidents.

---

* Most of these data are based on a variety of accident studies as reported in *Driver Education Task Analysis* by HumRRO (B 59).

Entering the Highway

The approach   When approaching the highway on the entrance ramp, begin scanning for vehicles on the highway as early as possible and note the amount of acceleration lane available. Search for a gap into which to merge; turn head to the left and use a brief glance technique to do so. Signal intention, and, if conditions permit, accelerate when entering the acceleration lane (Fig. 12.1).

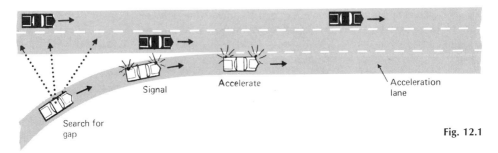

Signal   Accelerate   Acceleration lane

Search for gap

Fig. 12.1

   When vehicles are ahead on the entrance ramp, maintain an awareness of their position and movement and leave an adequate space cushion ahead (Fig. 12.2). Do not assume that they will accelerate and merge smoothly into the traffic lane—they may decelerate or stop at a time when you are checking to the rear. This could result in a rear-end collision (Fig. 12.3). Approximately 90 percent of on-ramp accidents are of the rear-end type (B 59). Also allow cars ahead in the acceleration lane to merge first.

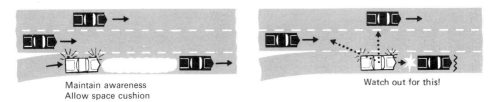

Maintain awareness
Allow space cushion

Watch out for this!

Fig. 12.2   **Fig. 12.3**

The entry   While proceeding in the acceleration lane, continue to search for an adequate gap in traffic, using the side-view mirror and a brief glance to check the blind spot, as necessary, and maintain an awareness of the amount of acceleration lane remaining to be used (Fig. 12.4).

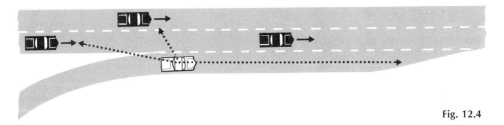

Fig. 12.4

When conditions are clear or an adequate gap exists, accelerate and move into the gap at or near the normal speed of traffic. Entering at the normal speed helps to reduce the possibility of rear-end collisions with fast-moving vehicles on the highway (Fig. 12.5).

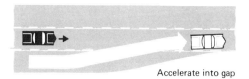

Accelerate into gap

Reduce risk of rear end collision

Fig. 12.5

When an adequate gap is not immediately available, reduce speed to allow the gap to reach you (Fig. 12.6). On roads with short acceleration lanes it may be necessary to stop. In doing so, however, recognize that an excessive speed reduction or a stop can be dangerous for two reasons: (1) It takes considerable time to accelerate from a slow speed to the normal highway speed, which increases the risk of a rear-end collision during entry. (2) The risk of being hit from behind by other vehicles in the acceleration lane is increased.

On highways where entrances are followed closely by exits, the acceleration lane is likely to also serve as a deceleration lane for exiting vehicles. Students should be alerted to this in advance and be ready to deal with exiting vehicles that move in front of them in the acceleration lane.

Some entrance ramps and acceleration lanes feed into the left side of the main roadway. In general, the procedures for entering from these ramps are similar to those mentioned above. Of course both student and teacher should recognize the increased danger associated with these entrances due to the fast speed of traffic in the left lane and to the fact that drivers on the highways are less likely to expect cars to enter from the left. In fact it is probably wise to avoid having students use left entrance (and exit) ramps unless they are well advanced in their driving skills.

Driving on the Highway

Lane selection   In many states and on many highways drivers are required to stay in the right lane except when passing a slower moving vehicle (check state laws). In any case, stay to the right if your speed is slower than that of some other drivers, which is likely to be the case during practice driving.

Passing entrances   Entering a limited access highway is a demanding maneuver—especially when a number of other vehicles are present. When passing an entrance, drivers can make it easier for the drivers trying to enter by trying to avoid reaching the potential points of conflict at the same time as the entering vehicle (Fig. 12.7). In many instances this can be done by simply maintaining speed and allowing the differences in speeds to bring you past the points of conflict first (Fig. 12.8). The selection of other alternatives for avoiding conflicts should be based on the specific characteristics of the situation. Some examples of alternatives are pictured in Fig. 12.9.

Whenever possible, try to avoid excessive decreases in speed that confuse the entering driver and increase the risk of a rear-end collision (Fig. 12.10).

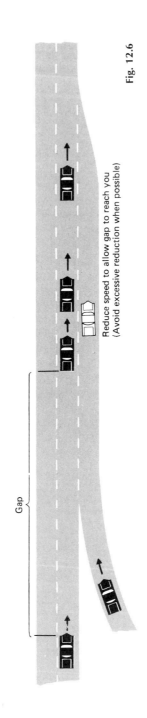

Reduce speed to allow gap to reach you
(Avoid excessive reduction when possible)

Gap

Fig. 12.6

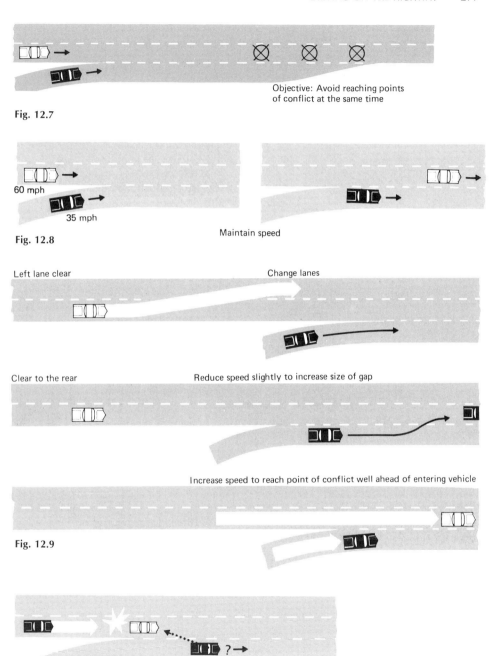

Fig. 12.7

Objective: Avoid reaching points of conflict at the same time

Fig. 12.8

60 mph

35 mph

Maintain speed

Left lane clear

Change lanes

Clear to the rear

Reduce speed slightly to increase size of gap

Increase speed to reach point of conflict well ahead of entering vehicle

Fig. 12.9

Excessive decrease in speed:

1. Increases risk of rear-end collision
2. Confuses entering driver

Fig. 12.10

Speed control and tracking   Whenever possible, maintain the normal speed of traffic, which is usually somewhere between the speed limit and 5 mph below the limit. Doing so reduces the risk of being hit from the rear and of causing the dangerous bunching of traffic behind.

Allow for a large space cushion between oneself and the car ahead. Since stopping distances at high speeds are so long (Fig. 12.11), the space cushion should be larger than the normal two-to-three-second gap—a four-second gap is desirable here.

When vehicles move into the lane a short distance ahead and reduce the space cushion available, decelerate slightly and reestablish an adequate space cushion (Fig. 12.12).

In heavy traffic it is frequently difficult to maintain an adequate space cushion because vehicles keep moving into the space ahead, and if drivers try to reestablish the space cushion by decelerating, they increase the risk of being hit from the rear. In such instances it may be necessary to accept a less than adequate space cushion, and compensate for it by maintaining an awareness of the movements of several cars ahead.

Whenever a driver ahead signals his intention to exit from the highway, expect him to reduce his speed substantially. Don't allow the differences in speeds to eliminate the cushion (Fig. 12.13). In addition, be alert to the possibility that drivers in deceleration lanes who are apparently preparing to exit may change their minds and attempt to re-enter the roadway.

Small tracking errors on limited access highways can be especially dangerous because the high speed magnifies the size of the error. Fortunately traffic lanes are normally wide and a centered lane position provides an ample space cushion on either side. Be especially careful to maintain an adequate space cushion in relation to roadway edges, fixed objects, and other obstacles bordering the lane.

Scanning and evaluating   High-speed driving on limited access highways requires major adjustments in scanning techniques. Most important, drivers have to scan and evaluate conditions very far ahead to allow for the substantial increase in stopping distances. Fortunately, the sizable sight distances available on highways permit this type of scanning. Also, since there are no intersections, no traffic signals, no pedestrians, and no busy adjacent areas, the need to scan to the sides of the road is reduced so that drivers can devote more attention to the road ahead. It may be necessary to periodically shift in scanning to check on the position of the car within the traffic lane and on the movement of other nearby vehicles.

Students should maintain an awareness of vehicles that are overtaking and passing them. Since "cutting in" is responsible for approximately one-fourth of all freeway accidents (B 138), students should be alert to the possibility that such vehicles may drift toward them or abruptly move back into the lane ahead of them. In addition they should watch for vehicles ahead in adjacent lanes that are trapped behind slower moving vehicles and might suddenly change lanes to pass.

Students should recognize that hill crests and dips in the roadway are particularly dangerous locations on limited access highways. At these points the accident rates are one and one-half times the rates on other sections of the roadway (B 138). Speed reduction is usually advisable when approaching these locations (see Unit 8).

Signaling for speed reduction or stop   On limited access highways when traffic is moving at a steady pace, drivers to the rear do not expect the cars ahead to stop. When an obstacle appears ahead on the road, such as a traffic bottleneck, stopped vehicle, or a closed lane, drivers should provide an early warning of their intention to reduce speed and/or stop, by using a hand signal or, if necessary, the emergency flashing signal.

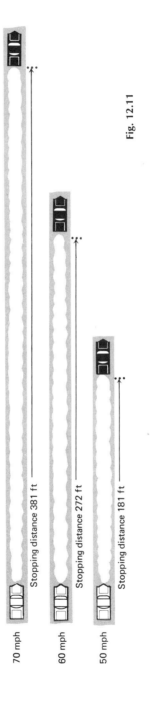

Fig. 12.11

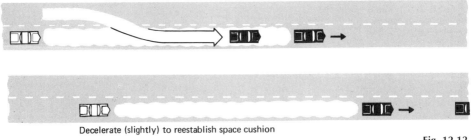

Decelerate (slightly) to reestablish space cushion

Fig. 12.12

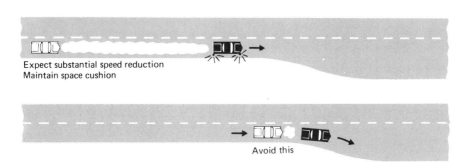

Expect substantial speed reduction
Maintain space cushion

Avoid this

Fig. 12.13

Maneuvers   Only a small variety of maneuvers are normally performed on limited access highways. Changing lanes and passing occur most frequently. When changing lanes or passing is required, use the reduced-risk procedures recommended in Unit 6.

U turns and backing up on limited access highways are prohibited. It hardly seems necessary to point out the dangers of such maneuvers. Yet a reasonably large number of drivers appear to be foolish enough to try them. Apparently, drivers attempt these maneuvers because they were inattentive, passed their exit, and want to return to it.

Stopping on limited access highways is usually prohibited, except in emergencies. If something does go wrong with the car, signal by using the emergency flashing signal, move to the right edge of the road, reduce speed, then move out well onto the shoulder of the road and stop. Get out of the car, stay well away from the traffic lane, tie a white piece of cloth to the door handle as a distress signal, and wait for the highway police to arrive.

Toll plazas   Students should obey posted speed limits as they approach toll plazas—a glance at the speedometer may be helpful here. They should be alerted to signal lights indicating open/closed booths, signs indicating exact change lanes, and other regulatory information. On the basis of this information they should be encouraged to pick an approach lane early and stay in it—avoiding sudden or last-minute lane changes. At the same time they should watch for erratic behavior of other drivers whose attention may be diverted by fumbling for money or searching for a toll card.

Exiting from the Highway

Before students enter the highway, they should know the route, including the exit they intend to use. When they reach the exit prior to the one they will use (which should also have been noted in advance), they should be mentally ready to get off at the next exit. Make certain that they are in the right-hand lane at least a mile or so before the exit, and are alert for the signs that indicate the approach to the exit.

Two important risks in exiting are (1) being hit from the rear while decelerating, and (2) entering the curved portion of the exit ramp at too high a speed. To reduce these risks check in the rearview mirror for traffic to the rear, signal intention to exit, move into the deceleration lane as early as possible, and decelerate rapidly when approaching the exit ramp (Fig. 12.14). Whenever possible avoid rapid deceleration in the traffic lane.

Students should recognize that off-ramps are especially dangerous because of the speed involved, the difficulty in controlling a decelerating car, and the presence of fixed objects, primarily signs (B 59). The tendency of drivers to underestimate speed when decelerating after driving at high speeds complicates the problem further. So as students approach and enter the off-ramp, they should check for posted speed limits, glance at the speedometer to check for adequate speed reduction, concentrate on tracking in the middle of the exit lane, and scan for other vehicles and obstacles ahead on the ramp.

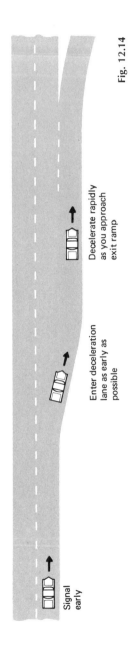

Fig. 12.14

CLASSROOM GUIDE FOR UNIT 12
Strategies for Limited Access Highways

Topics	Instructional Plan
1. The accident problem on limited access highways	1. Discuss special features and accident problem on highways.
2. *Driving practices:* a) Entering the highway b) Lane selection c) Passing entrances d) Speed control and tracking e) Scanning and evaluating f) Maneuvers g) Exiting from the highway	2. Discuss and explain reasons for adopting practices; show appropriate film if available.
3. *Strategy for Route 1:* a) Special roadway and traffic characteristics b) Driving strategy Continuous and recurring actions Actions at special locations	3. a) Specify route. b) Identify special characteristics. c) Develop strategy for route (see procedures in Unit 8).
4. *Strategy for Route 2:* (Same as above)	

PREPARATORY READING FOR STUDENTS

1. *Learning to Drive: Skills, Concepts, and Strategies.* Chapter 15, "Strategies for Limited Access Highways."

   —or appropriate section from another high-school text.

2. Articles, research reports, or other materials dealing with accidents on limited access highways.

RELATED SIMULATOR LESSONS

1. Aetna Drivotrainer System: "Expressway Excellence."
2. Link Simulator System: "Limited Access," "Expressways are Different."

IN-CAR GUIDE FOR UNIT 12

Strategies for Limited Access Highways

Teacher	Student

Phase 1: Strategy for Route 1

1. Prior to student performance, make certain route is clearly specified and understood.	1. Before starting to drive briefly review major elements of strategy: a) Basic rules: (1) "Be flexible, alter the strategy when unexpected events require it"; (2) "Be alert, concentrate on what you are doing now." b) See General Guides on following page. c) *Actions at specific locations:* _____ _____ _____
2. As student drives: a) Allow student to concentrate—use verbal cues sparingly. b) Use cues when necessary to help student remain flexible and alert.	2. Concentrates on applying the strategy. Also remains flexible (alters strategy when required) and alert (concentrates on what he is doing).
3. When trip is completed: a) Guide student's evaluation of his performance. b) Allow student to make observations about effectiveness of strategy. c) Discuss briefly required alterations in strategy.	3. When trip is completed takes part in evaluation of: a) His performance b) Strategy c) Alterations employed

Phase 2: Strategy for Route 2

(same as Phase 1)

General Guides for Driving on Limited Access Highways

Revise as necessary to suit the special characteristics of the limited access highways on which you will drive.

Entering the highway

Approach:

Begin scanning early.
Search for gap. (If vehicle is ahead on ramp, maintain awareness and allow space cushion.)

Entry:

Continue search for gap.
Use mirror and check blind spot, as necessary.
Maintain awareness of length of acceleration lane remaining.

When adequate gap is present:

Accelerate and move into traffic lane at normal speed of traffic.

When gap is not present:

Adjust speed as necessary. Try to avoid excessive speed reduction.

Driving on the highway

Lane selection: Use right lane except when passing.

Speed control and tracking:

Maintain normal speed of traffic.
Allow *large* space cushion ahead. (Maintain space cushion ahead, when possible.)
Maintain "centered lane position."
Maintain space cushion at road edge and by abutments, and so forth.

Scanning:

Scan *far ahead.*
Periodically check near points for lane position and other vehicles.

Signaling to the rear:

Use hand signal or emergency flasher to signal an unexpected speed reduction or stop.

Passing entrances:

Avoid arriving at points of conflict at same time as entering vehicles.
Adjust speed and lane position as necessary.

Exiting from the highway

At exit prior to one to be used get ready to get off at the next exit.
Enter right-hand lane early.
Signal.
Enter deceleration lane early.
Decelerate rapidly on approach to ramp. (Check speedometer.)

STRATEGIES FOR
DRIVING AT NIGHT

INTRODUCTION

This unit extends the capability of student drivers to enable them to cope with the special problems of night driving [1]. It is intended for students who have successfully acquired the skills and techniques in previous units—particularly Units 5–8. The unit concentrates on the development of scanning and evaluation techniques under conditions of low visibility and the driving adjustments required to ensure safety under such conditions.

Before planning night driving lessons, teachers should check state and local traffic regulations relative to giving instruction during the hours of darkness. In addition, local school district policies and regulations regarding evening instruction should also be consulted. Obviously, *instruction in night driving will have to be omitted in those locales where existing policies or regulations prevent it.* In addition, it would be wise to secure written permission from parents before allowing students to participate.

INSTRUCTIONAL PLAN

A classroom period should be devoted to a discussion of the special problems encountered in night driving and the appropriate driving techniques.

Practice should start in an off-street area, allowing students to become acclimated to conditions of low visibility. Then familiar routes should be used for initial on-srreet lessons— particularly routes for which strategies have been developed previously (see Unit 8). At first, it is advisable to avoid routes or locations that are particularly hazardous at night—such as high-speed winding roads or crowded intersections. Eventually, however, students should be exposed to a reasonable range of roadway and traffic conditions.

Existing strategies for roadway and traffic conditions, developed in Unit 8, should be modified to make them applicable for night driving. In particular, some of the recommended night driving practices (see Unit 8) might be added. However, the strategies that emerge should still reflect the basic roadway and traffic characteristics that prevail during the daytime as well as at night. Night driving strategies should *augment, not replace,* previously developed strategies.

Practice should include a variety of reduced-risk maneuvers, including turns, lane changes, and backing maneuvers. During the early stages of student practice, teachers should be alert to the possibility of increased tracking errors and failure to see potential obstacles. Teachers might use brief verbal cues to warn the students of such dangers.

Teachers should recognize that some students might have poor night vision. Results of a standard test for night vision given by the school or motor vehicle department should be used to screen out those with serious problems. Also, only those students who can successfully negotiate a route during the daytime should be allowed to drive on it at night.

In this unit the objectives for students are:

1. *To identify the risks created by the low visibility available at night*
2. *To describe the driving practices designed to compensate for the low visibility available at night*
3. *To be able to develop effective strategies for driving on given routes at night*
4. *To effectively apply strategies for driving at night on given routes*

SELECTED CONCEPTS AND PRACTICES FOR DRIVING AT NIGHT

The Problems of Night Driving

Nighttime is a comparatively dangerous time for driving. The mileage death rate at night is approximately two and one-half times the day rate in rural places, and three times the day rate in urban places (B 137). Unquestionably, conditions of low visibility contribute significantly to these high rates.

While in the daytime the road is often visible for thousands of feet ahead, at night visibility directly ahead is often limited to 150 feet (low beams) or 500 (high beams). However, since effective seeing distance decreases as the speed of the vehicle increases, clear sight distance traveling at 30 mph with low beams is only 90 feet (B 138). The problem is compounded by objects outside the lateral scope of headlight beams. For example, low reflectance objects at the roadside are not visible beyond 66 feet (B 59).

Glare from oncoming headlights can severely reduce a driver's night vision. Vision is adversely affected by oncoming lights as far away as 3,000 feet and maximum visibility when both cars are using low beams is 200 feet (B 138). When vehicles approaching each other are 100 feet apart, it is difficult to see objects beside or beyond the oncoming vehicle, and after passing the vehicle it takes the driver's eyes approximately seven seconds to recover from the glare (B 59). Of course the whole problem is exacerbated when oncoming vehicles use high beams, which can momentarily blind drivers.

Estimating speed and predicting closure of other vehicles can also be problems at night since distance perception at night is based on the angular separation of the headlights and distance between taillights of other vehicles (B 138). This can easily result in overestimating the distance of small cars.

Studies of driver search patterns indicate that there are substantial differences in the patterns used at night compared to those used during daytime (B 105). At night drivers have to fixate for longer periods of time on each area of the environment because of the longer times needed to acquire and process information. Also, on unlighted roads drivers find it necessary to substantially increase the frequency with which they glance at road edges and surfaces, apparently to aid in tracking.

Preparing to Drive

All of the preparatory actions normally performed prior to moving the vehicle are applicable to night driving (see Unit 2). In addition, several special actions are required:

1. Before entering the car, check conditions along the intended path—especially when the initial movement will be backing.
2. Turn the headlights on and check to see that they are adjusted to the appropriate beam position. In doing so it is sometimes advisable to flick the beams up and down to make sure they are working.
3. If necessary, adjust the panel light to an intensity that makes important instruments visible.
4. Whenever possible, check to see whether the taillights, stopping lights, and directional signals are working.
5. Switch the day/night rearview mirror to the night position.

Scanning, Evaluating, and Using Headlights

At night, it is advisable for drivers to keep their eyes moving in a way that allows them to see and evaluate conditions as far ahead as possible and to keep the car on path (accurate tracking). Three techniques should help accomplish this:

1. Regularly scan ahead to the limits of the headlight range.
2. Periodically scan beyond the headlight range and use visible clues to evaluate traffic conditions and roadway features ahead. (Taillights and headlights of other vehicles, street lights, and illuminated signs and signals usually provide the most important clues.)
3. When necessary shift eyes to near points to help in tracking.

Coordinating these techniques should help to compensate, to some extent, for reduced visibility. In addition, it should help prevent the common error of staring at the brightly illuminated portion of the road ahead and becoming oblivious to the dimly lit surroundings.

Students should understand that visible headlights and taillights of other vehicles provide important clues that help drivers evaluate the situation ahead. Maintaining an awareness of the taillights of the vehicle ahead helps drivers to gauge the proper following distance and alerts them to curves in the road. When taillights increase in brightness, it means drivers ahead are braking. Oncoming headlights provide advance warning of approaching vehicles and provide clues about road curvature ahead. Headlights approaching from the side allow drivers to detect intersecting vehicles early, and indicate the presence of intersecting streets.

However, it is important for students to be cautious in interpreting these clues. Often it is difficult to judge vehicle speed and roadway position when only headlights or taillights are visible. For example, taillights that may appear to be moving in the lane ahead may actually be on a parked vehicle at the roadway edge.

When driving at high speeds and when conditions allow, use high beams to increase visibility. Low-beam lights should provide visibility for at least 150 feet ahead; high-beam lights provide visibility for at least 450 feet ahead.

Switch to low-beam lights well before meeting an oncoming vehicle and when following another vehicle. Most state laws require that drivers switch to low beams at least 500 feet before meeting another vehicle and, when following, at 300 feet or less. Otherwise high-beam lights will shine directly in the eyes of the oncoming driver or reflect off the rearview mirror into the eyes of the driver ahead.

When meeting an oncoming car, the glare from approaching headlights will reduce visibility. In such situations avoid looking directly at the headlights. Instead, use the right edge of the road as a guide for lane positioning, reduce speed, and move to the right to provide an ample space cushion. After passing the vehicle it may take a few seconds to recover from the glare. It is usually advisable to maintain a reduced speed during this period.

When a following vehicle fails to dim its headlights, switch the day/night mirror to the night position if it is not already in that position. If the headlight glare is still bothersome, slow down gradually, position the car well to the right of the roadway, avoid looking directly at the rearview mirror, and allow the car to pass at the first safe opportunity.

Speed Control and Tracking

As a general rule, students should lower their speed to keep stopping distance within the range of the headlights; in other words, *they should not overdrive their headlights* (Fig. 13.1). It may not always be possible to do this, however, because they also have to adjust speed to the normal speed of traffic to reduce the risk of being hit from the rear. This is especially important in night driving because it is more difficult for other drivers (to the rear) to judge the speed of the car ahead.

When the normal speed of traffic exceeds a speed that is safe for headlight range, drivers have to decide whether to maintain a slower than normal speed, increasing the risk of being hit from behind; or to adjust to the normal speed, increasing the risk of not being able to stop in time to avoid hitting an obstacle in the path ahead. This is one of the difficult decisions that drivers often have to make. During practice driving the teacher's responsibility is to help the student choose speeds that involve the least overall risk.

Because it is so difficult to judge the speed and position of vehicles ahead at night, especially when only the taillights can be seen, leave an extra large space cushion ahead. And because other drivers will have the same difficulty judging speed and position from behind, whenever possible avoid stopping in or near a traffic lane.

Accurate tracking at night is more difficult than in daylight. Because the driver cannot see the immediate surroundings as well, it is harder to judge the immediate position of the vehicle. Frequently the driver cannot see far enough ahead to anticipate curves in the road and the corresponding need for steering adjustments. These conditions increase the risk of committing tracking errors, especially among beginning drivers. If students have difficulty staying on-path, have them reduce speed to reduce the size of their tracking errors, and have them use more frequent brief glances to near points to check on the position of the car in relation to the roadway edge and lane markings.

Performing Reduced-Risk Maneuvers at Night

For the most part, performing reduced-risk maneuvers at night is similar to performing them in the daytime. The procedures and techniques covered in earlier units are applicable to night driving. However, students should consider some special factors before performing these maneuvers at night.

Turning   Headlights do not go around corners. They clearly illuminate only that portion of the turning path that is directly ahead. To compensate for this, reduce speed on turns and scan ahead along the turning path beyond the headlights. Although it may not be possible to see clearly along the unlit portion of the path, it should be possible to see major obstacles ahead. In any case, avoid the common error of allowing "eyes to follow the headlights around the corner" (Fig. 13.2).

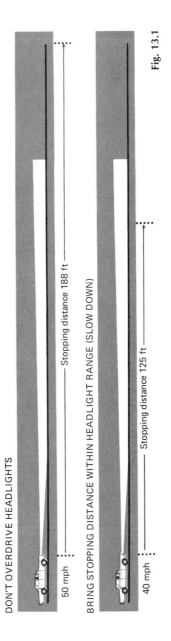

DON'T OVERDRIVE HEADLIGHTS

50 mph — Stopping distance 188 ft

BRING STOPPING DISTANCE WITHIN HEADLIGHT RANGE (SLOW DOWN)

40 mph — Stopping distance 125 ft

Fig. 13.1

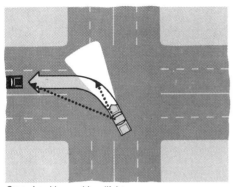
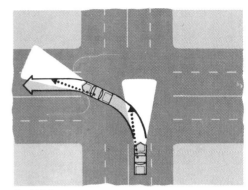

Scan ahead beyond headlights   Avoid this

Fig. 13.2

Backing   When moving backward at night, there is normally very little light to use as a guide in tracking. Back-up lights that go on when the driver shifts to reverse serve primarily as a warning to others; they do not provide much assistance for scanning. So in backing at night, drivers frequently have to cope with conditions of exceptionally limited visibility along the intended path. At times it may even be necessary to get out of the car and check conditions on the intended path before starting the maneuver.

Changing lanes   In scanning the critical area before changing lanes, the driver has to judge the speed of vehicles approaching from the rear, using the rearview and sideview mirrors. At night it will be possible to see only the headlights of these vehicles, so that judging their speed will be more difficult. It may take a while for students to become skilled in judging the speed of vehicles by the movement and position of their headlights. So, until they are experienced, encourage them to allow for extra clearance to the rear before initiating a lane change.

Passing   Passing on the left of center of the roadway is an inherently dangerous maneuver at any time of day; at night, it can be especially treacherous. Drivers can rarely see far enough ahead to be sure that the intended path is clear. The range of the headlights is simply not great enough; the road ahead may curve, there may be a hill crest, or there may be obstacles in the path. Drivers cannot adequately prepare for all these possibilities. In addition, as speed increases during the maneuver, drivers are likely to overdrive their headlights. Furthermore, other drivers approaching from side streets or from the opposite direction may have difficulty detecting the fact that a vehicle is passing, since they can see only the headlights (Fig. 13.3). In view of these multiple risks, the reasons for passing at night rarely justify the risks involved.

Parking on a shoulder   Students should be alerted to the dangers involved in parking on a road shoulder at night. When it is necessary to do so, however, make certain they position the car well to the right of the roadway and activate the four-way flasher to warn other drivers of their position.

1. Can't see far enough ahead

3. Others might not detect passing vehicle

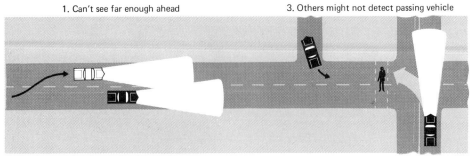

2. Likely to overdrive headlights

Fig. 13.3

CLASSROOM GUIDE FOR UNIT 13
Strategies for Driving at Night

Topics	Instructional Plan
1. *Safe driving practices:* a) Preparing to drive b) Scanning, evaluating, and using headlights c) Speed control and tracking maneuvers	1. Discuss limitations imposed on driver by low visibility. 2. Discuss and explain reasons for adopting specific driving practices under these conditions.
2. *Strategy for Route 1 night:* a) *Changed or new characteristics:* continuous and recurring, specific locations b) *Changed or new elements of strategy:* continuous and recurring actions, actions at specific locations	1. Use previously developed strategy for Route 1 as basis for building strategy for driving at night. 2. Use class discussion to arrive at most important changes in characteristics. 3. Use class discussion to identify major changes in strategy required by conditions at night. 4. Have students keep record of strategy.
3. *Strategy for Route 2 night:* same as above	

PREPARATORY READING FOR STUDENTS

1. *Learning to Drive: Skills, Concepts, and Strategies.* Chapter 16, "Strategies for Driving at Night."

   —or appropriate sections from another high-school text.

2. Articles, research reports, or other materials dealing with problems and/or accidents related to driving at night.

IN-CAR GUIDE FOR UNIT 13
Strategies for Night Driving

Teacher	Student

Phase 1: Strategy for Route 1, at Night

Teacher	Student
1. Prior to student performance, make certain route is clearly specified and understood.	1. Before starting to drive, reviews changed or new elements of strategy for night conditions (see General Guides on following page).
2. As student drives: a) Allow student to concentrate, using verbal cues sparingly. b) Use cues when necessary to help students remain flexible and alert.	2. Concentrates on employing strategy, including: a) Elements of strategy for roadway and traffic conditions (which still apply) b) Changed or new elements of strategy (for night conditions)
3. When trip is completed: a) Guide student's evaluation of her performance. b) Allow student to make observations about the effectiveness of the strategy. c) Discuss briefly the required alterations in strategy.	3. When trip is completed, takes part in evaluation of: a) Her performance b) Strategy c) Alterations employed

Phase 2: Strategy for Route 2, at night
(same as Phase 1)

General Guides for Driving at Night

Use these to supplement previously developed strategies for Route 1 (see Unit 8).

Preparing to drive:

Check intended path prior to entering vehicle.
Turn on and adjust headlights.
Adjust panel light.
Adjust day/night mirror.

Scanning techniques and using headlights:

Keep shifting eyes:
Regularly scan ahead to limits of headlights.
Periodically scan beyond headlight range.
When necessary, shift eyes to near points to help in tracking.

Use *high beams* (when conditions allow) to increase visibility.

Switch to low beam when approaching oncoming vehicle, and following another vehicle.

When meeting oncoming vehicle:
Avoid looking directly at headlights.
Use right edge of roadway as guide.
Reduce speed.
Move to the right to provide ample space cushion.

After passing vehicle, maintain reduced speed until eyes recover from glare.

Speed control and tracking:

Don't overdrive your headlights.
Adjust to normal speed of traffic.
Leave extra large space cushion ahead.
When necessary to improve tracking, reduce speed, and use more brief glances to near points.

Other new elements of strategy

unit 14

STRATEGIES FOR
SPECIAL CONDITIONS

INTRODUCTION

Driving in the rain on wet roads, or on snow or ice, requires special strategies and skills that have not been covered in other on-street learning experiences. This unit is designed to develop the students' ability to drive safely under these conditions [1].

The various special conditions are grouped into one unit because they pose common problems for drivers (reduced traction, limited visibility, and so forth) and require similar compensatory techniques (reduced speed, gradual acceleration and steering, and so on). Obviously, however, the conditions may differ significantly in terms of the degree of danger imposed and the level of skill required (for example, driving on glare ice is certainly more demanding and dangerous than driving on a wet roadway). Thus, teacher decisions regarding who should be allowed to drive under such conditions, which routes should be used, and so forth will have to vary depending on the severity of the special conditions.

Equally as obvious is the fact that teachers cannot plan to cover this unit in the same way as they can plan other units. Weather conditions are uncontrollable and essentially unpredictable. Indeed, in many regions of the country snow and ice are not present at all, and in other regions rain occurs only rarely. Even when these conditions prevail, they may not occur at appropriate times during the period in which the driver education course is offered. Therefore, teachers will have to remain ready to use this unit on those occasions when appropriate conditions arise. In any event, the strategies and techniques should be covered during a classroom session so that, at the very least, students are exposed to the basic concepts governing safe driver performance under special conditions.

Teachers should check school district policies and local traffic regulations to determine whether there are any restrictions against offering in-car instruction under special conditions.

In this unit the objectives for students are:

1. *To identify the limitations imposed on the driver by the following special conditions:*
   a) *Driving on snow and ice*
   b) *Driving in rain (and on wet surfaces)*
   c) *Driving under other conditions of reduced visibility (fog, twilight, and so on)*

2. *To describe the driving practices that are most appropriate for dealing with these conditions*

3. *To be able to develop a driving strategy for a given driving route under a given special condition*

4. *Having developed driving strategies for a variety of special conditions and routes, to effectively apply those strategies while driving over the routes*

INSTRUCTIONAL PLAN

Classroom   Since it is difficult to predict when special conditions will arise, it is also difficult to schedule a classroom session to coincide with this in-car unit. Nevertheless, a classroom session covering the key concepts in this unit should be scheduled at an appropriately early stage in the course. During this session, strategies developed for particular routes (Unit 8) should be modified to suit special conditions.

The decision to practice   Driving under special conditions is inherently dangerous. The teacher's first obligation here is *to not expose students to unreasonable risks*. When conditions are extremely severe, or when travelers' advisories warn against driving, it is probably wise to keep the driver education car in the garage or, at least, provide limited off-street practice. When students are at the very early stage of training, or are having difficulty mastering basic skills, they should not be expected to cope with hazardous special conditions.

Off-street practice and route selection   As a general rule, practice under special conditions should start in an off-street area. Students should become acclimated to the special condition in the off-street area and demonstrate the ability to cope with the condition before being allowed to drive on-street. When road conditions are very slippery, students should spend considerable time in off-street practice of basic skills in skid prevention and control. Generally, when roads are ice covered or severe storms are in progress, practice should be confined to the off-street area.

When conditions are sufficiently safe to allow on-street practice, the most familiar and least hazardous routes should be selected. Only students who have successfully negotiated these routes under normal conditions should be allowed to practice on them under special conditions. Avoid selecting routes with especially hazardous locations that will pose unreasonable problems for students, such as a slippery hill where cars normally get stuck when the road is snow covered.

Whenever there is any doubt as to the condition of the route, teachers should drive over it first to test its suitability for practice.

Development of strategies   The strategies used should include those driving practices appropriate for the special condition (see subsequent sections of this unit). However, they should also include appropriate elements of the strategy developed earlier for the roadway and traffic characteristics of the particular route being used (Unit 8). Thus strategies for special conditions should *augment, not replace,* previously developed strategies.

Teacher behavior   During practice, teachers must be ready to *modify their own behavior* to suit the requirements of the special conditions. Some suggested modifications include the following:

1. At the beginning of practice, test the traction available and practice braking by using the dual-control brake to bring the car to a stop.

2. Whenever the severity of conditions worsens or an extremely hazardous situation develops ahead, have the student pull over, stop the car, and allow the teacher to drive.

3. In general, place a more stringent set of restraints on student performance—for example, keep them well within appropriate speed limits, make sure there is an extra large gap available before allowing them to enter traffic, and so forth.

4. Scan ahead with particular attention to helping students predict the potentially erratic behavior of other drivers.

SELECTED CONCEPTS AND PRACTICES
FOR DRIVING UNDER SPECIAL CONDITIONS

Driving on Snow and Ice

The problem Snow and ice reduce the traction between the tires and the road surface. Reduced traction makes it more difficult to control the movement of the car. When the car is accelerating from a stationary position, the chances of wheel spinning and skidding are increased. Sudden changes in speed or steering adjustments can produce a variety of skids. The risks of skidding to the outside of curves and turns is increased. And braking distances are substantially increased. (See Fig. 14.1.) When snow is falling, the problem of reduced traction is complicated by the problem of reduced visibility. Furthermore, fallen snow often obscures roadway markings and road edges.

Accident statistics and special studies substantiate the dangers involved in driving on snow and ice. Close to 10 percent of all accidents occur on snow- or ice-covered roadways (B 138). More importantly, the *accident rates* on such surfaces are comparatively high. One study indicated that the accident rate on snow-covered roadways was five times higher than on dry roadways, and on icy roads was eight times higher than on dry roads (B 28). Patches of ice and snow are particularly hazardous; they account for one-third of all the ice/snow accidents (B 138).

Preparing to drive In addition to the normal preparatory actions (see Unit 2), special procedures need to be used to ensure maximum visibility:

1. Clean all snow and ice off the front windshield, *all* windows, and sideview mirrors. In addition, clean snow off the front hood and roof to prevent it from blowing on to the front windshield or rear window when the car is moving.

2. When necessary, wipe the interior of the windows with a cloth to clear them of condensation.

3. Turn on the windshield wiper and adjust it to an appropriate speed. Use the windshield washer as necessary to keep the windshield clean.

4. Turn on the defroster to melt ice and snow on the windshield and to keep the interior of the windshield free of condensation.

5. Open a window slightly to increase the circulation of air and reduce condensation.

BRAKING DISTANCES ARE INCREASED

Braking distances at 20 mph

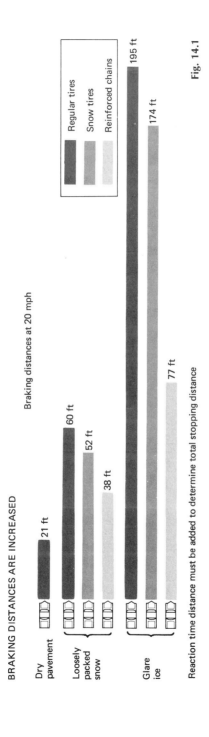

Regular tires
Snow tires
Reinforced chains

Dry pavement — 21 ft

Loosely packed snow — 60 ft / 52 ft / 38 ft

Glare ice — 195 ft / 174 ft / 77 ft

Reaction time distance must be added to determine total stopping distance

Fig. 14.1

Speed control and tracking   When starting the car on a snowy or icy road, *accelerate very gradually* to avoid spinning the rear wheels. Whenever possible, keep the front wheels pointed straight ahead. When the front wheels are turned, the additional force needed to move the car increases the chances of losing traction and spinning the wheels. If the wheels spin as the car starts to move, let up immediately on the accelerator because continued acceleration may cause the car to sink deeper into the snow or may increase the tendency to skid to the side. On the next attempt accelerate more gradually. In some situations it may be necessary to put sand or ashes under the rear tires to prevent spinning. In relatively deep snow, it may be necessary to rock the car to get it moving (Fig. 14.2).

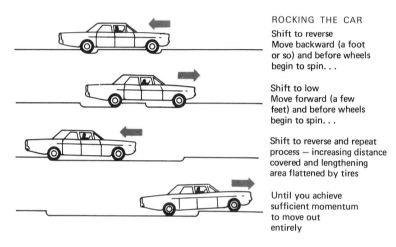

ROCKING THE CAR

Shift to reverse
Move backward (a foot or so) and before wheels begin to spin. . .

Shift to low
Move forward (a few feet) and before wheels begin to spin. . .

Shift to reverse and repeat process — increasing distance covered and lengthening area flattened by tires

Until you achieve sufficient momentum to move out entirely

Fig. 14.2

Once the car is moving, avoid sudden changes in speed and direction. Quick acceleration or deceleration, rapid and large steering adjustments, and quick braking responses are very likely to produce hazardous skids. Be particularly careful to avoid oversteering or overcorrecting, which can cause skidding. This is a common fault among beginning drivers because the steering wheel turns so much more easily under conditions of reduced traction. The need to avoid sudden changes in speed or direction is especially important on turns and curves. The only way to avoid skidding on turns and curves is to approach them and complete them at especially slow speeds, using gradual speed reduction, gradual steering, and gradual acceleration.

It is important for beginning drivers to appreciate the traction available to them on snow-covered or icy roads. Therefore, soon after starting to move they should test the brakes by applying them gradually at slow speeds and noting the stopping distance and the car's tendency to skid—of course this sort of test should only be performed when it can be done with complete safety.

In selecting paths to travel on, drivers should choose those lanes that offer the best traction, using dry pavement or loosely packed snow in preference to traffic-packed snow or ice. On multiple-lane roads, passing lanes frequently provide less traction and therefore should be avoided. In addition, drivers should be alert for icy patches on otherwise clear roads (especially in shady areas) and should steer straight and avoid braking on such patches.

Normal traveling speed has to be adjusted to bring stopping distances within safe limits. Since snow and ice increase stopping distances significantly, a substantial decrease in speed is required (Fig. 14.3). For the same reason, allow for an extra large space cushion when following another vehicle. For example, at 20 mph on dry pavement a 2-3-second gap is usually a reasonably safe following distance while on snow a 5-6-second gap is required, and on ice an 8-10-second gap may be necessary.

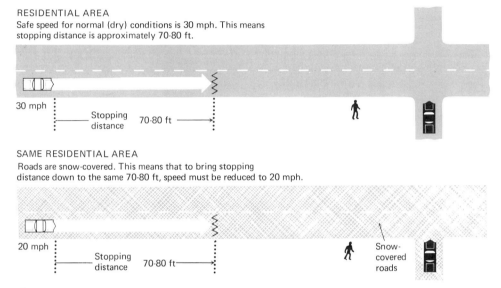

RESIDENTIAL AREA
Safe speed for normal (dry) conditions is 30 mph. This means stopping distance is approximately 70-80 ft.

30 mph · · · Stopping distance   70-80 ft

SAME RESIDENTIAL AREA
Roads are snow-covered. This means that to bring stopping distance down to the same 70-80 ft, speed must be reduced to 20 mph.

20 mph · · · Stopping distance   70-80 ft   Snow-covered roads

Fig. 14.3

Tracking in a centered-lane position is most difficult when roadway markings and roadway edges are obscured by snow. Frequently the driver has to be guided by the tracks made in the snow by other vehicles. When doing so, however, recognize that these tracks may not be in the center of the lane, and they may not provide an adequate space cushion between the car and obstacles at the sides of the path. So don't follow them blindly. In judging lane position and in determining needed space cushions, use as many other clues as possible, such as fences bordering the road, vehicles parked at the curb, and the position of oncoming vehicles.

The very gradual braking required to bring the car to a stop without skidding means that the driver will have to anticipate the need to stop earlier and begin braking earlier. On icy surfaces it may be necessary to pump the brakes when stopping to avoid a prolonged skid and to maintain steering control. To pump the brakes, apply them quickly, allowing the wheels to lock for a moment, release them immediately, then apply them again, repeating this on-off cycle until the car comes to a complete stop. Pumping the brakes is a difficult skill for inexperienced drivers to master, and it can be dangerous when performed incorrectly. Teachers should provide opportunities for students to practice pumping the brakes in a safe off-street area prior to allowing them to drive in traffic.

When driving on grades: (1) accelerate slightly, when it's safe to do so, prior to entering the upgrade to achieve adequate momentum to get up the hill; (2) maintain constant pressure on the accelerator while on the upgrade; and (3) slow down considerably before entering the downgrade to avoid the necessity of braking on the downgrade.

When driving in deep snow, shift to low gear and maintain speed to keep the car moving through the snow.

Skid control   A major objective when driving on snow and ice is to avoid skidding. However, should the vehicle begin to skid, the driver has to know how to control it. Although the specific type of skid and the nature of surrounding conditions at the time of the skid will determine the specific actions required, there are certain general rules that apply to most skidding emergencies. Unit 11, Phase 5 describes techniques for controlling skids.

Scanning and evaluating   A substantial adjustment in scanning and evaluating is required to compensate for increased stopping distances on snow and ice. During most of their practice driving, students have learned to adjust the distance they scan ahead to the speed of the vehicle. So at slower speeds they have become accustomed to scanning and evaluating conditions for shorter distances ahead. Now, however, they have to readjust their scanning techniques so that even at slower speeds they scan far enough ahead to compensate for increased stopping distances. For example, when driving at 20 mph on dry roads they may have become used to scanning ahead for relatively short distances. When driving on snow and ice at 20 mph this habit must be changed to allow for increased stopping distances, as shown in Fig. 14.4.

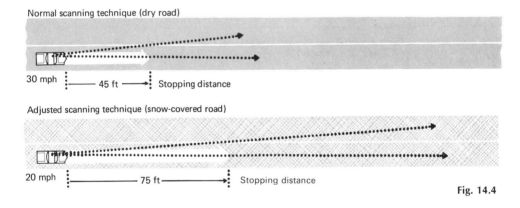

Normal scanning technique (dry road)

30 mph ┊———— 45 ft ————→┊ Stopping distance

Adjusted scanning technique (snow-covered road)

20 mph ┊———————— 75 ft ————————→┊ Stopping distance

Fig. 14.4

In evaluating the movement of other vehicles, allow for the increased stopping distances they will require. Don't assume that they will be able to stop in the same way they do on dry surfaces. This is especially important in situations where the student expects others to yield the right of way to him. For example, when moving through an intersection after a signal light changes, the student may have to adopt a different strategy in order to allow for increased stopping distances of the oncoming vehicles (Fig. 14.5). In these and similar situations, students should attend to the wheels of the other vehicle to detect early signs of skidding.

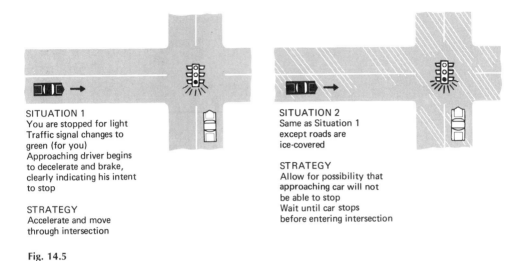

SITUATION 1
You are stopped for light
Traffic signal changes to
green (for you)
Approaching driver begins
to decelerate and brake,
clearly indicating his intent
to stop

STRATEGY
Accelerate and move
through intersection

SITUATION 2
Same as Situation 1
except roads are
ice-covered

STRATEGY
Allow for possibility that
approaching car will not
be able to stop
Wait until car stops
before entering intersection

Fig. 14.5

Driving in Rain and on Wet Roads

The problem   Wet roads also reduce traction. Although the loss of traction is not so great as it is on roads covered with ice or hard-packed snow, nevertheless it is substantial enough to cause large increases in stopping distances (Fig. 14.6) and to significantly influence the chances of skidding in a variety of situations. At the beginning of a rainstorm, roads are particularly slippery because the rain mixes with dust and oil on the road to form a slick film, which is slowly washed away.

When roads are heavily covered with water, driving at high speeds can result in hydroplaning, where tires lose contact with the road surface and ride along on a thin film of water. When hydroplaning occurs, steering and braking control are substantially reduced.

In addition, rain substantially reduces visibility. Not only does it affect sight distances ahead, but rain accumulated on the side and rear windows and on the outside rearview mirror significantly interferes with the visibility to the side and rear.

Given these difficult conditions it is not surprising that accident rates for wet roads tend to be double the rates for dry roads (B 138), and that 20 percent of all accidents occur on wet roads (B 59). Part of the reason for this is that drivers fail to modify their driving practices to compensate for slippery conditions (B 138).

Preparing to drive   In addition to the normal preparatory steps (see Unit 2), special procedures need to be used to ensure maximum visibility:

1. Turn on the windshield wiper and adjust it to the appropriate speed.

2. Wipe off the interior of the windows to clear them of condensation.

3. In situations where it will enhance visibility, wipe accumulated moisture from side windows and outside mirrors.

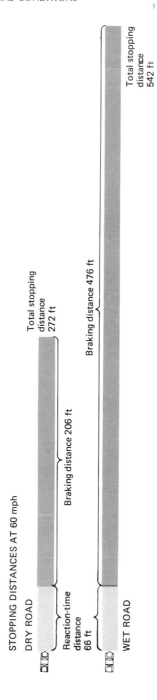

STOPPING DISTANCES AT 60 mph

DRY ROAD

Reaction-time distance 66 ft

Braking distance 206 ft

Total stopping distance 272 ft

WET ROAD

Braking distance 476 ft

Total stopping distance 542 ft

Fig. 14.6

Speed control and tracking   Most of the adjustments in speed control and tracking that were called for on snow and ice are also recommended when driving on wet surfaces—although to a lesser degree. In particular,

1. Use more gradual acceleration and braking.
2. Avoid sudden changes in speed and direction.
3. Reduce normal traveling speed.
4. Slow down further in advance of intersections, curves, and downgrades.
5. Use slower speeds on turns and curves.
6. Allow for larger space cushions ahead.
7. Periodically test brakes by pumping them.
8. When heavy rain coats a portion of the roadway, slow down even further to prevent hydroplaning.

When a portion of the roadway is covered with deep water, drive around it if possible. If it is necessary to go through the water, drive at very slow speeds, and after passing through it test the brakes to see that they are operating properly. If not, apply light continuous brake pressure to dry out the brakes, and retest them.

Scanning and evaluating   In addition to scanning farther ahead to compensate for increased stopping distances, be especially careful in situations that require scanning and evaluating conditions to the side and rear. Accumulated water on windows and outside mirrors reduces your ability to scan and evaluate effectively in such situations. In some cases it may be necessary to roll down the window to obtain an adequate view of conditions. In addition, recognize that other drivers have the same difficulties and so allow for errors they may make because of limited visibility.

Because of the reduced visibility in heavy rain, it is often advisable to put on headlights in order to help others to see you.

Other Special Conditions

Fog   In dense fog, visibility is severely limited. Extremely slow speeds are required to bring the stopping distance within sight distance. Use low-beam headlights—high-beam lights will reflect off the fog and glare back at the driver. Using lights is important even in daytime fog because taillights and headlights warn other drivers of your presence. When fog is dense, the only real reduced-risk alternative is to stay off the road. Postpone the trip until conditions improve.

Twilight   Twilight can be deceptive. Visibility is reduced more significantly than most drivers suspect. Since other drivers have the same problem, use low-beam headlights to enable them to see you more easily. (Check state laws for the times of day at which drivers are required to begin using headlights.)

CLASSROOM GUIDE FOR UNIT 14
Strategies for Special Conditions

Topics	Instructional Plan
1. *Safe driving practices:* snow/ice a) Preparing to drive b) Speed control and tracking c) Scanning and evaluating	1. Discuss limitations imposed on driver by snow/ice. 2. Discuss and explain reasons for adopting specific driving practices for snow/ice.
2. *Strategy for Route 1:* snow/ice a) *Changed or new characteristics:* continuous and recurring, specific locations b) *Changed or new elements of strategy:* continuous and recurring actions, actions at specific locations	1. Use previously developed strategy for Route 1 as basis for building strategy for snow/ice. 2. Use class discussion to arrive at most important changes in characteristics. 3. Use class discussion to identify major changes in strategy required by snow/ice. 4. Have students keep record of strategy.
3. *Strategy for Route 2:* snow/ice (same as above)	
4. *Safe driving practices:* rain/wet roads a) Preparing to drive b) Speed control and tracking c) Scanning and evaluating	1. Discuss limitations imposed on driver by rain/wet roads. 2. Discuss and explain reasons for adopting specific driving practices under these conditions.
5. *Strategy for Route 1:* rain a) *Changed or new characteristics:* continuous and recurring, specific locations b) *Changed or new elements of strategy:* continuous and recurring actions, actions at specific locations	1. Use previously developed strategy for Route 1 as basis for building strategy for rain/wet roads 2. Use class discussion to arrive at most important changes in characteristics. 3. Use class discussion to identify major changes in strategy required by rain/wet roads. 4. Have students keep record of strategy.
6. *Strategy for Route 2:* rain (same as above)	

The teacher should use discretion in determining the number of strategies for special conditions to be developed. It would seem advisable to encourage students to develop strategies for the same special condition on different routes, so that students can recognize both the similarities and differences in the strategies which emerge. For the same reason strategies for different conditions on the same route should be developed.

PREPARATORY READING FOR STUDENTS

1. *Learning to Drive: Skills, Concepts, and Strategies.* Chapter 17, "Strategies for Special Conditions."

   —or appropriate sections from another high-school text.

2. Articles, research reports, and other materials dealing with the special hazards of snow, ice, rain, fog, and so forth. Special conditions that are common to the area of the country where the driver education course is being given should be emphasized.

RELATED SIMULATOR LESSONS

1. Aetna Drivotrainer System: "Good Driving in Bad Weather."

2. Link Simulator System: "Winterproof Your Driving."

IN-CAR GUIDE FOR UNIT 14

Strategies for Special Conditions

Teacher	Student

Strategy for Route 1: (a) snow or ice; (b) rain and wet roads

Teacher	Student
1. Prior to student performance make certain route is clearly specified and understood. a) Use off-street area for initial practice. b) Allow only capable students to practice on-street. c) Provide off-street practice in skid prevention and control. d) Test traction available with dual-control brake.	1. Before starting to drive, reviews changed or new elements of strategy for: a) Snow/ice (see General Guides for driving on snow or ice) b) Rain/wet roads (see General Guides for driving in rain and on wet roads)
2. As student drives: a) Allow student to concentrate, use verbal cues sparingly. b) Use cues when necessary to help students remain flexible and alert. c) Set stringent restraints on student performance to suit conditions (speed, gap acceptance, etc.). d) Assist in predicting behavior of other drivers.	2. Concentrates on employing strategy including: a) Elements of strategy for roadway and traffic conditions which still apply (from Unit 8) b) Changed or new elements of strategy for snow/ice, or rain/wet roads
3. When trip is completed: a) Guide student's evaluation of his performance. b) Allow student to make observations about the effectiveness of the strategy. c) Discuss briefly the required alterations in strategy.	3. When trip is completed, takes part in evaluation of: a) His performance b) Strategy c) Alterations in strategy employed to suit special condition

General Guides for Driving on Snow and/or Ice

Use these to supplement previously developed strategies for Route 1 (see Unit 8).

Preparing to drive:

Clear off snow/ice.

Remove interior condensation.

Turn on and adjust windshield wipers.

Use defroster as necessary.

Open window.

Speed control and tracking:

Accelerate *very gradually*.

If tires start spinning, release accelerator immediately.

General Guides for Driving on Snow and/or Ice *(cont.)*

Test brakes.

Avoid sudden changes in speed and direction.

Choose least slippery lanes for travel.

Use especially slow speeds on turns and curves.

Substantially reduce normal traveling speed.

Allow extra space cushion ahead.

When snow obscures roadway, use all available clues to assist in tracking.

In stopping, use *very gradual braking;* pump brakes when necessary to avoid skidding.

Maintain constant acceleration on upgrade.

Slow before entering downgrade.

If car begins to skid:

Steer gradually in direction in which rear end is skidding.

Gradually release accelerator.

Avoid sudden steering, braking, or acceleration.

Avoid using brake until steering control is reestablished.

Pump brakes.

Straighten wheels.

Scanning and evaluation techniques:

Scan further ahead to compensate for increased stopping distance.

Allow for increased stopping distances of others; don't assume they will be able to stop the way they do on dry surfaces.

General Guides for Driving in Rain and on Wet Roads

Use these to supplement previously developed strategies for Route 1 (see Unit 8).

Preparing to drive:

As necessary, clean moisture and condensation off windshield and windows.

Turn on and adjust wipers.

Speed control and tracking:

Use more gradual acceleration and braking.

Avoid sudden changes in speed.

Reduce normal traveling speed.

Use slow speeds on turns, curves, approaching intersections.

Allow for larger space cushions ahead.

When appropriate, test brakes by pumping.

Scanning and evaluation techniques:

Scan further ahead to compensate for increased stopping distance.

Be careful scanning to side and rear to allow for reduced visibility.

Expect others to make unexpected movements because of reduced visibility.

PERFORMANCE EVALUATION AND PLANNING FOR FUTURE IMPROVEMENT

INTRODUCTION

The essence of this unit lies in its attempt to shift the responsibility for evaluation and improvement from teacher to student. During the in-car phase of the driver education experience, the teacher has accompanied the student and has borne the major responsibility for making judgments about student performance and for recommending improvements. Now, as the course nears its end, the time approaches when the students will be driving on their own and will have to serve as their own teacher and judge. They are more likely to carry out this responsibility effectively if they are prepared for it prior to leaving the course. This unit attempts to develop the students' ability to evaluate their own performance and to make subsequent improvements based on the evaluation.

Furthermore, this unit acknowledges the fact that students who leave a driver education course have not reached their potential as safe drivers; there is considerable room for further improvement. The extent to which students continue to improve (after they leave the course) will depend upon whether they recognize the need for continued improvement, and whether they are equipped to guide their own improvement. This unit attempts to develop among students an attitude that will lead them to seek further improvement and will equip them to guide this improvement.

Phase 1 consists of a formal evaluation of student performance by the teacher (a driving test). The results of this test are used to design further practice. In Phase 2 the teacher guides the students' evaluation of their own performance, and the students prescribe subsequent practice based on this evaluation. Phase 3 involves the development of a plan for continued practice and self-evaluation to be implemented after the student completes the driver education course.

In this unit the major objectives for students are:

1. *To demonstrate an attitude that acknowledges the need for continued improvement*
2. *To accept responsibility for guiding their own future improvement*
3. *To accurately evaluate their own driving performance*
4. *To develop (with the teacher's assistance) an appropriate plan for future improvement*

INSTRUCTIONAL PLAN

Phase 1: Formal Evaluation of Student Performance (Driving Test)

Toward the end of the in-car program the teacher should administer a formal driving test to each student in the course. The purposes of the test should be (1) to determine the status of the student's driving ability (which may be used as a part of the grading procedure), and (2) to provide students with information about their level of performance that will be helpful in planning for future practice.

The test should be taken on a prescribed driving route and should contain a standard number and variety of maneuvers so that the teacher can make appropriate comparisons of performance among students. In all cases, the test should provide for the performance of the important skills, maneuvers, and abilities that have been emphasized during the in-car program. An illustration of a test route appears in Fig. 15.1. Obviously, however, teachers will have to devise their own tests based on the unique characteristics of their course and the driving routes available. For those students whose progress has been slow and who have not progressed through all the units of instruction, the test will have to be limited to those elements of performance that the student has had an opportunity to practice.

Prior to the administration of the test the student needs to know its purpose, the procedures to be used, the route to be traveled, and the maneuvers to be performed. During the in-car administration of the test it is advisable for the teacher to remain relatively quiet—except when it is necessary to provide directions regarding what to do next. As the student drives, the teacher keeps a careful record of the performance. The record constitutes an evaluation of student performance in terms of the major elements of driving that have been emphasized during the in-car program. Any one of several types of rating forms might be used.* In all cases, however, the form should provide a *specific* record of what happened and should represent a relatively objective appraisal of performance. "Directions for Administering the Driver Rating Form" and a sample "Driver Rating Form" appear on pp. 314–318. The rating form is designed to include the important elements of performance emphasized in the previous units of instruction. Teachers are encouraged to revise the rating form to make it correspond more closely to the content of their own in-car program.

Notice that the score on this driver rating form is based on the number and severity of errors accumulated during the test period. It does not attempt to tally all of the things the driver does correctly. Given the complexity of the driving task and thus all of the things a driver has to do during an extended driving test, it is unreasonable to expect the teacher to note everything the driver does correctly. Instead, as long as the route and the maneuvers performed have been specified (see Fig. 15.1), the teacher will know from the record that the student performed all tasks correctly—except those for which errors are noted.

During the test special attention should be given to the students' ability to drive safely in response to existing roadway and traffic characteristics, instead of allowing smoothness of operation or skillful completion of maneuvers to be the dominant factor in test results. A recent study funded by the Department of Transportation (B 80) demonstrates that it is possible to design a road test that reliably measures the driver's pattern of safe performance in response to changing traffic and environmental characteristics—provided the test is carefully developed,

---

* Standard driving tests that do *not* reflect the content of the in-car program are *not* appropriate. See discussion in Chapter 2.

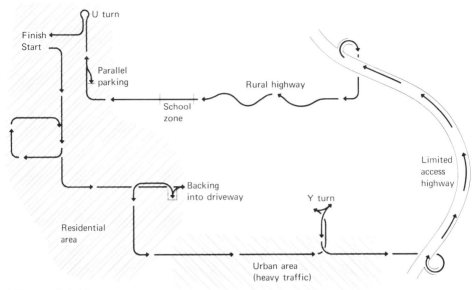

Miles traveled: 10

Total time (approximate): 30 minutes

Maneuvers included		Characteristics of route	
Number	Description	Number	Description
2	Starting engine and moving car forward	10	Traffic signals
		3	Stop signs
1	Parking the car	3	Yield signs
6	Lane changes (minimum)	1	Speed zone
8	Right turns	3	Miles limited access highway
5	Left turns	1	Mile heavy city traffic
1	U turn	2	Miles residential area
1	Y turn	4	Miles highway (rural)
1	Backing maneuver	2	Steep grades

Fig. 15.1   Route for driving test

observers are well trained, and driving locations are carefully selected in advance. The Driver Rating Form is designed to focus attention on critical elements of safe performance.

If this formal evaluation is to serve a legitimate educational purpose, the results of the test must be communicated to students in a meaningful way. Perhaps the best way to communicate and interpret the evaluation is through an individual conference between teacher and student. The conference may be used to (1) provide a concise appraisal of the student's level of achievement, (2) assess strengths and weaknesses, and (3) indicate the type of practice required to correct the weaknesses. If there is no opportunity for an individual conference, the students might be given a copy of their rating form, and the results might be reviewed and interpreted in a group meeting (classroom).

Finally, as part of the evaluation procedure, students should be given an opportunity to engage in post-test practice designed to correct the weaknesses discovered during the driving test. This practice session should take place during the in-car lesson immediately following the test. In fact, in the interest of efficiency, this post-test practice might be combined with Phase 2, "Guided Self Evaluation."

Phase 2: Guided Self-Evaluation

This phase of instruction is a formal attempt to develop the students' ability to evaluate their own performance. Although the development of this ability has been a secondary objective of several previous units, it is given exclusive attention at this point. The ultimate objective of such emphasis is to ensure that students recognize their responsibility for continual self-appraisal during the years of driving ahead and are reasonably well equipped to carry out this responsibility.

During an in-car period the students drive over an established route and, at the completion of the drive, evaluate their own performance. This self-evaluation may take the form of brief commentaries by the students that identify their most important actions, including effective actions as well as errors. The students then identify the corrections required and employ the corrections as they drive the route again. In addition, after practice it is wise to have students record their evaluations on an appropriate form (see the sample student self-evaluation form on pp. 319–320).

The teacher's primary role in this phase of practice should be to encourage the student to engage in rigorous self-appraisal. When the student makes a serious error in self-evaluation, the teacher should attempt to guide the student toward a more accurate appraisal (perhaps by using a series of carefully worded questions). In order not to defeat the purpose of the lesson, teachers should avoid imposing their own evaluation on students without giving students a reasonable chance to do the evaluation themselves.

Phase 3: Planning for Future Improvement: A Sample Plan

The intent of this phase of instruction is to develop an individual plan for each student that will encourage continued practice (and improvement) after the student leaves the driver education program. One plan is described below. A form that might be used in carrying out the plan appears later in this unit. Teachers might alter it or design a totally different one that is better suited to their own programs.

1. *Summary evaluation.*   The results of the teacher's evaluation (Phase 1), the self-evaluation (Phase 2), and any other available information on the student's driving proficiency are used to arrive at a summary evaluation. This evaluation is recorded and should indicate the important remaining deficiencies in the student's current level of performance. In addition, the evaluation includes a specification of those important driving experiences to which the student has not been exposed during the course, and which, in the teacher's opinion, should be a part of the plan for continued practice (see the sample "Plan for Future Improvement," pp. 321–322).

2. *Planning for additional practice.*   Using the summary evaluation as a guide, a plan for additional practice should be developed. The plan should indicate the major kinds and amounts of driving that should be undertaken, and it should provide some guides for student performance.

3. *Planning for future evaluation.*   As a part of the overall plan, students are encouraged to evaluate their performance (or have it evaluated by someone else) during and after they engage in periods of additional practice. Students are provided with a copy of the "Self Evaluation Form" as a basis for making the evaluation.

4. *Planning for implementation.*   Of course the implementation of the plan for continued practice is beyond the immediate control of the teacher since the practice will take place after the student has completed the driver education course. However, the teacher and student might explore alternatives for carrying out the plan. One possibility is to have competent parents supervise the student's future practice—in this case it would be advisable for the parent to meet with the driver education teacher for an orientation to the task of supervision. On the other hand, if the student is immediately successful in obtaining a driver's licence, she can provide her own supervision. Another possibility is that the student might be encouraged to meet with the teacher (at some future date) and discuss her progress since leaving the course. Planning for such a meeting might serve to ensure the implementation of the practice plan.

DIRECTIONS FOR ADMINISTERING DRIVER RATING FORM

The rating form is designed for rating those elements of driver performance that were emphasized during in-car instruction. Only those persons who have used the Unit Plan to guide their in-car instruction will be able to use the rating form effectively.

Test route   The test route should be carefully planned in advance. It should call for the performance of the variety of skills, maneuvers, and strategies covered during the in-car instruction program. The route should be standardized so that all students who take the test will be required to perform the same skills and maneuvers on the same segments of roadway. This will enable the teacher to make valid comparative judgments with respect to the driving proficiency of each student.

Recording performance   Prior to the beginning of the test, the nature of the test route and the maneuvers included are recorded on the form. As the student drives over the route and performs the maneuvers, the teacher records each error committed by the driver by placing a check (√) in the appropriate column next to the "Type of Error" committed. When, in the judgment of the teacher, the error committed is "dangerous," the check is circled (⊘). Although all driving errors are potentially dangerous, the circle permits the teacher to designate those errors that stand out by comparison as more dangerous than others.

In many cases when an error is recorded the teacher will want to make notations that more closely specify what happened. (A column for notations is provided.) In particular, the teacher will want to record the maneuver or the type of driving (that is, driving category) being performed at the time the error occurred, and, if appropriate, "the location and obstacles" involved. A "Code for Notation" is provided with the form. The initials of the code can be used to record the driving category, location, and obstacles associated with each error.

Example: In making a left turn the student approaches the turn at too fast a speed. Later on she fails to reduce speed for a pedestrian at an intersection. In the teacher's judgment the failure to reduce speed was a more serious error (Fig. 15.2).

Type of Error	Check (√) Each Error Committed, Circle Dangerous Errors ⊘	Notations
Maintains speed too fast	√	A/TL
Fails to reduce speed	⊘	PD/I

Fig. 15.2

Scoring   At the conclusion of the test run, the total score is calculated. One point is deducted for each check (√), and two, three, four, or five points are deducted for each circled check (⊘). The number of points deducted for a circled check will depend on the teacher's judgment with respect to the relative danger caused by the error. The student's final score is equivalent to the total point deduction (final page of rating form).

Summary comments   A section is provided for the recording of concise comments on the student's important strengths and weaknesses and additional practice required. These comments, together with the test record, should serve as the basis for a teacher-student conference.

Final rating   A final section (last page of rating form) is provided for recording a final rating of student performance that should be based on the student's final score. The form of the rating is left to the discretion of the teacher. Differences (from school to school) in test routes, maneuvers performed, and so on make it impossible to provide standardized ratings equivalent to various point deductions.

DRIVER RATING FORM

"Directions for Administering Driver Rating Form" should be consulted prior to using this form.

Only persons familiar with the "Unit Plan for In-Car Instruction" will be able to use this form effectively.

Student _____

Teacher _____

School (name and address) _____

Date _____

Student's prior experience (specify practice units covered and other important data):

_____

_____

_____

_____

_____

Test route and maneuvers (specify nature and length of route and maneuvers included):

_____

_____

_____

_____

_____

_____

_____

_____

DRIVER RATING FORM (cont.)

Type of Error	Check (√) Each Error Committed, Circle Dangerous Errors (Ⓥ)	Notations	Code for Notation of Driving Category, Location, and Obstacles (use appropriate combinations)	Type of Error	Check (√) Each Error Committed, Circle Dangerous Errors (Ⓥ)	Notations
Preparatory steps—omits or performs incorrectly:			*Driving Category:*	*Scanning*		
1. Enters or leaves vehicle			S = stopped	1. Fails to scan or scans improperly:		
2. Assumes driver's position			E = entering	a) Ahead		
3. Adjusts seat, belts, mirrors, starts engine			A = approaching	b) To the sides		
4. Checks instruments, doors, etc.			D = driving forward	c) To the rear		
5. Other (specify)			CL = changing lanes	2. Fails to scan in direction of obstacles		
Operating instruments and devices—omits operation or operates incorrectly:			TR = turning right	3. Fails to scan along intended paths		
1. Selector lever			TL = turning left	4. Fails to use mirrors (or uses improperly)		
2. Parking brake			TA = turning around	5. Other (specify)		
3. Other (specify)			B = backing	*Evaluating and responding to obstacles and potential obstacles*—when obstacles or potential obstacles are present, fails to:		
Speed Control			P = parking	1. Identify or see obstacles		
1. Improper acceleration			L = leaving	2. Predict movement or action of obstacle		
2. Maintains speed too fast			*Location:*			
3. Maintains speed too slow			SR = straight road			
			I = intersection			
			H = hill			
			C = curve			
			SD = location with limited sight distance			
			HW = limited access highway			

4. Fails to adjust speed to conditions _____

5. Other (specify) _____

Positioning—moves vehicle to incorrect position:

1. Too far right or left _____
2. Too far front or rear _____

Tracking

1. Moves off path to the right _____
2. Moves off path to the left _____
3. Selects improper lane _____

Traffic signs, signals, and regulations—fails to obey or respond appropriately to:

1. Traffic sign _____
2. Traffic signal _____
3. Roadway marking _____
4. Speed limit _____
5. Yield right of way _____
6. Other (specify) _____

Communicating intentions—fails to signal or signals incorrectly using:

1. Directional signal _____
2. Horn _____
3. Other (specify) _____

DW = driveway
OS = off-street area

Obstacles and potential obstacles:
OV = other vehicle
PD = pedestrian
FO = fixed object
CY = cyclist

3. Reduce speed _____
4. Stop soon enough _____
5. Adjust path or allow adequate space cushion _____
6. Sound horn or give other signal _____
7. Delay or postpone maneuver _____
8. Other (specify) _____

Adapting to roadway and traffic characteristics:

1. Fails to adapt to roadway characteristic (specify) _____
2. Fails to adapt to traffic characteristic (specify) _____

Other errors (specify) _____

DRIVER RATING FORM (*cont.*)

Scoring

Record total number of checks ($\sqrt{}$):_____ × 1 = _____

Record total number of circled checks ($\sqrt{}$): _____ × (2–5) = _____

Summary Comments

Specify most important strengths and weaknesses of test performance:

_____

_____

_____

Specify additional practice required: _____

_____

_____

_____

Other: _____

_____

_____

_____

Final Rating

_____

_____

_____

_____

STUDENT SELF-EVALUATION FORM

NAME: _____

Evaluation	Record of Errors
Evaluate your performance on the following skills and techniques. (When the skill was performed correctly on some occasions and incorrectly on other occasions—check ( ) both "Yes" and "No.")	When your evaluation indicates that you did not perform correctly, describe the errors you made in this column.

YES   NO

1. Did you enter and exit from the vehicle properly?

2. Did you perform the preparatory steps correctly and in sequence?

3. Before entering traffic, did you check conditions thoroughly?

4. During established path driving did you
   a) Control speed effectively?
   b) Maintain space cushion ahead and to both sides?
   c) Use proper scanning techniques including: Looking for obstacles and potential obstacles? Keeping eyes moving? Looking ahead?
   d) Respond correctly to obstacles and potential obstacles?

5. When changing lanes or passing did you
   a) Signal?
   b) Use appropriate scanning techniques?
   c) Maintain adequate space cushions?
   d) Choose reduced-risk alternative when obstacles were present?

6. When turning did you:
   a) Enter approach lane early?
   b) Signal?
   c) Use proper scanning techniques?
   d) Control speed effectively?
   e) Follow correct path using appropriate steering techniques?
   f) Choose reduced-risk alternative when obstacles were present?

7. When backing or turning around did you
   a) Stop and shift properly and assume appropriate driver's position?
   b) Signal when necessary?
   c) Use proper scanning techniques?
   d) Control speed effectively?
   e) Maintain adequate space cushions?
   f) Position vehicle accurately?
   g) Choose reduced-risk alternative when obstacles were present?

STUDENT SELF-EVALUATION FORM (cont.)

8   Did you use appropriate strategies for roadway
    and traffic characteristics (such as intersections,
    hills, curves, heavy traffic, limited sight distances,
    pedestrians, etc.)?

9. Did you respond properly to traffic signs, signals,
    and road markings?

10. Did you obey applicable traffic rules, including
    limits and "yield right of way" rules?

11. Describe and evaluate other important features of your driving performance (not included in items
    1–10:

12. Rate your overall performance on the following critical driving skills:

	Weak	Needs improvement	Acceptable	Strong
Speed control				
Tracking and positioning				
Communicating intentions				
Scanning techniques				
Evaluating situations				
Selecting reduced-risk alternatives				
Using strategies for road and traffic characteristics				

PLAN FOR FUTURE IMPROVEMENT

NAME: *John Smith*

Summary Evaluation	Additional Practice	Guides for Future Performance
1. Current level of performance (List important strengths and weaknesses at conclusion of course.)	Specify kinds of additional practice required:	List important guides for future performance.
Strong in speed control, tracking and positioning, communicating and scanning.	Practice backing maneuvers in off-street areas. Then on-street areas. Concentrate on maneuvers requiring accurate positioning.	Use Practice Guide for Backing Maneuvers; Concentrate on using slow speeds and on assuming proper driver position for scanning.
Strong in all maneuvers except backing maneuvers.	Practice several hours of night driving.	Use Practice Guide for Driving at Night.
Done well in residential areas and on rural roads.	If opportunity arises, practice in snow or ice (in safe area).	Use Practice Guide for special conditions.
Need improvement in evaluating conditions at busy intersections.	Practice at least two hours in busy city traffic — use of routes with busy intersections.	Concentrate on: 1. scanning intersections early. 2. keeping eyes moving.

PLAN FOR FUTURE IMPROVEMENT (cont.)

2. Driving experiences not covered
or covered insufficiently
(List skills, maneuvers, strategies, etc.,
not covered during course.)

Did not cover night
driving or driving in
snow or ice.

Did not have enough
practice in driving in
busy city traffic or
on limited access
highways.

Practice on limited
access highways;
concentrate on enter-
ing highway.

3. Driving at normal
speedal and main-
taining space cushion
wheel.

Use Practice Guide for
Limited Access Highways.

IN-CAR AND CLASSROOM GUIDE FOR UNIT 15
Formal Evaluation, Self-Evaluation, and Planning for Future Improvement

Teacher	Student

Phase 1: Formal Evaluation—Driving Test

Teacher	Student
1. *Orientation to test.* Prior to test, orient students to: a) Purpose of test b) Procedures of test c) Test route	
2. During administration of test, teacher: a) Remains quiet, except to give directions on which route to take b) Uses rating form to keep record of student performance	Drives over test route
3. *Post-test communication and interpretation.* Teacher arranges individual conference with student or uses classroom session to review and interpret results for each student. Individual copies of test results are made available to each student. Practice required to improve student weaknesses is specified.	Has opportunity to ask questions that will help her to better understand her strengths and weaknesses

Phase 2: Guided Self-Evaluation

Teacher	Student
Teacher selects driving route. Explains purpose of Phase 2: "to develop student's ability to evaluate and improve her own performance."	
During student performance, teacher remains relatively silent.	Drives over route, concentrates on taking note of her errors
At completion of performance, teacher encourages student to evaluate her own driving.	At the end of route, gives concise appraisal of her performance
Guides student toward accurate self-appraisal.	
Encourages student to suggest needed improvements in performance.	Specifies needed improvements
Allows for some additional practice that focuses on making improvements.	Drives route again, concentrates on making improvements
	After practice, fills out "Self-Evaluation Form"

IN-CAR AND CLASSROOM GUIDE FOR UNIT 15 (*cont.*)

Phase 3: Planning for Future Improvement

A classroom period, or individual conference, is used to design individualized plans for continued practice and evaluation. The plan might include:

1. Summary evaluation
2. Plan for additional practice
3. Plan for future evaluation
4. Planning for implementation

PREPARATORY READING FOR STUDENTS

1. *Learning to Drive: Skills, Concepts, and Strategies.* Chapter 19, "Performance Evaluation and Planning for Future Improvement."
2. *Laboratory Manual for Learning to Drive.* Section IV, "Self-Evaluations," and Section V, "Plan for Future Improvement."

RELATED SIMULATOR LESSONS

1. Aetna Drivotrainer System: "Road Check."
2. Link Simulator System: "Drive in Review."

REFERENCES AND NOTATIONS

UNIT 1: ORIENTATION TO THE
DRIVING TASK AND TO IN-CAR INSTRUCTION

1. Studies of driver performance have identified the relatively high frequency of errors made by experienced as well as novice drivers. One of the more revealing studies filmed five-minute segments of the performances of 304 drivers, who were unaware of the filming (B 77). The average number of errors committed per driver was 9.18 (for five minutes of driving), and 97 percent of the drivers made at least one error. After reviewing several studies of driver performance, a Department of Transportation report (B 41) concludes that "most drivers commit errors regularly." While deviant drivers (significantly high error frequencies) do exist, they are "few in number in comparison with the average drivers, who commit most of the errors and become involved in most of the crashes."

2. Several studies indicate that driver errors are a principal contributing factor in the large majority of accidents. For example, one multidisciplinary case study of accidents (B 31) found that driver errors were the "primary cause" of 93 percent of the accidents investigated, while another study of over 3,000 turnpike accidents (B 28) found that "86.5 percent were precipitated directly by human error." However, this does not imply that most traffic accidents are exclusively a result of driver error. Accidents are usually complex events involving interaction between driver, vehicle, roadway, and other variables. Most accidents grow out of a combination of several factors (B 12, B 16, B 20, B 36), all of which contribute to their occurrence.

UNIT 2: ORIENTATION TO GAUGES AND INSTRUMENTS,
AND PREPARING TO MOVE THE VEHICLE

1. The professional literature (B 119–B 147) as well as the more comprehensive analyses of the driving task (B 45–B 66) emphasize the need for familiarity with gauges and instruments and for the performance of preparatory steps prior to moving the vehicle. This emphasis seems reasonable in terms of the logical connection between these elements of performance and accident occurrence.

2. Some texts recommend specific hand positions on the steering wheel, such as "9 o'clock" and "3 o'clock" (B 120). Although no evidence has been found to support the superiority of a particular hand position, Lauer and Suhr (B 89) found that taking one hand off the wheel reduced steering efficiency. In addition an analysis of turnpike accidents (B 28) suggests that the driver should have a firm grip on the wheel to prevent it from spinning out of control in the event of a blow-out or similar emergency.

Apparently, however, experienced drivers adopt a wide range of hand positions—many of which are not consistent with maintaining firm control. In a study of the hand positions used by 4,257 drivers (B 96), 48.7 percent of the drivers held the wheel with one hand; 48.5 percent of the drivers had their left arm on the window ledge; only 7.6 percent of the drivers had their hands in the 10 and 2 o'clock position; and the most common single position (23.7 percent) involved holding the wheel with the right hand (only) at the 12 o'clock position.

3. The research supporting the value of seat belts in preventing injuries and death appears in several publications. A recent government study (B 23) of the accumulated data concluded that when lap belts are worn, the chance of incurring any injury is reduced 15–25 percent, the chances of being seriously injured are reduced 22–38 percent, and the chances of fatal injury are reduced 30–50 percent. Furthermore, the data showed that lap and shoulder restraint systems provided significantly more protection than lap belts alone. Despite this demonstrated value, studies show that seat-belt usage remains disappointingly low— ranging from 16 percent to 50 percent depending on the population studied, area of the country, and other variables (B 85, B 104, B 106).

4. The importance of thoroughly checking traffic before leaving a parked position or a driveway is reflected in accident data. In urban areas, 5.3 percent of all accidents involve vehicles that are leaving either a parked position or driveway (B 27). In 1972 in New York State alone, 19,557 vehicles collided with other vehicles when leaving a parked position (B 35).

Failure to observe conditions thoroughly before starting to move the vehicle appears to be a common error among beginning drivers. Brody et al. (B 70) found that failure to observe or signal before starting to move ranked thirteenth among all errors made by drivers taking road tests, and another study of road-test performance (B 116) obtained similar results.

UNIT 3: BASIC SKILLS IN SPEED CONTROL AND TRACKING ON FORWARD PATHS

1. Although most analyses of the driving task (B 45–B 66) emphasize the importance of basic manipulative skills in guiding vehicles, there has not been a definitive identification of these skills and their relationship to safe performance (B 65, B 36). The particular basic skills contained in Unit 3 represent the author's distillation of available evidence and theory in a form that is intended to be useful to the driver education teacher.

The results of a few studies have suggested that deficiencies in basic skills play a significant role in accident causation. For example, Bishop (B 5) found that a lack of skill helped to trigger the accident in 14 percent of the cases studied; in an investigation of accidents on the Pennsylvania Turnpike (B 28), 11.7 percent were attributed to "deficiencies in routine driving skills"; and a study of single-car accidents (B 8) indicated that the reasons for women's involvement in accidents seemed to cluster around the lack of manipulative skill.

2. Accident statistics (B 35, B 27) and other comprehensive studies (B 7, B 9, B 12, B 24, B 37, B 44) characteristically designate "speed" or "speed too fast" as a common contributing circumstance in accidents. In addition, studies of driver performance (B 77, B 70, B 116) have indicated that errors in speed control are common. For example, in a filmed study of five-minute segments of the performance of 304 drivers, "speed" was the most common error—it was committed by 87 percent of the drivers (B 77). However, the extent to which these excessive or inappropriate speeds are due to deficiencies in the driver's basic skills in speed control is not known. There is good reason to believe that factors other than deficiencies in skill cause drivers to select inappropriate speeds.

Of particular interest to teachers of driver education are the findings of an investigation of one-car accidents involving younger drivers (B 5), in which 7 of the 119 cases studied involved "inadvertently accelerating instead of braking." These figures correspond with the reports of experienced teachers of driver education (B 126), which indicate that inadvertent acceleration is not uncommon among beginning drivers.

As the beginning driver progresses, the teacher might expect him to exhibit greater efficiency and smoothness in his use of the accelerator and brake. Studies of driver performance (B 71, B 88) have found that the better or more experienced drivers tend to use fewer accelerator and brake actions.

Apparently, the task of judging the speed of moving vehicles (in miles per hour) is quite difficult. Even experienced drivers are not accurate in making such judgments (B 72, B 114). Teachers who choose to have their students achieve and maintain specified speeds (without looking at the speedometer) should recognize the inherent difficulty of this task.

3. The professional literature (B 119–B 147) gives considerable attention to the development of an awareness of required stopping distances from various speeds. Although no evidence has been found to support the relationship between this awareness and accident occurrence, it seems reasonable to assume that such an awareness might aid the driver in selecting appropriate speeds (speeds that would allow him to bring the vehicle to a stop in time to avoid a collision), and in selecting appropriate times to begin braking. Phase 2 attempts to systematically develop this awareness of stopping distances during in-car practice.

4. Most comprehensive analyses of the driving task (B 45–B 66) regard the driver's ability to control the movement of the vehicle in relation to the roadway (and to the intended path) as a fundamental component of driving. Furthermore, as a general rule, these analyses stress the importance of the driver's ability to accurately perceive the relationship between the vehicle's movement and the roadway as being prerequisite to effective control. The concept of tracking as presented in Phases 3 and 4 is based partly on these analyses.

There is some evidence to support the importance of accurate tracking in safe driver performance. A review of accident data (B 46) indicates that 3.75 percent of all accidents occur in situations where drivers inadequately track along a prescribed path—by, for example, drifting out of the lane of travel or failing to stay on path in a curve.

One study of driver performance indicates that there is a relationship between vehicle speed and accuracy in tracking (B 87). More experienced novices drove faster and made more tracking errors than less experienced drivers who drove more slowly. This indicates that there may be a critical stage in the acquisition of tracking skills where beginners have to integrate speed control and tracking.

Studies of driver performance indicate that failure to maintain proper lane position is a most common driving error (B 77, B 78, B 116). For example, Fine et al. (B 78) report that of the 2,270 incidents of driver behavior studied, 15 percent of all "bad" driver behavior involved failure to "maintain proper lane." In another study (B 77), which filmed five-minute segments of on-street driver performance, 63 percent of the drivers studied were guilty of at least one "failure to stay in lane." Although this error may not result exclusively from deficiencies in tracking ability, it might be argued that emphasis on accuracy in tracking during in-car instruction should encourage the student to be aware of and to avoid this error.

5. Encouraging the student to establish a point of aim well ahead of the vehicle is suggested as an aid in teaching accurate tracking. This practice is commonly recommended in the professional literature (B 119–B 147). However it is also recognized that students will have to shift their focus periodically to closer points in order to align the car with the roadway. In a study of drivers' eye fixations (B 81) the records showed "continuous visual shifts, forward to the limit of the road and backwards toward the vehicle." These shifts are explained by the need for "perceptual anticipation and alignment. . . Perceptual anticipation requires the driver to look far ahead to get a general idea of conditions that will have to be met. Alignment behavior requires viewing close up to ensure that the vehicle is on the road." Also, beginning drivers tend to look more closely in front of the vehicle and more to the right compared to experienced drivers (B 98), apparently because the beginners need to check more frequently on the vehicle's immediate position.

6. Hand-over-hand steering is advocated in the professional literature (B 119–B 147). However, no evidence has been found to support its superiority over alternative steering techniques. The hand-over-hand method is recommended in the Unit Plan partly because of its widespread professional acceptance. In addition, during the field testing of the Unit Plan, other methods of steering were explored and found to be less suitable for most beginners.

7. The skill of quick braking is introduced at an early point in the in-car program to equip the student to cope with situations that require an abrupt stop. When faced with the necessity of braking quickly, beginning drivers have been observed to commit three basic types of errors: gradually applying the brakes, "freezing," and jamming down the accelerator (B 126). Practice in quick braking is intended to overcome the tendency to make such errors. Field tests of the Unit Plan have indicated that most beginning drivers are capable of developing considerable skill in quick braking during the early stages of their training. However, the extent to which this skill is applied to subsequent on-street emergency situations has not been systematically observed.

UNIT 4: BASIC SKILLS IN SPEED CONTROL AND TRACKING ON BACKWARD PATHS

1. There is reason to believe that a sizable portion of all accidents involve vehicles that are moving backward. For example, in one year in New York State, 15,859 accidents (5 percent of all collisions) were classified as "backed into" (B 35). In a study of pedestrian accidents at selected urban locations (B 13), although "backing" accounted for less than 1 percent of all vehicle movement at these locations, it accounted for 11 percent of all of the vehicle-pedestrian accidents that occurred. So while backing maneuvers may not be among the most common elements of driver performance in terms of the total driving time devoted to them, they are a sufficiently prominent part of the accident problem and deserve attention in driver education.

Beginning drivers appear to have considerable difficulty in mastering the basic skills involved in backing maneuvers. The results of driving tests support this observation (B 70, B 116). For example, in a study of performance on the driver's license road test (B 70), the second and third most frequent types of errors were "excessive maneuvers in parking" and "parks too far from curb." Reports of experienced driver education teachers (B 126) also confirm the difficulties experienced in teaching and learning backing skills.

Unfortunately, systematic studies of driver performance (B 67–B 118) and analyses of the driving task (B 45–B 66) give comparatively little attention to backing. The professional literature (B 119–B 147), however, deals rather extensively with backing maneuvers and identifies some of the unique elements of performance involved in backing. Thus, the description of basic skills contained in Unit 4 is based partly on what appears in the professional literature, and otherwise on the author's own observations and analyses.

UNIT 5: ORIENTATION TO ON-STREET DRIVING, AND INITIAL TECHNIQUES IN SCANNING FOR, EVALUATING, AND RESPONDING TO OBSTACLES

1. Guide 3 encourages the beginning driver to adjust speed to the normal speed of traffic. This suggestion is based on a well-established principle in traffic engineering: "Accidents are not related as much to speed (measured by average speed or the speeds at or below which some percentage of the vehicles travel) as to the spread in speeds from the highest to the lowest. In other words, accidents result from the differences in speeds rather than from speed as a measure" (B 38). Several studies support this principle, including one of the most comprehensive investigations of the relationship between speed and accident occurrence, which found that "the greater the variation in speed of any vehicle from the average speed of all traffic, the greater its chance of being involved in an accident" (B 34). Rear-end collisions appear to be the characteristic outgrowth of these differences in speed. "Pairs of passenger-car drivers involved in two car rear-end collisions were much more likely to be traveling at speed differences greatly in excess of those observed for pairs of cars in normal traffic. For example, fully one-third of the accidents involved pairs of cars traveling at speed differences of 30 miles per hour or more, compared to only 1 percent of pairs of cars in normal traffic (B 34).

2. The method of counting off seconds to estimate following distance has been found to result in more accurate and consistent distance maintenance than other methods such as keeping a car length for each 5-10 miles per hour, or following at a specified number of yards (B 91).

3. The importance of scanning and search procedures in relation to safe performance is now well documented. Virtually all comprehensive analyses of the driving task emphasize the criticality of adequate search procedures (B 45-B 66). In-depth case studies verify that errors in scanning and search procedures lead to accidents (B 9, B 20, B 28, B 40, B 43). For example, in one study 19-25 percent of all accidents were due in part to "improper lookout" on the driver's part (B 40); and in another investigation (B 9) "failure to look" accounted for 21 percent of the accidents studied.

The problems involved in the study of perception and in the development of an effective training program for drivers are too numerous to discuss here. However, a few examples of these problems might serve as useful illustrations. Gordon (B 81) used a filmed record of driver's eye fixations in studying the "visual input" of ten drivers on a test road. His records "refute the notion that a common sequence of viewing is shared by all drivers." Assuming the validity of this finding, one might seriously question the advisability and the practicality of attempting to teach all drivers a common pattern of scanning. In addition, Gordon notes the inherent difficulties in studying what the driver perceives:

> We do not have communication lines to the driver's eyes or brain allowing us to determine how he selects and sorts this sensory input. If we ask the driver what he is responding to, we obtain suggestive, but in no sense trustworthy, answers. (p. 55)

The task of devising an effective and practical system for perceptual training poses special problems of its own. For example, how does one develop a system for scanning and perception that is simple enough to be taught and yet comprehensive enough to prepare the trainee for the great variety of driving situations she will encounter?

A system for training professional drivers in scanning and search procedures has been developed (B 147) and now appears in much of the professional literature in driver education. The system consists of five basic rules that are intended to guide the driver's "seeing habits": (1) aim high in steering, (2) get the big picture, (3) keep your eyes moving, (4) leave yourself an out, and (5) make sure they see you.

An experimental field test of the system has been conducted (B 142). A total of 131 truck drivers were divided into two groups; one group was trained using the system, the other was not. The accident records for the two groups were examined over a period of fifteen months subsequent to the training period. A comparison of the records showed no statistically significant differences between the accident rates of the trained and the untrained drivers. An additional finding of this study was that the effectiveness of the system depended, in part, on who did the training; drivers trained by one trainer had significantly better accident records than drivers trained by another trainer. (This reinforces the notion that the success of any plan for in-car instruction, including the Unit Plan, is highly dependent on the competencies of the teacher who uses it.)

More recently, this same training procedure has been modified to make it more useful with beginning drivers (B 143). Three techniques are emphasized during the initial stages of student practice: (1) aim high ahead, (2) visualize your intended travel path, and (3) sight down the center of the path. Two additional techniques are emphasized during the later stages of student practice: (4) scan the scene ahead, and (5) make regular checks inside and to the rear.

The scanning techniques included in Unit 5 have been developed to provide the beginning driver with a set of guides for performance that will facilitate her acquisition of effective (safe) response patterns. The techniques reflect ideas and evidence contained in several sources, although, as a group, the techniques are unique in that they do not appear elsewhere in the same form. In addition, the techniques have been refined as a result of informal field tests with beginning drivers. At the moment, however, there is no empirical evidence to support their value in the training of safe drivers.

4. Scanning Technique 1 encourages the driver to actively search for events within her visual field that are relevant to her continued safe travel so that she will be more likely to perceive those events. Research in other areas demonstrates that human perception is selective: we perceive what we are prepared or set to perceive (B 129). As Bloomer (B 48) states:

Experimental research in the psychology of perception indicates a stimulus object may be visibly available, yet not "tuned in" by the driver. The process of perception is necessarily selective: a driver paying attention to a child at the side of the road may inadvertently drive into another obstacle. (p. 549)

Several authors and researchers emphasize the need for drivers to selectively perceive events that are most crucial to the safe movement of the vehicle (B 4, B 48, B 60, B 63, B 64) and in so doing to avoid being distracted by unrelated events (B 63). The need for some kind of selectivity in drivers' viewing habits is evident, but the problem of deciding where to look and what to look for remains. Several analyses of the driving task (B 46, B 54, B 58, B 59, B 64) stress the fact that a driver's ability to perceive obstacles in relation to the intended path of the vehicle is a principal factor in avoiding collisions. Technique 1 uses these same key concepts (that is, "obstacles" and "path"). In addition, some indication of what to look for is provided by the illustrations of common obstacles. These illustrations are based on the most frequent types of collisions as described by national accident statistics (B 27) and on a recent government study of training requirements (B 46).

5. Scanning Technique 2 is based on one of the seeing habits included in the training system discussed earlier (B 147) as well as on the recommendations of other writers (B 64, B 138). Its basic purpose is to encourage the driver to see as many relevant events as possible, and, at the same time, to avoid overattending to a single event (to the exclusion of other critical events). In one series of case studies of accidents (B 32), a few of the cases involved drivers whose "attention was focused on one hazardous object or situation while a second hazard was operating simultaneously. The second hazard was not seen because of a focus on the first hazard." In another study a moderately high number of the accident reports reviewed (B 138) indicated that the driver's attention was diverted to other aspects of the traffic scene just prior to the accident, which led the researchers to conclude that "the eyes should be shifted frequently to avoid their freezing on one conflict while another is missed."

Some of the basic principles governing the operation of the human visual mechanism are related to the technique of keeping one's eyes moving while driving. These principles are discussed at length elsewhere in the literature (B 52, B 63, B 75, B 79). A few of the most relevant principles include:

1. "Higher levels of visual acuity are found only in an area on or immediately surrounding the line of sight; at 5° or above from the line of sight events are being seen by an eye whose vision is . . . equivalent to partial blindness" (B 52).
2. "The faster the speed, the narrower the clear zone [of vision]" (B 75).
3. "Clear vision occurs during fixation pauses between eye movements except when following a moving object" (B 79).
4. "A time interval of from 0.5 to 1.5 seconds is required to shift fixation and discriminate a detail at a distance after reading the speedometer or other dash instrument. A somewhat shorter fixation time is required to shift the gaze laterally without the near-far shift" (B 90).

In addition, Danielson (B 75) reports on a study, using himself as a subject, in which he was able to "leisurely" make 32 eye movements per minute while driving, but became dizzy when he forced himself to make 120 movements per minute.

These principles suggest that the driver will have to change her point of fixation to see clearly the range of events that take place in relation to her path of travel, and that she has a capacity for making relatively frequent changes in fixation. On the other hand, these principles indicate that excessively frequent eye movements may have deleterious effects—such as failing to allow sufficient time for fixation and discrimination, or causing dizziness.

Included among the actions to be performed in connection with Technique 2 is "periodically checking to the rear." This practice is commonly recommended in the professional literature (B 119–B 147). However, the effect of increased awareness to the rear on accident occurrence is as yet unknown. Although it would seem to be a logical precaution to take against one of the most common types of accidents (i.e., rear-end collisions (B 77)), every glance to the rear involves at least momentary inattention to the forward sector and thus increases the possibility that the driver might fail to perceive an important event in front of his vehicle. On the basis of a limited number of case studies of accidents, Ross (B 32) concludes: "In some accidents it appears that, had the driver been aware of a vehicle approaching from his rear, he could have avoided the accident, for instance by a less severe stop." However, he adds that "rear-end collisions are especially likely to result from stopping to avoid a collision in the forward sector, and accidents of this type do not appear potentially avoidable through increased attention to the rear sector." For these and other reasons, the Unit Plan cautions the teacher against overemphasizing the practice of checking to the rear.

6. Scanning Technique 3 encourages the beginning driver to look far enough ahead along the path of travel to enable her to anticipate the events she will encounter. This kind of anticipation seems to be fundamental to the driving task. Several writers (B 79, B 81, B 102, B 120) have noted the importance of being able to anticipate events well in advance of encountering them in order to allow adequate time for making the appropriate response. Also, in a study of 2,270 incidents of driver behavior (B 78), one of the principal distinctions between "good" and "bad" driving involved the driver's anticipation of impending events in the driving environment (hazardous situations, pedestrian movements, and so on).

The problem of determining precisely how far ahead the student should be looking is complex. What an appropriately distant focal point is will necessarily change with variations in the driving situation (increases in speed, traffic density, and so on). As a general rule, it is advisable to look further ahead as vehicle speed increases. Greenshields (B 82) reports findings (similar to those obtained by others) based on a trial series of runs in which the drivers focused on points approximately 510 feet ahead while driving at 20 mph and 1600 feet ahead while driving at 60 mph.

The general rule suggested in the Unit Plan of searching 8–12 seconds ahead is based on information provided in a government funded study (B 138) that indicates that "safe drivers assure themselves of information 8 to 12 seconds ahead."

In implementing Technique 3, teachers are advised *not to insist* that students continuously focus on points well ahead along the intended path. A study of the visual input of experienced drivers (B 81) strongly suggests that drivers periodically need to shift their focus from far to near points and that the fixations on near points enable the driver to maintain proper alignment between her vehicle and the roadway.

7. Evaluating, which includes identifying (or recognizing), predicting, and deciding, is viewed by many authorities as the most critical feature of the driving task (B 45–B 66). After reviewing recent research, the Department of Transportation has concluded that "recognition errors" account for a large percentage of the highway safety problem" (B 40). In one study (B 15), multidisciplinary accident investigation teams found recognition errors to be definite causes in 36 percent to 49 percent of all accidents. Among recognition errors, 18–20 percent were classified as due to inattention, and 19–25 percent were due to improper lookout. Another 9–17 percent of the recognition errors involved false assumptions (or predictions) about what other drivers would do. In another similar study (B 9), 22 percent of the accidents investigated were due to "misperception" and an additional 20 percent to decision-making errors. Another government funded review of research (B 46) identified eight critical situations (which account for 65 percent of all accidents) "where effective driver decision making would be a major contributory factor in accident avoidance." These situations include laterally moving vehicle, following, gap acceptance, laterally moving object, intruding approach, passing, tracking, and skidding.

8. Guide 4 suggests that the driver avoid overuse of decelerate and stop. Many beginning drivers have been observed to be overcautious in their use of the brake to the point where they create a hazard for other vehicles to the rear and confuse other persons in the vicinity (B 126). Although the extent to which such behavior contributes to the total accident problem has not been established, one series of case studies of accidents led to the following conclusion: "Equally dangerous, though not at first glance, is the overly cautious driver who hesitates and slows and is so courteous that he tries to wait until all traffic has passed before he executes his maneuver. Other drivers get false cues from him when he does not exercise his right of way. . ." (B 20). In addition, this type of behavior is likely to obstruct the smooth flow of traffic—a situation that has long been recognized by traffic engineers as a critical contributor to accidents (B 38).

9. Commentary driving is one of the major elements in a highly successful driver training program for the California Highway Patrol (reviewed in a report by the Department of Transportation (B 46)). One of the effects of this program was that cadet trainees dramatically increased the distance ahead at which they identified obstacles.

INTRODUCTION TO REDUCED-RISK PERFORMANCE

1. The reduced-risk approach to teaching maneuvers emphasizes the alternatives available to the driver, and his responsibility to select from these alternatives the ones that involve the least risk. In this respect the reduced-risk approach appears to be consistent with the nature of the driving task. Several analyses of the driving task (B 56, B 60, B 58, B 59, B 64, B 79) identify the driver's decision making and selection of alternatives as being fundamental to safe performance. Ross' (B 64) analysis is particularly relevant to the reduced-risk approach. He proposes that the driver's task may be divided into two parts: the obtaining of accurate information, and the effecting of appropriate action based on this information. After discussing the first part, he goes on to state:

> Having achieved accurate information, the operator is still faced with the problem of taking appropriate action. The first step, having judged the vehicle-roadway and the vehicle-vehicle relationship to be unsatisfactory, is to survey the alternative potentialities for action . . . For each alternative surveyed, it is necessary for the operator to estimate the consequences . . . A choice must be made among the various alternatives. We assume that the choice with the least risk will be made, allowing for miscalculations of risk as explained above. . . .(p. 9)

Furthermore, reduced-risk performance emphasizes the realistic possibility of reducing, not eliminating, risk. In this respect it encourages the driver to recognize that some risk is involved in all driving and, conversely, that no course of action is completely safe. Hurst's (B 56) comments are apropos here: "One reason that accident rates continue to increase, in spite of this 'common sense' approach [that is, educating drivers to avoid risk-taking], could be that it is patently ridiculous to urge the driver not to take any risks at all. It seems scarcely necessary to point out that following this advice, the 'driver' would never take his car out of the driveway . . . No action is ever completely safe, and it seems likely that most drivers realize this."

The ultimate objective of the reduced-risk approach to teaching maneuvers is to produce drivers who will select low-risk alternatives and thus experience fewer accidents. Excessive risk-taking has been associated with accidents and near accidents. In a study of near accidents (B 12), 27 percent involved drivers who were "pushing through" (squeezing through cross traffic, passing on right, starting before signal, and so on). Another study (B 28) reports on a limited number of cases in which the driver's "risky choice" of alternatives was associated with accidents. In addition, there is some evidence that suggests that more experienced drivers take fewer risks. In one study, more experienced professional drivers, when faced with the task of driving through gaps of varying sizes, took less "risk" ("attempts at performance when the person is not sure he or she will succeed") than did less experienced drivers (B 73). At this time, however, no evidence has been gathered (or uncovered) to support the contention that the reduced-risk approach to instruction will actually lead to accident reduction.

2. Communicating intentions is a basic element of content in the Unit Plan. This emphasis on communication reflects its acknowledged role as one of the fundamental components of the driving task (B 45–B 66). The word "communicating" is used instead of "signaling" because it more clearly indicates that the driver's task is to transmit a message to others and to make decisions based on the probability that the message is received.

An indication of the fundamental role of communication in driving is found in a study of over 2,000 critical incidents of driver behavior in which 14 percent of all "good" driver behaviors and 6 percent of all "bad" driver behaviors involved communication (B 28). Other studies of driver performance suggest that failures to signal intentions are among the most common driving errors (B 67, B 70, B 77, B 116). For example, in a study of performance on the driver's license road test, two of the seven most frequently made errors involved signaling. In contrast, a study of a selected group of "safe drivers" found that one of the characteristics common to all subjects was: "signaling intentions when slowing down, stopping, turning or changing lanes" (B 92).

Little evidence has been found that bears on the function of communication in accident causation or prevention. Accident statistics (B 27, B 35, B 39) do not list signaling failures or other aspects of communication among the common contributing circumstances. Although a large proportion of all accidents occurs when vehicles are performing maneuvers that require signaling—turning, stopping, leaving parked position, and so on (B 27)—the extent to which signaling errors contribute to these accidents has not been examined. In all likelihood the role of communication in accidents is quite complex. One study pointed out at least two types of errors in communication that led to accidents (B 32): some drivers failed to signal before turning, other drivers signaled for turns but proceeded ahead or stopped. In these instances drivers in the vicinity were led to believe that the vehicles would follow different paths from the ones they actually did follow, and accidents resulted.

UNIT 6: REDUCED-RISK TURNS

1.   Right and left turning maneuvers are distinctive and common segments of the total driving task. The professional literature (B 119–B 147) emphasizes these maneuvers, especially in connection with lesson plans for the in-car instruction of beginning drivers. Also, state driver's manuals (written for beginning drivers) normally stress the legal requirements governing turning maneuvers. Apparently there is professional consensus regarding the need to familiarize beginners with the elements of performance involved in these maneuvers.

Accident statistics (B 27, B 35) and special studies of accidents (B 12, B 29) support the fact that a relatively large number of accidents occur during the performance of turning maneuvers. For example, 8.6 percent of all urban accidents, and 4.6 percent of all rural accidents are two-car collisions in which one of the cars was turning (B 27). (It should be mentioned at this point that the total number of accidents associated with a given maneuver is not necessarily an indication of the inherent dangerousness of that maneuver. A large number of turning accidents may simply reflect the fact that driving involves frequent turns and that, by chance, accidents are more likely to be associated with those parts of the driving task that occur quite frequently. A more accurate indication of the dangerousness of a maneuver would indicate the rate of turning accidents in relation to the total number of turns performed. Information of this sort has not been uncovered.)

Evidence that associates specific features of turning maneuvers with accidents is sparse. Accident statistics (B 77) suggest that left turns are hazardous because they expose the vehicle to rear-end collisions with following vehicles as well as to collisions with oncoming traffic. Traffic engineering studies have shown that effective control of left turns can significantly reduce accidents. A summary of the findings of these studies (B 38) concludes: "Turn prohibition practically eliminates left-turn accidents and reduces rear-end collisions. Special turn-lanes bring a similar reduction in rear-end collisions and a reduction of turning accidents. Turn lanes with a special signal phase are most effective at signalized intersections." In a related study, Baldock (B 38) found an association between the rate of left-turn accidents and the volume of vehicles making left turns: at intersections where turning volumes were lower, the accident involvement per vehicle was higher. Apparently, left turns are more dangerous when made at locations where they occur less frequently and where they are inadequately controlled by roadway markings and signals. In a study of pedestrian accidents at selected urban locations (B 13), although vehicle turning maneuvers accounted for only 14 percent of the total vehicle movement, they accounted for 45 percent of all pedestrian accidents. Thus, vehicle-pedestrian accidents seem to pose a significant problem in relation to the safe performance of turns.

The findings of studies of driver performance (B 67, B 70, B 77, B 78, B 111, B 116) indicate that errors occur quite frequently in connection with turning maneuvers. A wide variety of types of errors have been identified in different studies. (Differences between studies are partly a reflection of the different methods used to observe and record driver performance.) In an investigation of performance on the driver's license road test (B 70), the fourth, fifth, and eighth ranking errors were: "swings wide right (turning corner)," "swings wide left (turning corner,)" and "fails to get in proper lane (turning corner)." In a similar study of road-test performance (B 116), the following were found to be among the most frequently committed errors in both right and left turns: "approaches from improper lane," "approaches (turns) at improper speed," "in improper lane during turn," "into improper lane after turn," and "shifts gear while turning." In another investigation, which used filmed records of five-minute segments of driver performance (B 77), 46 percent of the drivers turned without signaling and 11 percent made some other type of improper turn. In a study of critical incidents of driver behavior (B 78), 357 critical behaviors occurred in connection with turning maneuvers—the most frequent "bad" behaviors involved errors in deceleration, yielding the right-of-way, placement of the vehicle prior to the turn, and signaling intentions.

An intensive investigation of the turn-signaling behavior of 10,467 drivers at seven different intersections has uncovered some interesting data on this single aspect of turning maneuvers (B 67). Among the principal findings of the study were: (1)) Turn signaling behavior appears to be quite sensitively related to intersection and road characteristics (that is, speeds at intersection, presence of special turning lanes, and so forth). (2) At the seven intersections the percentage of drivers who signaled for a right turn ranged from 34 percent to 69 percent and for a left turn from 48 percent to 86 percent (per intersection). (3) A signal was given for approximately 49 percent of all right turns and 64 percent of all left turns. (4) At several intersections, the presence of opposing traffic tended to increase both right and left turn signaling. (5) Female drivers generally signaled more frequently than males. These data have two important implications for the driver education teacher: (1) the high incidence of failures to signal suggests that rigorous training procedures are needed to overcome this failure; and (2) the beginner needs to be alerted to the fact that a large portion of turning maneuvers are not signaled for by other drivers, and therefore he must make allowances for this behavior in maneuvering his own vehicle.

UNIT 7: REDUCED-RISK LANE CHANGES

1. Changing lanes is among the most common maneuvers and apparently drivers are prone to making frequent errors when performing it. In a study of the filmed records of five-minute segments of driver performance (B 77), 80 percent of the drivers changed lanes "without signaling" and 20 percent changed lanes "without caution." Also, in a study of 2,270 critical incidents of driver behavior (B 78), 11 percent of all "bad" driver behaviors involved improper "lane holding or changing." By contrast, a study of a select sample of "safe drivers" found that among the outstanding characteristics common to all the drivers were: "perfect timing when . . . changing lanes" and "signaling intentions when . . . changing lanes" (B 92).

The findings of some studies have indicated that a substantial number of accidents may be the result of improper lane changes. For example, in a study of turnpike accidents (B 28), approximately 32 percent of the 475 "illegal and unsafe" driver actions that contributed to accidents were committed in connection with performing lane changes.

Some clues to the errors in driver performance involved in lane-change accidents are contained in the study of accidents on the Pennsylvania Turnpike (B 28). The majority of lane-change accidents involved pulling into a lane that was already occupied by another vehicle. This would suggest that inadequacies in scanning and assessment procedures prior to initiating the maneuver were important factors. In addition, Ross (B 32) offers some evidence to support the contention that lane-change accidents occur partly because other drivers fail to expect the change of lanes; they are operating under the assumption that each driver will stay in his own lane.

SUPPLEMENT TO UNIT 7: PASSING

1. Passing is clearly among the more common and dangerous maneuvers performed by drivers. National accident statistics (B 27, B 35) and other special studies of accidents (B 12, B 28, B 29, B 46) support the fact that a relatively large number of accidents occur during passing maneuvers. In addition, studies of driver performance (B 77, B 78) indicate that passing is a common aspect of the total driving task during which errors in performance are frequent. For example, in a study of 2,270 critical incidents of driver

behavior, 21 percent of all incidents of "bad" driver behavior were associated with the passing maneuver (B 78). Recognizing the importance of the passing maneuver, the professional literature (B 119–B 147) normally gives considerable attention to it, with special emphasis on the need for certain precautions in initiating and completing the maneuver.

A variety of studies have pointed to some critical features of the passing maneuver, which in part explain its high degree of difficulty and risk. One of these critical features involves making judgments about the speed of the vehicle to be passed, and allowing a sufficient distance between it and the passing vehicle. McFarland (B 95) reports on a study of near accidents among professional bus drivers in which one of the "most important variables contributing to the situations" was "following too closely while approaching to pass." In another investigation of the performance of professional drivers (B 107), a significant relationship was found between "closest headway" (in performing passing maneuvers) and "highest accident rate." Also, in a study of turnpike accidents (B 28), a sizable number involved drivers who "misjudged distance (and rate of closure) of vehicle ahead while starting to pass." Another critical feature of the maneuver involves the variable behavior of the driver being passed. In the study of turnpike accidents cited above (B 28), 112 accidents occurred when a driver "pulled out in front of passing vehicle," and six accidents involved "vehicle being passed drifted over center line forcing passing vehicle off road." This same study pointed to other critical parts of the passing maneuver: "ran into median while passing and lost control" (30 accidents), and "cut in too quickly after passing" (18 accidents).

In a Department of Transportation review of several studies of driver behavior in passing (B 46), it was pointed out that while drivers are able to judge distances of oncoming cars, they are very poor judges of either closing rate or oncoming car speeds—and thus are unable to consistently judge the time available for passing and avoiding a collision with oncoming cars. In the same report, another study showed that drivers often violate no-passing zones when performing passing maneuvers—one-quarter of the sample of drivers observed violated the beginning of the no-passing zone and one-half violated the end of it.

Crawford (B 74) conducted a study that focused on the performance of the overtaking driver in situations where oncoming vehicles were present (at various distances from the passing vehicle). He used a two-lane road laid out on a 2,000-yard airfield runway to study the response of drivers who were given signals to pass other vehicles at various times in relation to the position of oncoming vehicles. One of the more interesting findings of this study was that response time increased as the interval (distance from oncoming vehicle) decreased, that is, a "decision required more time as the condition became more critical." On the basis of these findings, Crawford has suggested that "drivers should not attempt a maneuver about which they have any doubts, not only because they have a smaller safety margin for their action, but because they take longer to decide to act."

Another related study illustrates the difficulty of making decisions about the rate of closure of oncoming traffic when initiating a passing maneuver. Jones and Heimstra, as reported by A. D. Little, Inc. (B 36), asked subjects to judge "the last safe moment for passing" the lead car in the face of an oncoming car, but without actually passing it. The time between the subject's indication of the last safe moment and the arrival of the oncoming car was measured. The "actual time" it would have taken to pass the lead vehicle was also calculated. One of the more interesting findings of this study was that underestimates (estimated safety time less than "actual" safety time) were found to occur as frequently as overestimates. A part of the difficulty involved in making such decisions might be accounted for by the relatively long time-space normally required to safely complete a passing maneuver. Greenshields (B 82) reports on studies that indicate that "on the average a driver required a time-space of 9 to 10 seconds to pass."

UNIT 8: STRATEGIES FOR ROADWAY AND TRAFFIC CHARACTERISTICS

1. A substantial amount of data associates various roadway and traffic characteristics with accidents. A thorough examination of these data is beyond the scope of this report. A concise review of a portion of the data appears in *Traffic Control and Roadway Elements* (B 38). Some of the more commonly studied roadway and traffic elements that have been associated with accidents include traffic volume and speed, number and width of lanes, road surface, roadside features, limited access roadways, interchanges, types of intersections, intersection traffic controls, curves, hills, medians, illumination, one-way streets, and

pedestrian controls (B 38). In addition, an excellent resource for teachers is the HumRRO study of the driving task (B 138), which contains background information on safe driving in relation to various roadway and traffic characteristics. For example, sections of the report are devoted to such things as pedestrians, intersections, parked cars, hills, curves, road surfaces, road shoulders, and railroad crossings.

Although the results of some of these studies have implications for driver education, they are most directly relevant to the concerns of the highway or traffic engineer. Normally these studies identify features of the roadway or traffic controls that are more or less hazardous, and thus provide the engineer with the information necessary to make improvements in the roadway or controls. However, as a general rule they do not carefully study the specific actions of drivers in relation to these roadway and traffic factors and thus do not provide the kinds of information that would be most useful in driver education. For example, a review of studies of road curvature yielded the following conclusions: "To sum up, curves introduce an element of hazard on all types of highways. Sharp curves on grades are far more hazardous than curves on level alinement. Curves are also likely to be the scene of skidding accidents. There are a number of possibilities for reducing the accident potential of curves, including improvement of superelevation, visibility at the curve, and sign and markings, particularly by the addition of indicated speed signs and delineators" (B 38). These conclusions (and the specific data that support them) provide relatively definitive guides for the engineer charged with designing and marking roadways. On the other hand, the conclusions (and data) have limited value for the driver education teacher. Although they do indicate that curves (and particularly curves on grades) are dangerous and therefore represent features of the driving environment that beginning drivers should be exposed to, they do not specify the kinds of driver actions that are most effective (or ineffective) on curves and thus fail to provide a definitive guide for the teacher.

The professional literature (B 97–B 126) identifies driving practices that are appropriate for various roadway and traffic characteristics. Although no evidence has been found that directly supports the value of these practices in accident prevention, they represent the best available information on which to base the design of driving strategies in Unit 11.

2. After reviewing related research and theory in perceptual motor learning, Barrett et al. (B 46) conclude that films are "potentially useful in driving training, especially at perceptual and cognitive levels," although they also note that more research is needed to determine those critical driving situations that films should concentrate on and the optimal driving procedures for each of these situations.

UNIT 9: REDUCED-RISK BACKING MANEUVERS

1. See notations under Unit 4.

UNIT 10: REDUCED-RISK TURNING AROUND

1. The professional literature (B 119–B 147) emphasizes several methods for turning the vehicle around, including the U turn, the Y turn, and using alleys and driveways. In most instances these maneuvers appear in the lesson plans for in-car instruction. In addition, driver licensing procedures often include such maneuvers as part of the road test.

Despite the attention given to these maneuvers in driver education and road testing, no evidence has been found that bears on their relationship to accidents, or to the driving task in general. This lack of evidence suggests that such maneuvers are performed relatively less often than other maneuvers.

The driver education teacher might use this (lack of) evidence to justify limiting the practice time devoted to turning around. The Unit Plan includes these maneuvers in a separate unit primarily because they appear to have distinctive qualities that require special types of driving procedures not found in the common maneuvers, and because some of the concepts learned in relation to performing these maneuvers (such as selecting the safest location and method) have general applicability to other kinds of driving situations and maneuvers.

UNIT 11: EMERGENCIES: PERCEPTION AND RESPONSES

1. The way in which drivers cope with emergency situations appears to be a crucial factor in the total accident problem. There is some evidence that drivers make serious errors when faced with emergencies, and that these errors contribute to accidents. In one in-depth study of accidents (B 9), 10 percent of all accident-producing errors were classified as "panic reaction." In a series of case studies (B 5), 55 percent of the accidents were attributed, in part, to "faulty skill in attempting to correct for an emergency situation." Some of the errors that were made included "late correcting and/or compensating for skid, locking wheels in emergency stop, inadvertently accelerating instead of braking, turning steering wheel impulsively and failing to reduce speed after driving onto shoulder, failing to use brakes, 'freezing' at the wheel in emergency situation, [and] turning the steering wheel the wrong way in a skid." An analysis of turnpike accidents (B 28) has identified the following types of driver errors as precipitating factors in certain types of emergency situations (mostly skidding emergencies):

1. Discrimination (driver fails to discriminate)
    a) Loss of traction
    b) Change in vehicle's attitude in relation to road
    c) Failure to detect path of least probable collision

2. Decisions
    a) Failure to select path with least probability of collision

3. Motor responses
    a) (Failure to) turn steering wheel in direction of skid
    b) (Failure to exhibit) smooth control manipulation: abrupt slamming on of brakes

4. Habits
    a) Putting on brakes abruptly when in trouble
    b) Turning abruptly away from approaching danger

   (It should be noted here that although these errors seem to contribute to accidents, there is no assurance that the accidents would not have occurred if these errors were not made. This observation seems particularly relevant to making judgments about emergency responses since the "emergency" preceded the "response" and one can only speculate about whether a more appropriate response would have avoided the accident.)

   Recognizing this relationship between emergency responses and accidents, several authorities have strongly supported the need for training beginning drivers in perceiving and responding to emergencies. Indeed, the *National Highway Safety Standards* developed by the United States Department of Transportation gives special prominence to emergency procedures as a part of the driver education program. One of the major standards proposed for these courses is that each student should be provided with practice driving instruction in "basic and advanced driving techniques including techniques for handling emergencies." Most persons believe that such training should improve the driver's skill in coping with emergencies. Still others have suggested that such training is likely to have a beneficial effect on the driver's motives or attitudes toward the driving task—having experienced a simulated emergency during training, the driver is more likely to be alert to the possibility of its occurrence (later on) and to drive in such a way as to avoid the onset of the emergency.

   Despite the potential value of training in emergency procedures, no evidence has been found that has a direct bearing on the relationship between such training and accident involvement. It would seem that, among the many existing needs for research in driver education, one which stands out is the need to investigate the kinds of emergency training programs that might be most effective in accident prevention.

   For the most part, the simulated emergencies included in Unit 10, and the responses to these emergencies, have been based on information contained in the professional literature (B 119–147). In addition, the evidence from several accident studies (B 5, B 28, B 29, B 36, B 38) points to skidding as a relatively common factor in accidents, and at least one study (B 28) indicates that accidents resulting from blowouts are reasonably common. This evidence lends support to the advisability of providing training in these types of emergencies.

UNIT 12: STRATEGIES FOR LIMITED ACCESS HIGHWAYS

Selected research findings are reported in the text of the chapter.

UNIT 13: STRATEGIES FOR DRIVING AT NIGHT

Selected research findings are reported in the text of the chapter.

UNIT 14: STRATEGIES FOR SPECIAL CONDITIONS

1. Selected research studies and accident data used in the development of these Units are cited directly in the units, and so are not repeated here.

The teacher may wish to consult other sources for further information about the elements of the driving task covered in these units. The HumRRO description of specific instructional objectives (B 138) and the "Safe Performance Curriculum" (B 133) make excellent resources.

UNIT 15: PERFORMANCE EVALUATION AND PLANNING FOR FUTURE IMPROVEMENT

SELECTED BIBLIOGRAPHY

ACCIDENT FACTORS*

B 1. P. Abramson, "An Accident Evaluation Analysis," *Transportation Research Record*, No. 486, Transportation Research Board, Washington, D.C. (1974).

B 2. J. S. Baker, *Experimental Case Studies of Traffic Accidents. A General Discussion of Procedures and Conclusions*, Traffic Institute, Northwestern Univ., Evanston, Ill. (1960).

B 3. J. S. Baker and L. R. Horn, *An Inventory of Factors Suggested as Contributing to Traffic Accidents*, Traffic Institute, Northwestern Univ., Evanston, Ill. (1960).

B 4. J. E. Barmack and D. Payne, "Injury-Producing Private Motor Vehicle Accidents Among Airmen: Psychological Models of Accident-Generating Processes," *The Journal of Psychology* **52**, 3–4 (1961).

B 5. R. W. Bishop, *One Car Accidents and the Young Driver*, Safety and Traffic Division, Automobile Club of Michigan (1963).

B 6. H. H. Blindauer and H. L. Michael, "An Analysis of High Accident Rates," *Traffic Safety Research Review* **3**, 15–20 (December 1959).

B 7. Bureau of Traffic, Illinois Division of Highways, "Ran-Off-Road Motor Vehicle Accidents in Illinois—1963," Division of Highways, Springfield, Ill. (January 1965).

B 8. California Highway Transportation Agency, *Causes and Characteristics of Single Car Accidents*, Part I, Department of the California Highway Patrol (February 1963).

B 9. A. B. Clayton, "An Accident-Based Analysis of Road User Errors," *Journal of Safety Research* 4, 69–74 (1972).

B 10. P. K. Eckhardt, J. C. Flanagan, and T. W. Forbes, "Role of Roadway Elements in Pennsylvania Turnpike Accidents," *Highway Research Board Bulletin* **120**, 1–5 (1956).

B 11. R. L. Fisher, "Accident and Operating Experience at Interchanges," *Highway Research Board Bulletin* **291**, 124–133 (1961).

B 12. T. W. Forbes, "Analysis of 'Near Accident' Reports," *Highway Research Board Bulletin* **152**, 23–37 (1957).

B 13. J. J. Fruin, "Pedestrian Accident Characteristics in a One-Way Grid," *Pedestrians and Safety*, Highway Research Record, No. 436, Highway Research Board, Washington, D.C. (1973).

---

* The studies and reviews of data included in this section were useful in the development of the Unit Plan. Most of the studies deal with driver actions that contribute to accidents. Other useful studies and reviews of research dealing with traffic and roadway elements are also included. The section represents only a small fraction of the available research on accident factors.

B 14. D. F. Huelke and J. C. March, "Analysis of Rear-End Accident Factors and Injury Patterns," *Proceedings of the American Association for Automotive Medicine*, p. 174–199 (1974).

B 15. Institute of Research in Public Safety, *Tri-Level Study of the Causes of Traffic Accidents:* Interim Report I, 2 volumes, Institute for Research in Public Safety, Bloomington, Ind. (1973).

B 16. D. Klein and J. A. Waller, *Causation, Culpability and Deterrence in Highway Crashes*, U.S. Department of Transportation, Washington, D.C. (1970).

B 17. D. N. Levine and B. J. Campbell, "Effectiveness of Lap Seat Belts and the Energy-Absorbing Steering System in the Reduction of Injuries," *Journal of Safety Research* **4**, 106–118 (1972).

B 18. J. Logan, *The Child in Detroit Traffic*, Traffic Safety Section, Detroit Police Department, Detroit, Mich. (1972).

B 19. G. E. MacDonald, *A Report on the Intensive Investigation of Selected Fatal Motor Vehicle Accidents*, Department of Transport, Ontario, Canada (1962).

B 20. R. B. Mack and M. F. Young, *Derived Factors in Traffic Accidents*, The Traffic Institute, Northwestern Univ., Evanston, Ill. (1960).

B 21. R. A. McFarland and R. C. Moore, "Human Factors in Highway Safety," *New England Journal of Medicine* **256**, 792–799, 890–897 (1957).

B 22. C. J. McMonagle, "The Effect of Roadside Features on Traffic Accidents," *Traffic Quarterly*, **6**, 228–243 (1952).

B 23. D. F. Mela, *Review of Safety Belt Usage and Effectiveness in Accidents*, Office of Statistics and Analysis, National Highway Traffic Safety Administration (1974).

B 24. Minnesota Department of Highways, "The Relationship of Drinking and Speeding to Accident Severity," *Traffic Safety Research Review* **4**, 26–32 (1960).

B 25. B. F. K. Mullins and C. J. Keese, "Freeway Accident Analysis and Safety Study," *Highway Research Board Bulletin* **291**, 26–78 (1961).

B 26. National Highway Traffic Safety Administration, *Pedestrian and Bicycle Safety Study*, Washington, D.C. (1975).

B 27. National Safety Council, *Accident Facts*, The Council, Chicago, Ill. (1975).

B 28. Pennsylvania Turnpike Joint Safety Research Group, *Accident Causation*, Pennsylvania Turnpike Commission, Harrisburg, Pa. (1954).

B 29. D. F. Petty, *An Analysis of Traffic Accidents on County Roads*, Highway Extension and Research Project for Indiana Counties, Purdue Univ., Lafayette, Ind. (1961).

B 30. C. E. Preston and S. Harris, "Psychology of Drivers in Traffic Accidents," *Journal of Applied Psychology* **49**, no. 4, 284–288 (1965).

B 31. H. M. Robinson, *Multidisciplinary Accident Investigations (Boston)*, U. S. Department of Transportation, Washington, D.C. (Contract No. FH-11-7402) (1974).

B 32. H. L. Ross, "Awareness of Collision Course in Traffic Accidents," *Traffic Safety Research Review* **5**, 12–16 (1961).

B 33. L. Shaw and H. S. Sichel, "The Reduction of Accidents in a Transport Company by the Determination of the Accident Liability of Individual Drivers," *Traffic Safety Research Review* **5**, 2–13 (December, 1961).

B 34. D. Solomon, *Accidents on Main Rural Highways Related to Speed, Driver, and Vehicle*, Traffic Systems Research Division, Bureau of Public Roads, Washington, D.C. (1964).

B 35. State of New York Department of Motor Vehicles, *Accident Facts*, Albany, New York (1973).

B 36. *The State of the Art of Traffic Safety*, Arthur D. Little, Inc., Cambridge, Mass. (1966).

B 37. V. L. Tofany, "Factors Contributing to the Reduction of Motor Vehicle Fatalities in 1974," *Journal of Safety Research*, No. 3, 100–103 (1975).

B 38. *Traffic Control and Roadway Elements, Their Relationship to Highway Safety*, Prepared by the Automotive Safety Foundation in cooperation with the U.S. Bureau of Public Roads (1963).

B 39. U.S. Department of Health, Education, and Welfare, *Accidental Death and Injury Statistics*, Public Health Service Publication No. 1111, U.S. Government Printing Office, Washington, D.C. (1963).

B 40. U.S. Department of Transportation, *Diagnostic Assessment of Driver Problems: Volume I, The State of the Art in Driver Problem Diagnosis*, Washington, D.C. (D.O.T. H.S.-801-769) (1975).

B 41. U.S. Department of Transportation, *Driver Behavior and Accident Involvement: Implications for Tort Liability*, Washington, D.C. (1970).

B 42. J. Versace, "Factor Analysis of Roadway and Accident Data," *Highway Research Board Bulletin* **240**, 24–43 (1959).

B 43. F. R. Wagner and J. A. Austin, *Final Report of Multidisciplinary Accident Investigation Program*, U.S. Department of Transportation, Washington, D.C. (Contract No. DOT-HS-047-1-063) (1975).

B 44. J. T. Weston and C. V. Nakaishi, *Utah Multidisciplinary Highway Crash Investigations*, U.S. Department of Transportation, Washington, D.C. (Contract No. DOT-HS-047-1-063) (1974).

ANALYSES OF THE DRIVING TASK

B 45. J. S. Baker and L. H. Ross, *Concepts and Classifications of Traffic Accident Causes*, Traffic Institute, Northwestern Univ., Evanston, Ill. (1960).

B 46. G. V. Barrett, R. A. Alexander, and J. B. Forbes, *Analysis of Performance Measurement and Training Requirements for Driving Decision Making in Emergency Situations*, Department of Transportation, Washington, D.C. (Contract No. DOT-HS-167-2-512) (1973).

B 47. R. W. Bletzacker and T. G. Brittenham, "An Analysis of One-Car Accidents, *Highway Research Board Bulletin* **208**, 35–44 (1959).

B 48. R. H. Bloomer, "Perceptual Defense and Vigilance and Driving Safety," *Traffic Quarterly*, 549–558 (1962).

B 49. M. L. Braunstein, K. P. Laughery, and J. B. Siegfried, "Computer Simulation of the Automobile Driver—A Model of the Car Follower," *Highway Research Board Bulletin* **55**, 21–28 (1963).

B 50. R. M. Calvin and W. P. Quensel, "An Analysis of the Automobile Driving Task," *Journal of Traffic Safety Education* **20** (January 1973).

B 51. G. W. Cobliner and L. Shatin, "An Adaptational Perspective on the Traffic Accident," *Traffic Safety Research Review* **6**, 13–15 (December 1962).

B 52. P. L. Connolly, "Human Factors in Rear Vision," *Highway Research Abstracts* **34**, 27 (1964).

B 53. T. W. Forbes, "Traffic Engineering and Driver Behavior," *Traffic Safety Research Review* **9**, 87–89 (September 1965).

B 54. J. J. Gibson and L. E. Crooks, "A Theoretical Field Analysis of Automobile Driving," *The American Journal of Psychology* **2**, 453–471 (1938).

B 55. H. Haber, R. Brenner and S. Hulbert, "Psychology of Trip Geography," *Highway Research Board Bulletin* **91** (1954).

B 56. P. M. Hurst, "Errors in Driver Risk-Taking," *Report No. 2*, Division of Highway Studies, Institute for Research, State College, Pa. (1964).

B 57. W. Lybrand, "Driver Education and Training: Evaluation Requirements and Suggested Plans," *National Driver Education and Training Symposium Proceedings*, 161–178, The National Highway Safety Bureau, Washington, D.C. (1969).

B 58. J. L. Malfetti, *A Description of the Driving Task Adaptable for a Manual for Beginning Drivers*, American Association of Motor Vehicle Administrators; and Safety Research and Education Project, Teachers College, Columbia University, New York (1970).

B 59. A. J. McKnight and B. B. Adams, *Driver Education Task Analysis, Volume I: Task Descriptions*, U.S. Department of Transportation, HumRRO Technical Report, 70–103 (1970).

B 60. R. M. Michaels, "Human Factors in Highway Safety," *Traffic Quarterly* **15**, 586–599 (1961).

B 61. K. Perchonok, "The Determination of Environment Factors Controlling Driver Behavior," *Report No. 3*, Division of Highway Studies, Institute for Research, State College, Pa. (1964).

B 62. ————, "The Measurement of Driver Errors," *Report No. 1*, Division of Highway Studies, Institute for Research, State College, Pa. (1964).

B 63. F. N. Platt, *Operations Analysis of Traffic Safety*, Traffic Safety and Highway Improvement Department, Ford Motor Company, Dearborn, Mich. (1959).

B 64. L. Ross, "Schematic Analysis of the Driving Situation," Traffic Institute, Northwestern Univ., Evanston, Ill. (1960).

D 65. M. A. Safren and L. Schlesinger, *Driving Skill and Its Measurement,* Driver Behavior Research Project, George Washington Univ., Washington, D.C. (1964).

B 66. E. A. Suchman, "A Conceptual Analysis of the Accident Phenomenon," *Social Problems* **8**, 241–253 (1961).

STUDIES OF DRIVER PERFORMANCE

B 67. A. M. Barch, J. Nangle, and D. Trumbo, "Situational Characteristics and Turn-Signalling Behavior," *Highway Research Board Bulletin* **172**, 95–103 (1958).

B 68. N. R. Bartlett, A. E. Bartz, and J. V. Wait, "Recognition Time for Symbols in Peripheral Vision," *Highway Research Board Bulletin* **330**, 87–91 (1962).

B 69. J. K. Boek, "Automobile Accidents and Driver Behavior," *Traffic Safety Research Review* **2**, 7–12 (December 1958).

B 70. L. Brody, S. Yudin, and C. T. Gaza, *A Study of Performance on the Driver's License Road Test and Its Implications for Driver Education,* Center for Safety Education, New York Univ., New York (1958).

B 71. J. D. Brown and W. J. Huffman, "Psychophysiological Measures of Drivers under Actual Driving Conditions," *Journal of Safety Research* **4**, 172–178 (1972).

B 72. G. P. Chubb and R. L. Ernst, "Studies of Velocity Attainment," *Highway Research Abstracts* **33**, 78–79 (1963).

B 73. J. Cohen, E. J. Dearnaley, and C. E. M. Hansel, "Risk and Hazard," *Operational Research Quarterly* **7**, 67–82 (1956).

B 74. A. Crawford, "The Overtaking Driver," *Highway Research Abstracts* **34**, 3 (1964).

B 75. R. W. Danielson, "Relationship of Fields of Vision to Safety in Driving," *Traffic Safety Research Review* **2**, 8–25 (September 1958).

B 76. D. A. Dobbins, J. G. Tiedemann, and D. M. Skordahl, "Human Factors Research Reports—I. Field Study of Vigilance Under Highway Driving Conditions," *Highway Research Board Bulletin* **330**, 1–8 (1962).

B 77. D. S. Edwards and C. P. Hahn, *Filmed Behaviors as a Criterion for Safe Driving,* The American Institute for Research, Accident Research Center, Silver Spring, Md. (1970).

B 78. J. L. Fine, J. L. Malfetti, and E. J. Shoben, *The Development of a Criterion for Driver Behavior,* Safety Research and Education Project, Teachers College, Columbia Univ., New York (1965).

B 79. T. W. Forbes and M. S. Katz, *Summary of Human Engineering Research Data and Principles Related to Highway Design and Traffic Engineering Problems,* The American Institute for Research, Pittsburgh, Pa. (1957).

B 80. T. W. Forbes, R. O. Nolan and F. E. Vanosdall, *Driver Performance Measurement Research: Volume I, Technical Report,* U.S. Department of Transportation, Washington, D.C. (Contract No. FH-11-7627) (1973).

B 81. D. A. Gordon, "Experimental Isolation of Drivers' Visual Input," *Highway Research Abstracts* **34**, 55 (1964).

B 82. B. D. Greenshields, "Investigating Traffic Highway Events in Relation to Driver Behavior," *Traffic Quarterly* **15**, 664–676 (1961).

B 83. _____, *Changes in Driver Performance with Time in Driving,* Transportation Institute, Ann Arbor, Mich. (1964).

B 84. B. D. Greenshields and F. N. Platt, *The Development of a Method of Predicting High Accident and High Violation Drivers,* Transportation Institute, Ann Arbor, Mich.

B 85. R. L. Hix and P. N. Ziegler, *1974 Safety Belt Survey: N.H.T.S.A./CU Research Project. Final Report,* National Highway Traffic Safety Administration, Washington, D.C. (1974).

B 86. P. M. Hurst, K. Perchonok, and E. L. Seguin, "Measurement of Subjective Gap Size," *Report No. 7*, Division of Highway Studies, Institute for Research, State College, Pa. (1965).

B 87. K. A. Kimball, V. S. Ellingstad, and R. E. Hagen, "Effects of Experience on Patterns of Driving Skill," *Journal of Safety Research* **3**, 129–135 (1971).

B 88. A. R. Lauer, V. W. Suhr, and E. Allgaier, "Development of a Criterion for Driver Performance," *Traffic Safety Research Review* **2**, 24–27 (March 1958).

B 89. A. R. Lauer and V. W. Suhr, *Effect of Driving with One Hand off the Wheel*, Driving Research Laboratory, Iowa State College, Ames, Iowa.

B 90. B. A. Lefeve, "Speed Habits Observed on a Rural Highway," *Highway Research Board Proceedings* **33**, 409–428 (1954).

B 91. A. M. Mackie and K. Russam, *Instructions to Drivers to Maintain Safe Spacings Between Following Vehicles*, TRRL Supplementary Report 166UC, Transport and Road Research Laboratory, Berkshire (1975).

B 92. J. L. Malfetti and J. L. Fine, "Characteristics of Safe Drivers: A Pilot Study," *Traffic Safety Research Review* **6**, 3–9 (September 1962).

B 93. T. M. Mast, H. V. Jones, and N. W. Heimstra, "Effects of Fatigue on Performance in a Simulated Driving Device," *Highway Research Abstracts* **34**, 77 (1964).

B 94. B. L. McDonald, "Driver Work Load for Various Turn Radii and Speeds," *Driver Performance Studies*, Transportation Research Record 530, Transportation Research Board, Washington, D.C. (1975).

B 95. R. A. McFarland, "Human Factors in Highway Transport Safety," *Society of Automotive Engineers Transactions* **64**, 730–750 (1956).

B 96. D. C. Melton and J. W. Hutchinson, "Driver Steering Configurations" (unpublished), Univ. of Illinois, Urbana, Ill. (1962).

B 97. R. M. Michaels and D. Solomon, "Effect of Speed Change Information on Spacing Between Vehicles," *Highway Research Board Bulletin* **330**, 26–29 (1962).

B 98. R. R. Mourant and T. H. Rockwell, "Strategies of Visual Search by Novice and Experienced Drivers," *Human Factors* **14**, 325–335 (August 1972).

B 99. T. Ogawa, E. S. Fisher and J. C. Oppenlander, "Driver Behavior Study— Influence of Speed Limits on Spot Speed Characteristics in a Series of Contiguous Rural and Urban Areas," *Highway Research Board Bulletin* **341**, 18–29 (1962).

B 100. J. J. Pease and C. F. Damron, "The Effectiveness of Videotape Feedback on Driving Performance and Self-Evaluation," *Journal of Safety Research* **6**, 34–40 (1974).

B 101. K. Perchonok and E. L. Seguin, "Vehicle Following Behavior: A Field Study," *Report No. 5*, Division of Highway Studies, Institute for Research, State College, Pa. (1964).

B 102. K. Perchonok and P. Hurst, "The Effect of Lane Closure Signals Upon Driver Decision-Making and Traffic Flow," *Report No. 8*, Division of Highway Studies, Institute for Research, State College, Pa. (1965).

B 103. F. N. Platt, "Driver Behavior Research" (mimeo.), Presented before the Traffic General Session, National Safety Congress, Chicago, Ill. (October 30, 1963).

B 104. F. Preston and R. Shortridge, "A Study of Restraint Use and Effectiveness," *Hit Lab Reports*, **3**, 1–25, Highway Safety Research Institute, The University of Michigan, Ann Arbor, Mich.

B 105. N. J. Rackoff and T. H. Rockwell, "Driver Search and Scan Patterns in Night Driving," *Driver Visual Needs in Night Driving*, Transportation Research Board, Washington, D.C. (1975).

B 106. L. S. Robertson and W. Haddon, *The Buzzer-Light Reminder System and Safety Belt Use*, Insurance Institute for Highway Safety, Washington, D.C. (1972).

B 107. T. H. Rockwell and J. N. Snider, *An Investigation of Variability in Driving Performance on the Highway*, Systems Research Group, Department of Industrial Engineering, Ohio State Univ., Columbus, Ohio (1965).

B 108. T. Rockwell, C. Algae, and G. Chubb, "Human Factors Research in the Use of Electronic Devices as Traffic Aids," *Traffic Safety Research Review* **6**, 10–16 (September 1962).

B 109. N. J. Rowan and C. J. Keese, "A Study of Factors Influencing Traffic Speeds," *Highway Research Board Bulletin* **341**, 30–76 (1962).

B 110. E. L. Seguin and K. Perchonok, "Vehicle Interactions on an Urban Expressway," *Report No. 6*, Division of Highway Studies, Institute for Research, State College, Pa. (1965).

B 111. W. J. Shaw, "Objective Measurement of Driving Skill," *Traffic Safety Research Review* **2**, 13–16 (December 1958).

B 112. D. H. Shuster, "A Pilot Study of the Use of a Simulator in Retraining Problem Drivers," *Journal of Safety Research* **7**, 141–143 (1975).

B 113. B. W. Stephens and R. M. Michaels, "Time Sharing Between Compensatory Tracking and Search and Recognition Tasks," *Highway Research Record* **55**, 1–16 (1963).

B 114. V. W. Suhr, A. R. Lauer, and E. Allgaier, "Judgment of Speed on the Highway and on the Auto Trainer," *Traffic Safety Research Review* **2**, 27–31 (December 1958).

B 115. W. E. Tarrants, "A Study of the Relationship Between Driving Records, Field Driving Performance and Laboratory Driving Performance of Professional Automobile Drivers," *Traffic Safety Research Review* **4**, 22–27 (March 1960).

B 116. Traffic Engineering and Safety Department, American Automobile Association, *A Report of Driving Errors Made by 10,860 Licensed Drivers*, Washington, D.C. (1956).

B 117. F. A. Wagner, "An Evaluation of Fundamental Driver Decisions and Reactions at an Intersection," *Highway Research Abstracts* **34**, 46–47 (1964).

B 118. S. Wright and R. B. Sleight, "Influence of Mental Set and Distance Judgment Aids on Following Distance," *Highway Research Board Bulletin* **330**, 52–59 (1962).

PROFESSIONAL LITERATURE AND RESOURCES

B 119. J. E. Aaron and M. K. Strasser, *Driving Task Instruction*, Macmillan, New York (1974).

B 120. American Automobile Association, *Sportsmanlike Driving*, 7th ed., Webster Division, McGraw-Hill Book Company, New York (1975).

B 121. American Automobile Association, *Traffic Education Resources Catalogue*, Falls Church, Va. (1975).

B 122. American Driver and Traffic Safety Education Association, *Policies and Guidelines for Driver and Traffic Safety Education*, Washington, D.C. (1974).

B 123. W. G. Anderson, *Learning to Drive: Skills, Concepts, and Strategies*, Addison-Wesley, Reading Mass. (1971).

B 124. W. G. Anderson, *Laboratory Manual for Learning to Drive*, Addison-Wesley, Reading, Mass. (1971).

B 125. W. G. Anderson, Teacher's Manual for Learning to Drive, Addison-Wesley, Reading, Mass. (1971).

B 126. W. G. Anderson and J. L. Malfetti, *The Effectiveness of Teacher Performance in Behind-the-Wheel Instruction in Driver Education*, The Safety Research and Education Project, Teachers College, Columbia University, New York. (1963).

B 127. Automotive Safety Foundation, *A Resource Curriculum in Driver and Traffic Safety Education*, Washington, D.C. (1970).

B 128. R. Gagne, "Modern Learning Principles and Driver Education," *National Driver Education and Training Symposium Proceedings*, 127–136, The National Highway Safety Bureau, Washington, D.C. (1969).

B 129. L. G. Goldstein, *Behavioral Aspects of Highway Safety Relevant to Preparation of the Beginning Driver: A Review of Research*, The California Traffic Safety Education Task Force (1973).

B 130. M. Halsey, R. Kaywood, and R. A. Meyerhoff, *Let's Drive Right*, 5th ed., Scott, Foresman, Glenview, Ill. (1972).

B 131. Highway Users Federation, *Preparation and Use of Instructional Modules in Driver and Traffic Safety Education*, Washington, D.C. (1970).

B 132. Highway Users Federation, *The Multiple-Car Method: Exploring Its Use in Driver and Traffic Safety Education*, Washington, D.C. (1972).

B 133. Human Resources Research Organization, *Safe Performance Curriculum. Secondary School Driver Education Curriculum Development and Evaluation Project, Interim Specifications*, Washington, D.C. (1973).

B 134. Liberty Mutual Insurance Company, *Skid Control School*, Boston, Mass.

B 135. R. L. Marshall, R. L. Baldwin, R. Tossell, R. A. Ulrich, and J. S. Cunningham, *Safe Performance Driving*, Ginn, Lexington, Mass. (1975).

B 136. Maryland State Department of Education, *The Multiple-Car Method in the State of Maryland*, Baltimore, Md.

B 137. A. J. McKnight, "Evaluation of the Safe Performance Curriculum for Secondary School Driver Education," *Journal of Traffic Safety Education* **20** (June 1973).

B 138. A. J. McKnight and A. G. Hundt, *Driver Education Task Analysis: Instructional Objectives*, Human Resources Research Organization, Washington, D.C. (March 1971).

B 139. National Committee on Uniform Traffic Laws and Ordinances, *Uniform Vehicle Code*, rev. ed., The Committee, Washington, D.C. (1962); Annual Supplement (1970); and Supplement II (1976).

B 140. National Highway Traffic Safety Administration, *Safety Belt Instructional Booklet*, The Administration, Washington, D.C.

B 141. National Highway Traffic Safety Administration, *Statewide Highway Safety Program Assessment: A National Estimate of Performance*, National Highway Traffic Safety Administration, Washington, D.C. (July 1975).

B 142. D. E. Payne and J. E. Barmack, "An Experimental Field Test of the Smith-Cummings-Sherman Driver Training System," *Traffic Safety Research Review* **3**, 22–28 (June 1959).

B 143. W. P. Quensel, "A New Look at the Smith System," *Journal of Traffic Safety Education* **23**, p. 5 (January 1976).

B 144. M. C. Riley and R. S. McBride, *Safe Performance Curriculum For Secondary School Driver Education: Program Development, Implementation, and Technical Findings. Final Report*, Human Resources Research Organization, Alexandria, Va. (1975).

B 145. H. H. Shettel and W. R. Horner, *Functional Requirements for Driver Training Devices Volume I*, U.S. Department of Transportation, Washington, D.C. (DOT Contract No. FH-11-7322) (1974).

B 146. H. H. Shettel, S. P. Schumacher, and R. D. Gatewood, *Driver Training Simulator, Ranges and Modified Cars: A Review and Critique of the Experimental Literature*, American Institutes for Research, Pittsburgh, Pa. (DOT Contract No. FH-11-7322) (1971).

B 147. Traffic Safety and Highway Improvement Department, *Seeing Habits for Expert Driving*, Ford Motor Company, Dearborn, Mich. (1959).

INDEX